Hollywood on the Tiber

Hollywood on the Tiber

Hank Kaufman
and Gene Lerner

Sticking Place Books
New York

www.stickingplacebooks.com

Cover design by Virginia Brodie

A translation of this book was published in 1982 by Sperling & Kupler, Milan

ISBN 978-1-942782-85-8

Contents

Foreword by Sandy Lieberson

In 1961, I was a young agent at The Phil Gersh Agency in Hollywood, representing actors, writers and directors, when I was offered a job in Rome with Kaufman-Lerner Associates (KLA). In 1957, Hank Kaufman and Gene Lerner, two young Americans, in a romantic and professional partnership, had formed a talent agency and were soon representing some of the most exciting and gifted actors, directors, writers and cinematographers in Europe.

Anita Ekberg, Alain Delon, Romy Schneider, Anouk Aimée, Elsa Martinelli, Brigitte Bardot, Rossano Brazzi, Jack Palance, Robert Aldrich, Frank Sinatra were just a few of their glamorous and gifted clients. The films they were involved with included *L'Avventura*, *Rocco and His Brothers*, *Accattone*, *Salvatore Giuliano*, *The Battle of Algiers*, *The Leopard*, *La Dolce Vita*, *8½* and other landmarks of Italian cinema.

I had never been to Europe and had little or no idea what to expect, but I felt that one of the greatest adventures of my life was about to begin. *La Dolce Vita*! I had seen Fellini's film – and here I was about to live it.

The first thing I discovered in Rome was that being an agent in Italy was actually illegal. A leftover law from the Fascist era, originally designed to eliminate organised prostitution, prohibited anyone from earning a living off someone's services. Technically Hank, Gene and I could be arrested for doing our jobs, so KLA had two offices: a secret one where we kept all our contracts and correspondence, and another where we practiced our "illegal activities" as agents.

Rome was a revelation: sex, drugs, open homosexuality and, most important, the opportunity to represent some of the most talented and gifted filmmakers. No one was beyond reach. I was amazed that I could just pick up the phone and get through to almost anyone: Fellini, Visconti, Rosselini, Antonioni, Ferreri, Germi, Bava, Monicelli, Bertoluccci, De Sica, Godard, Resnais,

Chabrol, Pasolini, Leone and many others. There was genuine camaraderie, and a distinct lack of hierarchy, between filmmakers, writers, cinematographers and actors.

Rome opened my eyes to a new and different kind of cinema, a way of working and politics. Italians worked hard to distance themselves from the Fascist era, and being a part of the Communist Party was the surest and easiest way to repudiate your recent past. In Italy you could be a communist and have a secret Swiss bank account.

Hollywood on the Tiber is a love letter to the vibrant days of Italian filmmaking that brings to life Hank and Gene's unique, unsung contribution to one of the most exciting periods in modern culture. It's the story of how two young Americans arrived in Rome "with absolutely nothing and ended up with a very great deal" – for themselves, and for cinema.

Introduction by Stefano della Casa

There are many images capable of evoking the presence of American actors and directors in Italy during the postwar period, a phenomenon that film (and also fashion) history has defined as Hollywood on the Tiber. In no particular order: Gregory Peck and Audrey Hepburn riding a scooter through the center of Rome. Lex Barker, clearly drunk, confronting Anita Ekberg. The four hundred extras who for a month trained under the master of arms Musumeci Greco, preparing to perform the turtle formation commanded by Rex Harrison as Julius Caesar. Sergio Leone, then an unknown second unit director, filming a frenzied chariot race. The films, of course, are *Roman Holiday*, *La Dolce Vita*, *Cleopatra* and *Ben-Hur*.

This glorious book by Hank Kaufman and Gene Lerner evokes those years and that atmosphere, and stands above all others because it doesn't limit itself to the lights, glamor or legendary moments of the era. It is rich with facts, characters and suspense, with sensational details of the parties and glitz, but also the underworld – that of blackmail, failure, promissory notes and despair, the one not so visible to those outside looking in. Hollywood on the Tiber represents modernity. An Italy that had, until then, been agricultural, frugal and religious suddenly came to know opulence and consumerism. Kaufman and Lerner's book is among the rare works that vividly capture the intricacies of such a transformative era.

Hollywood on the Tiber has a strictly economic origin (film, after all, is an art inseparably linked to financial considerations) that gives rise to a completely unexpected development. American studios came over and shot in Italy because production costs were much lower than any they could ever find in Hollywood. The Italian technical departments (especially set designers and stuntmen) knew how to do everything, and did it quickly, at prices a quarter of Hollywood's union wages. In particular, the stuntmen were much more skilled than their overseas colleagues. Musumeci Greco, the greatest master of arms in Italian cinema, who built a formidable team, offered a detailed price list (a certain fee for a fall from a horse, double if the horse was among other horses, etc.), and the stuntmen, for their part, agreed to any request. Their refrain was always: "We do everything, sir. We do everything."

The great Hollywood stars were happy to spend time in a place where they were served and revered in ways not possible in California, where their various excesses were tolerated and even became a reason for admiration. As director Giuliano Montaldo explained, U.S. Marines were the vanguard that, in 1943, swept away the Nazis and prepared the ground for Fox, Universal and other Hollywood studios.

And so, after enjoying this particular book, readers will surely crave more on the subject, including, perhaps, the wild arguments between the Italian and American sides on the set of *Ulysses*, which pitted star Kirk Douglas and his entourage against director Mario Camerini, or the chronicles of the 1953 wedding in Turin between Lex Barker and Lana Turner, where journalists made readers' eyes widen with the announcement of the wedding lunch menu (seven T-bone steaks for him, a salad for her), or the case of Christa Wanninger, a German model who, like so many others, came to Rome to become part of the international film community and was found murdered in an apartment near Via Veneto, the pulsating heart of Hollywood on the Tiber.

The myth, the legend, but also the abyss and its squalor, one full of drug addiction, unrealized dreams and sexual favors – *Hollywood on the Tiber*, with its modern, brisk and wildly captivating narrative, is all these things together. It is Heaven and Hell.

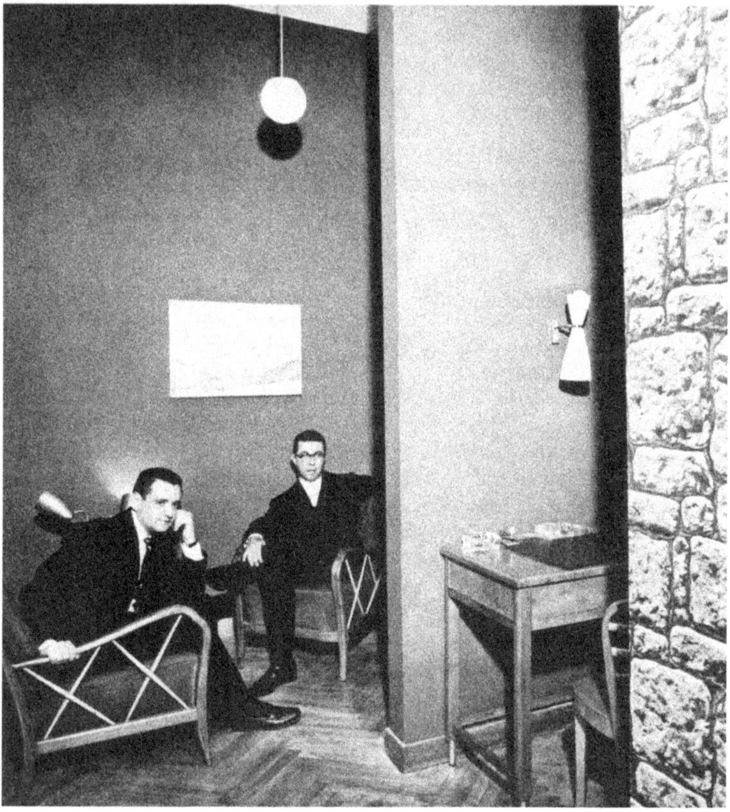

Gene Lerner and Hank Kaufman, Rome, 1970

To our dear families

To the film critics and journalists of Italy,
past and present,
and to their colleagues around the world,
because together with the directors, producers,
screenwriters, cinematographers, musicians,
set designers, costume designers,
and all the other people
involved in the making of a film,
they contribute significantly to the art of cinema.

Hollywood on the Tiber

with

Anna Magnani

Ava Gardner

Anita Ekberg

Simone Signoret

Rossano Brazzi

Margaret Truman

Robert Aldrich

and

Dawn Addams
Josephine Baker
Ingrid Bergman
Lydia Brazzi
Richard Burton
Maria Callas
Charles Chaplin
Walter Chiari
Franco Cristaldi
Bette Davis
Dino De Laurentiis
Queen Elizabeth
Federico Fellini
Mel Ferrer
Micol Fontana
Anthony Franciosa
Judy Garland
Vittorio Gassman
Audrey Hepburn
Hedy Lamarr
Belinda Lee
Gina Lollobrigida
Sophia Loren
Elsa Martinelli
Vittorio Massimo
Filippo Orsini
Irene Papas
Pier Paolo Pasolini
Pier Angeli
Gillo Pontecorvo
Burt Reynolds
Roberto Rossellini
Giuseppe Rotunno
George C. Scott
Frank Sinatra
Susan Strasberg
Elizabeth Taylor
Shelley Winters
Franco Zeffirelli

Prologue

Hollywood on the Tiber refers to the epoch of the 1950s and the 1960s which marked a frenzied increase of international film production concentrated in Rome, rivaling Hollywood and coinciding with what historians refer to as Italy's "economic miracle."

After desolate and war-scarred centuries, in which even the Vatican lived in the *chiaroscuro* of history and events, Rome once again became an empire – but not as a result of military might or geographical position. Its renewed hegemony came through the magnetism of celluloid and the illusion wrought by the motion picture camera.

The vast film studios of Cinecittà, built as a monument to Fascism, became the new Palatine of the Empire of the Silver Screen. Rome itself became a gigantic, breathtaking cinema set to accommodate the innumerable deities and idols of motion pictures, who came from their various domains of the world, trailed by servants and sycophants, to reincarnate their new Hermes, the *paparazzi.*

Like the Roman Empire of ancient times, Hollywood on the Tiber stretched its tentacles far and wide. Neither continent nor nation was exempt from involvement in the euphoric adventure to seduce larger audiences in every corner of the globe and to conquer mass markets in every town and city. Larger and costlier productions and co-productions emanating from Rome made the lands and seas of the Earth the city's location sites.

Thus, Rome once again seemed Glory, delighted by the play of klieg lights which blotted out centuries of wrinkles and millennia of darkness and disinterest. Once again seemed Narcissus, adoring its reflection in the massive artificial lake constructed by Metro-Goldwyn-Mayer at Cinecittà. Once again seemed Courtesan, abandoning itself to the marvelous sensation of make-believe through the sorcerous ministrations of makeup artists, hairstylists and costumiers.

And once again, Rome became a magnet for peoples from all parts of the world. Rome became the place to be. Rome became the place to see.

Two young Americans who had no useful relationship to, or contact with, the world of cinema found themselves caught up in the Hollywood on the Tiber phenomenon. Unexpectedly present during an epoch no Pliny, Edward Gibbon or Henry James could possibly have predicted, they found themselves participants and prisms of the era which once-was… and which will never-again-be.

PENSIONE GIGLIESI
Via di Porta Pinciana No. 6
ROMA

Telefono: 841-273

July 7, 1953

Mr. Gene Lerner
Hotel Perreyve
86 rue Madame Paris, 6me
France

Carissimo Gino

This is going out express, so hopefully you get it fast. My impulse was to phone but you know our damned money situation, and there would have been so much to talk about. This is my fourth letter to you and I've so far received two. Did you get mine, and are you okay?

The month of investigation down here is up. I've had day-and-night talks with dozens of people who seem to know the ins-and-outs of what's going on. I have asked endless questions. I have researched. I have listened. And I have done more pondering in these four weeks than in any given four years of my life. And at last I have an idea which is the answer for our be or not to be, and it's absolutely beautiful. I deliberately didn't say anything about it in my previous letters. It first had to jell in my own mind, and finally it has.

Everybody senses that Rome is on the verge of a fantastic film boom, far beyond doing an occasional picture here on location, like Three Coins in A Fountain, Roman Holiday or Ben-Hur. What the insiders think is that there's going to be a vast movement of international production based on millions of dollars in frozen assets the American major companies have got to spend in Europe. Production costs are cheaper than in Hollywood and there are tremendous advantages for America stars, directors et al. tax-wise, if they work abroad, particularly if they take foreign residency.

Helen Tubbs, who is the Variety stringer here, and a wonderful gal, told me that part of what's happening also has to do with the ambitions of Italian financial and artistic elements to enter the world film market in a big way. She and others tell me that with all of Rome's excellent studio space (I paid a visit to Cinecittà and Titanus-Farnesina), mild weather, marvelous creative people such as cameramen, costume and set designers, and cooperative, experienced technicians, Rome has everything going for it to become a great film capital, possibly out-Hollywooding Hollywood.

So, impatiently, you are asking what does all that have to do with you and me? All right. I know I can get carried away. I know that sometimes I don't dig deep into every facet of things. What else do you expect from a Gemini? But you're still a Pisces, so who else but a fish will understand what I'm talking about and will let imagination and instinct dive into the murky waters of the future?

What we do is open a talent agency. That's what I said, a talent agency! Pause for your reaction. Are you still there? Or have you keeled over in a dead faint? But after the Paris disaster with our bitterly lamented TV-series idea (I'll never forgive those fucking Frenchmen for insisting that we come over and then walking out on all their promises), we decided we still wanted to stay and live in Europe, didn't we? That's still our dream and our goal, n'est-ce pas? And the reason for my coming down to Rome to investigate prospects in Italy, non è vero? I'm convinced my talent agency idea is worth a try. I'm convinced that it'll work.

In all the ferment of activity down here, there just ain't any such animal, at least not in the American sense. There are a couple of so-called agents like Lilliana Bianchini and Franz de Blasi, who seem to have a bit of standing. But from what I'm told, there's no such thing as exclusivity or any sense of career-building. And commissions aren't fixed at ten percent but anything the traffic can bear. You see sleazy guys standing around in hotel lobbies and near the studios, hanging on to an album of photographs. They try to sell hungry, panting actors and actresses to producers and directors they buttonhole. If they succeed, they take as much as fifty percent of the money and sometimes find a way to pocket all of it! And an integral part of the deal is more often than not a certain amount of performance in bed and bedroom.

Then there are hundreds of foreign, mostly American actors – real, would-be's and used-to-be's – floundering about, desperate for work, desperate for representation. If they're employed, they often don't get paid. Or they get paid in I.O.U's (cambiale is the Italian word) that turn out to be toilet paper. What applies to them applies in spades to the Italians. The Italian actors live in fear of being blackballed by hot-shot Mussolini-type producers if the poor slaves don't "collaborate." There's nobody around with the guts to stand up against these guys.

And there's something else. Publicity, public relations and promotion. That's a field I know something about. There's a big need for that here, but outside of a few Americans (like Helen Tubbs and Bob Edwards, who heads the Italian film information office) and an occasional Italian like Mario Longardi (who works for Metro-Goldwyn Mayer here), no one understands what the hell you're talking about when you try to explain the long-range importance of publicity and promotional programs.

So my idea is really two ideas meshed into one. We set up a two-pronged organization. One prong will be the handling of Talent. The second prong will be a Publicity and Promotional Department. I elect you to head the Talent operation, and I think you'll be great at it. I'll take charge of Publicity and Promotion. And, of course, we'll be there to help each other in every way that we can.

If you're doubtful, maybe you should come down right away anyway, for your own on-the-spot analysis. You should get down here pronto anyway. With all the political tension and all the talk of civil war and general strikes in France, it looks like an explosion might be just around the corner. And three months of search and disappointment in Paris, as much as we love it, is enough to show there's no apparent future for us there.

Rome maybe isn't Paris, at least not yet for me, but Rome has its own special appeal. It's a wonderful spectrum of pastels to primaries. Every street has a surprise. Every nook-and-cranny is a discovery. Museums, art, history, churches. And what architecture. What pink in the evening sky and what celestial blue in the morning. And the people! The parade is just fantastic. They're beautiful, alive, sensual, exciting. And it's contagious, because you begin to feel the same. Well, Eternal City it's called and the Eternal City it is.

This pensione is okay. Nothing special and a bit too expensive. I'll stay here till I know what you decide. If it's yes, our first order of business is to find ourselves a cheap apartment. But one thing at a time.

So, a telegram, please, and please, please take the next train to... bella, magnifica, splendida, favolosa ROMA!

I can't wait, partner!

Hank

One

Che sarà, sarà

Rome. July 13, 1953.

Hank was up early. His night had been fitful. He had had a convulsive parade of dreams, most of them suffocating and confusing, "no foundation all the way down the line," in the words of William Saroyan. A few had been delightful.

In one, he was back at the Massachusetts School of the Arts or at Boston University, he couldn't now remember which. He had just left his class in Advertising Design, where he had been enthusiastically lauded for the creativity of his layouts and sketch-work, and was, like a bird sailing through the air, entering his much-preferred ambiance of Set Design. As he was intensely absorbed in his sketches for an imagined production of Eugene O'Neill's *The Emperor Jones*, he heard a babble of excited voices. When he looked up, he was startled to see Florenz Ziegfeld, George Abbott, George White, Max Gordon, Sam Harris, Alfred de Liagre and Leland Hayward beaming at him while jockeying for position to be the first to congratulate him.

There was another that was still vivid, of his adolescence in the modest Dorchester house which had been his home since birth. There she was, his only sister, Estelle, eight years younger than he, a singing, dancing, mimicking Theda Bara in the musical revue of his invention. A dark, mysterious, biblical-looking little beauty, Estelle, in his eyes, made Shirley Temple seem a puppet made of gold dust. Glittering marquees, reflected in an endless series of mirrors, were flashing, "Written, Directed, Designed and Costumed by That Fifteen-Year-Old Genius of the Epoch – *Hank Kaufman*!"

There was an opening in the Kaufman home between living room and dining room. The separation between the two rooms was to Hank what the Red Sea was to Moses and the pair of blue-velvet drapes were perfect as dividing line between stage area and the non-existent audience. Various lamps covered with tissue paper of varied colors were turned upwards to give magical lighting effects. While Estelle was pirouetting like a top and singing as if her heart and lungs had converged, he kept confidently awaiting the arrival of his father, indefatigable, life-time salesman for Prudential Life Insurance, to announce that all tickets for every performance had been eagerly grabbed by the neighborhood.

Hank did not notice smoke from the scorched tissue paper covering the lamps and the beginnings of flame which gave the revue a Wagneresque atmosphere. Walls, armchairs, the precious drapes were saved by the fortuitous entrance of his Mother, who loved him so overwhelmingly that she was convinced no other woman in the world had a son to equal him. The near conflagration seemed to him a perfectly normal consequence of genius-at-work. Hank watched unperturbed, until he felt growing excitement as he watched his screaming, wild-eyed mother frantically working to save furniture and home from destruction. Yes, yes – what a discovery! She would be a sensation opposite Charles Chaplin, Buster Keaton or Harold Lloyd in a film written, directed, designed and costumed by… Hank Kaufman.

Recalling the dreams, Hank shook his head. Show business is eating my brain, he said to himself. And what a driving compulsion I have for recognition! Wow! But what's new about that, he added silently with a sigh.

There was another dream, so sharp and distinct that it seemed an incision across his head. It was 1946 and winter and spring were intermingled. He was in New York just after completing three-and-a-half years of service in the Army Air Force. Led by Gene, he was for the first time entering an art house showing foreign films, like the Fifth Avenue Playhouse. The theaters became myriad and the pictures Gene was showing him became a crescendo of fascinating, sublime images blurred by English subtitles. There was the Russian-made *Alexander Nevsky*, with its Sergei Eisenstein spectacle and Prokofiev music. Then the language he was listening to was French and he was watching shifting images of such classics as *La Kermesse héroïque*, *The Baker's Wife*, *La Symphonie pastorale*, *Grand Illusion.*

The French was being overwhelmed by Italian when suddenly an explosion thundered.

Roberto Rossellini's *Open City*. Gigantic ocean waves overwhelmed Hank. Emotions consumed him like fire. The World Theater on New York's West 49th Street to which Gene had taken him no longer existed. Frightened, frantic, Gene and he were racing through the streets of Rome, terrorized by the Nazis. They did not know where to go, where to hide. Then, like a dilating vision, they found themselves face-to-face with Anna Magnani. Hank was in ferment as he saw the look in her eyes and watched stunned as she was shot in the barren streets of the barren city. His whole body was assaulted by unbearable pain when he heard her final cry of grief as, like a stricken animal, she raced far beyond her physical powers in her final effort to save her doomed husband.

Hank fought back the tears as he recalled the dream and an onrush of thoughts pressed down on him. If the scenario the Fates had decreed was that he and Gene, who had known one another for a mere three months, had impetuously decided to go and see some picture that particular May evening in 1946; if that film happened to have been *Open City* with Magnani; if, when it was over, Gene and he shook hands good night, never again to see one another, he still would have remembered Gene with deep feeling for the rest of his life.

Gene.

Still no reply to the letter Hank had written and rewritten over so many concentrated hours. The talent agency idea could have shocked Gene. Being an agent was certainly far from Gene's image of himself. He had tried so hard and made so many sacrifices to make it as a playwright and three times had nearly made the breakthrough to Broadway with one of his plays. Yes, it would be most understandable if Gene were upset by the agency scheme. Should I spend the money and call Paris, Hank asked himself? Out of the question, we can't afford it, was his instantaneous answer.

As he sipped his caffè latte, an Italian grammar open beside him, Hank was beset by all kinds of doubts. He started to reread the copy of the letter he had so laboriously typed to Gene. How and why could he possibly have been so upbeat? His idea now seemed to him so tenuous, all risk and no assurance. He decided to write up a detailed memo based on all the conversations he had had and all the information he had gathered that had led him to his plan. He did it longhand. Pencil-and-paper better suited his thought processes when he really had to think something out. The more he wrote, the better he felt. And by the time it was noon, he found himself once again assured. He had pulled himself back to the top of the cloud. Feeling good, he decided he deserved a stroll.

The Pensione Gigliesi was a short walk from the Via Veneto. He stopped at the corner newsstand to buy the *Daily American*, and Rome's morning daily, *Il Messaggero*, which he read every day in his effort to familiarize himself with Italian. Glancing across the Via Veneto, he noted that Rome's most fashionable outdoor café, Doney, had every one of its tables filled with the usual concoction of gazing tourists, gabbing and gesturing ladies, and a healthy sprinkling of boys and girls on the make if the price was right. As he passed Doney, engrossed in the front page of the *Daily American*, he thought he heard his name called. Surprised, he turned to look and saw no one he recognized. Now I'm hearing voices, Hank said to himself.

Once again, he started in the direction of the Excelsior Hotel and the American Embassy. Once again, he heard a shout of what sounded like his name. Again, Hank stopped and turned. A man was standing at one of the tables, waving.

Lester Grady, of all people!

More than an acquaintance, not close enough to be a friend, Grady was editor of two of the world's most widely read film fan magazines, *Silver Screen* and *Screenland*. Waving back, Hank made his way to a smiling, back-slapping, typically dressed American. Pumping Hank's hand, Grady quickly passed through the banal how-are-you's. "What do you say to a little walkie-talkie?" he asked.

"Great with me," Hank replied. "But do you have time? I thought you would be surrounded by a bevy of beauties offering their favors in return for a hot interview in your magazines."

"Yeah, yeah. I need to get away from all that for a while. I've got a problem to resolve which has been bugging me for weeks."

They started up the Via Veneto towards the Villa Borghese. "I didn't know you were in Europe," Grady said.

"I came across with Gene Lerner in April. You've met Gene."

"Yeah," Lester said uncertainly, trying to capture an image.

He brightened. "Yeah. Now I remember," he said, recollection now in focus. "Gene's about five-foot-six, dark. Very intense and smart as a whip, right? He's a playwright, isn't he?"

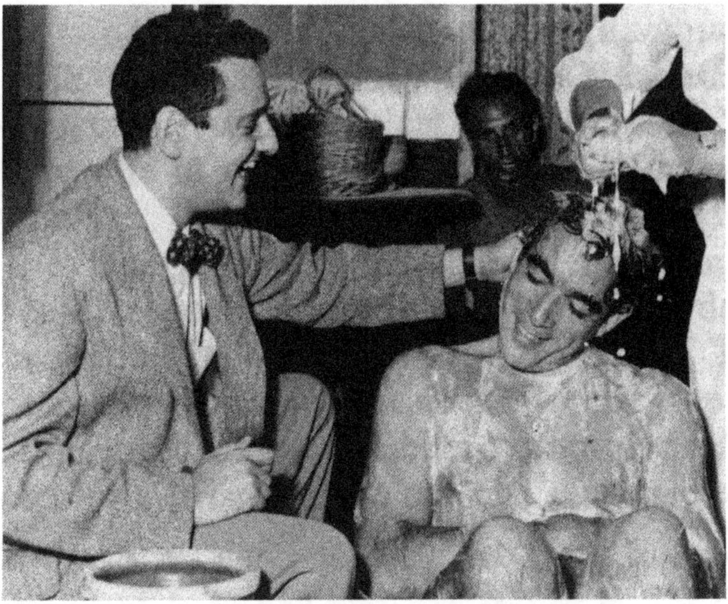

Gene Lerner and Anthony Quinn on the set of *Fatal Desire* (1953)

"He sure is. He was selected by the New Dramatists Committee as one of the thirty most promising playwrights in America, alongside such guys as Paddy Chayefsky, Robert Anderson and Arnold Schulman."

"Yeah? Where is Gene?"

"In Paris. We're trying to figure out a way to stay on in Europe."

"You mean really stay? To *live*? But you were doing so great in advertising and promotion, Hankele."

"It's like this, pal," Hank went on to explain. "We *thought* we were making a dream come true: achieving a creative, successful show-biz activity based in Europe. So Gene and I worked three years to develop a TV series which required shooting over here. A Paris agent said she had a deal set for some French outfit, to finance us ten percent, and we should get our asses over as fast as we could. So we gave up our respective jobs, sublet our apartment for two years, packed everything up, and sailed off for Cherbourg. On the Liberté on April 10, 1953, if you want to be specific about it."

"So what happened?" inquired Grady as they crossed into the gardens of the Villa Borghese.

"Fiasco's what happened. It all sank into the Seine," said Hank, not without bitterness. "And thus, dear Mr. Grady, Gene and I were left stranded. We can't go back because we've got no place to live. Anyway, we want to stay. We're determined to stay." The thought that maybe he should reveal the talent agency plan to Lester flitted across Hank's mind.

"Too bad, too bad," commiserated Grady, as they continued to saunter. Unexpectedly, the editor stopped and put his arm around Hank's shoulder. "You're coming with me, Hankele. I'm taking you to lunch. At Capriccio's. It's the Chasen's, Brown Derby and Sardi's of Rome, as you must know. Okay with you?" he asked Hank with a broad smile.

Very okay, thought Hank. I've never been able to afford the place.

They turned back towards the Via Veneto. Hank felt a slight change of atmosphere. He glanced at Grady through the corner of his eye, trying to figure it out. "Tell me about Gene," said Grady after they had walked silently for a moment. "How did the two of you meet?"

"By coincidence. Warren Shearer, an old army buddy of mine, went to live in New York when he was mustered out. He and Gene became friends. When I came through the Big City at the end of my three-and-a-half years of service for God, country and civilization, Warren introduced us. We got to be very close, Gene and I. I think he's a very special guy."

"Special in what way?"

"A lot of ways. The fact that he was a conscientious objector in the war, for example. The government put him in a Maryland work camp, planting trees for eighteen months. He wrote a damn good play about it. I've always admired him for his guts. You see, such a thing wouldn't have entered my mind. Personal character, strong beliefs, things of that sort, of course play their part in such a radical decision, but family background also has its influence. I come from a lower middle-class, apolitical, socially uncommitted, Orthodox-Jewish immigrant mother and father of Polish-Austrian origin. Gene's mother and father were socialist pacifists in Omaha..."

"Omaha? Omaha, *Nebraska*?" Grady interrupted, astonishment widening his eyes.

"Dat's da place," replied Hank, grinning. People were always surprised when they learned Gene came from Omaha.

"The same Omaha that gave the world Marlon Brando, Montgomery Clift, Henry Fonda, Dorothy McGuire, Fred and Adele Astaire?"

"The same Omaha 'with the dirty face,' as Carl Sandburg described it."

Grady looked thoughtful. "I wonder if there's another town in the States that per capita has given Hollywood so many stars. And I certainly never thought of Omaha as having socialist-pacifists," added Lester.

"Well, it'll never forget that it had the Lerners, I'll tell you that," said Hank, warming up to the subject. "What a family! Gene's parents came from Russia and his mother always refused to marry Gene's father, even though they produced six kids. She had her undeviating principles. No belief in God, but faith in life. No religion but love for humanity. Equality of the sexes. Spiritual and moral freedom for women. Six kids in eleven years! What kind of freedom is that for a woman, I ask you?"

Grady grunted in amusement. Hank recognized that Lester was interested in his account of Gene and the Lerners, and wanted to keep him talking. As they continued their slow walking towards Capriccio's, Hank found his own desire to reminisce compelling. Perhaps it was nerves, confusion, Gene's silence. But there was also something else and he couldn't put his finger on it.

"Gene's mother's quite a gal. You would describe her as an ever-replenishing fungus of yeast," Hank went on, his fondness and appreciation for Mrs. Lerner evident. "She's spent her life trying to lift anything and everyone to the level of her over-fecund hope for mankind, a socialist nirvana for all but the rich. She adores poetry, drama, opera, music, and is mad about dance.

"When Mrs. Lerner was younger, she used to stage shows and literary readings of all cultures for workers and their families in the Workmen's Circle meeting hall in Omaha's black ghetto, where the Lerners lived, one of the few white families which did."

"Love it, I love it," Grady commented, slapping Hank's shoulder. "C'mon, tell me more."

"Well, Gene's father spent most of his life as painter-and-paper-hanger and state secretary of the Socialist Party. Every two years he was a candidate for some local or state office. Gene, his older brother and his four sisters used to be his campaigners – six kids boldly marching out to the meatpacking factories to sing

The Internationale and pass out Socialist propaganda. Gene's dad always ran a close race. One percent of the votes for him, 99 percent for the other candidates."

Grady laughed. "Great copy. Fascinating as hell," he said, clearly savoring Hank's revelations. They were turning the corner of the Veneto up Via Liguria. Hank realized that Lester's previously affable, smiling face was now serious, and that his step had quickened.

"You went to the Massachusetts School of the Arts and Boston U., didn't you?" Grady asked Hank.

"I plead guilty."

"And Gene?"

"George Washington University, where he graduated Phi Beta Kappa. Then on to Catholic University for a master's in Speech and Drama. All in Washington, D.C."

They walked even more quickly as they neared the "in" restaurant, Grady remained silent, lost in thought. They were immediately shown to a table on the covered terrace. Without speaking, Lester motioned to Hank to sit. As they settled in their seats, Grady asked, "Would you like a drink?"

"I would, thanks. A Negroni would be great."

"Two Negronis," Grady said to the head waiter. Hank sat waiting for Lester to pick up the thread… something…

Finally, Grady spoke.

"You've been here before. When was that?"

"1949. I did France, Germany, Austria, Switzerland, Italy."

"In how much time?"

"Fifteen months. Mostly in Paris. I studied Art at the Sorbonne and French at the Alliance Française. All on the G.I. Bill, of course. It was then that I swore I was going to find a way to get back to Europe to live."

The Negronis were served. The Grady-Kaufman glasses clicked and a portion of their contents were sipped.

"And Gene?" Lester asked, his mind unmistakenly on single track. "Gene was one hundred percent for it. You see, after his stint in that conscientious objector's camp…" Hank paused, struck by the awareness that he was being interviewed. And so was Gene, in absentia. As nonchalantly as he could, he savored another sip of his Negroni as a cover for the realization. Interviewed. What for?

"After his stint in that conscientious objector's camp," Hank repeated, speaking more slowly, carefully studying Grady's face, "and a couple of years of fighting it out on Broadway, Gene became a purser-pharmacist mate in the Merchant Marine. From '46 to '48, he came across to Italy maybe a dozen times on those creaking Liberty Ships for UNFRA, bringing food, clothing, machinery, the whole bit, to help Europe recover."

Grady fondled his glass, only glancing at Hank from time to time, but there was no doubt in Hank's mind that he was absorbing every word being spoken.

"After each trip," Hank went on, conscious of the new atmosphere, "Gene used to recount to me his reactions to Italians struggling to overcome the destruction and deprivations that Fascism, Nazism and the war forced upon them. He seemed a troubadour as he described the people and the country. The images he evoked rocked my mind. My compulsion to travel, see and feel it all for myself grew steadily through all the things Gene described."

There was a pause. "We had better order," said Grady, as the waiting maître d'hôtel handed each the menu.

Hank gave Grady a long look, then made the decision. He would tell Lester about the agency plan. "And Les, after we've ordered, I want to tell you about a plan I've presented to Gene. I would like your reaction," Hank said carefully.

The glance from Grady was sharp. "I would love to hear it."

And so, in the palate-stimulating atmosphere of the elegant restaurant, Hank combined forkfuls of exquisite cannelloni with explanations of his agency concept. While the fan-magazine editor played with his food, he listened attentively, rarely interrupting. By his head nods and the responsiveness evident in his eyes, it became clear to Hank that Grady saw the promise in the project.

"Let's face it," Lester said as Hank finished the cannelloni and was ready to enjoy his piccata di vitello, topped with fresh parsley sprigs and surrounded by slices of lemon. "More and more action is taking place here. It seems that every American star, director or writer is either in Europe or is willing to come.

"Every Hollywood agent, business manager and lawyer is telling their clients to consider foreign residence, so they can keep every last penny they own. If you're a foreign resident, you don't even have to file a tax return on earned income, did you know that? Tax havens are tax heavens not only for corporations, the corrupt and the rich-bitches, but for everyone climbing up or falling down in Hollywood.

"Let me give you just a few examples of some of the biggies in Europe right this minute or who are due here in the next couple of months. Ingrid Bergman. Marlon Brando. Kirk Douglas. Shelley Winters. Pier Angeli. Lana Turner. Ava Gardner. Humphrey Bogart. Zsa Zsa Gabor. Claudette Colbert. Errol Flynn. Charlton Heston. Hedy Lamarr. Anthony Quinn. And let's not ignore some of those top Hollywood directors like Joseph Losey, Robert Rossen and Jules Dassin who have set up shop in Europe to be as far as possible from Joe McCarthy's halitosis. Or some of the august untouchables like Joe Mankiewicz, William Wyler and Robert Wise.

"Ol' buddy, you said you wanted my reactions to this agency idea of yours," Grady went on. "For my money, it makes a hell of a lot of sense."

"It's still only an idea, Les," replied Hank. "I think it'll work. But I haven't yet heard from Gene. So there's nothing sure about it."

"Let's go on the premise that you'll go ahead. That means the two of you will be here on the spot. Now I want *you* to do the eating and let *me* do all the talking. No interruptions, please." At last Grady was coming to the crux of what had been simmering in his mind, Hank realized.

"I want to make a deal with the Kaufman-Lerner duo." Hank's heart leaped. "I want the two of you to track down all the stars and personalities flocking over here. I want you and Gene to get some good, fat, exciting stories out of them." Hank fought to keep any exhibition of astonishment from his face. "Away from home, far from studio influences," Grady continued, "I have a hunch that they'll be more open and available. And I know I can count on the two of you to give me stuff that's more revealing and substantial than the drivel we normally get back home."

Hank was no longer eating. What Les was saying had all of Hank's concentration. Stunned by the offer, Hank needed a little time to get his thoughts together. "But Les, I don't know…" he stammered.

"I said don't interrupt," reproached Grady, shaking a finger at Hank. "And I'll tell it to you up front. There'll be no cheap bargaining. I'll pay you guys top prices, because I've learned enough about Gene and more about you to assure me that you're going to give me really high-level stuff."

"Look, Les, I *have* to interrupt," Hank interjected. "I'm not sure this is anything Gene or I will want to do – particularly Gene. What he wants to write are plays. And if we go ahead with the agency, writing interviews for *Silver Screen* and *Screenland* may not jibe."

"Baby, you are wrong. So way, way wrong," responded Grady. "You'll get official press cards, I'll see to that. They give you status, entrée, the right to residence and work permits, and big reductions on travel. You want all that, my friend. I'll make the two of you exclusive for the entire continent. And that means when you make a trip for an interview, it's all on me, and I'm not going to ask you if you do other business at the same time. It's going to help, not hinder, your agency plan, I'm telling you. And if Gene really wants to be realistic, I don't see how he or anybody else could have the time and energy to be a serious playwright and serious agent simultaneously."

"I don't know, Les," Hank replied, shaking his head. "I can't tell what the future will bring." But man, you are getting through to me, Hank was saying to himself. Legal status. Residence permits. Entrée. Greenback money, money, *money*! Yes, Lester, old buddy, you are indeed getting through to me!

"I've still got a long way to go, so will you please not interrupt me, Hankie-pankie," remarked Grady, cocking his head. "And if I haven't sold you by the time I'm finished the first round, then I'll just start in all over again." His intensity was genuine and infectious.

"I want a story on each and every one of the artists I've already mentioned. And I want more. It's time to give Europe its due. French ooo-lala's like Martine Carol, Michèle Morgan, Simone Signoret, Danielle Darieux. And Mr. Savoir-Faire, Charles Boyer. And the Italian contingent. Sensational. Tremendous. That Anna Magnani. All glow and burn."

"Don't I know it," Hank broke in, enthusiastically.

"The titsy titillators like Gina Lollobrigida and Silvana Mangano. And that young new babe who out-balloons them all, Sophia Loren. Rossana Podestà, all that young innocence packed in a keg of dynamite. Vittorio Gassman, the husband Shelley Winters has been trying like hell to housebreak. Rossano Brazzi, who's got every female from eight to eighty twitching over his 'I love you' vibrato."

Hank kept listening to Grady's recital of names. He tried to recall when he had last read a fan magazine. He couldn't remember. But he did recall that it had all seemed to him cheap trash concocted for adolescent-minded kooks who sought to escape from reality by identifying with stars they so adoringly watched on silver screens. And yet, the more Grady went on, the more Hank began to feel that what Grady really wanted was more depth and more honesty in interviews with great movie personalities, and the idea of getting involved seemed to Hank very intriguing.

"There are more – American, French, Italian, English, all nationalities and sexes. And there'll be even *more*," Lester went on. "Now, listen carefully, Hankie boy. I want not only your ears, but your *kop* and your pocketbook all at strict attention to what Lester Grady is saying. I'm counting on you and Gene and I'm dead serious. I know it's going to be great for me, great for the fans, great for you. A touch of class, courtesy of Hank Kaufman and Gene Lerner, and you solve the problem which has been bugging me for weeks."

Hank looked at his host and his host looked at Hank in a dangling moment of silence.

"If we end up saying yes," Hank finally replied, "do we have total carte blanche? Let's say we set up a system whereby we agree, you, Gene and me, on the personalities to be interviewed. After that, do you eat what we write, the way we write it, without change or censorship?"

"Basically, no problem," Grady answered.

"Look, Les, you're wonderful and I love you and I've loved the lunch and your offer is very tempting…"

"Don't give me any buts, pal."

"But I have to…" responded Hank. "I have to talk it over with Gene. We have to reflect. And if we decide to go ahead, we have to agree on money and expenses."

"We'll agree! We're friends, aren't we?" said Grady, as if that settled everything. "You talk to Gene. You and he tell me how much you want per story, a good but fair price, no holdups. I'll do everything I can to come up with the dough. Today's July 13. I want an answer no later than August 1. That's the deadline. But I want you to tell me right now, do we, in principle, have a deal?"

What do I say, Hank asked himself. It makes sense, so much damn sense from a practical point of view. The situation we're in doesn't offer much choice. Why turn down something tangible at a time when nothing else is? And it certainly is a plus in our effort to make it in Europe, where we want to be.

Finally, Hank spoke. "Mr. Lester Grady," he said, stretching his right hand towards the editor of *Silver Screen* and *Screenland*. "I have the pleasure of announcing to you that in principle, you have yourself a deal with Hank Kaufman and Gene Lerner."

Lester beamed. Pumping Hank's hand with exuberance, he alternated a series of "great"s with a number of "I'm thrilled, just thrilled." "This calls for champagne," Grady announced with a flourish.

Hank shook his head, then wiggled his finger in front of Grady's face in admonishment. "Not champagne, pal. We're in *bella* Roma, remember? Spumante is what we want. The best spumante from the finest vineyard in good old Italia!"

*

July 18, 1953

HANK KAUFMAN
PENSIONE GIGLIESI
PORTA PINCIANA 106
ROMA, ITALIA

LETTER ARRIVED STOP NO MONEY NO AGENCY BACKGROUND NO CLIENTS NO SPEAK ITALIAN SO WHAT HAVE WE GOT TO LOSE STOP AVANTI STOP ARRIVING ROME EXPRESS 7H43 TUESDAY MORNING IF GENERAL STRIKE PERMITS.

LOVE, GENE

On September 9, 1953, Hank Kaufman and Gene Lerner moved into Via Aiaccio 12-bis. They were talent representatives without clients or experience, publicists without an account. But thanks to Lester Grady, as journalists they were fully accredited with Italian ministries, and joined the Foreign Press

Club. The Kaufman-Lerner arrival on the Rome show business scene was heralded by the distribution of more than a thousand announcements to every conceivable element of the local motion picture industry. They made an absolutely spectacular impression – on wastebaskets...

Ah, *bellissima* Italia! Thank you and bless you for giving two American Columbuses, with 620 US greenbacks between them, their chance to discover you and to be discovered! That was Hank's prayer when, in Gene's presence, and under the watchful eyes of Count and Countess Luigi Colisi-Rossi, from whom they had rented the premises for roughly $70 a month, he nailed an engraved and polished brass plate reading, "Kaufman-Lerner Associates" to one side of the wrought-iron gate leading down to the apartment, which was now home and office. The Colisi-Rossis, an impoverished couple from the lesser nobility, occupied a rambling apartment fronting on Via Aiaccio. Hank and Gene's garden flat was considerably more modest.

Via Aiaccio curved in a gentle arc in a middle-class residential area off Corso Trieste, a minute's bus ride from the Via Veneto. "You might as well be in Florence," was the sneering reaction of an assistant director who eventually made his way there. "Nobody, but nobody, will take you seriously out here in this suburbia."

Suburbia? Maybe to him, and maybe he was accurate in his snide prediction. But on September 9, 1953, what in hell difference did it make? The iron gate proudly embellished with the "Kaufman-Lerner Associates" brass plate opened onto a stone paved, oleander-lined path leading to a lush Roman garden. What other talent agency in the world had a grape arbor, pomegranate trees and gigantic multihued rose bushes? True, agencies normally had clients, made deals for them and earned ten-percent commissions. But did they have a garden that in good weather (which was most of the time) would double as a waiting room? And such high-beamed ceilings? And such wonderfully baroque furnishings and tapestries provided by the Colisi-Rossis?

Not that the Colisi-Rossis ever quite comprehended what the Signori American were up to. Talent agency? Public relations consultation? They understood that there was some connection with cinema and that in itself was suspicious. From time to time, Hank caught Il Conte or La Contessa peering through their windows, awaiting some proof of illicit trafficking, or some indication of wild orgies or unspeakable perversions.

For months, their suspicion was aroused by Hank's and Gene's wearisome morning-and-night ritual of moving much of the Colisi-Rossi furniture so as to convert the Kaufman-Lerner home into Kaufman-Lerner offices, and vice versa once the long day's work was finished.

The two bedrooms had to be transformed into private offices, one for each of the partners. Beds became respectable divans. Tables and chairs were moved in to create an un-bedroom-like setting for those who were to be received. The long, antique table in the living-cum-dining room, upon which Hank and Gene shared their self-cooked midday and evening meals, were transformed into a receptionist's desk, and all of the Colisi-Rossi-owned furniture rearranged to project the appropriate waiting-room aspect. The mite of a kitchen was cleaned, then shut off to avoid any aroma of cooking oils or scent of appetizing pasta sauces. An office, alas, is not a home, particularly when transformation from one to the other and back again is required six days of every week, month after month.

Two very telling facts helped allay the Colisi-Rossis' dark conjectures. Kaufman and Lerner were Americans, and the Italian love affair with the USA had not yet cooled. Americans were still considered to exemplify idealistic Emersonians rather than shrewd Machiavellians. And they had paid the Colisi-Rossi's three months' rent. Cash in advance.

Gene's talent department started with excruciating slowness and the revenue it provided over the forthcoming months barely reached the postage stamp level. Sadly, it became clear to him and Hank that to build it would require a great deal of time, stubborn effort, painstaking organization and preparation to enter a jungle wild with outdated practices and a gamut of problems.

Fortunately, the Grady connection went into immediate gear. Ingrid Bergman. Anna Magnani. The rising starlets of Italy, including Rossana Podestà. Anonymous dubbing artists like Lydia Simoneschi, who provided Italian-voiced histrionics for the throats of Katharine Hepburn, Ava Gardner, Rita Hayworth, Bette Davis and virtually every other American or British female star. Interviews in Paris with Claudette Colbert and Zsa Zsa Gabor. Errol Flynn, back in Rome. Kirk Douglas. Lana Turner. Pier Angeli.

But what about Hedy Lamarr, whose naked run through the woods in a European import inspirationally entitled *Ecstasy* provided her springboard to world stardom?

"Why don't we have lunch together tomorrow?" she asked Hank with dripping sweetness, when he was finally put through to her Hassler Hotel suite after eighteen tries over a period of four days. "Would it be convenient for Mr. Lerner and you to make it at Capriccio's at one o'clock?" she added.

"That would be lovely, Miss Lamarr," replied Hank, images of his wonderful lunch with Grady bringing aromas in his nose. "Gene, she's invited us to lunch tomorrow," he announced to his partner, adding, almost salaciously, "At Capriccio's."

They had been waiting at the second-floor entrance to the dining room when, nearly half an hour late, she finally appeared. Beautiful she was, but she struck Hank and Gene both as being too thin. Her face seemed strangely unfeminine and her movements and gestures were angular and constructed. She was more curt than polite as introductions took place. Her telephone graciousness had disappeared.

Maître d'hôtel obeisance, hovering waiters, elbows, whispers and glances from other diners as she preceded Hank and Gene to a table of honor. She accepted the attention matter-of-factly. When the menu was placed before her, she took endless time to examine it, as a biologist would examine cells under a microscope. Hank and Gene both had a sensation of being erased by her. How were they ever going to find a channel of communication with this expert in non-communication?

She ordered appetizer, pasta, fish course, meat dish, dessert, accompanied by aperitivo, wine, liqueur and coffee. Hank and Gene also ordered an ample, but less plentiful repast. As she ate and drank with sensual relish, the two interviewers made an effort at conversation. Any and every question asked seemed to her an interruption to her eating rhythm, or a challenge. They were ruthlessly examined but never really answered.

It was a miserable, futile lunch. Even the luscious *cucina* that made Capriccio so famous seemed bland. Both Hank and Gene grew increasingly depressed by their incapacity to get anything substantive from Madame Ecstasy. Although they were getting lunch, they certainly were not getting an interview.

The ordeal finally came to an end, thank the Lord. Hedy did not ask for the check. Hank did not ask for it. Neither did

Gene. Finally, she said, "It's late and I must go." The waiter, overhearing her statement, took it as an order to bring the check. With a graceful sweep, he returned with a silver tray with the discreetly folded bill, placing it in neutral territory on the table.

Miss Lamarr simply eliminated it from her line of vision. She opened her compact to check her makeup. Gene and Hank became hypnotized by the folded monster lying threateningly on its silver bed. The compact closed with a resounding click. The star looked to her left. She looked to her right. The sound of her voice startled Gene and Hank. Addressing neither of them in particular, she spoke her command. "Will you pay the check so I can go?"

"Miss Lamarr," a blushing Gene began. "There seems to be a misunderstanding. Hank... Mr. Kaufman... and I thought you were inviting us to lunch."

"What?!" she crescendoed. "Why should I have invited you and..." She haughtily stared Hank down. "And him? I'm not accustomed to taking men to lunch. And you were desperately trying to get an interview with me. Look at the break I've given you."

"But Miss Lamarr," Gene insisted, both embarrassed and resentful. "It was you who proposed lunch. It was you who selected Capriccio and set the time. We never doubted for a moment that we were to be your guests."

"Well, you're *not*! So kindly pay the check." Hedy's enraged eyes darted from Gene to Hank, then back again to Gene. "Or I'll just get up and leave!"

Hank virtually jumped. "You can't do that," he said. "The truth is... well... the truth is... Look, Miss Lamarr, we haven't got the money. All we have between us is a little more than five dollars, and..." Hank gulped and fumbled into silence, as he and Gene waited fearfully for the reaction.

The glare in her eyes could have doubled for a lighthouse beam on a stormy night. "You mean..." She was spluttering. "You mean... you two came to... to have lunch with me, me, with..." She almost couldn't bring herself to say it. "With *five* dollars? *Five* lousy dollars? ABSOLUTELY UNHEARD OF!" she screamed. All action stopped. Open-mouthed, every other diner in the room froze, knives and forks suspended in midair. With all his might, Gene wished that he was back in New York with his two fried eggs, ham, toast and coffee at the 57th Street

Automat instead of sitting at Capriccio's on the Via Liguria in Rome with Hedy Lamarr.

Mouthing obscenities, she opened her purse with as much clicking and clacking as she could make. With ill-contained rage, she plopped several bills on the tray, then shut her purse and ungraciously pushed away the waiter who courteously tried to help her rise from her seat. As all the diners and most of the restaurant personnel stared, she started to make her exit without another word to the two shaken young men, who didn't know where to look or hide.

To Hank's and Gene's horror, they saw her stop, turn, and head towards their table. Shakily, both rose. Hank was certain she had decided to ask for the five dollars. She didn't even bother to look at him or Gene. She simply scooped up the change that had been placed on the table under the paid bill, stuck it in her pocket, and made her second exit, which, to Hank's and Gene's relief, was also her final one.

Fortunately, Hank's publicity and promotional activities were catching. He was selected to handle press for actress Nadia Gray, of Hungarian origin, who, while already somewhat established in Italian and French films, including *La Dolce Vita*, wanted to make an international career. Hank was also chosen to mount an industry campaign on behalf of Marisa Pavan, Anna Maria Pierangeli's 19-year-old twin, who, at Momma Enrichetta Pierangeli's relentless urging, had decided to enter the career race. Marisa finally emerged with a personality of her own and, as Anna Magnani's daughter in Hal Wallis' *The Rose Tattoo*, was nominated for an Oscar in the category Best Supporting Actress.

When Hank was hired to act as Gina Lollobrigida's foreign press representative, she had already made such film successes as *Fanfan la Tulipe*, opposite the great French actor Gérard Philipe, *Belle de Nuit* and *La Provinciale*. La "Lollo Nazionale," as she was referred to, was fast emerging as a star of the first magnitude in Italian and French films. The *Daily American* referred to her as "a sort of moving version of an historical novel's book-jacket."

In the six years since this curvaceous country girl from Subiaco, a village on Rome's outskirts, had been chosen Miss Italy, she had become one of Europe's biggest box office attractions. Dr. Milko Skofic, her ambitious husband-manager of Yugoslav birth, had decided to limit his medical practice to Lollo. He felt

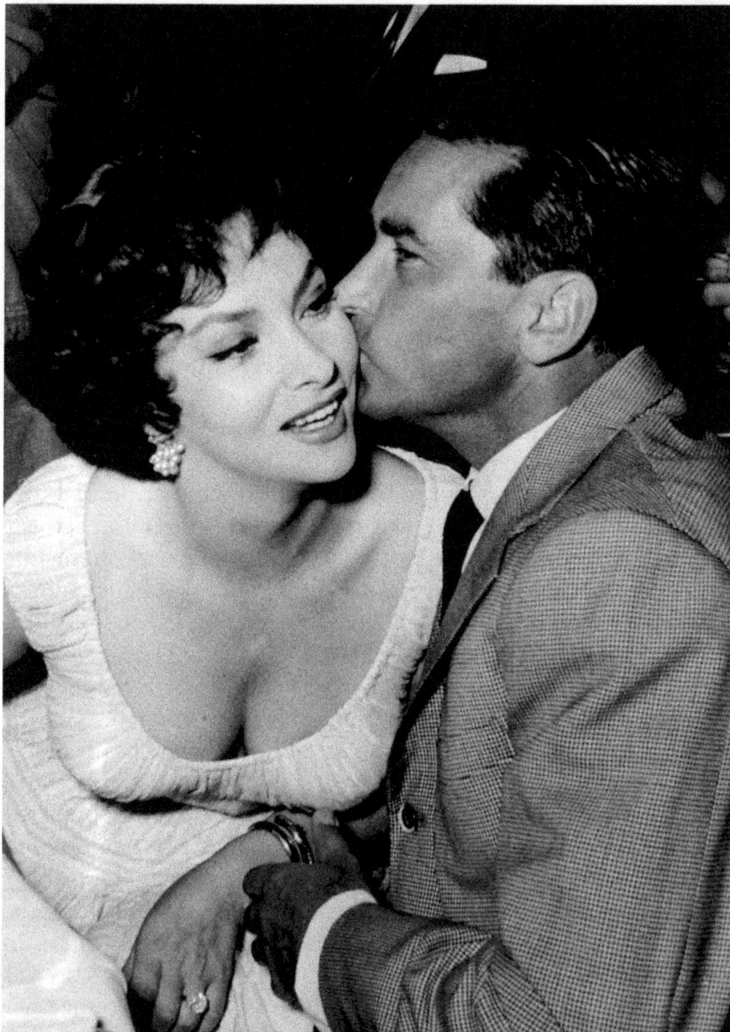

Gina Lollobrigida and Milko Skofic

the time had arrived for her succulent physical proportions, talent and name to reach every corner of the globe, with particular emphasis on the U.S.A.

Gina basked totally, blissfully, under the firm thumb of her very handsome Milko. It was perfectly okay with her that he chose her films, supervised her deals, handled all her business affairs, decided what she should wear, declared what she should utter to the press. Rumor had it that they were both so concerned with preserving her unblemished, splendiferous body that it was unwise to risk any damage by subjecting it to any type of sexual activity.

When interviews with the foreign press were arranged, Gina would glance helplessly towards darling Milko to take her cue from him or to allow him to answer posed questions. Admittedly, her knowledge of English at that time was limited. And there was another factor. She was embarrassed by her country hands, which, she felt, were unattractive and unfeminine, unfit to be attached to the rest of her exquisite body. She did everything possible to hide or disguise them.

When Hank entered the picture, Lollo was filming what was perhaps her most challenging film to date, *La Romana*, based on the novel by Alberto Moravia, under the direction of Luigi Zampa. In *La Romana*, she was facing her real test as an actress. Skofic took up a burning question with Hank. "Surely her name is unpronounceable to you Americans. Should we change it now so she is prepared for greater American identification?" Lollo's doctor queried. Gina glared but listened quietly. "Lo-lo-*bri*-gi-da," Hank repeated several times, savoring each syllable. "It's never going to be pronounced right," Hank concluded. "But it's Gina or Lollo here, so why wouldn't it be the same in the States and everywhere else?"

A broad grin appeared over Gina's face. She rarely opposed Milko on anything, but now she spoke up. "My name is my name. I'm not going to change it." And Gina was right.

Called everything from Lo-llo-bree-*gee*-da to Lollo-frigida, thanks to Humphrey Bogart, her co-star in her first American film, *Beat the Devil*, she achieved fame in the United States as much for the seeming inability of the public to pronounce her name correctly as for her spectacular physical qualities. The importers of that delicious Italian white wine, Fazi Battaglia Verdicchio, took a leaf from the Lollobrigida book. Their recent stateside advertising campaign, including costly television commercials, was based on American inability to pronounce the wine's name correctly, and it resulted in soaring sales.

Beat the Devil, a cult classic, was a cinematic romp put together by John Huston for a few of his drinking buddies, shot mainly in the resort town of Ravello overlooking the Bay of

Naples. Gina was mystified by, but played along with all their in-talk and in-jokes, which Bogart, Peter Lorre, Robert Morley and Huston all participated in. "She's really a great sport," Bogey said. "She's really the wide-open type, with a hell of a lot to her. And all of it meets the eye! That gal is molten ore, and boy, she's really got heat. Look at me, I'm a crisp."

Huston, never one to be left out of any intellectual debate, had this to offer: "In any serious discussion of Gina's talent, you can't ignore her bosom. That is an extraordinary talent to have and to hold. In fact, every time Gina comes to mind, I find myself seeing even her elbows as bosoms."

Finally, Errol Flynn, her leading man in *Crossed Swords*: "What a department store! She has everything you could want on every floor and plenty of overstock too."

As Hank was to discover during one of his first meetings with Lollo and Skofic, she possessed a kittenish sense of humor. Bosley Crowther, eminent critic of *The New York Times*, in his review of *Fanfan la Tulipe*, labeled her "that Italian doll." "How do you feel about Crowther's comment?" Hank asked her. La Lollo glanced at Milko, turned to Hank, giggled. "*Molto bene.* A doll is something you love to play with," she replied, rolling her eyes suggestively. Hank then asked if she understood the meaning of "doll" in the Damon Runyonesque sense. While Skofic looked on primly, Gina's big brown eyes assumed a too-innocent look, as she nodded. "It's like *pupa* in Italiano. A *pupa* can be loved and looked after by daddy, but it does not always have to be her own daddy," she explained in her spaghetti-flecked English. Milko gave her a disapproving look.

"But Hank, now you know me a little. I'm a very simple, a very good girl. I don't gamble. I don't smoke. I don't drink. I don't take drugs. Gina has no vices. Yes, Gina is a very good girl." She cast a mischievous glance at her husband, enjoying her moment of teasing him. "And I am never wicked with other men. Yes, Gina is a very good girl. How could I be anything else? Milko never leaves me for a second. When I was on location with Bogey, there were so many stories that we were having a wild affair together. I ask you, how was such a thing possible when my darling was there all the time? When we went to England to finish the picture, I met Lauren Bacall for the first time. Mrs. Bogey looked me up and down and down and up with those burning green eyes of hers, not saying anything. She made me very nervous. Then she turned to Milko and said to him, 'I hope you kept both your eyes on them. In these matters, I don't believe in lend-lease.'" Gina looked questionably at Skofic. "I never understood this lend-lease business. What does it mean?"

The good doctor looked at his wife for a moment, in silence. "It's what you do not do with other men, darling. And what Bogey should not do with other women but his wife!"

Gina's success made her rich. Skofic felt that they should leave their modest penthouse on the Via Taro off the Via Salaria and buy something more in keeping with her star standing. They purchased an elaborate villa on the Appia Antica, surrounded by high walls, thick shrubbery and huge trees to keep out prying eyes. Shortly after they moved into the sumptuous, ostentatiously furnished and decorated mansion, Hank had to accompany Ted Richmond, Tyrone Power's producer, to the new premises to explore a prospective film with Lollo.

The Italian actress had begun to shed some of her former reserve. Perhaps aided by her new role as "chatelaine" of such an impressive establishment, she was becoming somewhat more self-assured. Practicing some of her newly acquired English, Gina asked, "May I offer you some whiskey? I think all Americans love their whiskey, no?" Richmond and Hank opted instead for cognac. The request obviously took Gina by surprise. Skofic's eyes were trained on her as she surveyed the rows of glasses in the gilt and lacquer cupboard by the bar. To her husband's horror, she hesitantly selected the tallest tumblers in the collection. She blithely proceeded to fill each glass to the brim with Courvoisier Napoleon brandy, as if it were Pepsi-Cola.

As the years went by, there was no longer a Milko Skofic. But Gina had become too habituated to those of the Hippocratic faith to make too sudden a change in her species of worship. Though in any examination of her vital organs there was no manifestation of heart difficulty, she became attracted to Dr. Christiaan Barnard, the South African medicine man who astounded the world by performing the first human heart transplant in the history of mankind.

Barnard was tall, urbane, charming, attractive, and at that time, perhaps the most front-paged male on the globe. Gina delightedly basked in her friendship with a genius applauded by the world. Barnard kept making excuses to the international press about his frequent visits to Rome, but neither he nor Gina really made a serious effort at discretion, even though Barnard was still very much wived. With all the photographed comings-and-goings of a smiling, happy Gina clinging to the arm of a proud, affectionate Barnard, it seemed foolish to try to deny that Gina was the focus of his Italian medical practice.

Soon there was no more Christiaan Barnard, soon less and less of a movie career. Never again marrying after her divorce from Skofic, Gina turned to world traveling and photography, and became an amusing *raconteuse* in several languages. She shrewdly found ways to keep herself in the public eye. But whatever the activity, the presumed romance of her contact with the powerful and famous, she could not hide the growing desperation one sensed in her. The legend of the untouchable body had already collapsed through her apparent increase of interest in sex and in games women play with men. As time went on, she seemed to have less and less compunction in making a male aware of her interest, obviously weighing his attributes as she examined him from toe to head. If the man intrigued her sufficiently, she did not seem to mind putting all her attributes into the fray.

March 13, 1967 was one time she lost the game, and lost it bad.

With the conclusion of the Command Performance of *The Taming of the Shrew*, stars Elizabeth Taylor and Richard Burton and director Franco Zeffirelli were limousined to the Grand Ballroom of London's Dorchester Hotel to preside over the lavish party organized by Columbia Pictures to celebrate the gala premiere.

Elizabeth and Richard were charming, radiant and graciously majestic. Zeffirelli was sparkling, wittily fending of all the exuberant tributes to his genius. The toasting, which began immediately, seemed never to end. Much of it was due to the presence of a considerable number of Burton's relatives and friends, who had come over from Wales for the occasion. The more they imbibed, the more they sang, ranging from the most bawdy to the most tender. Elizabeth, her radiance sometimes in conflict with her quaffing, tried to join in with the infectious Welsh harmonies, which continued well into the London dawn.

Among the guest-glitter was another queen of the cinema, looking particularly ravishing in an astonishing décolleté of white satin that seemed in constant peril of popping. It was Lollobrigida, concentrating all her wiles on her companion, named

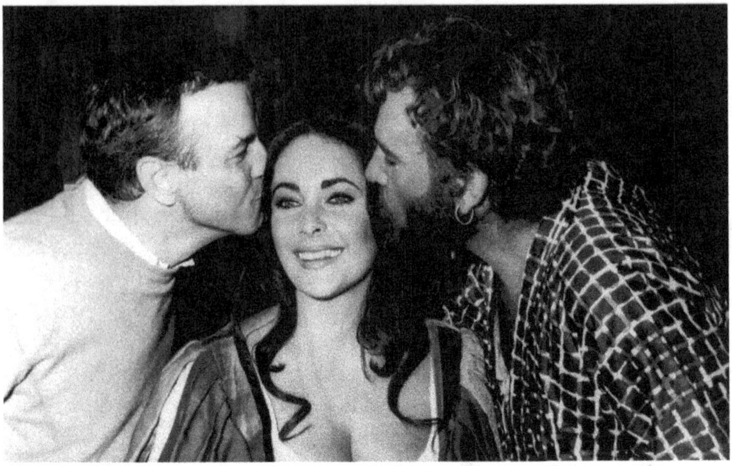

Franco Zeffirelli, Elizabeth Taylor and Richard Burton

Rudolf, whom she clutched on the dance floor. The two had met for the first time while in the receiving line to meet the Royal Family prior to the showing of *Taming of the Shrew*. Now they whirled, twirled, held each other close dance after dance, her partner cutting a splendid, dashing figure, which entranced not only her but most of the guests. At a certain moment, after whispering a few words into Gina's ear, a generous smile and a sweeping bow, Rudolf took his leave.

He was not again seen that night.

"But he promised me he would be back in no more than an hour," a tearful Gina later confided to Zeffirelli.

"What a silly little idiot you are," Franco replied, shaking his head in disbelief. "Why, you're just a babe-in-the-woods. How can you be so unsophisticated? *Carissima mia*, he panicked. It's as simple as that. And he's not coming back. You women! You're all so convinced that your femininity will conquer all and everyone. You're so certain you can surmount any obstacle to getting what you want from a man," Zeffirelli concluded.

A dazed Gina looked at Franco. She? Lollobrigida? The sex-symbol desired by millions of males? Rejected? How was it possible that she had been rejected by… Rudolf Nureyev?

Gina's bewitchment did not seem to fail her back in Rome on the night of October 18, 1969. It seemed that Gina had made up her mind to "make it" with one of the magnificent astronauts who had participated in America's first moon landing on July 9 of that same year.

The astronauts and their wives were making a good-will tour of the world, and Gina felt a great deal of good will for the space heroes. She gave a fabulous party in their honor at her Appia Antica villa, an exciting throwback to the *Dolce Vita* days. According to friends, Gina clearly had an underlying purpose for the event, and if solemn oaths on mothers' heads are to be believed, she achieved it. Intimates swear that when the party was at its glittering height, one of the astronauts "lost" his wife among the milling crowd in order to meet Gina in upper-floor privacy, and that Lollo's once so sacrosanct body went swirling into orbit with one of America's stratospheric valiants.

Hank had a Rome reunion last March with one of his favorite "old-timers," whose "Photo by Pierluigi" trademark was so well known everywhere that few in the film world knew he had a surname. An indisputable star in his profession, Pierluigi Praturlon, in his 35-year career, has photographed every male and female star of international cinema, building longtime friendships with greats like John Wayne and Frank Sinatra. Very much a man's man he is, though wizen-faced, raucous-voiced and scraggy as a scarecrow, a man for whom women feel strong affinity.

The conversation turned to Gina, whom Pierluigi has known for thirty years. The photographer spoke of her with unquestionable affection. "As magnificent as she was and as she still is, she's lost. What she and Skofic had was a business partnership instead of a marriage. She genuinely loved him. She truly wanted only him. But when a career booms, you don't stop to weigh the basic things of life you really need. Everything gets confused, distorted by the demands of the career. It's always a more damaging problem for girls of simple origin because they're less able to cope. You can't blame Milko for what happened, you can't blame Gina. Today, she's alone. Yes, she has a beautiful son, but she's really alone. And I've seen her be so aggressive, brazen even. And that's not the Gina that was meant to be." Praturlon couldn't continue. He shook his head sorrowfully, avoiding Hank's gaze in order to hide his emotion.

Hank and Gene had previously met Marlon Brando in New York, but the first professional connection came when the unorthodox actor, who fused hero and anti-hero into a unique personage unequaled in postwar show business, hired Hank to handle his press relations during his October 1954 visit to Rome for the continental premiere of Elia Kazan's *On The Waterfront*. Brando carefully placed American Express travelers checks in Hank's left hand. Hank's right hand had been rendered useless by a cracked elbow resulting from an accidental fall and had just been put in cast and sling.

Hank's primary task was to coordinate Brando's many press activities with Enzo De Bernart, head of the Rome publicity office of Columbia Pictures. A Roman film premiere normally elicits as much excitement as the swearing in of yet another prime minister. However, the flood of demands for interviews and photographic sessions, which came to Hank and to De Bernart, served as a warning that Marlon was in for a tussle with the ladies and gentlemen of the fourth estate.

It was another of those repeated "delicate" moments in the Brando saga. The man's every peccadillo, romantic or otherwise, always became instant front-page news for the tabloids and fodder for columnists' mills. In recent weeks there had been a stunning development. Endless reams of copy had been written over Marlon's probable marriage to a now completely forgotten mademoiselle, Josanne Mariani, from the French Riviera village of Bandol. The international press was impatiently awaiting an opportunity to pounce on Brando for the inside story.

Brando and marriage. Irresistible force versus immovable mass. Erudite, intellectually eclectic, Brando undoubtedly knew the meaning of the word "bachelorhood." It was, of course, the state of being an unmarried man. That definition only proved to Brando the serious limitations of the dictionary. Bachelorhood, at least to him, was the infinite freedom to seek full satisfaction for his androgynous sexual appetite. His field-to-field capering to sow wild oats led journalists to schools of agriculture to study everything from plows to animal husbandry.

Then, too, Brando, whatever he did, whatever he said, was copy. After all, he was Brando. Elusive. Disdainful of the press. Guru of non-conformists. Puppeteer of the unexpected. The hottest male star in the world. The thrilling macho sex symbol, violence and tenderness wrestling in the night. The press was down on hands and knees, sniffing his tail, and it had no intention of letting him escape unscathed.

So Hank and De Bernart agreed that unusual security precautions were in order for the Brando premiere, against both press and public. Enzo arranged for an expanded staff. A large police contingent was requested for the Cinema Fiamma, where the sold-out event was scheduled. It was agreed that De Bernart would hold the fort at the Fiamma, while Hank and Gene, in one of those hearse-like Cadillacs, would escort Brando to the theater.

At the prescribed time, Hank and Gene appeared at Brando's hideout, the Albergo Nazionale, a simple hotel looking out onto Italy's Chamber of Deputies. When K and L arrived, Brando, clearly preoccupied, was lying down in the small room he had rented. He was anything but happy about making a public appearance. It was not his speed. Besides, he was concerned over the reaction to the film in Rome, even though it had aroused so much excitement and praise in the States. But he had given his word, and he was going to keep it, so through a rear exit, unobserved, the trio departed from the hotel in the Cadillac.

Brando kept anxiously peering through the window of the black limousine as it moved from the Albergo Nazionale to its destination. Suddenly, he pulled back, stiff and tense. "Do you see what I see?" he asked K and L. Hank and Gene looked at the unfolding scene as the Cadillac moved down the Via Bissolati towards the Fiamma. Anyone who has seen newsreels of ecstatic mobs in the Piazza Venezia listening to a Mussolini harangue will immediately get the picture. Brando sank miserably into his seat and slapped his forehead to show his disgust. Hank and Gene quickly rolled up the open car windows.

Somehow the limousine managed to keep moving through the throng of thousands that had gathered to get a glimpse of the grand Marlon. Hank frantically searched for De Bernart, who was supposed to be waiting under the marquee with the police escort. He ordered the chauffeur to honk three times, the signal agreed upon with De Bernart. De Bernart and the phalanx of uniforms quickly moved forward to the street, struggling to clear space in front of the theater's entrance. The car slithered into it, fortunately causing no casualties among the increasingly maddened throng.

As the chauffeur opened the rear door of the limousine, Gene emerged first, then Brando, followed by Hank. Brando was totally unprepared for the hysteria that ensued. A clutching,

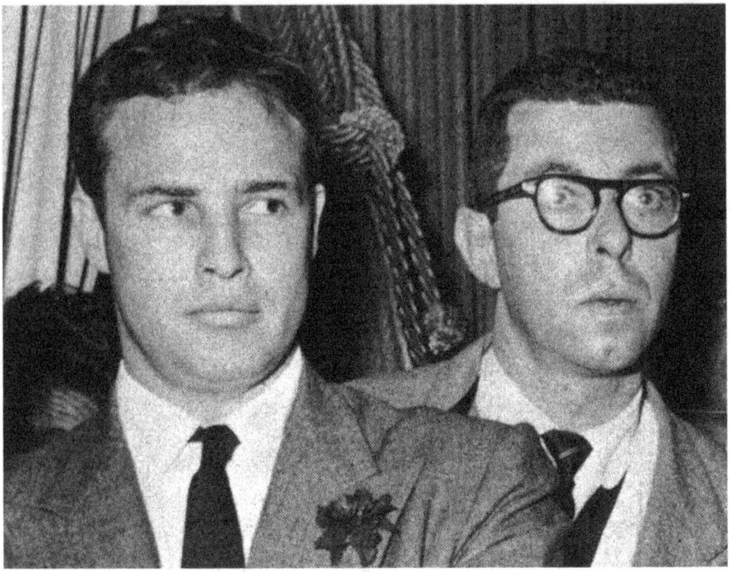

Marlon Brando and Hank Kaufman

pulling, pummeling, screaming mob that was struck by Brando-fever engulfed him. The frenzy caused shock waves in Marlon. Terrorized as he was, he was caught by the alarm in Hank's eyes, who seemed petrified that the cast on his arm could be torn off and his injured elbow wrenched from its socket. Understanding Hank's fear, Brando changed character instantaneously. He grabbed Hank's good arm and shouted at Gene, "Stick close behind us!" With excellent football technique, he began to run interference through the crowds. Protecting Hank, he pushed past De Bernart and the police, Gene desperately trying to cover the rear. The tactic got them through unscathed.

Safely inside, Brando's nervousness once again began to show. He was immediately escorted to the first row of the mezzanine by De Bernart and other Columbia officials, flanked by a relieved Hank and Gene. His seat of honor was beside that of an opulent 19-year-old Italian actress. Even before Brando turned towards his seat, he was aware of her. His primitive juices began to flow.

Hank introduced him to Sophia Loren.

Brando had made art out of mumble. But in no film had he yet achieved the total inarticulacy which now overcame him, nor a gasping double take as extraordinary as the one prompted by Loren's frontal apparatus brimming over the mezzanine railing. Whether by design or accident, Sophia had chosen a gown with a décolletage closer to history than obscenity.

Marlon's efforts not to stare were as farcical as his double take. He was unable to utter a word, and outside of an occasional smile at each other, the two sat in fidgeting silence. Whenever Sophia seemed to be looking elsewhere, Marlon turned with open mouth and bulging eyes to stare at Sophia's twin mountains and the gorge between them. A photographer recorded one of the most comic of his surreptitious glances. For years, the photo was one of the prizes in the Kaufman-Lerner collection. It has disappeared. Would Marlon have stolen it? Or Sophia? Or someone planning to write a Freudian treatise on the female mammalia and the male stare? Or a lascivious film museum curator?

The house lights finally dimmed. Warm applause from the packed theater. The film titles began to roll. "Marlon Brando in..." Not in *On the Waterfront* but... *Fronte del Porto.* Puzzled, Marlon glanced over at Hank, then continued to watch, aghast. What was all this Italian? When finally his face flashed on the screen, he heard himself speaking not in English, not with his own voice, but in an Italian facsimile. The shock struck him like a knife. Staggering up from his seat as if from a heart attack, he grabbed Hank, in his consternation forgetting the arm injury. "Get me out of here! Get me out, get me out," he frantically whispered, panting for breath. Marlon and Hank started up the aisle, Gene anxiously following. Sophia observed the departure with a look of confusion on her face.

Marlon was sputtering in fury. "Why didn't somebody tell me I was going to see a dubbed version? I've never seen myself dubbed. I'm an actor, not a ventriloquist's dummy, for Christ's sake. Can you imagine what it's like to hear somebody else's voice come out of my mouth? You feel like a goddamn freak in a sideshow. Christ, why didn't somebody prepare me? Didn't you guys know?"

"No!" Hank replied angrily. "Nobody told us. We thought for the premiere they would show the original English-language version. I never dreamed it would be otherwise."

The ushers and policemen in the lobby looked surprised when they saw Brando leave the theater. Gene caught Brando

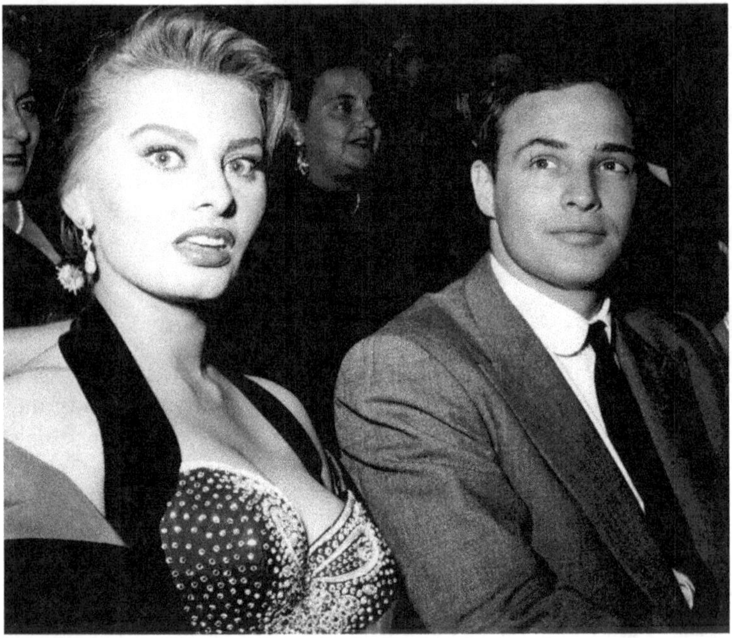

Sophia Loren and Marlon Brando

by the arm. "Marlon, hold it. Everybody will write about your leaving. They'll say you hated it, disowned it, whatever. They'll write reams on the incident and say nothing about the quality of the film." Hank nodded his agreement.

Brando lowered his eyes, then looked from Gene to Hank and again lowered his head. "Okay," he finally said. "Is there a bar near here?"

"The California, across the street. It's pretty lousy," Gene answered.

"We'll go there. Five minutes before the end of the picture, we'll sneak back in. Nobody will ever know the fucking difference."

And as the lights went up at the end of the picture, there was Brando standing by his seat, leaning over the mezzanine railing to acknowledge the wild applause and shouts of bravo that greeted his triumph. Then, in a gesture which brought further cheers and feet-stomping, he turned towards a standing and applauding Sophia. He lifted her right hand and with perfect continental aplomb brushed it with a kiss. As he straightened up, he stared once more at the incredible bosom and sighed.

Clenching his fists in frustration, he turned to leave the cinema, nodding right and left at the applauding, shouting public. As he quickly moved up the aisle, he muttered to Hank and Gene, "That dame's great. Great. Both of her. I've never ever seen such a double feature."

Robert Rossen, famed for his *Body and Soul* with John Garfield and Lilli Palmer and for his 1949 Oscar-winning picture, *All the King's Men*, starring Broderick Cranford, was hired in 1953 to direct *Mambo* for Carlo Ponti and Dino De Laurentiis.

Rossen was perhaps the most noted cinema professional who bowed to the McCarthy-like pressures of the House of Representatives' Committee on Un-American Activities when it brought its witch hunt, its paranoic search for Communists, to Hollywood. Without unequivocal proof, he named names and made statements that forced important Hollywood colleagues like Joseph Losey and Jules Dassin to flee the country in search of work. Others who remained faced blacklisting, their livelihoods and reputations impaired. Rossen was obsessed by his role in one of the most abominable scandals in the history of show business, and alcohol became more and more a necessity to assuage his self-hatred and guilty conscience.

When the director made his deal for *Mambo*, nobody bothered to describe to him what it was like to direct an Italian-produced, "English-language" musical film in Rome, since nobody had ever done one before. Nor did anyone describe to him the confusion that stemmed from a cast of actors whose tongues had different mothers, or from the gibberish of dialogue that inevitably emerged. Or the on-set shouting and chattering of assistant directors, cameraman, crew and sundry individuals while the director was trying to guide performers struggling to sustain emotion under three-ring circus circumstances.

Rossen was bewildered by the bedlam, the babel of languages, the disorganization, the improvisatory atmosphere, and, in spite of his intake of alcohol, he could not cope with the film. In fact, he simply could not cope. He had all the symptoms of an extremely sick man, mentally, emotionally, physically. One day, maddened by frustration and drink, he opened his fly in full view of cast and crew, whipped out his penis and masturbated.

It was on the set of *Mambo* that Hank first met Shelley Winters. Shelley was only one of several stars in the film, but when it came to off-screen performance, she was definitely, deafeningly and defiantly the show-stealer. The cast of the Rossen musical included Shelley's adored husband Vittorio Gassman; Silvana Mangano, only recently Mrs. Dino De Laurentiis, world pin-up girl as a result of the earthy, black-stockinged rice picker in Giuseppe De Santis' *Bitter Rice*, followed two years later by Alberto Lattuada's commercial smash, *Anna*; Katherine Dunham, the American dancer-choreographer-anthropologist, with her extraordinary troupe of dancers; and the excellent British actor, Michael Rennie.

A young Italian actress reaching for stardom, Anna Maria Ferrero, was not in the *Mambo* cast, but was definitely the key character in the off-screen Shelley Winters Show.

Only fireworks failed to erupt when Shelley, violently jealous, discovered that her one and only Vittorio was playing his Latin version of "hanky-panky" with the delectable Signorina Ferrero. And just where was hubby performing with the nubile Anna Maria? Where else but in Gassman's portable dressing room, just off the set of the picture. Suddenly, Shelley was overcome by a mirror fetish. She smashed several against Gassman's roulotte walls while screaming epithets and insults of Teamster Union caliber at a protesting husband and a terrified actress. Fortunately (or unfortunately, depending upon the point of view) the shards of flying glass caused no injury to anyone's private parts, and everybody's career, onscreen and off, went on.

But a really great Shelley Winters Show doesn't end with a few broken mirrors. She was, after all, Mrs. Vittorio Gassman, and had a hell of a lot more to say, so she decided to hold a press conference in her Hotel de la Ville suite, which Hank, as correspondent of *Silver Screen* and *Screenland*, attended. She looked at one and all before making her announcement. And then it came. Her marriage to Signor Vittorio Gassman, after only two years, was over, ended, finished, dead, *finito*, *finitissimo*!

The rage, anguish and upset exhibited by Shelley at the press conference was counterpointed by flashes of her piquant wit, mingled with an occasional sob and a sprinkle of tears that turned her eyes into a mass of swell, as if they had been bitten by a swarm of bees.

Swollen eyes have always been an unmistakable sign of Shelley's insecurity and stress. In July 1978, Costanzo Costantini, one of Italy's brightest and most widely read feature writers,

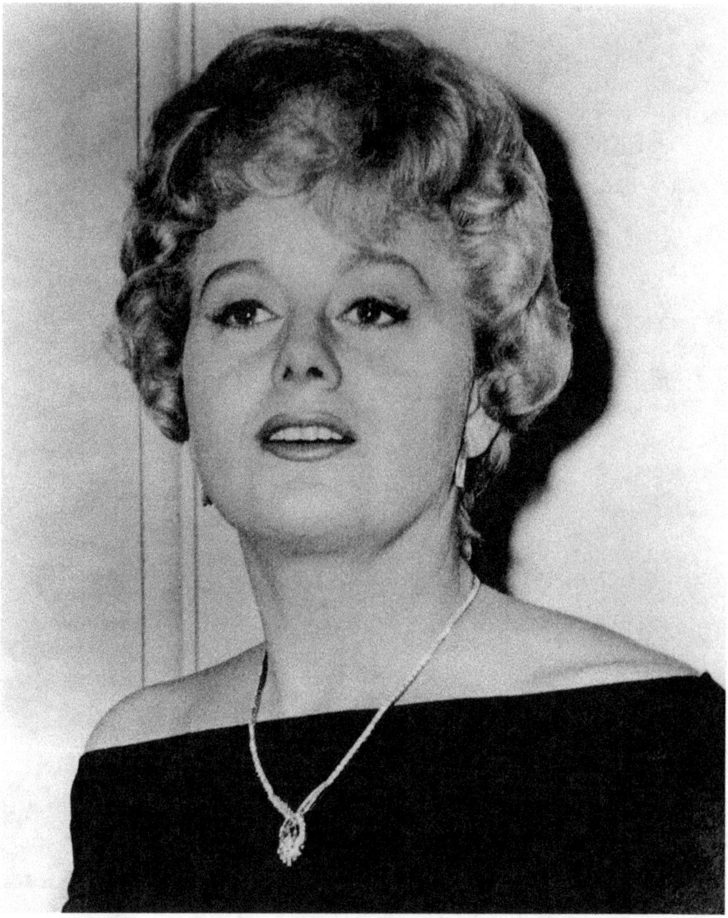

Shelley Winters

referred to the actress' ballooned peepers in a delicious interview with Shelley, who was in Rome on a visit. In reading some of her comments on Gassman, Italy and herself, it almost seemed that her eyes had remained swollen ever since that melodramatic press conference of 25 years earlier.

"Vittorio only taught me dirty words to amuse himself. So, beside those, the only other Italian I learned from him was cheese, table, pasta and *spaghetti al dente*. He had a fixation for *spaghetti al dente*. One day he invited an Italian professor friend to dinner, telling him that I made sensational *spaghetti al dente*.

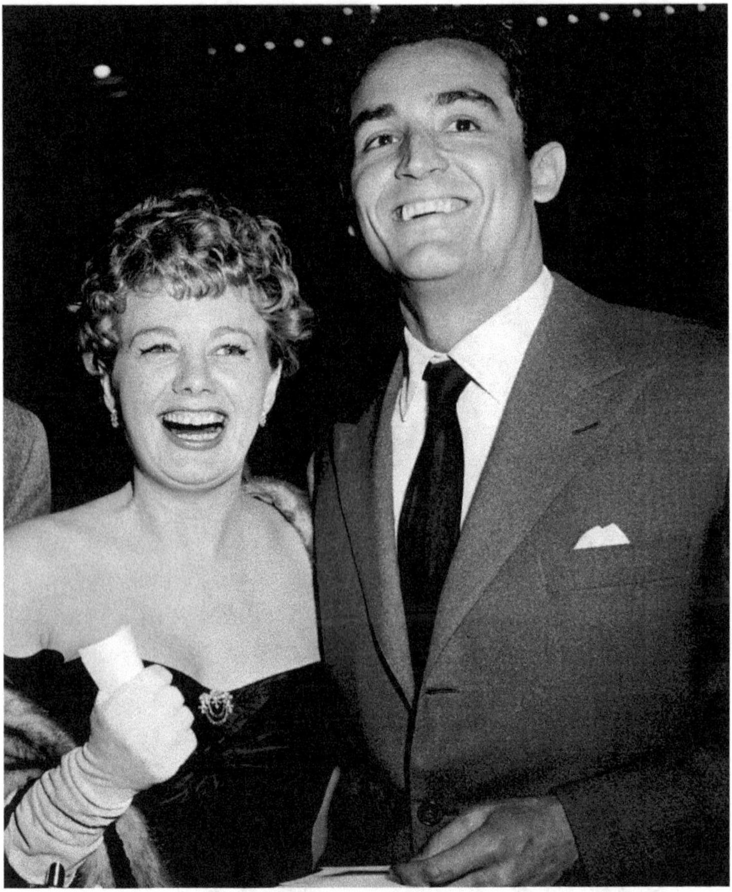

Shelley Winters and Vittorio Gassman

When I brought the bowl of pasta to the table, Vittorio took one taste and began to scream that I had overcooked it. So back to the kitchen to cook another batch. Another screaming fit. This time it was too undercooked. So off I went to fix a third batch, but even that didn't satisfy him. So I took the bowl full of hot spaghetti and dumped it over his head."

"Have you ever been in analysis?" Costantini asked.

"For only about thirty years," replied Shelley. "You forget that I was once married to Gassman. After our divorce, I headed straight to a psychoanalyst. Vittorio, all by himself, could keep every psychoanalyst in the Western World in business. During the two years we were married, he supported virtually half the world's airlines. Back and forth, forth and back, Los Angeles-Rome, Rome-Los Angeles, psychoanalysts and airplanes, airplanes and psychoanalysts."

"Did you feel abandoned when Vittorio left you?" the journalist asked Shelley.

"Abandoned? To be left by an Italian is to be liberated," she trumpeted.

Italian males, like certain wines, lose flavor and bouquet in travel. However, Italian-American men, so long as they keep faith with their natural origins and reject restrictive WASP influences, can also be deliciously savory. So Shelley's move from Gassman to Anthony Franciosa, brought to instant prominence as Shelley's co-star in the Broadway production of *A Hatful of Rain*, was not without libidinous logic, and Shelley became Mrs. Anthony Franciosa.

Ironically enough, Anna Magnani played a role in both of Shelley's Italianate matrimonies. It was Magnani who introduced Shelley to Gassman when he was appearing on the Roman stage in a *Hamlet* that seemed to Shelley more Wagner than Shakespeare. And Shelley and Magnani were engaged in a tug-of-war over the affections of Franciosa while Anna and Tony were making *Wild is the Wind* in Hollywood. The two were drawn to one another by a powerful and complex attraction that neither was able to shake off completely. It was only the passage of time and eventual separation, when Magnani returned to Rome and Franciosa continued with his rapidly rising career, which calmed the intense relationship.

The Winters-Franciosa-Magnani triangle turned into a quadrangle when, shortly thereafter, Tony came to Rome to shoot *The Naked Maja* as co-star to Ava Gardner. Magnani hovered nearby in her Palazzo Altieri, but wisely kept her distance, and, except for a few intimates, her silence. But Shelley, convinced that her husband was more than superficially involved with Gardner, once again threw tantrums any Italian would be proud of. It made no difference to her whether they took place in private or in public. Once again, she was betrayed. Once again, she was deeply hurt. Once again, it was *matrimonio finito*, but she held no press conference to announce it.

Franciosa returned to Rome twenty years later to star in Alberto Lattuada's *The Cricket* opposite Virna Lisi. Tony was asked by a Rome journalist to recall his impressions of the aforesaid three ladies. "Magnani was a woman of formidable temperament," he commented. "She overwhelmed me with her oceanic sense of humanity. Gardner was an extraordinary woman of electrifying physical beauty. But her inner immaturity and fragility were unbelievable."

Franciosa didn't bother to comment on Shelley.

Hank was contracted by Robert Favre Le Bret to serve in an official liaison capacity at the 1954 Cannes Film Festival. His responsibility was to handle illustrious invitees, with particular concentration on the Hollywood flock. He worked side-by-side with a vivacious, green-eyed blonde of Belgian origin, Anne Buydens. After the festival, Anne became foreign press representative on *Ulysses*, still shooting in Rome. Cautiously and intelligently riding out the Pier Angeli-Kirk Douglas affair, she eventually became Mrs. Kirk Douglas by making herself indispensable to him. To this day, more than a quarter of a century later, Anne has not only been fully involved with Kirk's production activities, but her European chic, charm and practicality have made her one of the most knowledgeable ladies of show business as well as Hollywood hostess par excellence.

The American turnout for the annual Festival was exceptional. Grace Kelly, who was shooting Alfred Hitchcock's *To Catch a Thief* on the French Riviera, was a guest. It was there that she met Prince Rainier of Monaco. Meanwhile, French actress Gisèle Pascal had turned to one of Hollywood's most sought-after princes, Gary Cooper. Virginia Palance was distraught over the disappearance of her moody husband, Jack. Hank remembered seeing Palance standing alone on the beach across from the Carlton Hotel in the early evening, transfixed, immobile, gazing at the falling sun and the endless Mediterranean. The next time anyone heard from him was when he reached San Remo. Without passport or identification, in some amnesia-like state, he had managed to cross the Italian border. Robert Mitchum's wife was also deeply concerned about her husband. Mitchum was fresh, too fresh, from his marijuana bust in Hollywood, and she lived in trepidation during the entire festival over the possibility of Bob once again succumbing to temptation.

There were Olivia de Havilland and her French journalist husband, Pierre Galante, and the lovely Arlene Dahl, who, between husbands, had come to Cannes as a beauteous solo act. Arlene's fresh and friendly personality made pleasure out of responsibility, and it thus became Hank's pleasure, not duty, to escort her to a number of festival events. On one particular occasion, Hank found himself accompanying two noted specimens of the female sex, with character, personality and physical appearance in startling contrast, but each fabulous in her own way. One of them was Arlene Dahl. The other was Shelley Winters.

When Shelley completed *Mambo*, she took off for Cannes, where her growing bulk and Italian obsessions were plunked heavily on the shoulders of Hank, who, as her staunch admirer, never seemed to feel the weight. Hank greeted her on her arrival at Nice Airport and accompanied her to the Carlton Hotel. Hank could not help but observe that while momentarily having shed her obsession for the Italian male through the break with Gassman, she had more passionately than ever embraced her adoration for pasta.

Shelley was euphoric. Fresh from the emotional impact following the definitive split with Vittorio and her blazing encounter with the Rome-based press, she was eagerly looking forward to the festival as diversion and consolation. Instead, she was faced with immediate crisis.

"You're invited to a big party tonight after the showing of the film," Hank told her. "It's going to be a really special Cannes splash. Everybody will be there in all their finery." Hank expected Shelley to be delighted to commence her festival stay with such a glittering event.

"Oh, no. God almighty," she responded in agitation. "I haven't a darn thing to wear. Nothing fits me anymore. We'll have to shop for a gown right away."

"There are some fabulous shops on the Croisette," Hank said cheerfully, hoping to soothe her.

"You've got to come with me and help me pick out something," said a Shelley taut with nerves. "Christ Almighty, how can I make myself resist my appetite for pasta and vino that slides over my palate so divinely? And why do I always keep buying dresses? I did that in Rome and never wore any of them. Why do I do it? Somebody told me that Mary Todd Lincoln used to buy bolts and bolts of material, tons of it, which she would hide away in trunks and never used. She ended up loony. Do you think I'll end up loony too? *Oy vey, oy vey, Oy VEY!*"

So Shelley and Hank immediately rushed to find some appropriate covering that would camouflage the unwelcome bloat. They went from elegant salon to elegant salon, Dior, Balenciaga, Dessès. They had absolutely nothing ready that would fit. Finally, at Ricci's, they ran across an ice-blue satin confection that was all wrong for Shelley's burgeoning curves. It was just going to have to do, or Cinderella would have to stay home from the ball. Seamstresses worked frantically to make all possible alterations. While they were working, Hank, suddenly realizing that the festival had made no arrangements to provide Shelley with an escort to the film and the subsequent festivities, quietly phoned Favre Le Bret, who suggested that Hank, as official liaison to American stars, serve as escort on behalf of the festival.

When Hank came to pick up Shelley that evening, she was actually being sewn into her gown. Disconsolate, she was trying not to burst her seams, or into tears. Her eyes swelled. Hank tried not to betray his discouragement. Shelley had thrown a short white fox jacket over the mishmash of a gown and added a few diamond trinkets in her effort to simulate the image of glamorous movie star.

As soon as the weary seamstress left, Shelley looked tearfully at Hank. Then, out of her mouth came a really schmaltzy wail. "Ohhhhhhhhh, God! Gooooooooodddddddd! I look like some elegant hooker in this outfit. I've just got to lose some weight. I've got to, I've got to, I've got to. This can't go on. It can't!" Hank gently put his arms around her, then gave her a big hug. "You look great, Shelley," he said, grinning. "Really, you do. So will you stop this carrying on? You and I are going to go out and have a ball."

She looked up at Hank through the puff engulfing her eyes. "Hank, why did Marco Polo have to come back from China with pasta? Why were Italian men allowed on this Earth to torture me? Why? Why do I ask *you*? Why don't I ask *me*? To hell with it. Let's go out and have ourselves a ball." She looked at Hank again. The swell of her eyes began to give way to a wicked gleam. "Hey, maybe we'll run across Rossano Brazzi!"

*

In the summer of 1954, Mel Ferrer passed through the iron gates of Via Aiaccio 12-bis and entered the Kaufman-Lerner Associates offices for a meeting with Hank. He was the first truly international name to pass through the Agency portals.

Tall, stolid, sad-miened, Ferrer was propelled by an unquenchable ambition to reach the top of the heap. At the highest salary that he had ever received to date for his American films, he had agreed to appear in his first Italian film, *Proibito*, a daring exposé of Sardinian kidnapping that was to become a Cassandra-like precursor of what had, by the 1970s, become a staple in the Italian way of life. *Proibito*, scheduled to be shot in a remote area on the island of Sardinia, was one of the early and less appreciated efforts of director Mario Monicelli, later to achieve world acclaim for his delicious heist film *Big Deal on Madonna Street.*

Ferrer hired KLA for a personal publicity campaign for the duration of his *Proibito* engagement. He wanted to widen his industry status and public appeal in Europe. Weeks of shooting in a secluded and obscure location would isolate him dangerously from major publicity sources and he had to keep his name and image alive in the media and the trade press through KLA's facilities. And then, there was a gamine, elfin-like star who, through *Roman Holiday*, zoomed like a rocket towards being filmdom's number one female attraction.

Miss Audrey Hepburn.

While Ferrer was busy making *Proibito*, the very-much-in-love Audrey had quietly made her way to a hideaway in Switzerland. The official announcement said that she desperately needed quiet and rest, and whispers of a nervous breakdown, were spreading. The truth was that Audrey's Swiss hideout was a secret trysting place for her and Mel, who utilized KLA as cover for these hidden encounters. Unfortunately, he never troubled to advise Hank that during these secret rendezvous, he and Audrey were making preparations for their wedding.

Hank was romantic enough to love lovers and more than willing to do what he could to help them be together whenever it was possible. He took over the coordination of complicated, top-secret trips from Sardinia to Audrey's lair of love, whenever Mel was able to sneak away from shooting to embrace his waiting wife-to-be. Hank fully agreed that not only the ever-watchful press but also the producers of *Proibito*

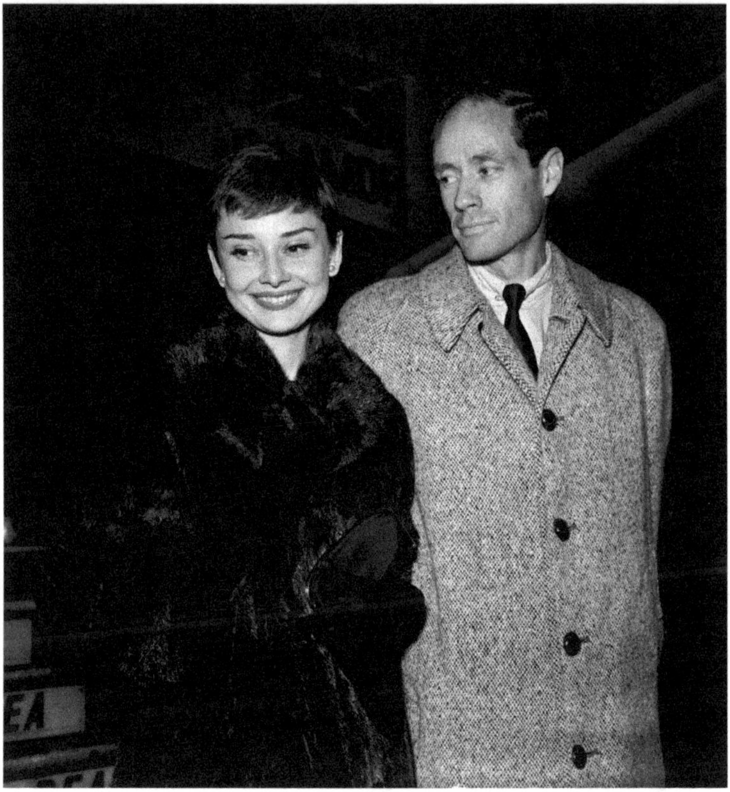

Audrey Hepburn and Mel Ferrer

had to be kept in the dark, to prevent the picture's press office from tipping off the frustrated, already suspicious fourth estate of the trysts, and thus reap rich publicity rewards for the film.

The wedding took place in the utter secrecy sought by the couple. That secrecy lasted approximately ten minutes. Phone calls from an infuriated press jammed the telephone lines at Via Aiaccio. All through the night they came. Nobody believed Hank when he admitted that he had no information to provide, and while fielding the curses, he became more and more enraged over Ferrer's thoughtlessness, which prevented the execution of his responsibilities and manifested a warranted lack of faith on Ferrer's part in the press representative he had chosen.

Pressing Gene into service, the two partners began a systematic effort to find either Mel or Audrey, get the details of the marriage, and agree on an official statement. This was NEWS! The kind of headline story that suited the film-crazed climate of Rome. The type of romantic event to excite readers around the world.

But no word from Mel. No peep from Audrey. All efforts to get through to the newlyweds failed. Finally, a call came in from Switzerland. Hank heard the less-than-mellifluous Ferrer voice repeating, "Hello, hello." "It's him," Hank said to Gene. "Keep it cool," Gene replied.

It wasn't easy. His voice shaking with rage, Hank warned Ferrer of the hysteria the re-entry to Rome was certain to provoke and urged an immediate press statement as well as the formation of a plan for the couple's return.

Ferrer was adamant. No interviews. No photographers. Their entry into Rome was to be secret. They would travel by night and hide by day behind drawn shades and locked train doors. Once they arrived at the Central Station in Rome, they would race to a waiting car to speed to the Villa Rolli, which they had rented, a short distance from Castel Gandolfo in the Alban hills.

"Look, Mel, it's up to you and Audrey," Hank replied, deliberately adding Audrey's name as a subtle expression of doubt that Audrey was in complete agreement with all that cloak-and-dagger stuff. "The more furtive you become, the more intense the chase to trap you," Hank continued. "And I won't take any responsibility for the plans if they don't work out the way you expect."

And did the newlyweds get the business! Secret arrival, indeed! The Central Station arrival was not tumult. It was riot. A traumatized Audrey and a shocked Mel barely managed to escape into their limousine and flee to the Villa Rolli. A 24-hour night-and-day siege was on at their insignificant little love nest of only twenty rooms, eight baths, two guest houses, servant's house, swimming pool, African-style cabana and gardens, gardens, gardens.

The couple was distraught, their first days of marriage fraught with nerves. They hated being prisoners and recognized that some step had to be taken to rectify the intolerable situation. So Hank, Gene and Viero Nicoli, head of Paramount's Rome press office, were called in for an urgent strategy council with the unhappy couple.

Hank repeatedly stressed the need for the organization of an official press conference for the Ferrers to be held as quickly as possible. Nicoli and Gene argued in support of Hank's position. Much to Audrey's relief, Mel relented. It was agreed that Nicoli would assist KLA in the preparations and that the press conference would be held in the private salon just above the lobby of the Grand Hotel, a charming and elegant room with a museum quality which rarely failed to put people on their best behavior.

Of course, the press corps turned out en masse. The photographers and various ladies and gentlemen of the written word were at first resentful and arrogant, but Audrey's radiance and Mel's smiling countenance helped disarm then.

Audrey remained fresh, cool and bride-like through it all and Mel was warm and ingratiating. Hank then asked the photographers to give the reporters their chance, and with some cajoling by the tactful Nicoli, they finally moved to the rear so the journalists could move forward. "Ladies and gentlemen," Hank announced, after a quickly whispered conference with Audrey, "Mrs. Ferrer would like to say a few words to you."

"I've come full circle," she began in her sweet, modulated British tones. "And the circle is now complete. Rome was the beginning for me, the real beginning," she said, her huge eyes misty. "With *Roman Holiday*, my life suddenly seemed to assume shape and... direction." Then, turning a love-lit gaze towards Mel, she continued with that studied combination of wistfulness and frankness that has fascinated millions. "And now, after two years, I'm back in Rome, and I'm in Rome with Mel. The Princess now has her Prince for her very own special Roman holiday." And she and Mel went on from there.

The press was jubilant. It got what it came for and more than it had anticipated, but the "honeymoon" with the fourth estate was not destined to last even a week, thanks to Mel and Audrey Ferrer's goddamn wedding cake!

Gene and Frank Gervasi, the Rome chief of the Motion Picture Export Association of America, were invited to the Villa Rolli for tea with Audrey and Mel. Hank, also supposed to have been a guest at the intimate affair, had left for the States. Gene and Gervasi were served dainty slices of wedding cake on silver salvers, and the cake, even if a week old, was more or less holding its own.

On the morning of November 9, Kaufman-Lerner's part-time secretary, Vera, was startled by a furious phone call from Ferrer, who referred to Hank and Gene as "those two Jackals, Shylocks only interested in pounds of flesh, Judases ready to betray for thirty pieces of silver," and continued his diatribe with similar laudatory comparisons. Knowing Hank was in America, he demanded to speak to Gene forthwith.

"He's out, Mr. Ferrer," stammered the frightened Vera, "but I expect him back before lunch. Would you like him to telephone you?" she managed to ask.

"No, I would *not* like him to telephone me. Tell him that I'm sending a messenger with a letter. He should have it within the course of the afternoon. I have nothing more to say!" Vera looked stunned at the soundless receiver.

Within an hour after Gene's return to the office, the Ferrer chauffeur appeared and handed him a pale blue envelope with the engraved monogram "MGF." Gene quickly opened it, pulling out a one-page handwritten note on matching stationery and a Thomas Wiseman article from the London *Evening Standard* dated November 2. Wiseman, a popular, widely read English columnist, found the Ferrer attitude towards the press distasteful, and among some unflattering contents he included the following:

> To reach the Ferrers I drove for half an hour to an isolated villa high above the sea. Outside the villa, hired guards patrol night and day to discourage uninvited guests. When I called... they were having coffee among the flowers, the grapevines and the six cats that go with the villa, and serving the last pieces of their everlasting wedding cake.

The letter from Ferrer did not bother with the usual salutation of "Dear":

> Gene,
>
> I enclose the Wiseman article. I urged you to keep away from this man and tell him nothing. Why you chose to betray a courtesy and the hospitality which my wife offered you the afternoon you visited here is beyond my understanding. The only people who were ever offered

wedding cake in this house were you and Frank Gervasi that afternoon on the terrace. There is such a thing as decency, even among professionals, and I need hardly tell you that I could not recommend someone who thought so little of the people with whom he is associated.

And please be kind enough not to call me again, or use my name in any way as connected with your and Hank's business.

Mel Ferrer

Gene jumped up in anger, throwing both Ferrer's letter and Wiseman's article to the floor. He then phoned Gervasi. Frank was horrified by the attack.

"Why in the name of Christ would either one of us think it worthy of mention?" he asked. "And even if we had, what the hell is so sacred about that tired old wedding cake? Ferrer's an idiot not to realize that underpaid, overworked servants are only too eager to pocket handsome tips for revelations about their masters and mistresses. He should ask his staff some questions. And raise their salaries!" concluded Gervasi, angrily banging down the receiver.

Sitting down in front of his prized Royal Standard, which had come from the States, Gene wrote Ferrer a reply and arranged to have it brought over to Villa Rolli by hand the next morning. Among other things, it said the following:

November 9, 1954

Dear Mel,

I can understand your anger, but cannot at the same time allow charges without factual or moral foundation to go unanswered. I have never "betrayed the courtesy and hospitality" offered me in someone's home and am deeply sorry that you felt it necessary to make such charges without first seeking the truth.

Can't your practiced eye see that the Wiseman article was made out of whole cloth? He was no more near the Villa than Eisenhower was. He did not drive out. He saw no armed guards. He saw no one having coffee. He saw no everlasting wedding cake being served on the terrace.

God knows that by now you should understand and accept the difficulties and dangers involved in dealing with the press, while at the same time appreciating their ingenuity for good as well as for evil. KLA was your official press representative but it was the press which kept *us* better informed of many of your activities than you did. It was the press which informed us of your Swiss plans. And several journalists have described the Villa and your and Mrs. Ferrer's living habits far better than either Hank or I have been allowed to know them.

Gene

No reply ever to the letter. Hank returned from the States, but months went by with no contact whatsoever from the actor.

Discussions vital to the future of KLA were taking place at quickening pace. The reference in Ferrer's November 9 letter to "I need hardly tell you that I could not recommend someone who thought so little of the people with whom he is associated," had ominous overtones in connection with those crucial discussions.

As enemy, particularly though his increased prestige resulting from his marriage to Audrey, Ferrer was perhaps powerful enough to sabotage them. He was a time bomb. If it were to explode, the KLA saga might well be blown to bits.

Che sarà, sarà, Hank and Gene kept telling one another, but something inside them wasn't really convinced.

Two

Bridgehead on the Tiber

In order to give impetus to the flagging talent division of KLA, Gene decided to set up a central casting registry. Every English-speaking actor of whatever nationality living or available in the Rome area would be listed. This turned out to be an arduous task. Each individual had to be interviewed, his experience carefully noted and then as carefully checked for accuracy. Each applicant had to provide a suitable set of photographs. With such a registry, KLA would then be ready to demonstrate to producers and directors that much of their requirements in the bit or supporting role echelon could be covered locally, thus eliminating travel and living expenses for imported actors.

As part of this effort, Gene and Hank scheduled a weekly open house on Wednesday afternoons, to which anyone who fancied himself an actor and claimed familiarity with English was welcomed. As the months rolled by in 1953 and '54, many of Rome's foreign colony, plus some minor Italian and other European actors, converged on Via Alaccio 12-bis. A few, like Tonio Selwart, Gertrude Flynn, Richard Camp and Stephen Garrett, had a legitimate stateside professional background, but most had little or no actual experience. Rome and the Roman way of life had taken possession of them, and they desperately wanted to earn a living in order to remain.

One indubitable star did emerge from these Wednesday afternoon open houses and she was to have a career of seventeen-year duration. She walked into Gene's office about four o'clock on a Wednesday in February 1954. A tall, handsome woman of forty, she had piercing black eyes, raven hair, a startlingly transparent complexion and a bone structure that signaled aristocracy. A tailored black suit, spike-heeled black pumps and a dripping silver-fox stole enhanced her excellent figure.

Gene was fascinated. "Tell me about yourself," he started, waving her to a seat. She continued to stand.

"*Che cosa?*" was her reply. "*Mi dispiace.* English, don't speak. No speak."

Christ Almighty, thought Gene. That's really a pity. Lady, you're an exceptional type of character actress we can do something with and you don't understand a word of English. Why are all of these Italian actors so damn lazy? Why can't they get it through their heads that they have to know some English if they want jobs in international films? Still, this dame is great looking. You never know.

"Tell me something about your past experience, please," continued Gene in his basic Italian.

"My name is Maria Petrin, but everybody calls me Marion," she replied. The name meant nothing to Gene. What pictures could he have seen her in, he wondered?

"I'm from the Veneto and came to Rome a few months ago. I come from a good family. My father was mayor of our town. My husband has run off with some other woman and my only son has disappeared." She seemed ready to cry.

Not your life story, Signora, if you don't mind. Only your professional experience, please. The career facts are what I'm after.

"My sister Lina works for the Alexanders, those friends of yours. They told her that you were looking for a housekeeper…"

And so a star *is* born! When Hank came into Gene's office to meet her, it was love at first sight. For months, the unique, very special Marion slept on a cot in the kitchen. For seventeen years, an immaculate housekeeper, watchdog and protectress *straordinaria*. Keeper of the exchequer, scrupulously honest, who walked miles to markets whenever she could save "Commandante" Kaufman or "Baby" Lerner a few pennies. Surrogate mother to her two adopted American sons, upon whom she lavished the care and affection she was unable to give to the son who had vanished forever. For seventeen years, this remarkable character and ardent film fan reigned in the various Kaufman-Lerner establishments, respectfully but firmly exercising what she considered her right of co-star billing with the luminaries for whom she would eventually be preparing repasts and parties. Over the years, she managed to upstage some of the most experienced and noted actors and actresses in the world.

Marion was a co-star as Member of the Family. And as Marion had her domain in the various homes Hank and Gene occupied, so Enzo Barbato made KLA his realm. He came to the agency at the age of fifty as its chief accountant. His decade of service as an officer in the Italian armed forces in Libya and Ethiopia was indeed a precious asset in the endless war to collect monies from producers for clients of the agency.

Not that one could understand a word he said. When he opened his mouth to speak, out came mumbled, swallowed half-syllables of Pugliese dialect at missile speed. Although he had studied English for years, he spoke not a word of it, but there was never any question that his silent English was superior to his abomination of Italian.

An arsenal of action, ramrod straight, he moved as quickly as he spoke, and seemed always to be marching on the double. His military training was so ingrained that every time he walked into the offices of his bosses, he virtually clicked his heels and saluted.

As for the money-collecting war front, he was daring, ruthless and inventive. He became cavalry, infantry, commando, guerrilla and regiment combined. Depending upon the situation, he would attack the enemy frontally, sneak in from the flank, infiltrate from behind the lines. He refused to settle for anything less than unconditional surrender.

Barbato loved food as much as he loved to cook, and showed admirable taste in loving and marrying Lea Vittoria Paggi, who was the finest creator of Italian delectables ever to appear on a dining table. After eating one of Lea's banquets, which she always claimed was some simple thing she had whipped up, one staggered home, and, before collapsing from gleeful overeating, threw out *Larousse Gastronomique*.

Enzo was trusted by everybody, respected by everybody, including his producer-enemies. Few, however, had the opportunity of knowing his human decency, his generosity, his loyalty and devout religious faith, his despair over the misery of mankind.

Barbato was not a man of heart. He was the heart of a man.

As time went on, Barbato was joined by a welcome companion, an ex-employee of the Banca d'America e d'Italia. Massimo Frosi was a toothpick of a man with a face so pallid, one could easily believe that he was a refugee from a Dracula film. For most of the life of Kaufman-Lerner Associates, Frosi served as expert tax counsel and special adviser on bureaucratic red tape, which always required unraveling on fiscal matters. The more one knew him, the more one recognized that he was a surprising contrast to his undertaker aspect. His mind was electricity. His knowledge of his field vast. He had a smile that came from the sun. He was always available, always in good humor, and had enough lively comedy in him to make even Dracula laugh.

Frosi was another of the blessings Italy gave Hank and Gene.

The first positive use of the KLA Registry came in September 1953. A still-untitled television series was to be shot in English for the American market and a considerable number of English-speaking performers were needed. Tele Cinema was the name of the company. Augusto Fantechi was the producer.

Fantechi, a tall, vigorous, authoritative man, and his assistants, Renato Tonini and Masimo Rocchi, spent hours over a number of days poring over the voluminous file cards and photos gathered by the agency. They made notes of some forty possible selections and politely asked whether they might borrow a photo of each to show to the director. With the proviso that the pictures be returned in a day or two without fail, Gene assented. Fantechi heartily agreed. Shaking hands with exaggerated warmth, the producer profusely thanked Gene for his invaluable assistance and promised to be in telephonic contact the next day.

The phone call never came.

In setting up the registry, Gene had written the home phone number and personal address of each actor on his photos. And what the ever-so-grateful, ever-so-courteous Fantechi and Assistants Tonini and Rocchi had done was to have telephoned each of the actors directly, setting up appointments for the eighteen artists finally selected. It was the intention of the ever-so-grateful, ever-so-courteous producer to negotiate with each, thereby eliminating any further contact with Kaufman-Lerner.

Gene and Hank discussed the critical situation. The agency concept had been challenged. If KLA was to maintain credibility both with actors and industry, the challenge had to be met. Each of the selected actors was telephoned. Gene listed the time of appointment each had been granted, noting that they had been spaced at ten-minute intervals. It was agreed that Hank remain in the office, available for instant action if necessary, while Gene was to serve as war-front general.

A half-hour before the first actor's appointment, Gene presented himself in the offices of Tele Cinema at Via Lucullo 8. Embarrassed, assistant Rocchi told him that Fantechi was not in. "Then I'll wait," responded Gene, plopping himself down on a stuffed chair in the receiving room. Rocchi did not hide his consternation. "You can't wait," he said. "Oh, yes, I can. And oh, yes, I will," replied Gene, staring Rocchi down.

The assistant hurried from the reception room into an inner office. Moments later, Tonini, the other assistant who had been to Via Aiaccio, appeared. With smile and charm, he repeated Rocchi's words. Gene simply folded his arms and sat even more firmly in his chair. And into the inner office went Tonini, too.

Gene heard angry voices. Fantechi appeared, hurriedly followed by the two assistants and others Gene had not seen before. Gene rose, trying to hold a smile on his lips. Fantechi's color was deep purple. "GET OUT!" he screamed. "I permit no agents in my office."

"I will not get out," Gene replied. "You made full use of our facilities and you made your selection of actors at our offices. I am their duly appointed agent. And it is my right and responsibility to negotiate their contracts," Gene shot out all in one breath.

"NEVER!" hurled Fantechi. Rocchi, Tonini and the others all vehemently nodded their heads in agreement. "Never! Never! If you don't leave, I'll have you thrown out." Gene realized that Fantechi was not kidding.

"You imbecile! You half-liter shit, you! What the devil do you think, that we're still in the period of occupation? Don't pull this American dictator stuff on me! Never, never, NEVER will I agree to negotiate with an idiot like you. You go stick yourself and your actors up your ass!" Fantechi raged in Italian. Then came a pause as pregnant as sextuplets, a pause which fortunately gave Gene time for quick reflection.

It's not that he missed Fantechi's point, though Gene certainly had no intention of placing it anatomically where the producer had recommended. "Hold tight, Lerner. Violent confrontation is not going to solve this crisis. The actors have to work. I haven't got the right to jeopardize that right," Gene was reminding himself. "But I also can't jeopardize the agency concept. Those actors came to us for protection from arrogant snakes like Fantechi, with his fangs hanging out. I've got to find a way to give them the help they came for, while not compromising KLA's status." Such were the things running through Gene's mind.

"Are you going to leave, or am I going to have to throw you out?" Fantechi hissed, his fists opening and closing. He stood over Gene, glaring. Gene glared back, preferring to sit there and see what would happen. Instinct, however, kept telling him that if he made himself the issue, he would be making a serious, perhaps fatal blunder. He made his decision.

He rose with deliberate slowness. "I'm going to leave. But don't think this is the end of it. It very definitely is not." Another glare of defiance at the hulking Fantechi, a turn, an exit. As he went down the stairs, Gene heard another explosion of expletives. There are all sorts of ways to learn Italian, he said to himself, as he listened to Fantechi's thunder of colorful insults.

He walked over to the street corner which the actors would have to pass to enter the building. The first of the appointees appeared. Gene told him what was happening. "We have to stand together," he explained, "or we'll never get to the point of protecting you or anybody else. Producers have to learn that they must deal with the representative, and they'll only accept that if they know there's nothing they can do if the actor refuses to deal directly with them. Recognition of the agent is recognition of the rights of the artist."

The actor looked sad, uncertain. He stared at the sidewalk, up at the sky. As an ex-actor, Gene understood. "You know if you refuse to negotiate directly, without me, you may lose the job," Gene added. "I would hate like hell to see that happen. I want you to know that you're free to decide for yourself. It's your livelihood and your choice. Whatever you decide, I'll understand."

The actor shifted uneasily, looked at Gene. As the second appointee appeared, the first showed his relief. Let's see what he does, was what the first was obviously thinking. The second was apprised of the situation by Gene. The two actors moved away to discuss the pros and cons. The third appeared. Then the fourth. Not a one had yet gone into the Tele Cinema office. Though none of the four had committed himself to a policy, they were at least still on the corner debating the issue.

Rocchi came out of the building. Nervous but tactful, he reminded the actors that they had appointments with Fantechi. Trying not to look at Gene but extremely conscious of his presence, Rocchi underlined the point that if they wanted work, they would have to come to the office *immediately*. Just then Tonio Selwart appeared and the situation was quickly explained to him. A pro, a member of Actors' Equity and the Screen Actors Guild, he needed little explanation. He spoke out firmly in Italian. "I'm not coming without Signor Lerner," he said to the assistant. His words were a catalyst. The other four nodded their heads in agreement. Rocchi looked shocked. He cajoled. He virtually begged. But it was no use.

With a deep sense of gratitude, particularly to Tonio, Gene stood and watched this manifestation of solidarity.

A stunned Rocchi left. Two more actors appeared, one of them Gertrude Flynn, who, like Tonio, was a Guild and Equity member. Explanations were made. Gertrude improvised one of her best performances in support of the decision to stand with Gene. By now, the crisis had become a show. Forgotten was the promised work. Forgotten was the real need, the strong desire. This was an exciting event. This was what it meant to "make history," even if a miniscule footnote. Somebody mentioned the word "strike." By then, all of the eighteen actors were standing on the corner. Everybody started talking at once. They were actually "on strike." Wasn't it exciting? And wasn't it great that Italy's first actors' strike involved a bunch of foreigners like them? The atmosphere was party. Beer and orange drink appeared. If street dancing had begun, it would have suited the sense of celebration. There were jokes, laughter, reminiscences, a rare sense of brother/sisterhood.

Then, there he came, followed by his two faithfuls, Fantechi in person, charging forward like a red-seeing bull. The group fell silent. Gene stepped forward to meet the *toro*. Glaring at Gene in speechless hatred, the producer walked around him to address the actors. He ordered them to his office. If they didn't come, not one of them would be hired for this series. Not one of them would ever be hired for any other project he had in mind. Not one of them would ever be hired by anybody else in Italy. So they had their choice: either come and make deals with him, or starve in the streets of Rome.

Gene watched and listened with anger and trepidation. He had to do something. He turned to the actors. All eighteen simply stood in silence, staring back at Fantechi. Then Selwart walked over to Gene. Playing his scene to perfection, he carefully put his arm around his agent. The symbol could not have been more dramatic. The shock on Fantechi's face was atomic. He began to scream profanities.

No one deigned to respond to the vituperation. The silent reaction brought disbelief to Fantechi's face. Uncomprehending, he turned to Rocchi and Tonini for explanation. The two bewildered assistants simply shrugged their shoulders. The producer stared at them with dilated eyes, then turned again towards the actors. Silent stares met and collided. Fantechi looked over at Gene. Wordlessly, Gene looked back at Fantechi. His face contorted in a desperate effort to comprehend. Fantechi marched back into the building, followed by Rocchi and Tonini.

The party spirit was over. Actors started to say their goodbyes and leave, convinced of defeat. "No," said Gene, perturbed. "Nobody leave. Please! Let's all of us stay. That man has just had the shock of his life. He's got 26 half-hour shows to make. Who is he going to do them with? Either he goes to London or flies in actors from the States, or he's got to come back to us – unless he just cancels the series. So we wait and see what happens."

There was a flurry of whispers and considerable gesturing, then general agreement to go along with Gene's recommendation. A half-hour passed. The actors became more and more restless. Another fifteen minutes. Then an abashed Rocchi appeared, all eyes glued to him. Il Commendatore Fantechi would be pleased to receive Gene. Each actor would be called up individually to hear about his role, Rocchi continued, but Gene would always be present and would do all the negotiating.

The cheer from the group startled passers-by, the hugs and kisses among the actors causing many to stop and watch in curiosity.

Led by a much-relieved Rocchi, Gene started towards the office building. He stopped and turned, tears in his eyes. He smiled at those courageous, no-star human beings who, at that moment, seemed to him the biggest stars on Earth. They smiled back.

"We've won," Tonio said. "Yes, yes, we've won," repeated Gertrude, nodding happily.

"Thanks to both of you and each and every one of you. You're all heroes."

Tonio, Gertrude and the others watched Gene disappear into the office building with Massimo Rocchi.

*

The September 1953 street-corner strike became a topic of conversation in the film milieu for months. Producers who had never before heard of KLA now became aware – and wary – of its presence. Italian performers who previously dismissed Kaufman-Lerner as the agency formed to represent only foreign actors began to show interest, of particular gratification and importance to Hank and Gene, while a number of imported actors resident in Italy and of considerable renown became intrigued by KLA and those two "American boys."

Some of them began to make their way down the Via Aiaccio garden path:

Marc Lawrence, his pockmarked face a trademark for dozens of Hollywood gangster films, such as *The Asphalt Jungle*, and one of the victims of McCarthyism.

Doris Dowling, the sympathetic prostitute in Ray Milland's triumph, *The Lost Weekend.*

Steve Barclay, mustached swashbuckler (*The Three Musketeers*), who was doing well in Italian costume potboilers.

Frank Lattimore, who seemed to be on a climb towards stardom on the lot of 20th Century Fox, when suddenly it was toboggan time, with Italian films coming to his rescue.

Valentina Cortese, who had achieved little in Hollywood with her formidable acting talent and off-beat personality during years under contract to 20th Century Fox.

Richard Basehart, her American husband, who had insufficient success in Hollywood but reached an artistic pinnacle in Fellini's *La Strada.*

Joseph Calleia and Eduardo Cianelli, two veteran character actors of Italian-American origin, both of whom could portray Mafia plug-uglies and gentle father roles with equal aplomb.

Tulio Carminati, remembered for his brief burst of fame as loading man to Metropolitan Opera Star Grace Moore in the unforgettable Columbia Pictures musical romance, *One Night of Love.*

And Tamara Lees, who came from Yugoslavia or Rumania or Czechoslovakia or Austria, but let Italian producers believe she had sacrificed a promising career in England to come to Rome to marry the Italian she loved. Tamara had fair skin, blue eyes, blonde hair and a hefty bosom, and in dozens of class

"C" pictures portrayed with immense success the woman of temptation, perdition, sin. Tamara was the first foreign actress to make a real career in Italy after the war.

Chief producer Alberto Manca's voice was obsequious as he spoke over the phone to Gene. It became eloquent when he referred to the great costume film with its fabulous story and its sensational role for that exquisite, charming Tamara Lees. Would Signor Lerner be so gracious as to come over to discuss the matter on behalf of his marvelous client?

Of course Signor Lerner would. His first negotiation for an artist of Tamara's level. He hoped his limited Italian and minimal negotiating experience wouldn't blow the deal. He prepared himself for this baptism by talks with Tamara, her husband, her brother-in-law and Hank.

When Gene arrived for the appointment at P.A.M. Films on Via Livenza, he found himself confronting not only Manca, but six of his associates, none of whom were ever introduced. The seven-to-one proportion seemed to Gene somewhat excessive, but if that's how it's done, that's how it's done.

The first half hour was spent in the seven's overwhelming paeans over the beauty, gentility and talent of Signora Lees, who clearly outranked Garbo, Davis, Crawford, Hepburn, Bergman and Magnani combined. They then expressed profound gratitude to great America for its generous and unselfish help to impoverished Italy after the war. They went on to extol the extraordinary caliber of their film entitled *Frine, Courtesan of the Orient*, which not only was going to be a sensation all over the world with the marvelous Mario Bonnard directing, but was going to make *la splendida* Signora Lees an even greater star than she already was.

Then the pause. The ingratiating smile. The obsequious voice. Producer Manca at last was coming to the point.

"How much are you asking for your *beautiful* client?" came the telling question. "We will need her only for five weeks. We know she has many, many offers, so we will concentrate our work plan so she can complete her part in that period." Seven nods, seven broad smiles, seven pairs of eager eyes on Gene.

Gene was comfortable, surprisingly calm. It all seemed so cut and dried to him. "Her price is seven million lire in cash," he said, a sum approximating $10,000.

A tornado struck the room. The seven dwarfs jumped from their seats, shouting and screaming at Gene, at the walls, at Lord Jesus, at each other. What have I said, Gene asked himself in horror. What have I done? Holding on to his seat amidst the hysterical din, he kept turning towards one after another of the seven, trying to understand what terrible crime he had provoked to cause their frenzied reaction.

One of the men grabbed Gene's arm, another took hold of Gene's free arm, lifting him out of his chair. Then a ring-around-the-rosy roundelay began, the shouts, screams and imprecations to Heaven rising to fever pitch as Gene, the centerpiece, found himself pushed and pulled into the mad dance. One of the screaming associates rushed to the window, opened it, and to Gene's horror, prepared to jump out, shouting, "I'm going to kill myself. There's nothing left but suicide! Your demand kills our film. I have nothing left to live for!"

Then dead silence. The suicide threat ended with one leg out of the window. The victim and everybody else again took a seat. Producer Manca, back behind his desk, reassumed his smiling, gracious, obsequious manner. "So how much are you asking for your *delicious* client?"

Gene took his time. He glanced at each of his seven antagonists, all considerably puzzled and shaken. He then fixed his eyes on Manca. "Seven million lire in cash," Gene repeated.

A second explosion. The end of the world had come and Gene was responsible. All the expostulating and shouting was now directing at Gene. Fingers were pointed at him. Arms gestured in his face. Gene was getting angry. This, a negotiation? To hell with it. Holding his head high as he could, he stood up. Mouth set, he looked at the seven twerps. The room fell silent. All eyes upon him, he started to the door. As he was about to walk through it, several of the un-magnificent seven pounced on him. With tender solicitude, they led him back to his seat and gently sat him down as if he were a precious piece of porcelain.

Manca now made an impassioned speech about their finances, the budget of the picture, their absolute determination to have Signora Lees since the film and their lives depended upon it. But it was impossible for them to pay her such a sum. Oh, she merited it ten times over, twenty times over! But they just didn't have the funds, so couldn't Gene show his collaboration by agreeing to three million lire, or at the outside three-and-a-half million? The six associates sat smiling, convinced that Manca's moving appeal had had its effect.

"I'm sorry, gentlemen. Her price is seven million lire in cash."

After a tense moment, Manca stood up, leaned over his desk towards Gene. All eyes, including Gene's, were upon him. His face was dark and serious.

"You are an American," he began. "And you do not understand our psychology. Permit me to give you some advice. To be inflexible is considered by us arrogant, even unprincipled. You defy tradition and human nature when you renounce the pleasure of give-and-take. You must never start a negotiation with demands you really expect to be met. Straightforwardness and honesty are vices, not virtues in such situations. It is an insult to refuse to give us a right to bargain, no matter how much time is spent or how much energy is involved. I know it was not your intention, but you have hurt me by your attitude. I feel stabbed in the heart. Is there not some gesture you can make to assuage the affront? Some small gesture?"

Pain in his eyes, he stood waiting for an answer, as the Six looked on, sharing the anguish. Gene felt like a student being taught a lesson by a professor. An unexpected ball had been thrown to him.

"I much appreciate your comments and your frankness," Gene said to Manca in reply. "And to show my appreciation, I am happy to make a gesture. I am prepared to accept..." Gene paused for effect. "I'm ready to accept the sum of... six million lire for Signora Lees. And to give you one additional day of shooting, free of charge."

Manca clenched his fist, keeping his eyes fixed on Gene. Like an auctioneer accepting a final offer, down came the fist on the desk. "I accept," he roared. Exaltation from the Six. They kissed. They embraced. They slapped one another on the back. Manca came from behind his desk, arms outstretched, exhibiting his broadest smile.

Gene rose uncertainly. What next? He warily watched as Manca approached. Before Gene knew it, he was in a bear hug. The ecstatic Six came forward to surround the embracing Manca and Gene. The negotiation ended. There was no reprise of the ring-around-the-rosy roundelay.

The mixed bag of new KLA clients kept growing. Edmund Purdom, who replaced both Brando in *The Egyptian* and Mario Lanza in *The Student Prince*, in perpetual escape from his wife Alicia and inseparable from the widow of Tyrone Power, Linda Christian, became a permanent and popular Rome habitué and an instantaneous success in Italian costume pictures. A decided addition to KLA's list was Kerima, a smoldering Algerian beauty discovered by Carol Reed to play opposite James Mason in Joseph Conrad's *Outcast of the Islands.* When Magnani rejected *The She-Wolf*, the film adaptation of the Giovanni Verga classic, prepared especially for her, director Alberto Lattuada selected Kerina to replace her.

Added prestige came to KLA with two noted stage and film performers, Gino Cervi, so vividly remembered for his superb portrayals of Don Peppone in the Franco-Italo film series of *Don Camillo*, co-starring Fernandel, and Lea Padovani, brilliant in the Italian-American co-production of *Christ in Concrete*, opposite one of Hollywood's political refugees, Sam Wanamaker.

There was also Milly Vitale, whose loud-mouthed, garrulous, Russian-born mother, Natascha, would have been ideal for the Ethel Merman role in a Russian-Italian co-production of *Gypsy*. Natascha claimed to have been a ballerina, but by now had the build of a shot-put thrower. Blue-eyed, honey-haired and slightly infantile, Milly had a sweetly voluptuous quality which made her popular in agonizing love stories adored by frustrated adolescents of all ages. Because of her particular type and her capacity with English, KLA won her co-starring roles with Kirk Douglas in Stanley Kramer's *The Juggler,* shot in Israel, and in Hollywood with Bob Hope in *The Seven Little Foys*.

Hank found himself to be Milly's most constant cavalier and was anything but displeased. He escorted her to galas, parties, theater openings and film premieres. When Natascha learned that Hank was also a passionate opera buff, he was amazed to be offered a private box at the Rome Opera house by its managing director, so Hank could take Milly to performances at any time. When Hank learned that Maestro Riccardo Vitale, the managing director, coincidentally happened to be Natascha's husband and Milly's father, the uneasy feeling slowing growing in him that he was the victim of a conspiracy leading to matrimony with Milly, suddenly became a realization. He therefore was not surprised by the following item nationally syndicated, in Walter Winchell's May 21, 1955 gossip column:

> The woomance of Milly Vitale and Hank Kaufman is the top buzz in Rome movie circles.... Though attracted to Milly, he could not see Natascha cast in the role of *his* mother-in-law, so from that time on, Hank, in his spare time, listened to the opera on records at Via Aiaccio – alone.

And there was also Belinda Lee. Blonde, green-eyed, rising English starlet of prominent physical attractions under contract to J. Arthur Rank, Miss Lee, barely 20, definitely underlined the fact that she intended "to become a real actress, not some kind of animated decoration." Shortly thereafter, at the 1955 Cannes Film festival, she was applauded as an exciting new personality in the film *Footsteps in the Fog*, which co-starred Stewart Granger and Jean Simmons.

When Belinda was introduced to Hank at the 1955 festival and was told that he owned a talent agency in Rome, a glow made sunshine out of her face as she enthused, "Oh, Mr. Kaufman. How I would love to come and work in Italy. I feel there's something there which I've been waiting for all of my life."

All of her life.

Her affirmation about becoming a "real actress" would be confirmed as her feeling that "there's something there which I've been waiting for all of my life" would turn out to be tragically prophetic.

Hers was instant popularity with the Italian public with the release in 1958 of her first of a series of extremely forgettable costume pictures, *La Venere di Cheronea*, followed by *The Nights of Lucrezia*, *Messalina*, the somewhat superior *Joseph and His Brethren*, and others.

Francesco Rosi's *I Magliari* was the first of Belinda's Italian-produced films that gave proof of her artistic development. *I Magliari* led Belinda to an even more important step in the enhancement of her career. On seeing the film in the winter of 1959, Florestano Vancini was stunned by the face and performance of the girl who had previously been to him only a shapely figure in costume pictures and innumerable magazines, only a name in gossip columns and sensationalized articles in the press. He

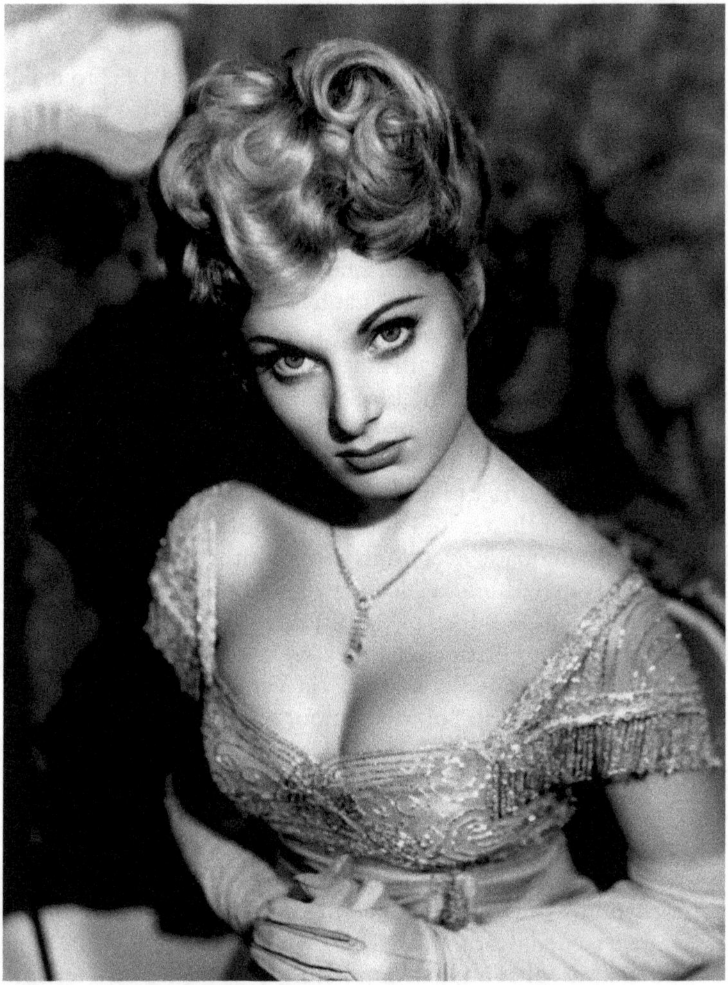

Belinda Lee

rushed to the phone to tell his producers that he had at last found his female lead for his courageous and eloquent anti-fascist drama, *La lunga notte del '43*, released in 1960.

"I was surprised by her seriousness, her courtesy, her discipline, her intense professional commitment," Vancini told the well-known journalist Mino Guerrini, in 1960. "*La lunga notte del '43*, was my first film experience, but even the electricians, the grips, the carpenters, the stagehands, some of whom had been on hundreds of pictures, didn't know how to hide their incredulity over the sweetness of character Belinda demonstrated."

Soon after her arrival in Italy in the summer of 1957 to make *La Venere di Cheronea*, Belinda took a swim some distance from the shore of Fregene. Without having the slightest idea who she was, a young man swam swiftly towards her to warn her that a shark was in the area and that it was dangerous to go out too far. He spoke excitedly, making broad gestures of peril. He realized that the attractive girl did not understand Italian and he went through the scene in English. What he told her was, of course, an invention to give him an opportunity to get acquainted.

The young man was Prince Filippo Napoleone Orsini, perhaps number one in the black aristocracy, attendant to the Pope, which is the maximum honor to which a layman could aspire in the Vatican hierarchy and for generations was the post reserved for the Orsini family. The fairytale about the vicious shark lurking in the tepid, listless waters of Fregene catapulted into a highly dramatic event only five months later. Belinda and Filippo had entered into a suicide pact and on January 28, 1958, Belinda took an overdose of barbiturates and the Black Prince slashed his veins. Both their lives were saved, but for many months afterwards, the gossiping Via Veneto crowd sneered at their act as pyrotechnics of infatuation.

The traumatic event revealed a vital and basic element in Belinda's character. When she loved, it was total, complete, definitive, absolute. Anyone who really knew her, understood that she was not the kind to undertake suicide attempts for the sake of sensation or in a morbid effort to hold on to a man. Love, to her, had no limitation. It superseded career.

It superseded death.

Theirs was, of course, an impossible love. Each paid a terrible price for it and it had to end. It had to, and it did. By the end of 1959, Belinda's first of two impossible loves had been crushed by Fate.

She met the second of her impossible loves while she was making *La lunga notte del '43* in early 1960. The man was Gualtiero Jacopetti, director-writer of exposé documentaries of sensational nature, such as the world-successful *Mondo Cane*. Fourteen years Belinda's senior, Jacopetti was judged by many not only as nonconformist, but as a sinister, morally corrupt and

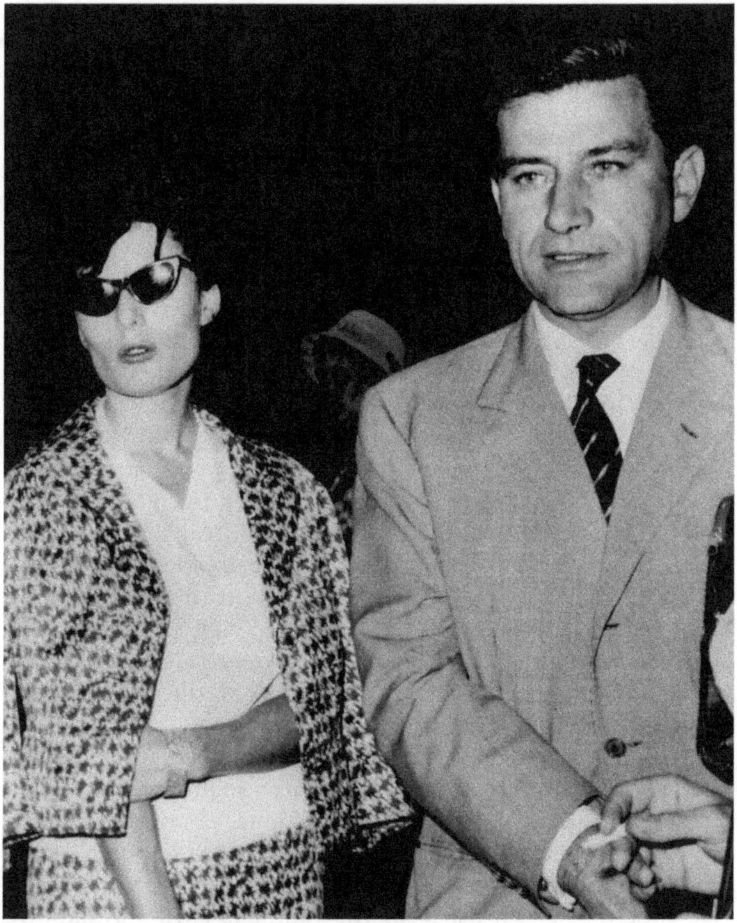

Belinda Lee and Gualtiero Jacopetti

cynical being. Belinda saw him as cultured, intelligent, witty, simple and capable of both speaking vividly and listening intently.

Yes, when Belinda loved, it was total, complete, definitive, absolute. Love, to her, had no limitation. It superseded career.

It superseded death.

On March 13, 1961, at the age of 26, death came to Belinda. Her life was torn to shreds in a car accident in California on a Hollywood freeway. She and Jacopetti were on their way to Los Angeles from Las Vegas in a rented car driven by Nino

Fallanga. Fallanga lost control of the speeding vehicle. Both he and Jacopetti were injured. Belinda was killed instantly.

Alive, so alive, Belinda carried her vulnerability as a monarch her scepter. Her luminescent persona never seemed to diminish. She was fairylike in the delicate and unassuming way she created her special aura in every space she entered. She seemed a captivating visitor from an enchanted world, and in embracing her, one had the scintillating feeling of embracing a creation of fantasy.

Yet she was real. Very real. Real in mind, spirit, body. Had producers the imagination to cast her as Saint Catherine of Siena instead of Catherine the Great of Russia, or Saint Joan instead of Messalina, they would have been awed by the thin line of separation between actress and personage, as they would have been stupefied by the undefiled emanations of her attributes of women that would have distinguished her portrayals. Had she lived to fulfill her prophecy "to become a real actress," these revelations might well have come to inspire millions of filmgoers.

When Belinda died, a child died with her. It was discovered that the blond, green-eyed, 26-year-old English actress was several months pregnant. In Hanks' and Gene's absence from the office on March 1, 1961, Enzo Barbato took the call from Los Angeles with the news of her death.

He prayed for the soul of Belinda Lee, and later, when he learned of the mangled, unborn child, he also prayed for its soul. "There will never be another like Belinda," Barbato said to a shaken, unbelieving Hank when he returned to the office.

As Barbato wept in his arms, Hank found himself remembering her words, "Oh, Mr. Kaufman. How I would love to come and work in Italy. I feel there's something there which I've been waiting for all of my life." All her 26 short years of life, five of them in the country she loved, he said to himself bitterly.

When Belinda Lee loved, it was total, complete, definitive, absolute. Love, to her, had no limitation. It superseded career. It superseded death.

There would never be another like her.

One means for discovering talent is to accept an invitation to a Mingolini-Guggenheim fashion show. KLA client Audrey MacDonald, English actress, model and lady-about-town, asked Hank to a showing of the new fall line of the then-famed Roman house of high fashion. As chic and attractive as Audrey was among the models, it was not Audrey that Hank was seeing. His heart was racing and his blood pressure rising as he watched the materialization of an apparition, a dazzling vision of loveliness who seemed to move in floating mist.

At the conclusion of the showing, Hank rushed to Audrey to ask her about the incredible creature. "That's Elsa Martinelli," replied Audrey. "She's just 17 and straight out of the Trastevere ghetto. Can you believe that she's got eight sisters and a brother? No father. And that she's got to support the whole lot of them plus mum? She was working in some bar only a couple of months ago, when somebody brought her to Micol Fontana's attention. I've never seen anybody get the hang of it as quickly as Elsa. I don't think I've seen another model around to equal her."

Nor had Hank. An idea began to shake up his brain. Director-writer Joseph L. Mankiewicz had told him there might be difficulties in springing Ava Gardner from Metro-Goldwyn-Mayer for *The Barefoot Contessa*, in which KLA had gotten Tonio Selwart and Gertrude Flynn featured parts. The director had said that he might reluctantly have to go forward with an unknown, if Gardner really turned out to be unavailable. Elsa could well be the answer, Hank told himself excitedly. "You've got to introduce me to her," he told Audrey. Audrey nodded, shrugged her shoulders, took Hank by the hand, and led him to the dressing room, where Martinelli was hurriedly getting into her street clothes.

Hank introduced himself in Italian, explaining to Signorina Martinelli that he was an agent and felt she had marvelous opportunities for a film career. She kept staring at him, wide-eyed, not in innocence but in wariness, but Hank failed to note the difference, so overwhelmed was he by her bearing, way of movement and piquant dark beauty. He revealed to Elsa the particular idea he had in mind. "As I watched you," he said admiringly, "I felt that you had exactly the combination of earthiness and etherealness that Mankiewicz has in mind." Elsa agreed to a date to discuss the matter further.

She neither appeared nor bothered to telephone her excuses. Hank was furious. He phoned Audrey for help. The English actress-model sighed philosophically. "You'll get used to it, darling, unless you let your American background become a mental block. Elsa's Roman, and typical. Indolence and disdain are both seasoning in any Roman dish. I wouldn't take it to heart if I were you."

So convinced was Hank of his instincts about Martinelli that he hadn't the slightest intention of halting his pursuit. He went to see Mikhail Wasczinski, Mankiewicz's casting consultant. Wasczinski was one of the most intriguing rogues in Rome's show business. A Polish refugee of presumed noble lineage, he lived the role of His Royal Highness Prince Mikhail to the hilt. He resided in a magnificent, antique-laden flat in a palazzo of Via Paisello. It served not only for casting assignations but also as setting for some of Rome's most swinging parties. By accent, malapropisms and male bitchery which left nothing sacred, he earned and enjoyed his subtitle of Clown Prince.

Mike used his stranglehold over casting for American producers shooting in Southern Europe to benefit his favorites, as well as his pocketbook. Agents were looked down upon as if they were peasants and a threat to his position and payola. Yet he was an utter charmer with whom one could spend many pleasant hours. It took that long, when Hank went to see Mike, to get around to the subject of Elsa. Mike seemed impressed by Hank's enthusiasm and agreed to present Elsa to Mankiewicz.

So Hank turned detective to track down Elsa. She no longer worked for Mingolini-Guggenheim. Audrey had lost contact with her. No one else at Mingolini knew where she might be found. The family had no phone. He was warned not to go to her Trasterere home and knock at the door asking to see her because Mamma Martinelli and the army of sisters would just throw him out. He finally settled on leaving an urgent message, then another, followed by another always more urgent, at the local coffee bar above which the Martinelli family resided.

Finally, Elsa phoned. As nonchalantly as could be, she said, "I forgot about our date." With ill-controlled patience, Hank explained once again about the importance of the role in the Mankiewicz picture and carefully went over his talk with Prince Mike. She agreed to meet Hank at Masczinski's apartment, assuring Hank that this time, she would really come. "That's an absolute promise. Word of honor. I'll see you there, I swear," she insisted.

She didn't show. Nor did she phone. Embarrassment and ire led Hank to utter some juicy curses of Roman origin that Elsa would have no difficulty in understanding. When

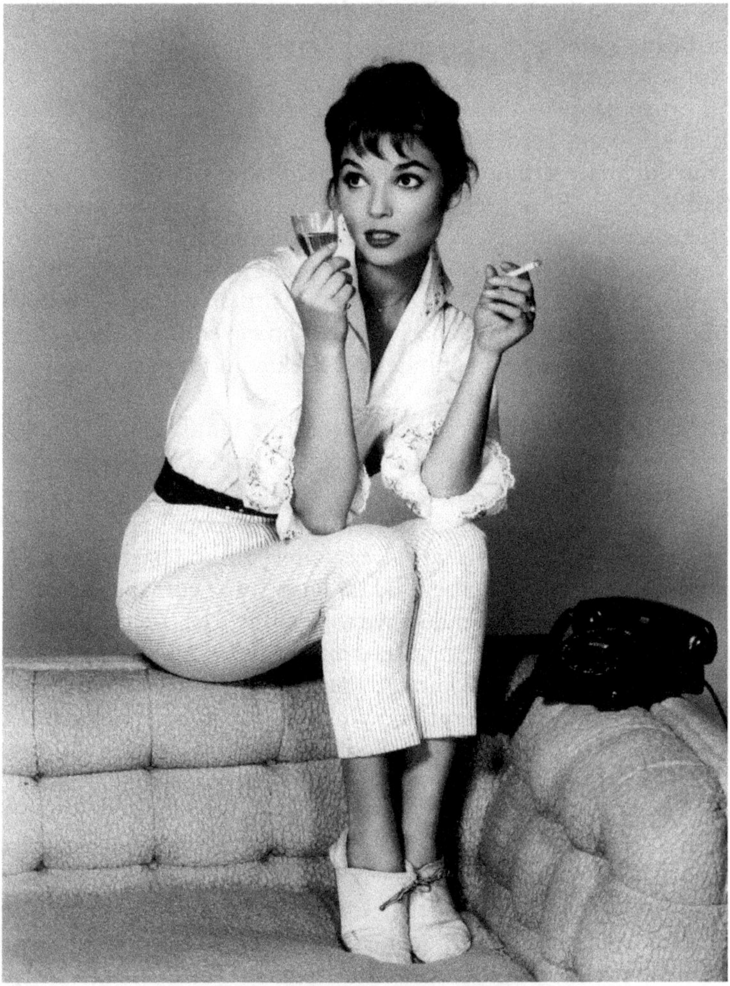

Elsa Martinelli

he was soon advised that Metro had finally agreed to release Gardner to United Artists for Mankiewiez's picture, he ceased his efforts with Elsa. But not without a resounding *chi se ne frega*, Roman slang for "who gives a goddam?"

Chi se ne frega notwithstanding, Hank just couldn't forget Elsa. And he went through a series of chest-beating, "I was right, I was right, I was right," when, during a *Life* cover session in New York, she was spotted by Kirk Douglas and began her film career opposite Kirk in *The Indian Fighter*, cast as an extraordinary-looking Indian speaking English with an unmistakable Roman accent.

It so happened that Hank had to go to Milan soon after the film was completed. When he went to a nightclub that evening, who did he see sitting at a corner table? Walter Chiari and a styled and stunning brunette, with whom Walter was having a serious romantic relationship. Elsa! Hank made a beeline to their table, determined to trap his quarry. Prodded by Chiari, Martinelli finally succumbed to Hank's blandishments and agreed to become a KLA client. Chiari himself, however, was still holding out, continuing a game of hide-and-seek with the agency, not yet ready to take the plunge.

When, after the contract signing, Hank asked for an explanation for her earlier behavior, Elsa leveled as she often can and does. "I was sure all agents were pimps. And I thought, me – a movie star? I had just started being a model. That for me was already a Cinderella world, so wonderful and paying so well. I couldn't see anything beyond it. Then I was convinced that to make it in pictures, I would have to become a whore. Who needs it? I asked myself. You were so enthusiastic, Hank. How could I be so heartless as to discourage you? So I took the *romano* way out. I just agreed to everything you said, everything you wanted me to do. But I never had the slightest intention of going through with it, *capisci*?"

Irene Papas also came with her extraordinary gifts as an artist and exceptional qualities as a woman. Few on the agency roster had the theatrical skills of the Greek actress, developed through years of classical training, nor matched her open, frank and human sensibilities. Irene adored Italy and for many years has kept an apartment in the seaside village of Sperlonga, filling it with canvases, easels, paints and paintbrushes, books and coming-and-going friends whom she considered precious, even when they were penniless and homeless. Irene's qualities and personality make another noted Greek actress, Melina Mercouri, seem papier-mâché, marionette-like and artificial, characteristics that do not seem to detract from her current role as Minister of Culture in Greece's Socialist government.

Papas was scheduled to make her Hollywood debut in 1955 opposite Spencer Tracy in the Western *Tribute to a Bad Man*, the

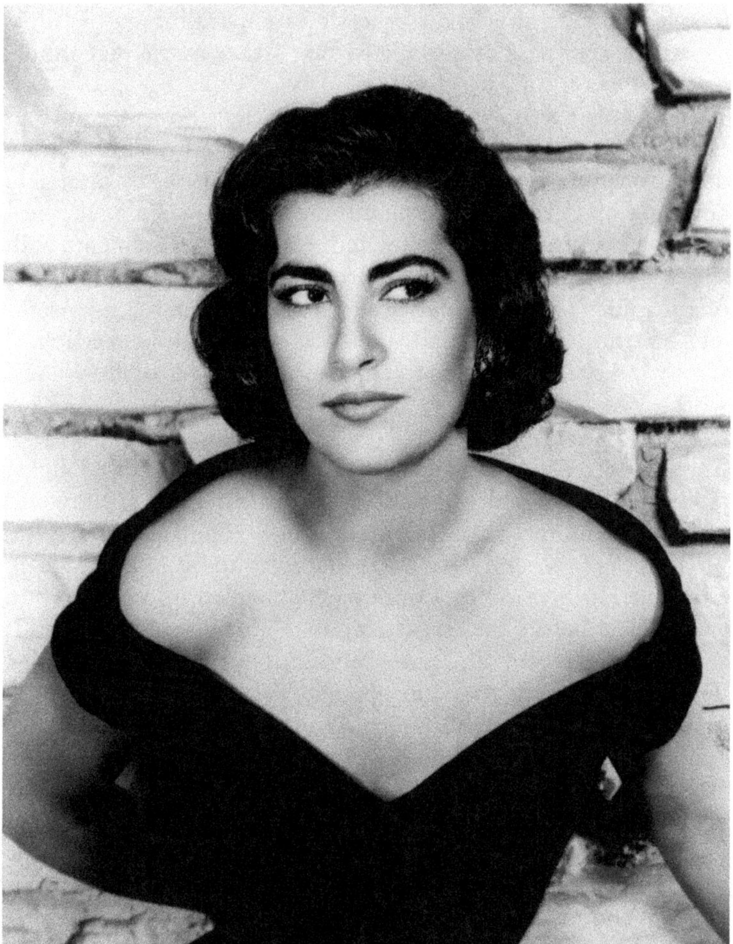

Irene Papas

first picture of the exclusive, seven-year contract with Metro that KLA had negotiated on her behalf. Because of some unspecified illness, Tracy was replaced by James Cagney. Sensational critical reactions ecstatically hailed Papas as the new Garbo. Nevertheless, her Hollywood career never took off.

Poet, painter, philosopher, romantic idealist, realistic romantic, iconoclast, money-come and money-go, Irene baffled the big studios and their concept of "commerciality." All her remarkable talent, all the hosannahs from critics, failed to overcome Hollywood's practice of concealing its inability to handle greatness by placing certain artists in the pigeonhole marked "too special."

Papas is the only actress in the world who can emote in English, Greek, Italian, French, German, even Arabic. With a degree of philosophic fatalism rare in an ambiance of insatiable ambition and greed, she has continued her career on even keel in many countries, mixing film and television engagements with stage appearances, such as her Broadway portrayal, in English, of Euripides' *Medea*, a performance memorable for its insight and emotional power, and, in 1980, her triumph in Michael Cacoyannis' New York presentation of another of Euripides' works, *The Bacchae.*

English-born Dawn Addams became one of KLA's most sought-after clients. She had gained a certain notoriety in Hollywood in Otto Preminger's film adaptation of F. Hugh Herbert's *The Moon is Blue*. When Dawn's career seemed to be going nowhere either in Hollywood or London, she decided upon migration to Italy just before the mass invasion of foreign actors began. It was a wise decision. She gained instant popularity in an Italian underwater epic called *Mizar* opposite Franco Silva, a new hunk of Italian beefcake, who later provided Rome with a piquant scandal when he combined his sex appeal with blackmail in an affair with Anita Ekberg. Dawn's flamboyant romance with the patrician of Roman patricians, Prince Vittorio Massimo, plastered her name and photo in virtually every newspaper and magazine on the peninsula, putting her more and more in demand for films. She was soon ready for a vehicle that might have borne the title "Every English Girl's Fantasy Come True."

If the Hepburn-Ferrer wedding was maximal understatement and discretion of nihilistic extreme, the Addams-Massimo nuptials set some kind of record for disorder, overt publicity pandering, and that special brew of Roman brouhaha. The over-adrenalized couple had been living together for some time prior to their marriage and had accidentally or deliberately provided miles of tasty copy to the Italian gossip magazines, which seemed to have been read by three Italians out of every two. Neither Dawn nor Vittorio seemed to be the least perturbed by the neverending attention. They were the darlings of the sensational press, the darlings of the photographers, just darlings.

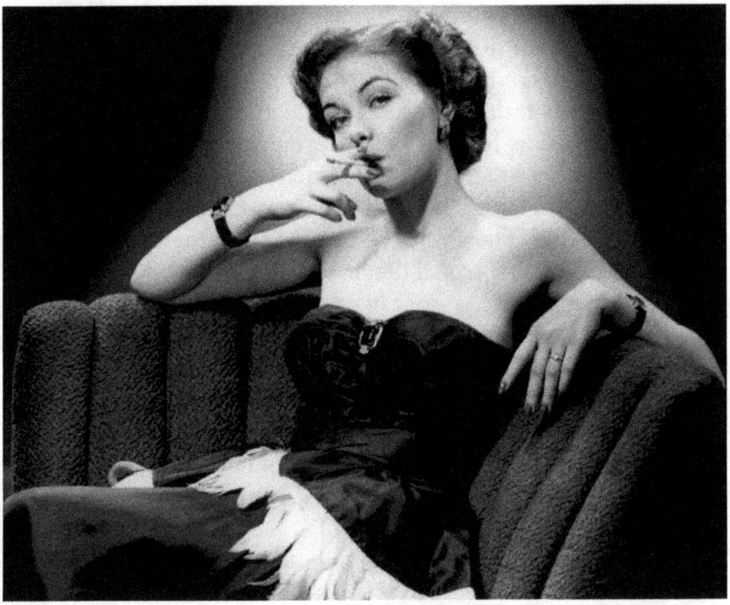

Dawn Addams

The wedding was set to take place in the historic church of Ara Coeli, "Gates of Heaven," majestically perched on Capitoline Hill. The spectacular church could only be reached by a climb up several hundred gracefully graded steps. Rome had not forgotten the cinematographically inspired Roman wedding of Tyrone Power and Linda Christian a few years earlier at the Church of Santa Francesca Romana, and excitement to match that event was mounting daily. Dawn asked Hank not only to be a witness but also to take charge of the press.

The great day arrived. A perfectly serene Roman afternoon in June 1955. The brilliant ultramarine sky accentuated the weathered gray-brown facade of the Ara Coeli edifice. The vast interior, rococo and severity effectively interwoven, was adorned ostentatiously with every kind of white flower: roses, tuberoses, lilacs, gardenias, magnolias, lilies. They were almost obliterated by the surging crowd of spectators and the press. Perhaps a hundred photographers were literally swinging from the eaves, ensconced around marble columns, perched on ledges, pedestals, fountains and even in the choir-and-organ loft. Pandemonium reigned.

Anxiety was mounting. Nerves were fraying. Where were the bride and groom? Already twenty minutes late. Even by Rome's standards of punctuality, this was unpardonable. Captain James Addams, father of the bride, a dashing ex-British Air Force officer in his forties, kept peering stealthily at his watch, cursing under his breath. "You had better keep an eye outside," he suggested to Hank, "and I'll keep the vigil inside. Where in hell can they be? They've probably had another of their wild arguments over some trivial detail."

At that moment, a roar was heard from outside. Hank forcefully pushed his way through the crowd. The couple had finally arrived. Hundreds lining both sides of the flight of steps cheered as bride and broom slowly ascended the steep rise. Hank quickly rushed towards them and was quick to note that the two were alternately smiling to and acknowledging the delighted public, while stage-whispering filthy curses at one another in both English and Italian.

At last they reached the great brass portals of the church. Dawn broke away from Vittorio and locked arms with Daddy Jimmy. Vittorio joined members of his illustrious family, attired in formal Vatican dress, as dictated by custom. Dawn smiled divinely. The public applauded. The wedding march commenced. Then sheer bedlam broke out. Photographers began hurling instructions at bride and groom. Invited guests and uninvited curiosity seekers brutally shoved each other for a better view. The church authorities looked at the turmoil, aghast.

The police were competing with one another in an effort to get themselves photographed with the bride. Foreigners, unused to such a spectacle in a site of sanctity, were horrified by the sacrilege and the hysterical violation of a haven of God. However, the Romans looked upon the wild proceedings as a comparatively normal demonstration of the Italian penchant for spectacle, which after all had roots in ancient history.

Somehow, the ceremony commenced and continued to its conclusion. In spite of the noise, interruptions, flashbulbs and constant jostling for position, it had its lovely moments. A beaming Vittorio and an exquisite Dawn traditionally exchanged simple gold wedding bands.

Afterwards, a huge reception, picnic-style, took place in comic disorganization on the Massimo country estate at Scorano, about fifteen miles outside of Rome. The basic *cucina*?

American-style barbecue. And Dawn and Vittorio? Off with their wedding finery and into blue jeans, twin pairs of Western boots and matching cowboy hats on both. Hollywood actress of British birth, the last descendent of a noble family traceable to the days of the Roman Empire, representatives of the Church and of Vatican nobility, members of Roman aristocracy, an international film crowd and dozens of the local *contadini*, photographers by the score, newspaper men and women, members of the police made up an *insalata capricciosa*, oiled, vinegared, herbed and spiced to salivate the palate of 1950s Rome.

Rossana Podestà, fresh, young and luscious, an unusual amalgam of innocence and sensuality, became a client after her portrayal of Helen of Troy in the 1956 Robert Wise epic for Warner Bros., opposite that magnificent specimen of malehood, Slavic-born Jacques Sernas, who regrettably confused acting with wood-pecking. And, head held high, grand in manner, Isa Miranda turned to KLA after her re-entry into Italy, embittered by Paramount's campaign to "sell" her as an alternative to Marlene Dietrich rather than utilize her own specific quality and talent to bring her to world stardom.

Anna Maria Pierangeli, also known by her Metro-Goldwyn-Mayer pseudonym of Pier Angeli, came too. And when Anna Maria came, Mamma Enrica Pierangeli – plus canyon smile, white, white teeth, a trumpet voice and star-glitter splatter in her eyes – was not far behind.

The first contract made by KLA on Anna Maria's behalf was to co-star as Edith, Lot's wife, in Robert Aldrich's *Sodom and Gomorrah* for Titanus Productions. Her name on the screen preceded such well-known European artists as Anouk Aimée, Rossana Podestà and Stanley Baker, following only the name of Stewart Granger, who portrayed Lot.

It was when Hank was still writing for *Silver Screen* and *Screenland* that he first met "Pier-Anna Maria." It was in 1954, just after Mamma Enrica had brought Marisa to Hank for a special promotional campaign to launch the second of the twins in films. Metro-Goldwyn-Mayer had taken over the ballroom of Rome's Grand Hotel for a gala press cocktail to honor Lana Turner and Pier Angeli, co-stars in *The Flame and the Flesh*. Under her seven-year contract to Metro, which began in 1950, Anna Maria had already done *Teresa*, directed by Fred

Zinnemann; *The Light Touch*, with Stewart Granger; *The Devil Makes Three*, with Gene Kelly; *The Story of Three Loves*, with Kirk Douglas, James Mason and Leslie Caron; and *Sombrero*, with Ricardo Montalban.

Lana Turner was the first to arrive, all startingly blonde, extravagantly hairstyled, glamor-varnished and maximal Hollywood. The photographers swooped all over her and had her twirling in one pose after another, each of which ended up with the same expression. Then came the moment for questions. "Miss Turner, will you please tell us how you like Rome?"

Lana looked at the reporter as if he had asked her to explain Einstein's theory of relativity. Fluttering her stretched-open eyes, agitating her what-do-I-do-with-these hands, she stood silent with a twitching smile, trying desperately to provide an answer to a question of such import.

"Well," she started. The reporters leaned forward eagerly, pencils and pads at the ready. "Well, I just… I just… LOVE Rome." Pause. The twitching smile. "I just love it, but to tell you the truth, I thought, well, I thought, you know what I mean, that there would be a little ruin here, a little ruin there. But ALL THOSE RUINS!"

It was fortunate that just at that moment, 22-year-old Anna Maria walked in. Poor Lana found herself hopelessly upstaged by the "Pier-Anna Maria" vision that had amalgamated Hollywood with Rome. She strode through the ballroom with an authority and dignity that seemed impossible for someone so young. She combined an intensely dark beauty with an indisputable "I am a star" hauteur. Everyone crowded around the Cagliari-born girl, applauding and cheering her homecoming as the first Italian actress who had been triumphantly transformed into a genuine Hollywood star.

"Anna Maria Pierangeli represented a certain type of Italian girl who appeared in the first years after the War," Léonide Moguy, who discovered her for his *Domani è troppo tardi* when she was 17 years old, said of her years later. "She symbolized the life which continued with all of its daily problems but which substituted the long cataclysm of the conflict with quietude, slowly rising from the ruins. Hers was the youth upon which our new society would be constructed. Hers the sweetness, the innocence after the ferocity. Her face expressed all this with an

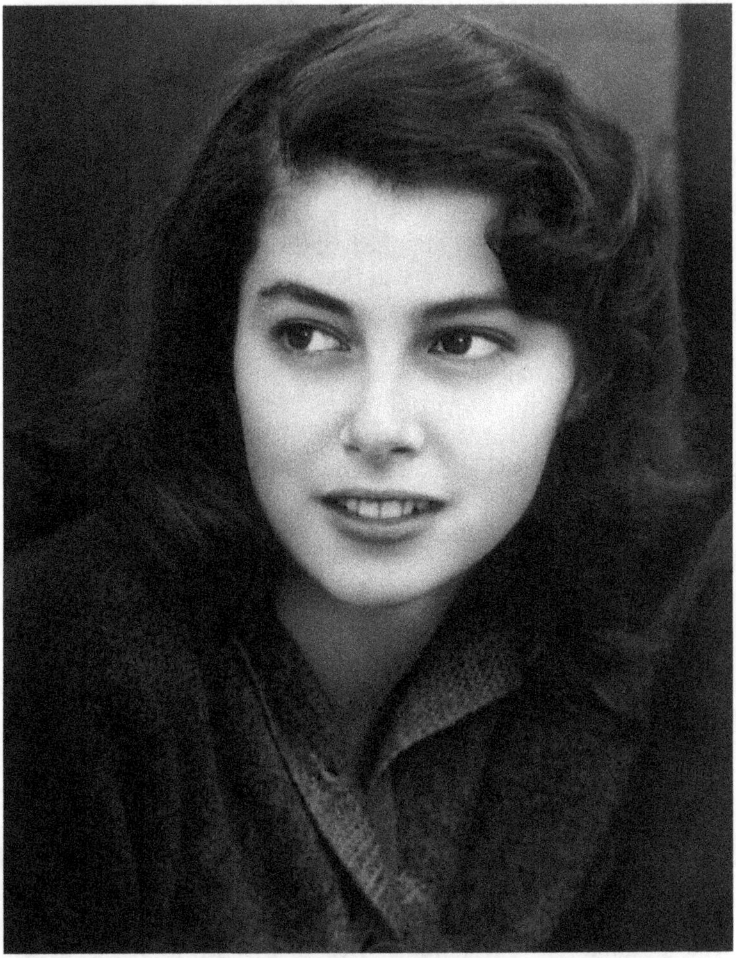

Pier Angeli

incredible perfection, and provided a new image both in the human and cinematografic panorama."

Hollywood had tampered with that "new image" but covered its manipulations with a stunning makeup job. And six years after the *Flame and the Flesh* press conference, Hollywood and "Pier" seemed to have had it with each other. "Pier" returned to Italy as "Anna Maria" and a KLA client. Following *Sodom and Gomorrah*, she immediately shot two other Italian films,

The Sea Musketeers and *The Mutiny*. Hank and Gene were concerned about the type of pictures she was being offered and made strenuous efforts to secure first-quality projects for her, but Mamma Enrica was always impatient for action. It was Moguy, her discoverer, who understood the heart of the problem when, years later, he said the following about Anna Maria-Pier:

"When she came back to Italy, her homeland, in its social and human aspects, had changed, and consequently so had the cinema. A changing society had become interested in new types of female – obviously 'sexy' women, buxom, broadminded, promiscuous, adulterous, possibly also a bit vulgar. In other words, the sensual female who confronts the world without complexes. The cinema naturally grabbed hold of these changing attitudes of and towards women and put all of its cards on them, producing pictures that exalted and deified the new concept of femininity. With her sentimental, romantic, intimate baggage, Anna Maria could not meet the requirements of the trend. Thus, contrary to all her hopes, her opportunities were limited. Yes, she did several films, earned a good deal of money, but underneath it all, she was considered passée."

Unfortunately, Moguy, in hindsight, had correctly analyzed the situation. As the 1960s went on, Pier appeared in such productions as *Shadow of Evil*, *Spy in Your Eye*, *Red Roses for the Führer* and others of similar theme and level. "I often get the impression that I don't exist," she once said, "that I'm only a character in a picture." Her impression was painfully astute. The films she played in were less and less interesting, and the life she stumbled through became a harrowing, demeaning accompaniment. The real issue had been camouflaged by years of Hollywood razzle-dazzle and the know-it-all domination of Mamma Enrica: how to avoid being sucked under by life's quicksands.

The issue had become brutally apparent as early as 1962.

Her decade of the 1960s in Rome was a jarring, inevitable slide into Hell, a vilification of all her innocence, all her promise and dreams. There were a few who understood, who sought to help, but how could they reverse time? How, in some Alice-in-Wonderland miracle, could they lead her back to her childhood years so that, alone and undisturbed, she could build herself a marvelous castle in the sand? Or create some sprawling architecture with diverse sizes and shapes of colored blocks? Or sketch a crazy-quilt of animals, flowers and trees? Or fascinate herself with abstract scrawls that liberated her spontaneity? And thus, through her own solitary deeds, through her own private fantasy, mark out that indispensable individual space of self-confidence and self-structure so critical to her growth into maturity?

"I don't think that Anna Maria ever really had fun in her life," said Carlo Delle Piane, recalling those adolescent days of *Tomorrow Is Too Late*, in which he also appeared. "She seemed a slave to her mother, who didn't want Anna Maria to join us in our diversions. The poor thing was never young. I saw her many years later. She was always with her mother. She never freed herself from her mother, even up to the end. She seemed always conditioned, maneuvered, only rarely liberated, light-hearted, but for a moment."

Yes, there were some who tried to understand. Hank and Gene were among them, but the professional barrier in her particular case was a fence that separated them from the truth of her private existence. Bob Aldrich, too, was among them, sensing her fears and despair after so many months of working together on *Sodom and Gomorrah*, and he developed a project for her and Marisa to do together – *The Angry Odyssey*, to be shot in Greece – but he was unable to raise the financing to make the picture.

In that Dantesque, Hollywood on the Tiber decade of the 1960s, there were two men with whom she had particularly intimate, romantic and serious ties. One was Armando Trovajoli, one of Italy's most noted postwar composers of popular music, whom Anna Maria married in a civil ceremony in London on February 14, 1962, with Hank being among the few invitees. The other was lawyer, builder, developer and, above all, world offshore racing champion Vincenzo Balestrieri, whose powerful motor boat, Black Tornado, won him more world-point races than any other offshore racer in history.

Trovajoli was fourteen years older than Anna Maria. He appeared solid, steady, and self-controlled—qualities crucial for Anna Maria if there was to be any chance of escaping the depths that threatened to consume her. She seemed genuinely happy about the marriage and he seemed madly in love with her. "I finally know that I am being loved, not because I'm a famous actress, but because I'm a woman," she said. In 1963, the birth of a boy, whom they named Andrea "Andy" Rugantino, gave her an added sense of comfort and normalcy.

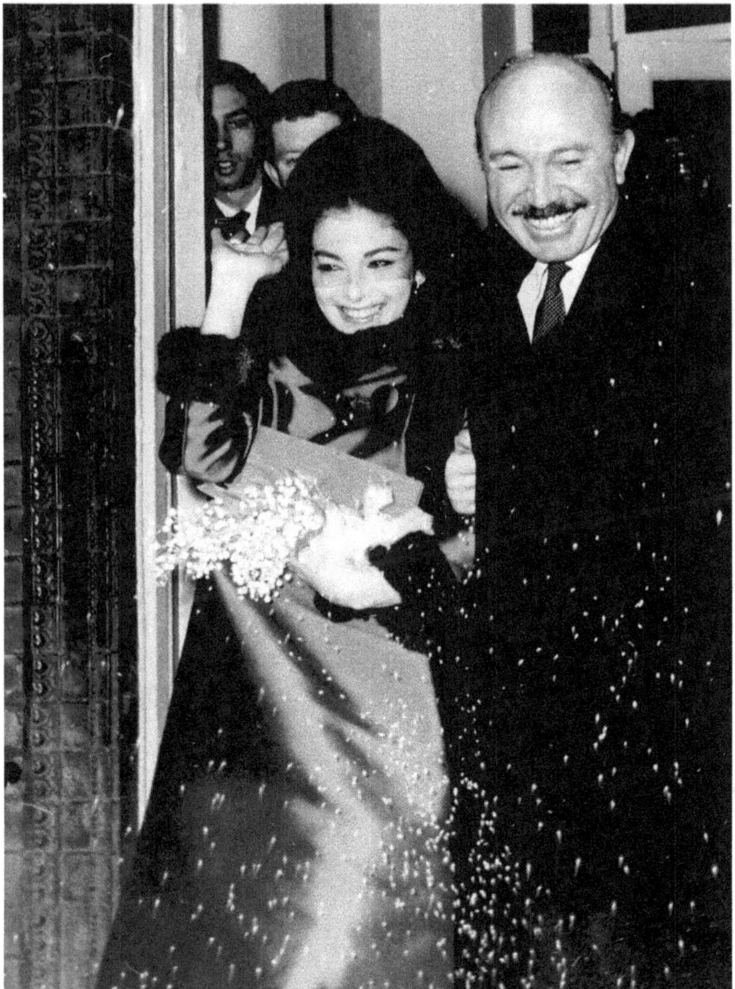

Pier Angeli and Armando Trovajoli

But by 1964 it was all over, terminated in a morass of gossip from other men, particularly popular singer Fred Bongusto. Suspicion, bitterness, recrimination – not much different from the atmosphere that had disfigured the end of her 1954 marriage to the Italo-American singer Vic Damone, a matrimony openly manipulated by Mamma Enrica as a highly satisfying antidote to the poison of the love affair between James Dean, whom Mamma despised, and her "superior" Anna Maria. It was Dean, out of wry retaliation, who dubbed Mamma "Signora Pizza," and who soon after the loss of Anna Maria smashed himself to death in his Porsche.

The marriage with Damone, certainly no romantic idyll, lasted four years. It, too, produced a son, who was named Perry, and who would go on to graduate from the West Point Military Academy. When the conjugal alliance between Vic and Anna Maria shifted into divorce proceedings, it turned into a ferocious war of accusations, below-the-belt lies, a marketplace fight for material possessions and a no-holds-barred battle for the custody of Perry. The issue of Perry's paternity raised its primitive head. It was repeatedly gossiped that he was actually Jimmy Dean's child, that "Signora Pizza" always knew it and that Damone himself suspected it. And soon after the final break between Anna Maria and Travajoli, the paternity issue again appeared on the agenda. To Anna Maria's dismay, the composer denied that he was the father of Andrea Rugantino and adamantly refused to speak, write, or in any other way be in contact with the brokenhearted child, who could not understand why his father did not want him. Andrea is now the legally adopted son of Marisa and Jean-Pierre Aumont.

The second of the two men to establish an intimate, romantic tie with Anna Maria during the 1960s, Vincenzo Balestrieri, was approximately six years older than Anna Maria. Short, electric-charged, sculpture-faced, grey-haired, his dry thinness kneaded into tight muscle, he established a relationship with Anna Maria in 1965. He placed her in a handsome apartment at Via Polibio 52. He provided her with a motor launch. He saw to it that she had funds to buy things she needed or fancied.

How the Balestieri-Pierangeli rapport began, what it represented to him, what it gave to Anna Maria in emotional, spiritual and economic sustenance, why and how it ended, was never made clear by either of the two. But it was the last of her relationships with men that had either meaning or relative duration. And when, in the latter part of 1966, it ended, he carefully consigned to her many items of value, including diamond, sapphire, ruby and pearl rings, bracelets, pins, clips and earrings, objects of gold and silver, antiques and paintings, including a Renoir.

No one knows where these precious articles ended up, or with whom. Anna Maria seemed to be turning into a jellyfish, tossed by violent seas to disintegrate on some vacant shore. Men sensed her inner formlessness, the weakening of her sting, her incapacity at self-protection and her acceptance of herself as a degraded, sexual animal. Giacomo Rossi Stuart, a featured actor in *Sodom and Gomorrah*, who was having an affair with her in the Morocco desert, could abuse her, bruise her with violence, foaming at the mouth with such foul comments as, "All you want is miles of cock."

Men might have been saddened by the torn remnants of the sweetness, gentleness, courtesy, tenderness and submissiveness that seemed basic elements of her character. Yet in their cynicism, they were also quick to understand that she had so little faith in herself, such fragile possession of herself, that they actually did not feel that she existed either as a person or a woman. She was a species of protoplasm – pulsating, palpitating, twitching, contracting. Her humiliations often turned her wild, angry and foul-mouthed. They also left her bewildered soul to suffocate in terrifying solitude.

The intake of alcohol increased. The orgies of meaningless coupling intensified. The insomnia became more and more relentless. The use of barbiturates accelerated.

Anna Maria's exquisite villa at Porto d'Ercole, which she had bought as love nest and refuge during the brief interlude with Trovajoli, was fought over by the separated couple, sequestered for her failure to pay taxes, then sold for a pitiful sum at public auction. Neighbors denounced her to the police for nightly brawls. In the summer of 1969, as a result of a screaming battle with her lover, 30-year-old Piero Ranieri, son of a prominent builder, she was put in the hospital for two weeks with a fractured nose and a suspected injury to her spinal column.

She was condemned by the tax authorities to ten days' arrest for failure to file a tax return, fortunately rescinded in 1969. She lived in total poverty and heartrending decomposition. She was filthy, unwashed, hair matted, in the clothes of a street bum. She had no money for food, no room in which to sleep. She was saved by KLA's own Enzo Barbato, who, from his modest income, and knowing he would never be repaid, saw that she had food, clothes and a roof over her head, a mini-apartment on Rome's periphery, a cot and a trunk her only furniture. It was reported that three times she tried to kill herself and that three times she was saved in extremis.

In the summer of 1970, she entered a clinic specializing in nervous disorders. After nearly a month of treatment, Anna Maria went to the French countryside fifty miles from Paris to try to rebuild her physical and emotional resources. Hope seemed to be reborn. She stopped drinking, taking drugs, swallowing sleeping pills and gained a few pounds. Soon thereafter, she made the decision to return to Hollywood, believing that she would be returning to the home at 1075 Sunset Boulevard she had bought in the early 1950s with her earnings in the golden period of stardom at Metro-Goldwyn-Mayer. She had forgotten that she had given her mother a power of attorney years before and that Mamma Enrica had used the authority given her to sell the house.

"I have returned to Hollywood only to die," she said, soon after her return.

When Barbato heard the news bulletin that September 1971 night, announcing the death of Anna Maria Pierangeli, he wept more bitterly than he had for Belinda Lee, who, ironically, a decade earlier, had also come to her tragic end on the sun-drenched soil of Southern California. Many times in the last six years of Anna Maria's wretched struggle to survive, she had said to Barbato, "You're like a father to me."

And many times, Mamma Enrica, in her endless streams of letters to him – beginning in 1963, asking for and about money, money, money and more money, accountings, terms of contracts; lamenting debts, obligations and financial problems; vituperating against the gangsters, criminals, idiots, connivers, thieves and profiteers who had robbed her daughter right and left of her property, income and rights; whining over the indifference with which Anna Maria, in September 1963, permitted her to go away, "as if I didn't exist or never existed," pleading over and over again through the following years for news of her estranged daughter – also commented, "You've been like a father to her."

There is a marvelous cartoon drawn by noted American artist-satirist Saul Steinberg years ago, published in *The New Yorker* magazine. It is now part of American folklore. It shows a map of the United States as seen by a native of the miniscule island of the City of New York, the Borough of Manhattan. In Steinberg's cartoon, Manhattan covers nearly half of the United States as far as Chicago, the other four boroughs of the New York metropolis and the state of New York representing most of the nation up to the Rocky Mountains. The remainder of the fifty states is squeezed into a strip along the Pacific Ocean and nearly requires a microscope to decipher.

The Steinberg drawing is a delicious and imaginative projection of an insular and insolent geographical concept.

The giant American talent agencies such as MCA – soon to be put out of business by the United States government for violation of the anti-trust acts – and William Morris, particularly the latter, seemed to see the European continent in a similar manner. The Continent was a thumb across an ocean which could fit into Texas. Instead of skyscrapers, Disneyland and modern conveniences, it was crumbling with ruins, bearable for quick holidays, a tour here or there, shopping sprees and the fulfilment of depraved and lascivious fantasies. What a pity that millions of overcrowded, illiterate and unfortunate humans had made the fatal error of having been born so ingloriously on foreign soil, nor having the joyful pride of saluting the Stars and Stripes as their national flag.

But business is business, the buck the buck, and prestige not so bad if it doesn't diminish profit. The powerful William Morris organization had its headquarters in an unassuming office building on El Camino Drive in Beverly Hills, California, with offices in New York, Chicago and wherever else it could make a deal for its clients. Whether by fortune or foresight, it had worked out a reciprocity arrangement with the London agency of Christopher Mann, whose preeminence stemmed not only from his extraordinary overall comprehension of the motion picture business but also from a clientele which included most of England's greatest filmmakers, including David Lean and Carol Reed.

Mann was brilliant, authoritative, jealous of his terrain and light years more erudite than his highly respected and extremely capable William Morris peers. Neither Abe Lastfogel, President of William Morris, nor Bert Allenberg, its admired motion picture department head, could match Mann's stylistic brilliance or his rapier-like wit or sarcasm. Mann's elegance in phrase and measured fluidity of words were without equal.

It was Chris Mann who first took notice of Kaufman-Lerner. His sharp glance was not at first trained on Hank and

Gene just because of their existence, or even because of any accomplishments they might have achieved. From his austere London observation desk, free of William Morris astigmatism, he was above all aware of the importance of the European continent in the broad scheme of picture-making. That KLA was in Rome and was seemingly functioning seemed to him worthy of note.

In the 1950s, production in England was riding at a fast gallop. There was a huge American financial involvement, and the British government's Eady Levy not only offered attractive subsidy for investment but also offered American companies greater in-depth distribution of their British-financed product throughout the United Kingdom.

Mann recognized that the American-British honeymoon was not going to blossom into a lasting marriage. He therefore developed a twofold strategy: first, to make the USA-Great Britain effort as fruitful as possible for as long as it lasted, and second, to forge alliances between England and the Continent's major production centers to increase the world potential for European films, whether or not there was American financial involvement.

As for the second basis of his design, he worked on both governmental and industry-wide levels, seeking co-production agreements between England and individual Continental countries, foreseeing the Common Market and the simplification of barriers among member nations in the financing, distribution and talent exchange in European films.

Chris had already established a reciprocal arrangement with Paris-based Olga Horstig-Primuz, who years earlier had left Yugoslavia with husband Vjeyko, their daughter Vera, and Olga's mother. Olga quickly became a perfect Frenchwoman with an absolute command of the language, an unerring business instinct, and her own very special gallic femininity. She rapidly made a reputation for herself in the agency field, planting roots both in cinema and theater.

By the time Chris was undertaking his international knitting process, Olga had amassed a client list of enviable quality. Among others, it included Brigitte Bardot, Michèle Horgan, Edwige Feuillère, Annie Girardot, Pierre Brasseur, Michel Simon, Nadia Gray, Jane Fonda, Juliette Gréco, Pierre Brice, Claude Dauphin, Robert Hossein, Gérard Oury, Jean Servais, Line Renaud, Dany Saval, and for a period of time, Alain Delon and Romy Schneider.

Horstig and Mann had a number of things in common. Integrity. Authority. Prestige. Ability. Coolness under fire. Incorruptibility. Unmitigated passion for work. Limitless devotion to clients.

And cigarettes.

Both were obsessive chain-smokers. Olga's conversations, whether in French or in her equally perfect English, whether by phone or face-to-face, were, like Chris', limited to three-quarters of her mouth, the other quarter caressing and puffing the cigarette dangling from her lip. Chris was plagued by a heavy stammer and nervous giggle, which, with cigarette in mouth, made Marlon Brando's mumble seem a Laurence Olivier declamation. Olga had no such problem. Through the thick of nicotine fumes, her voice came across loud, clear and precise.

Although they chain-smoked different cigarette brands, Chris suited Olga and Olga suited Chris. In spite of the fact that both Hank and Gene were mere take-it-or-leave-it smokers, the London-Paris axis demonstrated its capacity for tolerance. Before long, a business compact was to be established between them and Kaufman-Lerner, and a deep, affectionate friendship was to give it warmth and meaning.

Mann began his campaign to secure William Morris' recognition of the European continent, concentrating on Italy, where the Hollywood on the Tiber boom was reverberating louder and louder. Chris appreciated KLA's daring in entering what he considered "the Italian jungle." The Italian way of doing business was beyond his concept and not his style. It puzzled, irritated and unnerved him. The fact that KLA was showing stamina and seemed to be growing, the fact that Gene and Hank were Americans, made him decide that an association with Kaufman-Lerner Associates was worthy of a gamble.

After advising Olga Horstig of his decision and recommending to her that she follow suit, Mann, in the latter part of 1954, brought KLA to the attention of Lastfogel and Allenberg of William Morris. He told them of his decision to associate himself with "those two American boys." He suggested that William Morris give consideration to doing the same. Chris found a strong ally in Martin Jurow, a William Morris vice president working out of its New York office. Jurow, young, bright and exuberant, welcomed an opportunity which, if shrewdly utilized, could lead to his becoming chief architect of William Morris International. He immediately took the lead in propagandizing Mann's vision with Lastfogel, Nat Lefkowitz, head of the Agency's New York operation, business manager Morris Stoller and television department chief Sam Weisbord, the tightly knit "Sanhedrin," or supreme council, which held all power in William Morris and interpreted all its sacred doctrine.

In 1955, Man and Jurow were finally able to convince the WMA power group that it was in the Agency's interests to look out across the Atlantic and decide on a Continental setup. Mann endorsed KLA as the best solution. When Jurow came to Rome to investigate, he was delighted with what he found, returning to the States to urge that the mandate go to Kaufman-Lerner.

Suddenly, the Tavel & Marouani agency of Paris got into the act. For years, it had had a reciprocal arrangement with William Morris in the lucrative variety act field. The French agency now claimed that it was always understood that it would have exclusive control on the Continent of all William Morris clients in every field of activity, including the rapidly growing motion picture area. It expressed its willingness to make KLA its subagent for Italy if given the overall continental WA franchise. Hank and Gene fiercely opposed the plan. It would be impractical in its application. It was economically unjust and failed to recognize KLA's achievements. As a result, Félix Marouani, on behalf of his organization, not only graciously withdrew Tavel & Marouani in favor of Kaufman-Lerner, but heartily endorsed the choice.

It seemed that at last there would be a positive conclusion.

But, in the wings, waiting to make an entrance, was Mel Ferrer.

Having sworn vengeance on Hank and Gene, he set out to sabotage the WMA commitment to KLA. "I need hardly tell you that I could not recommend someone who thought so little of the people with whom he is associated," were the words he had written to Gene on November 9, 1954.

It was Allenberg who advised Hank and Gene of Mel's opposition to a WWA-KLA deal, and Bert demanded a complete explanation from K and L. Hank and Gene concluded that long explanations to Bert would not contribute to a clarification of the delicate situation, so they wrote Bert a brief note, expressing their deep appreciation for his sense of fairness in giving them an opportunity to respond to the charges and suggesting that he play

Solomon to pass final judgment after he had perused the exchange of correspondence between Mel and Gene of November 9.

Allenberg then phoned from Los Angeles. He said he had received the KLA letter and the enclosures. He spoke of his great respect for Ferrer. He referred to him as both a good friend and a valued client, whose views had to be given every consideration. He had weighed the matter carefully. He had discussed it with Lastfogel, Mann and Jurow. He had reached his judgment. WWA was to proceed with the association with KLA.

Thus, with the Ferrer time-bomb defused and the conclusion of the agreement with William Morris, another chapter in the KLA saga began. The WMA deal meant crucial financial help. More important, KLA, while exclusive representative of the William Morris colossus and all its world-renowned clients, retained its freedom and independence, and remained in control of its own destiny and its own clients.

The William Morris connection and the associations with Chris Mann and Olga Horstig required three basic policy moves by KLA. The promotional and public relations prong, though it had been valuable in establishing contacts and providing income, had to be rooted out. Hank's abilities and time had to be concentrated totally on the overwhelming demands on the talent department, which from that moment on was to be the sole activity of Kaufman-Lerner Associates. Furthermore, the *Silver Screen* and *Screenland* involvement had to be terminated. It was farewell to star interviews and the variety of pseudonyms Gene and Hank had so often used. They sent Lester Grady their resignation, with deep gratitude. His contribution in getting them work at the very commencement of their Italian years, as well as residence status, had been vital, not to speak of his having been essential to their financial survival. Bottles and bottles of the finest Italian spumante were sent to Lester. And heartfelt thanks, dear *Silver Screen*, and warm embrace, dear *Screenland*.

Whereas the break with the fan magazines was KLA's most painful policy move, the most pressing was the need for new quarters. The Via Aiaccio home-cum-office was leaning towards schizophrenia even before the WMA deal was seriously discussed. Marion had slept on the kitchen cot for too many months and the daily changeover from house to office, office to house, even with her help, had become unbearable. For the equivalent of a mere forty dollars a month, Hank found a handsome suite of rooms on the ground floor of Corso Trieste 85, a rococo turn-of-the-century building six stories high. Corso Trieste was just a few blocks from Via Alaccio, where Hank and Gene, and their Marion, still intended to reside. If Via Aiaccio was a tiny vessel in the blood-conveying mechanism of Rome, the Corso Trieste would have been considered a vein. It fused with one of the Eternal City's major arteries, Via Nomentana, and was not far from another, Via Salaria.

The move was scheduled for September 1, 1955. Hank and Gene owned no furniture at that time and had only a modest budget to furnish a reception area and the four private offices. The search was on, via classified ads, flea markets such as the famous, fascinating Porta Portese, and secondhand furniture shops. Hank fortunately had a talent for "make-do," and things were assuming a respectable aspect.

But it was not sufficiently stylish for the new Principessa Massimo, the former Dawn Addams.

"Honey, it's okay. But it's so… functional. A bit drab, don't you think?" she said to Hank the first time she came to take a look. "We need elegance. Rich style. An office that's really the last word in *soigné*. We're in Rome, sweetie. History, art, monuments, paintings. The office, *my* office, has got to reflect that. Let's make it an office which could be no other place in the world but Rome."

Hank felt his heart sink. With what? "We can only do the best we can, Dawn. We're very limited. We can't afford museum pieces and magnificent paintings. Splendor we can't afford, but good taste we'll have."

Dawn broke out into a big smile and affectionately tweaked Hank's cheek. "Splendor you are going to have, my darling. Right out of the attic of Palazzo Massimo!" She looked at Hank triumphantly, arms akimbo. Hank felt excitement course through him. He found his imagination racing through the nearly bare rooms as he imagined a sumptuous spectacle of opulence.

"Vittorio's attic is piled to the top with fantastic things, part of the treasure trove the Massimo family has been gathering for centuries. And they're all there in the dark just gathering dust. I'm sure Vittorio will be glad to lend you some of the things. He won't give them to you, but he will lend them." She looked questioningly at Hank. "That is, if you would like to borrow them."

Hank swallowed, surprised by the shaky voice that emerged from his throat. "I'm speechless, can't you see? This is marvelous of you, Dawn. Of course, Gene and I would love to borrow them."

"Good. I'll talk to Vittorio today. Fortunately, he likes you guys. Then you come over to the Palazzo and we'll climb up to the attic and we'll pick out whatever we think is appropriate." Enthusiasm burst out all over. Dawn slapped her thigh with glee. "By God, there won't be an agency office on this planet as fabulous as yours. Anybody who walks in will know he's coming in to Roman magnificence of the highest pedigree. And he'll know it's cinema, too. Otherwise, he would never believe it."

Dawn was right. The effect was startling. It looked like a film set. Clusters of gold-leaf, ornately carved armchairs upholstered in old-rose damask. A magnificent throne chair embroidered in gold. Splendid inlaid tables of precious woods. Lustrous, crystal-prismed chandeliers made by brilliant glass artisans of Venice. Antique carpeting. Huge, gold-encrusted mirrors that could easily have graced the Court of the Este family at Ferrara or the Medicis in Florence.

When all the furnishing was completed, Hank and Gene stood together to survey the new quarters of Kaufman-Lerner Associates, decor courtesy of Principe and Principessa Vittorio Massimo. Gene literally pinched himself. Grinning, Hank said to his partner, "Maybe we'll have to come to work in full Renaissance garb." Gene burst out laughing as they embraced. They walked wordlessly from room to room. Dear Abe, dear Bert, dear Marty, dear Chris, dear Olga, come look at these KLA-William Morris headquarters in *bella Roma*, courtesy of a family that was bandying about the Circus Maximus even before the Holy Temple of Jerusalem was destroyed.

Dawn had unwittingly provided the magnificent setting of KLA's offices for the revelation, in less than two years, of the most rewarding moment of her career.

Only she, Prince Massimo, Hank and Gene knew that she was being seriously considered by Charles Chaplin for the key female role in the film he was secretly preparing. The great Charlot had created a smokescreen around story, script, potential cast and production plans. Its title, *A King in New York*, was known, but it took espionage techniques to ascertain that it would be a critique of a McCarthy-ridden USA, which Chaplin had hurriedly abandoned, carrying bag, baggage, cash, jewels, gilt-edged securities, animals, Oona and the family brood to the financial and personal serenity of Switzerland.

One morning, half deranged by emotion, Dawn phoned Gene from the post office of Vevey, Switzerland. Having sworn secrecy to Le Grand Charles, she had gone there as a guest of the Chaplins. She assured Gene that she was, at last, the first choice. The time had come to pin down the role for her. Gene was to phone Charlot right away and would have to be ready to take the first train up to Vevey. She would wait at the post office and call Gene back in an hour to see how the conversation with Chaplin had gone.

It had gone well. Before putting in the call, Gene had checked the Vevey-Rome train schedule. When the Master Comic of Cinema came to the phone, he was polite, gracious, hospitable. Yes, the first train Saturday morning would be satisfactory. A car would meet Gene at the station. Could Gene be their guest for the weekend? Gene sensed the wisdom of time restriction. Unfortunately, he replied, he would have to take the last train back to Rome that same Saturday evening. When Dawn phoned for a report, she was in ecstasy. "I knew it was the right moment," she screamed in triumph. "But how are you going to get it in writing?"

I'll have a maximum of seven hours to get a document, Gene thought to himself, and it could easily take seven months. "Honey, I'll bring up my portable typewriter. The moment Chaplin sees it, he'll guess I brought it with me for a reason," Gene replied.

There was a luncheon with Dawn, Oona, Chaplin and several of the children. Gene asked Chaplin, "If you had to select the four most important political figures of the twentieth century, who would they be?" Chaplin rose from his seat at the head of the table and for more than a half an hour put on the most remarkable display of imitative genius Gene had ever seen. How this one man, even with all of his renowned genius, with gesture, stance, facial expression, pantomime, use of words intermingled with invented language and snatches of music, could be first Franklin Roosevelt then Winston Churchill then Charles de Gaulle and last and most unbelievably Mahatma Gandhi, defies description.

After the luncheon, Chaplin led Gene to the studio. There, the negotiations continued for two hours, train time coming closer and closer. Chaplin was friendly, charming, warm-voiced, always laudatory of Dawn. There were, of course, alternatives if she was too expensive, he commented with extreme gentleness. He spoke of poverty, of months of agony as to whether he and Oona could afford to finance the film from personal funds, of Oona's insistence that if the film meant so much to him, they absolutely had to be ready to make the necessary sacrifices. The budget was probably no more than $500,000, which according to estimates at the time represented less than one percent of the Chaplin wealth.

Gene said that he fully understood the financial problem, though he was thinking, "Charlie, old boy, everybody knows you're a tightwad par excellence." Gene knew that Dawn would be glad to come out with just enough to keep her in pizzas for a while, and felt he should just leave the salary issue completely in Chaplin's hands. He then outlined to Chaplin the terms of Dawn's compensation for her last two films. Could Mr. Genius afford to meet those terms? It was up to him. Chaplin mumbled-fumbled calculations as if arithmetic were a subject he had never learned. His voice weak in resignation, he said he would find a way to meet them.

Gene then asked if as a mere token, a good-luck charm, a small gesture, a talisman Dawn could treasure throughout her life, Mr. Chaplin could give her a percentage of the profits, something insignificant, four percent, two percent, one percent, it didn't matter. Chaplin's eyes widened in horror at the very idea. Oh, no, impossible, impossible, he said, then emphatically shook his head. No, no, no, out of the question.

They then discussed other factors like billing, living expenses, period of engagement, the script, starting date, all of which were ultimately concorded. Gene then picked up his typewriter and removed its cover. He said he was so sorry time was so short and what a magnificent treat the day had been, and how unfortunate the world was not to have seen the imitations. Might he sit in the study and prepare a brief Memo of Agreement? Chaplin stared at the typewriter as if he had never before seen the monster. He then rose from his seat and said courteously, "Please. Go ahead. I'll join the others. When you're ready, come and call me."

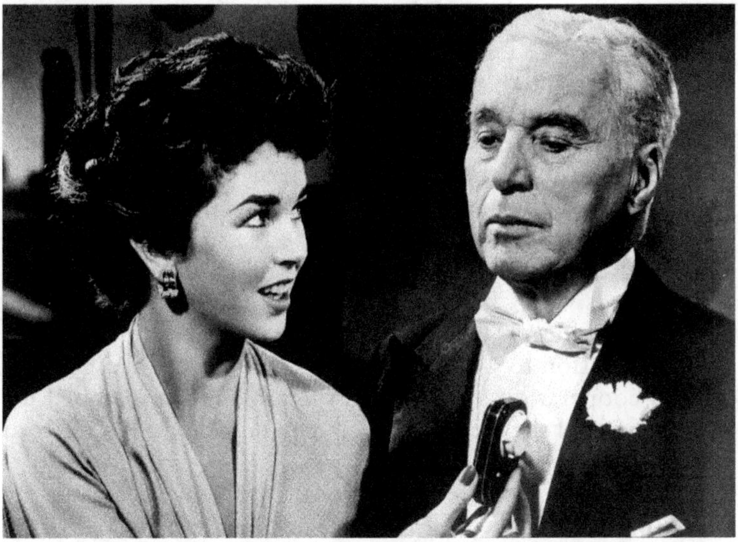

Dawn Addams and Charlie Chaplin in *A King in New York*

Gene furiously went to work on a page-and-a-half Memo of Agreement that would irrevocably bind the two parties. He had no need to consult Dawn on any of the provisions. She was only interested in the Great Man's signature. Summoned by Gene, Chaplin re-entered the study. He took the original copy of the document and read it carefully. He read it carefully a second time, then a third. Gene kept nervously glancing at Chaplin's face, nervously glancing at the passing time. Chaplin finally spoke. "It seems fine to me. Clear. Simple. Yes, it seems fine to me."

Pulling out his pen, Gene said, "I'm authorized to sign on behalf of Dawn." Without waiting for a reply and as Chaplin watched, Gene signed the carbon copy of the Memo, then passed it and the pen to the producer-director-writer-star-financier of the film to affix his eagerly awaited signature.

"Mr. Lerner, I'm going to sign this," Charlot then said. "But you must never let it out of your hands. Nobody must know it exists, not even my lawyers. They'll be furious." He bent close to Gene. "You see," he confided, "I've been ordered not to sign anything. It's all very complicated. And dangerous. Those awful taxes, you know. Eventually, the Agreement will be transferred to some corporation. I still don't know which one. When that happens, we must destroy these two copies, you understand. Do I have your word?"

"You certainly do, Mr. Chaplin. I want you to know how much I appreciate your confidence in me. Nothing will be done by Dawn or me to jeopardize the deal or your personal situation."

Using Gene's pen, Chaplin then signed the original with a flourish. He then handed it to an elated Gene, saying, "You'll keep this strictly confidential, now. You're sure?"

"You don't have to worry, sir," said Gene as he warmly shook hands with Chaplin. He returned to the living room with Charlot to inform Dawn, amidst hugs and kisses, then expressed his appreciation to Oona for the hospitality, thanked Chaplin for his cooperation and the unforgettable lunch, grabbed his typewriter and the secretly signed memo, and was rushed by a Chaplin limousine to the train.

A plan was coordinated between Chaplin and KLA for the announcement, once the production became official. At the precise hour of the given day, Chaplin would release the news in London, while KLA would do the same in Rome.

John Francis Lane, dean of the foreign press colony in Rome, correspondent for major newspapers of England and the States, and film historian, recalled the event in a March 12, 1978 article in the *Rome Daily American*:

"I'll never forget that afternoon when the press was mysteriously summoned to the spacious Kaufman-Lerner offices in Corso Trieste. With the type of theatrical gesture that made a newspaperman's job so much easier, Hank and Gene both looked at their watches, counted the seconds, and then with a flourish bade a minion to open a door, through which came the actress who had been chosen to play the lead in Charles Chaplin's new film. Chaplin was making the announcement at the Savoy in London at that very moment as Dawn Addams was ushered into our presence and the corks popped from champagne bottles."

Chaplin's *A King in New York* had its world premiere in London in September 1957. It was bad. The script was confused, the direction indifferent, and Chaplin had substituted polemic and resentment for entertainment and sense of humor. It was a brutal disappointment to Dawn, though she successfully continued her European career, particularly in Italian and French films.

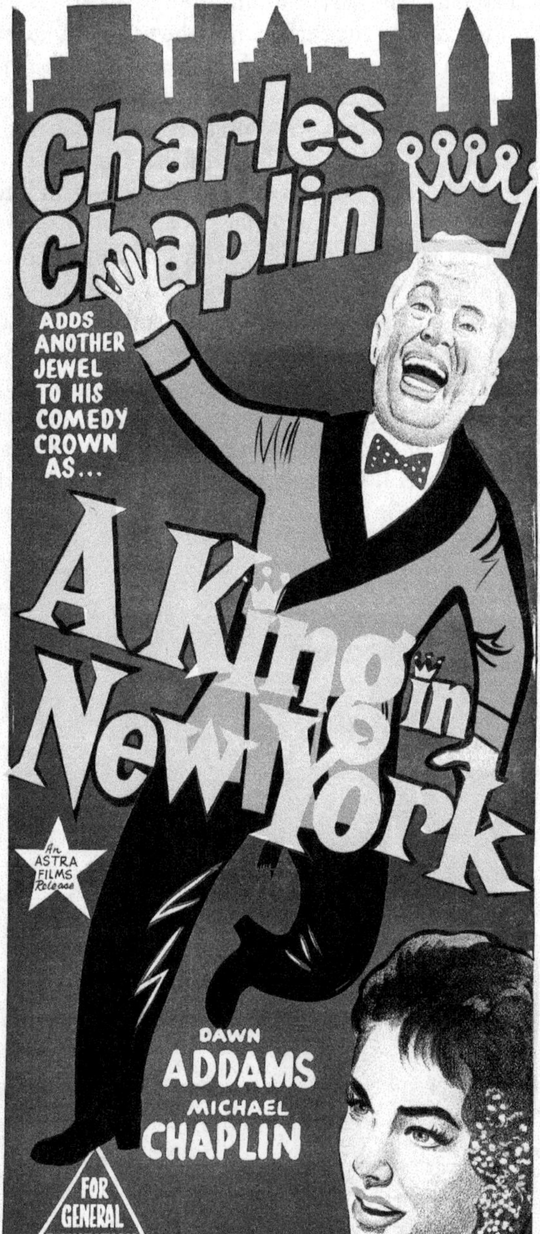
Charles Chaplin
ADDS ANOTHER JEWEL TO HIS COMEDY CROWN AS...
A King in New York
An ASTRA FILMS Release
DAWN
ADDAMS
MICHAEL
CHAPLIN
FOR GENERAL EXHIBITION

Nikita Khrushchev, still at the height of his power, was visiting London during the early run of the film. A huge reception was organized in his honor at the Dorchester Hotel. Among the throng of hundreds invited were Chaplin and Dawn.

Khrushchev held private court in a salon off the main ballroom, to which he asked certain of the dignitaries. Chaplin was invited in and took Dawn with him. Through an interpreter, the hearty, gregarious Russian leader passionately hailed Chaplin as great artist, great humanitarian, great lover of freedom. Then came the blunt question: why didn't the great Soviet nation have the privilege of seeing Chaplin's pictures? Chaplin's blunt answer came without pause. "The great people of the Soviet Union will have the privilege of seeing my films when the Soviet Government is ready to pay the price their greatness warrants." And so, courtesy of Professor Charles Chaplin, the head of the world's most powerful Communist state learned a good, tough, old-fashioned lesson in capitalistic doctrine.

Three

How Can You Tell An American?

It was Marty Jurow who wrote to let Hank and Gene know that Margaret Truman and Guri Lie, daughter of United Nations Secretary-General Trygve Lie, would be coming to Rome. Marty expressed his confidence that Hank and Gene would go all out in providing them with every possible courtesy and assistance.

Hank and Gene were enthusiastically ready to "go all out." They were looking forward to knowing Miss Lie, but since she had never much been in the public limelight, nor had they ever had the opportunity to meet her, they didn't have much of an idea as to what they might do for her.

But Margaret Truman!

"It's such a natural," Gene said to Hank, as they sat discussing Jurow's communication. "New offices. The deal with William Morris. Margaret Truman the first WMA client due in Rome since we set the deal. Somebody up there is telling us something."

"Telling us to celebrate!" Hank replied promptly. "A party. A real blow-out. Our first official Roman soirée!"

"No stinting. We'll go all out!" enthused Gene.

"I think Margaret will go for it," Hank went on.

"There's only one way to know. We cable and ask her."

"She's had enough of all those formal receptions. And I can't believe she would want to waste her time going to a bunch of Embassy-type dos. She's coming to us as show business, and that's what our party will be."

"She meets Rome's show-biz world and vice versa," Gene added.

"I'm sure she will welcome the change. So let's prepare the cable!" Hank said.

The only child of Harry and Bess Truman, Margaret had been in the limelight for much of her life, but not always in a manner she would have preferred. Rather-plain-Jane Margaret

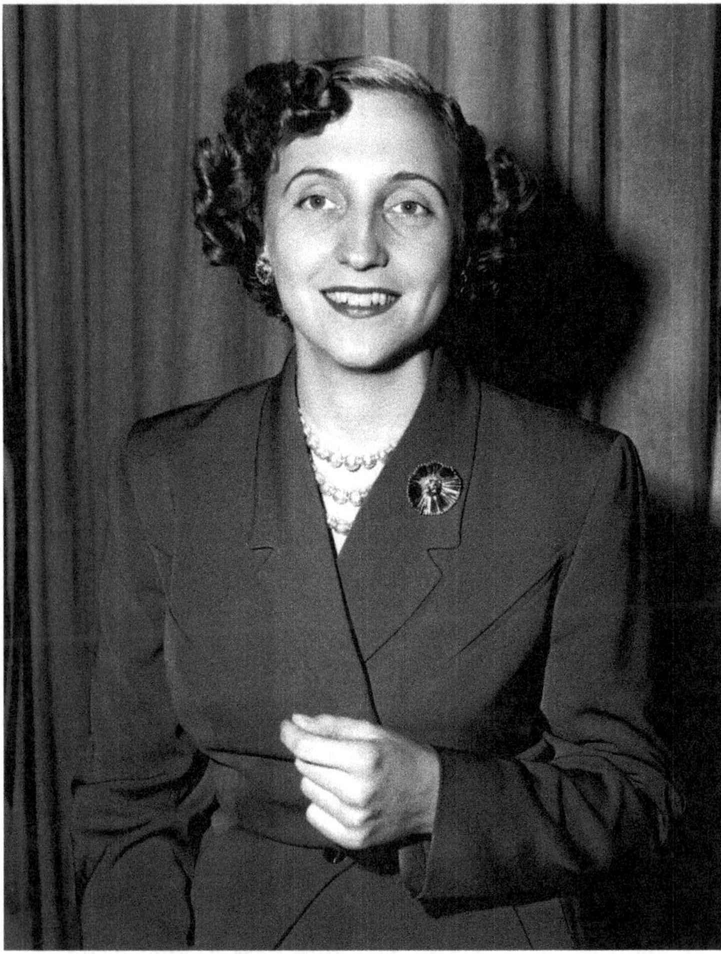

Margaret Truman

was daddy's darling. Her attempts to be professionally accepted on her own merits as a serious singer-actress were frowned upon, though her aspirations were fully endorsed by a proud, understanding father. The American public remained skeptical of her role as performer, preferring to think of her as the circumspect, dutiful White House daughter who so perfectly fit the Truman image.

Margaret was often seen at the side of Mother Bess or Dad Harry, or both, in an undistinguished-looking family portrait.

As befitting the daughter of the unpretentious Trumans, her conduct was exemplary. She seemed without surprises, very, very apple pie, which no one could even imagine her tossing in somebody's face. There were only rare anecdotes about Margaret and a male companion in the gossip columns and it was exceptional for her to be seen or photographed with beaux.

Like her father, however, Margaret was endowed with an obstinacy to succeed at any chosen task. She had guts, a straightforward manner, a rich Midwestern sense of humor and a no-nonsense moral code. She had become a William Morris client with the hope of making a career, but the Truman name had, in the long haul, more hindered than helped her.

Micol Fontana of the Fontana Sisters fashion house of Rome had met Margaret when the Trumans were still White House occupants. Once Hank and Gene received Margaret's reply to their cable, expressing her "being honored and delighted" to be guest of honor at the KLA inauguration party, they went into a huddle with Micol, who was also a KLA friend. They wanted to know more of Margaret's preferences, dislikes, hang-ups, character, anything Micol could tell them so they could get a handle on the noted young lady.

It was decided that on the night of Margaret's and Guri's arrival, there would be a small dinner of just "the family": the two famous daughters, Micol, Hank and Gene. This would be the best opportunity to get acquainted and to lay plans for the holiday visit. The restaurant selected was the Trattoria Angelino, nestled in the shadows of Capitoline Hill. The dinner was out-of-doors and quintessentially Roman: excellent food, strolling singers, sad-faced flower sellers and Signor Armando, the owner, who could have made it into the *Guinness Book of Records* with his amazing ballet of bowing, scraping and servile hand-wringing.

Margaret was warm, winning, clearly pleased, as was Guri. It was a good beginning. The magic of Rome was beginning to take effect.

During the meal, Hank and Gene couldn't help notice that Micol's eyes were constantly moving over Margaret. She was studying Margaret's conservative and basically formless attire, and, with experienced eye, Micol was analyzing the attributes and flaws of the body underneath. A native of Parma, Micol was nevertheless enamored by Rome as much as she was by her business. "Rome is in another period of glory," she was saying.

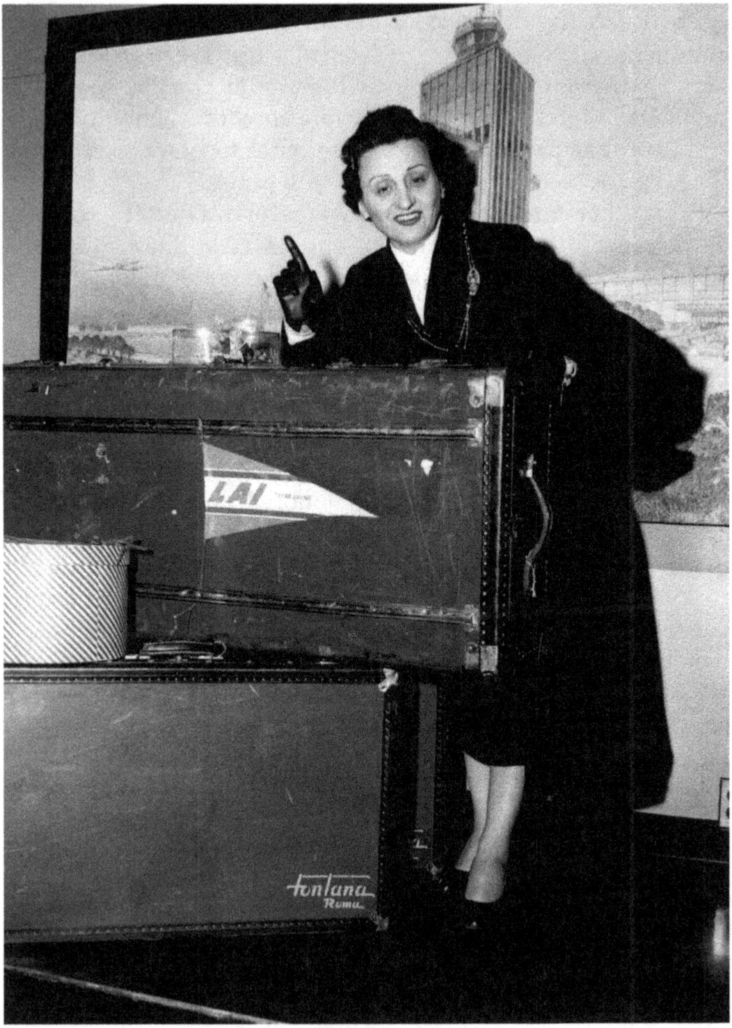

Micol Fontana

"I see it. I feel it. It has always had a genius for survival. And Romans have always had a remarkable capacity for bending and shaping conquerors, foreigners, visitors to their own image. Those who come to partake of Rome are irrevocably altered."

She was making a point deliberately, one which was to have a direct application. As outgoing, animated and fun as Margaret could be, her femininity seemed entombed and had to be released. The young woman who was soon to meet the glamor and elite of Rome had to be transformed from the Margaret-that-was into the Margaret-to-be.

Micol, whose English was good, turned quietly to Margaret. "Why don't you and Guri come to the atelier on Monday? I want to give you a private preview of our new collection. We've prepared some stunning outfits." Guri immediately nodded her approval of the idea.

"Sounds great to me," said Margaret. "But I have to check with my agents first." She turned to Hank and Gene. "Fellas, can I be free to spend a few hours at Micol's on Monday? Hank's immediate reply was "No problem."

"What time, Micol?" asked Margaret.

"Well, I would like the morning to prepare some things for you. So let's make it three in the afternoon, *se va bene con te*," replied Micol.

"*Va bene con me. Puntualmente alla tre lunedi*," confirmed Margaret in Italian. "You see, the Italian I studied in opera training comes in handy," she said, pleased with herself. Applause and bravas from Micol, amplified by Guri, Hank and Gene.

"We had better go over some of the other plans," said Gene. "We'll start with the most important of all."

"Which takes place Wednesday evening," Margaret jumped in to say. "You'll want Guri and me there no later than six, right?"

"Right," chimed in Hank and Gene.

"On Saturday, Prince and Princess Vittorio Massimo – she's Dawn Addams – have asked us to lunch at some marvelous sixteenth-century restaurant near their country estate. It's not far from Tivoli," announced Hank.

"What about Tuesday?" Margaret asked.

"That's a big day," began Gene.

"It's an all-day visit to Cinecittà, and you're going to have lunch with Vittorio de Sica."

"De Sica? Well, how about that!"

"*War and Peace* has taken over most of the lot," continued Hank. "David Hanna's the press rep and a good friend. He used to be Ava Gardner's press agent, and happens to be one of your greatest admirers," Hank went on. "You'll meet King Vidor, who's directing, and some of the stars, like Henry Fonda."

"I know Hank Fonda. He's such a darling. I would love to see him," Margaret interpolated.

"And Audrey Hepburn's also shooting, and you and Guri will meet her – all arranged by David Hanna."

It was really a glorious day for Margaret, thanks to David. According to his later report to Hank and Gene, she was received with warmth wherever she went, greatly enjoying the contact with the highest echelons of filmmaking in the studio ambiance. Fonda was a dream. De Sica at his elegant, courtly best. Audrey, on the other hand, just couldn't be bothered. Only Hanna's persistence and Fonda's deepfelt courtesy finally forced her to agree to Margaret's and Guri's calling on her. When Audrey received two of the most distinguished daughters of our times, she couldn't have performed with greater sweetness or charm, her consummate technique camouflaging her lack of conviction in the role she was required to play.

The luncheon hosted by the Massimos on Saturday began ominously. The proud owner of the ancient restaurant, followed by two of his maîtres d'hôtel, marched out ceremoniously with his precious guest book for Margaret and Guri to sign.

"It is only for the most famous of personages," he said proudly. One maître d'hôtel opened the yellowing book, the other presented Margaret with a thick-pointed, black-inked pen. They stood marveling the signature-writing ritual.

Margaret Truman was not brought up to sign anything she had not first read. She began leafing through the album. Suddenly, she stopped turning the heavy parchment pages. Her face whitened, its expression becoming grim. Something was amiss. She placed her finger near two signatures on the page, simultaneously gesturing to Gene to look. To Gene's horror, he saw two names that made his skin crawl.

Margaret resoundingly clapped the album shut. Without another word, she handed it back to the flustered owner. She was finding it difficult to contain her temper.

"What is wrong, Miss Truman?" he asked.

"What is wrong, Signore? I will not add my name to a book which includes signatures of..." She stopped, biting her lip to prevent an explosion. "Of Heinrich Himmler and Joseph Goebbels," she said frostily, enunciating the two dreaded names as if they were part of an elocution lesson. Guri, Dawn, Vittorio and Hank could hardly believe their ears.

"But Miss Truman. Forgive me if I say that all kinds of people have come here over the centuries. There have been wars, invasions, catastrophes..."

"And Nazis!" Margaret couldn't resist adding.

"Unfortunately, we were occupied."

"But nobody forced you – or whoever preceded you – to ask for their autographs, did they?"

Margaret turned to Vittorio. "Do you mind if we order lunch?"

The owner and two maîtres d'hôtel retreated in consternation.

"We can go somewhere else," a humiliated Massimo suggested.

"No. It's okay. Boy, would I have liked to have torn that darn page into pieces. But I'm okay now. Honest. The place really is lovely. It's so nice out here in this bowered grove. And the view! Mile upon mile of rolling green. And the view! No – we'll stay, if it's okay with all of you." Massimo glanced at Guri, who was definitely not smiling, and Gene, Hank and Dawn, who were still in shock. There was a nodding of heads and murmurs of "Okay, let's stay."

How you can tell an American!

On the Monday that followed the Trattoria Angelino dinner, Margaret and Guri arrived at the Fontana salon for their private showing. All key personnel had been alerted, along with a makeup and hair expert summoned by Micol for the occasion. Micol had spent the morning carefully studying her entire collection for what seemed to her the best suited for Margaret. She selected three gowns, including one for the KLA-WA reception. It was a black taffeta confection, form-hugging with a rather daringly low-cut sweetheart neckline. Micol loved it. Guri looked at it wide-eyed with envy, but recognized that for her petite height, it wouldn't work for her. Margaret examined it from top to bottom, then looking questioningly at Micol, she asked, with that typically sharp side-glance of hers, "That? For me?"

Micol began talking. She referred to Margaret's hidden assets. It would be foolish – no, *criminal*, not to take advantage of them. After all, when one is a woman, why should her womanly qualities be smothered? Her naturalness, her honest sex appeal be obscured? Shouldn't one have pride in one's sex? In what God

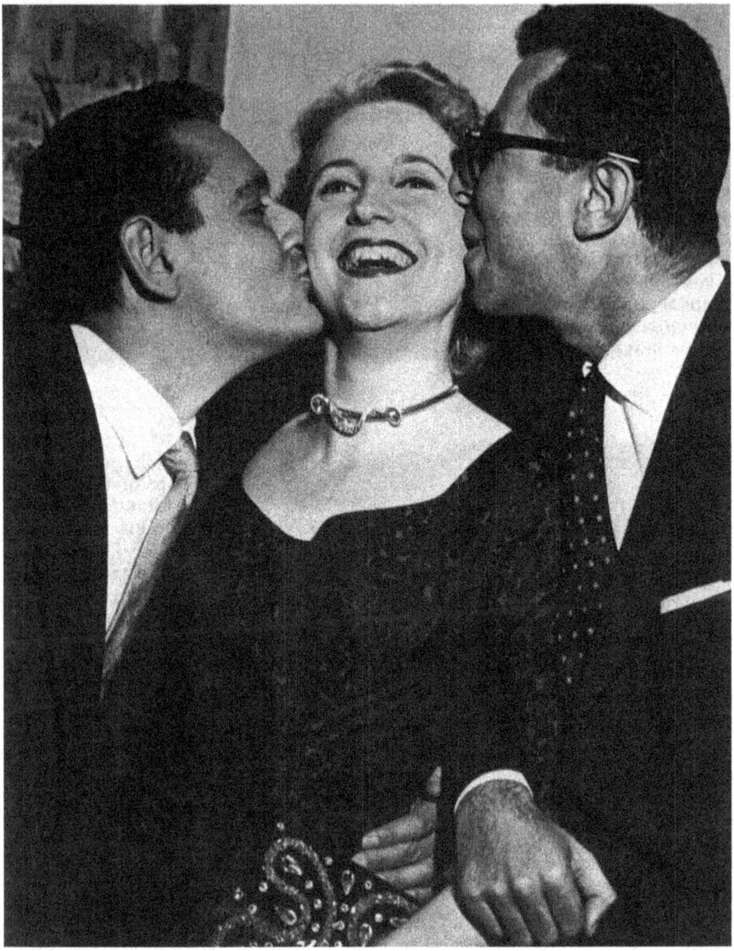

Gene Lerner, Margaret Truman and Hank Kaufman

had given? And if one had weaker points, what was wrong in minimizing them? Isn't that what good common sense dictated? The three gowns she had selected with such care were chosen not to make Margaret something she was not, but to bring out her best. And along with them, of course, there would have to be special foundation garments.

Margaret listened to Micol's comments with skepticism. Micol moved close to the ex-President's daughter, looked deep into her eyes. "You must trust me," she said with unmistakable sincerity. "*Hai fiducia in me?*" Long pause from Margaret. Another analytical examination of the particular dress. Then, similarly, of the other two. "Okay, Micol," Margaret finally said with Truman decisiveness. Guri clapped her hands with glee. "I'm in your hands. All of me!"

"That's what I want," Micol responded, giving Margaret a kiss on the cheek. "We'll do something about your hairstyle, something a little more 'today,' more sophisticated. And I want our makeup analyst to get to work and bring out all your loveliness. You have such skin, *mamma mia*, and such good bone structure. And so much life in that face of yours. We're going to see that your personality and the dramatic effect of that gown look like they were born for each other."

"Boy, it looks like I'm in for it," Margaret said to Guri. "Okay, Micol, do your worst. I'll never be competition for Lollobrigida, whatever you do!" Micol just grinned.

"Shoes," Micol said, snapping, her fingers. "Something really sleek to show off the form of the leg. Italian women know very much about the overall importance of a shapely leg." She turned briskly to an assistant, rattling off precise orders. Micol had it all worked out in her mind.

And so began the transformation of the gal from Independence, Missouri, George Washington University and the White House, into a modish, truly attractive and elegant female. When Margaret appeared with Guri promptly at 6 p.m. on Wednesday, ready for the reception, Hank and Gene were stunned. Micol's creation wasn't just mode and mannequin. She had simply fulfilled the true qualities that Margaret possessed but that she had shrouded. Margaret radiated an assurance that in the past lacked elan. The new Margaret was now ready to meet, head on, the Roman show business contingent and press corps.

She and Guri took a tour of the new KLA quarters and enthused over the plush decor. Just then, Dawn and Vittorio, who had not yet seen the completed offices, arrived. Hank made the introductions. "May I have the honor of presenting our esteemed interior decorators, La Principessa and Il Principe Vittorio Massimo?" he said with mock formality to Margaret and Guri. Vittorio was noted for his violent temper, but he also possessed a delicious sense of humor. He laughed, then proceeded, with Dawn as usual interrupting, to explain how the KLA offices came to be so opulent. "There just happened to be a few old trinkets lying around in my palazzo for a couple of centuries and when Dawn said what she wanted to do, I agreed. I told her we'll just make Corso Trieste 85 an annex."

There was enormous curiosity to meet and know the daughter of the former President of the United States. The turnout was brilliant. It included many leading figures of the Roman film scene, a carefully selected group of journalists, including Oriana Fallaci, and a cross-section of Roman society. Margaret's poise and loveliness were second to none, as evidenced by the dozens of photos shot that evening with Hank and Gene, the various celebrities and an exquisite array of film beauties, each one an individual jewel, including a new KLA client, Gianna Maria Canale, oft referred to as Italy's most beautiful woman. In the days that followed, the pictures were plastered all over the dailies and in weekly magazines in Italy and around the world as permanent record of the event.

Neighbors and passers-by were quick to realize that something unusual was taking place in the relatively quiet, bourgeois *quartiere*. With growing excitement, they watched the continuous parade of chauffeur-driven luxury automobiles disgorging their glamorous cargo at Corso Trieste 85, as well as the increasing commotion in the open-windowed ground-floor suite. Word spread swiftly that not only in-the-flesh film stars but also the daughter of the *presidente degli Stati-Uniti* were on the premises. The rumor, while drawing greater and greater crowds, failed to place the "ex" before the *presidente.* Soon the mass of people became so great and unruly that all traffic along the Corso Trieste was blocked.

There were loud and insistent knocks at the agency's front door. Wondering who was trying to break it down, Gene rushed to open it. To his astonishment, he found a breathless platoon of carabinieri facing him. The *capitano* saluted smartly, then immediately demanded to know where the daughter of the President was. They had been ordered to come at once to protect her. Margaret was brought over to the door. There were even more smart salutes and stiff attention. Margaret graciously told them that really, she was fine and that she needed no protection.

"But it is our duty," the captain insisted. "We must protect you. If anything should happen to you, we Italians would be mortified. After all, you are the daughter of the president of a great country, which is our friend."

"Ah, *Capitano*, there is a grave misunderstanding," replied Margaret. "I am not an Eisenhower and I am not a Republican. I am a Truman and a Democrat. My father is the *ex*-president of the United States." The *capitano* and his men looked at each other, stunned. For a moment, they did not know what to do. However, the Italian talent for improvisation quickly came to the rescue. "But why should such a small matter make a difference?" asked the suave captain. "We will protect you all the same."

Margaret was enchanted. Smiling in delight, she took the captain's arm and beckoned to his fellow carabinieri. Drinks were brought and her protectors, totally enchanted, became members of the party.

Applause, cheers and shouts of "Come to the window" grew stronger. So Margaret, Guri, Dawn, Gianna Maria Canale, Isa Miranda and other luminaries appeared at the windows to wave and throw kisses to the happy crowd. A number of men scrambled up towards them. Dangling with amazing acrobatic prowess from the window ledges twelve feet above ground, they managed to kiss the outstretched hands of the bevy of beauties. Meanwhile, drivers of stalled buses, taxies and cars were screaming and gesticulating in hysteria. The *capitano* and his fellow carabinieri were too occupied in "protecting" Margaret Eisenhower… er, Truman… to be bothered.

The reception at KLA's new offices, celebrating the William Morris affiliation and presenting Margaret Truman, was a smash success. But Margaret's enchanted evening had only just begun.

K and L had planned a supper in the private dining room of Palazzi's, Rome's then "in" restaurant, sitting high on Monte Mario with a dramatic view of the entire city. It was once the palatial villa where Mussolini had his trysts with Mistress Clara Petacci, and it was easy to understand why Il Duce had chosen that particular site. Was Margaret aware of the scandalous origin of the exclusive eatery to which she was being transported? And if she knew, would it have made much difference at this point?

Rome, seductive courtesan of the night, was continuing to exercise her sorcery. As supper was ending, a special dessert was created for Margaret and Guri by two of Italy's most irresistible symbols of masculine glamor: Rossano Brazzi and Walter Chiari. In hilarious competition and to gasps of laughter, they did imitations of themselves, each other, male and female American and Italian stars, climaxing the vaudeville portion of their show with wow portrayals of Charles Chaplin being directed by Vittorio De Sica and De Sica by Chaplin. Then, at not quite the level of Enrico Caruso, they moved on to a duet of Neapolitan and Sicilian folk songs that roused the entire party into a free-for-all chorus.

Despairing, anguished pleas accompanied by beseeching fallings-on-knees finally overcame Margaret's "I'm not in voice," "I haven't practiced in months," "But I need accompaniment" protestations. Everyone listened entranced to her moving a cappella rendition of Puccini's *Mi Chiamano Mimi*. Margaret made no effort to hide her emotion over the applause and the repeated "bravas."

Someone then came up with the idea of driving out to the Appia Antica. Piling into cars, the happy group raced each other in crazy Italian style, snaking through traffic, past the Via Veneto, the Piazza Venezia, the Colosseum and Gina Lollobrigida's villa to the portion of the Appian Way paved with two-thousand-year-old cobblestones.

The moon was Hollywood full and van Gogh yellow, the star-glitter astonishingly bright. The statuary, tombs and monuments of early epochs lining the historic throughway glowed fantastically. Margaret, Guri, Rossano, Lydia, Walter, Gene, Hank and the others began racing back and forth in unleashed joy, dancing and twirling and leaping. The daughter of the Ex began singing at the top of her lungs. After all, it was only three o'clock in the morning! Everybody else chimed in, no one singing the same song. It was doubtful that for centuries, if ever, the Appia Antica had heard such operatic disharmony. It was madness – wonderful, unbelievable, unrestrained madness, so exuberantly romantic that romance itself became a participant.

And now came the *de rigore* pilgrimage to the shrine of the Fontana di Trevi. This, of course, was Rossano Brazzi's moment. His association with that iconic location was solidified by his tremendous success in *Three Coins in the Fountain*, which endeared him to film fans around the world. As Margaret and Guri tossed their coins and wished their secret wishes, he sang in his rich, natural baritone:

Three coins in the fountain,
Which ones will the fountain bless,
Three coins in the fountain,
Which will bring me happiness.

Dawn – not Dawn Massimo but Aurora – was near. The time had come for good nights, good mornings, goodbyes. There were still two days left to Margaret and Guri's visit, but they knew it was time for:

Arrivederci, Roma;
Goodbye, au revoir.
Mentre l'americana s'allontana
Un ragazzinetto s'avvicina
Va nella fontana
Pesca il soldo e se ne va!
Arrivederci, Roma…

Arrivederci, Roma. In English, "Rome, I'll be seeing you!" Arrivederci. You can tell an American by the hundreds of thousands of them who had echoed the phrase. You say it, not really believing. You're overcome by sadness, a smidgen of a tear, a lump in the throat, an aching in the heart. But if you're a Truman, you mean what you say. And what you mean, you say, and *that's* how you tell an American!

The letter Gene and Hank received from Margaret was dated March 9, 1956. The typewritten text of it related to professional matters and some personal chitchat. Then, after the initials "M.T." as a signature came a handwritten postscript. And it was a stunner.

"The first and only husband has shown up," wrote Margaret. "He is so nice, so handsome and such fun. And smart, too! I am of course not at all prejudiced! He says I can continue with my career, so there we are. Am in a flap, but it's so nice. *Lerve*, it's wonderful."

Within weeks after her return from Rome, Margaret had met and captivated her Prince Charming. His name: Clifton Daniel, Jr. Within six months of her visit to the Eternal City, she had *definitely* captured him. Scion of a noted North Carolina family, Clifton was indeed handsome, indeed fun. He was also urbane and world-traveled. He was once foreign correspondent and then an associate editor at *The New York Times*, and until he had met the post-Rome Margaret, he had seemed a perennial, adamant candidate for bachelorhood.

And who, in spite of a storm of criticism from American fashion editors and designers, did Margaret select to make her wedding gown? The Fontana Sisters of Rome, of course. Handwoven, champagne-colored, three-hundred-year-old Venetian lace to form the bodice. Over it, a butterfly-treated tulle skirt of the same pale honey color, a wonderfully harmonious tint for Margaret's golden blonde hair and cream complexion. The neckline, a yoke of pleated tulle in a "Marguerite" pattern of lace that delicately frosted the tulle.

Micol herself brought the gown to Independence and supervised the final fitting. As Margaret exited from the limousine to enter the church with Dad for the wedding ceremony, Micol noticed with horror that the hem was caught on Margaret's pump. Just in the nick of time, Micol succeeded in unloosening it so that a torn gown or worse, a possible fall, was avoided.

"I was frantic," Micol recalled. "Think of the embarrassment. And what fun the press would have had if Margaret tripped or fell. But that wasn't what first came to my mind. I'm supposed to be worldly, sophisticated. Hah! I'm just another Italian. And my head swam with all those catastrophic superstitions we associate with a wedding which starts in such a way. I was ready to light a dozen candles to the Madonna for my having seen it in time. *Mamma mia*, what an awful moment!"

And so on April 21, 1956, some eight months after her Roman holiday and that enchanted evening, Margaret Truman, without the protection of the *capitano* and his carabinieri, became Mrs. Clifton Daniel, Jr.

Was there any question that Rome and honeymoon were synonymous?

Hadn't Margaret repeated "Arrivederci" and meant it?

The newlyweds picked the Hassler as their hotel. Of course, they had already accepted Hank and Gene's cabled invitation for a dinner party to mark another inauguration. Well… two in fact. Leaving the sad and tearful Conte and Contessa Colisi-Rossis waving in sad *addio*, Hank and Gene had at last moved into a spacious apartment at Via Salaria 290, with Marion, of course, immediately taking charge.

Margaret asked about the guests. There would be ten, Gene said: the Daniels, the Brazzis, Micol, Erna Stenbuck (Joe Mankiewicz's sister and a United Artists Rome executive Margaret had met and liked), Chiari, Anita Ekberg, K and L.

Gene detected a diffidence in Margaret's reaction. "Honey, is there something wrong?" he asked. Margaret tried to avoid answering him. "What's bothering you?" Gene insisted. Margaret, whose middle name might have been "frank," still hesitated. "C'mon, out with it, Truman," Gene insisted.

There was a pause. "All right, then," she said. "I don't dig the idea of dining with Anita Ekberg. There have been so many scandalous stories about her. Meeting her just casually for a passing hello, okay. But a formal event like yours? It kind of bothers me."

Gene was surprised. "Margaret, Anita's very pleasant. She knows how to behave. In fact, there's a simple, prim side to her that most people are never exposed to."

"Well, I don't know, "demurred Margaret. "Let me talk to Clifton and I'll call you back."

It was Clifton who phoned back. "Gene," he said. "First, I would like to say that Mr. and Mrs. Clifton Daniel, Jr. are delighted to be your and Hank's guests, as you, of course, already know. Second, Mr. and Mrs. Clifton Daniel, Jr., will be delighted to have the pleasure of Miss Anita Ekberg's company. Particularly, Mr. Daniel. I hear Miss Ekberg can be charming and I know that she's very attractive to look at. Now where are you planning to seat her?"

Suddenly it was Margaret on the phone. "Don't you dare put her next to Clifton! Remember you're *my* pal!"

Gene was getting a bang out of the situation.

"Well, actually, Margaret, we were planning to," he replied.

"You had just better un-plan it!" Margaret broke in.

Gene began to laugh. So did Margaret. Then, her voice muted, she said: "Clifton gave me a little lesson in tolerance. I deserved it. That's what happens when you get yourself a husband. So let's just remove the whole conversation from the record, okay?"

"Okay," was Gene's reply.

"Are you really putting Ekberg next to Clifton?"

"We're putting Brazzi on your left."

"Well, in that case, Clifton can have her... Who cares?"

*

Anita was beautifully but circumspectly dressed in black. She sat at the table with that little girl primness which sometimes emerges as part of her character. Her conversation was modulated and unusually void of self-reference. Margaret soon found herself back in her natural groove and there was some "girl-to-girl" chatting between the two. Clifton was indeed charmed, as everyone was charmed by him. He had an enviable capacity for adaptability and instinctively knew how to put people at ease.

As everyone got comfortable after dinner with their wine, cognac or liqueur, Walter, who had brought his guitar, plopped himself down on the living-room floor and began to plunk out Roman *stornelli.* In the midst of his second effort, the doorbell rang. Marion went to admit the caller. It was a special after-dinner surprise the hosts had arranged, and it was greeted by excitement and applause.

Wearing a floor-length, grass-green jersey gown, Anna Magnani, another WMA-KLA client, bowed. There were cheek-to-cheek kisses with Hank and Gene. She was then led to the newlyweds, who had risen to greet the great Italian actress and to express their delight at her coming. Anna's thickly accented, "Thank you, I'm very happy to meet you," was buried in shyness. There were formal introductions to Anita, Micol, Erna, and a kiss blown to Brazzi, a gesticulating salutation to his rotund, vivacious spouse, Lydia. The greeting for Walter – peals of laughter and warm embrace – was an insulting rejoinder, Roman style. They had been friends from the time they had made Luchino Visconti's unforgettable, heartrending *Bellissima*.

Marion handed Anna the glass of red wine she had requested and Anna immediately joined Walter on the floor. They finally decided on the *stornello* they would sing. Walter started to play the guitar. After a few plunks, Anna pulled the instrument from Walter's hands, with a "What do you know about guitars? Anyway, who said a Milanese *stronzo* like you could ever sing a *Roman* song? You need a real *romana*, like me!"

As Anna put down her glass of wine, the room fell quiet. She ran her fingers through the guitar strings, then began the first notes of *Quanto Sei Bella Roma*. She then stopped, clearing her throat. Typically Anna, she said, with a deprecatory laugh, "My voice. How do you say? A mess." She drank down the wine, once more cleared her throat, and recommenced.

The spell wrought by that green-clad figure, her hair half over her face, as in her deep vibrato voice dug from Roman earth she sang one *stornello* after another, remains fixed in indelible memory as a scene on film celluloid is forever recorded.

The camera of time pulls back slowly. Margaret and Clifton are seated on the sofa, Clifton with eyes closed, absorbing words he cannot understand, yet understanding all, Margaret with head leaning back, eyes set on unleashed visions, identifying with Magnani's artistry, sharing the depth of her emotion. Walter is on the floor, back turned to Anna, head down, his hands hugging his knees. Seemingly hypnotized, Lydia stares at the hand plunking the guitar. Brazzi watches Anna's every gesture and every nuance of expression, as if recalling their portrayal of lovers in *Vulcano* in 1949.

Anita is sitting on her dinner chair, quietly fingering her drink, casting furtive glances at Magnani, then as quickly turning away, too awed, too admiring, not wanting to reveal how deeply moved she is by *that* voice and mesmerized by *those* songs of the Rome that had conquered her. Micol, Erna, Hank and Gene, all still seated at the dining table, caught by vibrations which each know come so infrequently in life, are feeling a rare affinity. Marion is standing against the living-room wall, her lips tight and trembling, fighting back tears.

"As I look back at it, I realize that my visit to Rome with Guri might have been a turning point in my life," Margaret said later. "I've often wondered while I was there, what is Rome doing to me that makes me respond so deeply?

"That September '55 was the first real honest-to-goodness holiday I ever had since I grew up. Ever since Dad was in national politics, and that was most of my childhood and growing up, there was no such thing as running off and doing what you wanted to do, what the hell, who gives a damn. There were always press or Secret Service or relatives or some responsibility. And always an image. No, that's not quite the word. It wasn't external, but internal. Reserve. Caution. Watch your step. The wish to do and to be what Dad and Mom wanted of me, even though once in a while there was some Missouri mule acting up. Sure, it was burdensome and boring a lot of the time. And frustrating. But boy, it was exciting, too! Would I have changed it for all the money in the world? You can bet your sweet life I wouldn't.

"It's so wonderful when things happen to work out perfectly. How could I realize how ready I was for Rome? Everything from beginning to end was a kind of improvisation. Yet, there was a solid core which only became apparent later on. Micol convinced me that I needed a different kind of wardrobe. Okay, what the heck? She was probably the first person in my life who really studied me from that point of view, and had the ability to turn theory into practice, with taste. She saw things I sure never saw. And she had made up her mind to work on my good points and camouflage my not-so-good ones. If someone had tried that on me at that particular given moment anywhere else but Rome, I doubt that I would have gone for it.

"You spend your life trying to be yourself. Then, if you're lucky, you discover that you've only really been part of yourself, and you open up. You feel what you haven't felt before. You see what you haven't seen before. It's glorious! Like you can burst out singing in the middle of the street, or start dancing out in the open, just like I did in Rome. I was suspicious of most people, of what they would say and what they would want from me, finding it tough to accept real, honest motivation. How revved up you feel when you're able to give yourself over to chance, to, well... *che sarà, sarà*.

"Would I have been ready for Clifton and marriage if there had not been that Roman trip? Would Clifton have been ready for *me* is probably the better way to put it. I really don't know. I do know I wasn't quite the same after Rome. I felt something different. Fuller, fresher. I was more confident, more, okay, I'll say it, more attractive. Maybe all of that showed. I guess it must have showed.

"I got Clifton. And then four male children. Ye Gods! A five against one set-up. Five guys against one gal! Isn't that a real battle of the sexes? But I'm not bad at defending myself even with odds like that. I'm a Truman, remember?"

Hank was not present at the Truman-Daniel nuptials. It must be pointed out at this time that if any couple is planning marriage and expects the "until death do us part" oath to be fulfilled, they should never ask Hank Kaufman to be a witness. Any marriage for which he has served in that capacity has not survived for long.

Elsa Martinelli's eventual matrimony with Count Franco Mancinelli Scotti, attended by Hank in the miniscule Republic of San Marino, ended in disaster. There was Dawn Addams' marriage to Prince Vittorio Massimo. Disaster. There was Pier Angeli's London wedding to Armando Trovaioli. Disaster. Add Walter Chiari's matrimonial venture to actress Alida Chelli in March 1969, in Sydney, Australia. Disaster. Whereas each of the official couplings provided the protagonists with a single offspring, it was nevertheless disaster every time!

Happily, in 1980, the Daniels' matrimony is now in the 26th year of its run.

If, for Margaret Truman Daniel, Jr., the Roman connection was instrumental to the shape of her future, her appearance in Rome coincided with a new phase in the lives and professional development of Kaufman-Lerner, another series of adventures and encounters which ranged from achievement and excitement to confrontation and delusion.

On November 24, 1958, the agency moved into its expanded offices at Via Lisbona 12 to accommodate the onrush of new business and additional personnel. For a rental of 75,000 Lire (slightly more than a hundred dollars), Kaufman-Lerner Associates occupied the entire ground floor of the handsome, streamlined tan-and white palazzo crisscrossed by flower-decked terraces. Each room of the offices had spacious windows that looked out on public gardens bordering the tranquil street. Via Lisbona was in one of the most attractive residential areas of Rome, located between the Parioli and Salario districts of the city and a mere fifteen-minute walk from Rome's throbbing nerve center, the Via Veneto. Just up the street from the new headquarters was the Piazza Ungheria, with its cafe, which deserved the equivalent of the Oscar for the most delicious assortment of fruit ice cream on the Italian peninsula.

It was Hank who again took over the responsibility for the décor of the new KLA headquarters. With the Dawn and Vittorio Massimo furnishings no longer available, Hank worked out a soothing, harmonious blend of Swedish modern, French provincial and Italian antique as the theme of the new KLA HQ. Photos of the most noted of the agency's clients were framed and hung in the reception area and along the corridors. But in both Hank's and Gene's private offices, a particular photo had its place of honor. It could easily have been entitled *How Can You Tell An American?*

In the middle of the picture was a lovely laughing Margaret, Hank kissing her right check, Gene her left. In the years to come, Margaret always seemed to hover nearby, a true "guardian angel." And the new era at Via Lisbona began with an event so unexpected that it only seemed to prove the existence and the prowess of that mystical clan that Margaret personified for the two men. For yet another popular American girl with renowned and powerful parents was about to have her life altered, radically and forever, by Hank and Gene.

The fairytale occurrence ironically and shudderingly had its roots in the Nazi Holocaust. Together with Moris Ergas of Zebra Film, Franco Cristaldi, head of Vides Cinematografica, had agreed to co-produce a cruel and yet human film about a Nazi concentration camp entitled *Kapò*, written by Gillo Pontecorvo and Franco Salinas, to be directed by Pontecorvo.

A *kapò* was a Jewish inmate who volunteered to collaborate with the Germans to maintain order among the prisoners and was an object of particular contempt from the Jewish captives. The *kapò* envisioned by Pontecorvo and Salinas is Edith, a 14-year-old French-Jewish girl shipped to the concentration camp. She sees her parents murdered by the Nazis and is saved from death by a camp doctor. Her animal instinct gives her the necessary impetus to survive. She becomes a hardened criminal, uses her body as a tool, and eventually achieves her goal of *kapò*. But when a young Russian soldier is brought into the camp to be gassed along with the Jews, her humanity is revived through her love for him and his for her. With the film ending in a cry of protest against barbarianism and racism, Edith dies a heroine, sacrificing herself in an attempt to save the lives of her fellow prisoners.

Hank had read the script. It had left him in emotional shock.

Cristaldi, Ergas and Pontecorvo had conducted a fruitless search for a European girl to portray the role. With shooting scheduled to begin in Yugoslavia in only a matter of weeks, Pontecorvo still hoped to find a European unknown to play the part, while Cristaldi and Ergas became more and more convinced that it was essential to have an experienced actress of talent in the role.

January 26, 1960. Four o'clock, Tuesday afternoon. Hank was ushered into Cristaldi's private office at Vides just off Piazza Pitagora, easy walking distance from Via Lisbona. After a quick handshake, Hank was asked to sit. With Cristaldi were Ergas and

Pontecorvo. Hank was startled by the sparkling luminosity of the royal-blue eyes of the director, whom Hank had never met, and whose later *Battle of Algiers* would be recognized as an all-time cinema achievement. Cristaldi quickly introduced the two.

The usually overheated Ergas, prone to violent outbursts of enthusiasm or of vitriol, mutely shook hands with Hank. Ergas' eyes then concentrated on Cristaldi, waiting. The deep blue pools of Pontecorvo followed suit, and so, of course, did the paler blue eyes of Hank.

The question which then came from Cristaldi's lips stunned Hank.

"Do you know Susan Strasberg?" he asked.

Before Hank was able to reply in the negative, Cristaldi continued, pacing the floor slowly. "I know you don't represent her and I haven't been able to find out who does. I saw her on Broadway two years ago in *The Diary of Anne Frank*. I want her for *Kapò*. You read the script?" he asked Hank. As Hank nodded his head, Cristaldi went on. "It's an incredibly difficult part and makes terrible emotional and physical demands. Strasberg is the only one who can play it. Do you agree?" He ceased pacing, stared at Hank.

"Wholeheartedly," replied Hank. "I'm positive that she'll be absolutely remarkable."

Pontecorvo winced, looked at Hank, troubled, suspicious. "But everybody says she's completely controlled by her parents. The way people talk, Lee Strasberg's a god and his Actors Studio is Olympus. The Method, the Method. What is this 'Method'? I don't trust it. It's a cult, religion. And her mother, what's her name...?"

"Paula," replied Hank, sympathetic to Pontecorvo's doubts over working with the daughter of a couple so powerful in the American theater and who, to many, were divinities. Struggling not to betray his impatience, Cristaldi listened. Ergas made no effort to hide his irritability. Hank realized that the issue had been argued and argued many times before.

"Yes, Paula," Pontecorvo said. "People tell me that every time Marilyn Monroe speaks, it's Paula who's really talking. It's Paula who gives Marilyn every gesture. Every intonation is Paula's. Marilyn is only Paula's puppet. There's no Marilyn if there's no Paula. Is this true?"

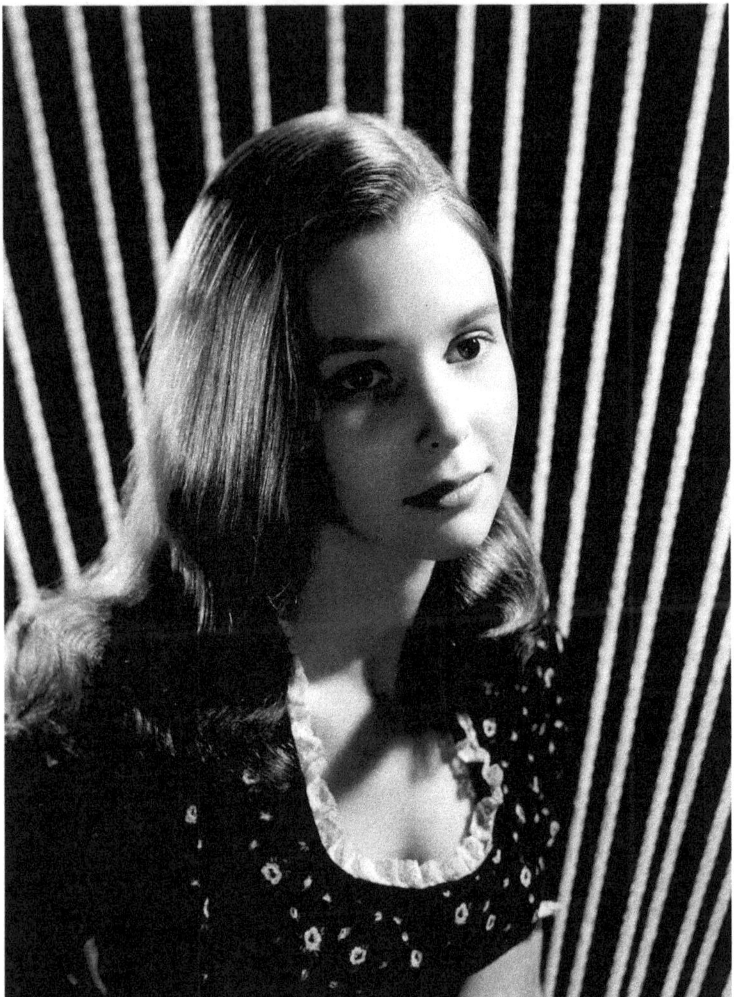

Susan Strasberg

"Let's call it a half-truth, Gillo," answered Hank, seeking to comfort the disturbed director who felt that his destiny was at stake. "But none of us here know if Susan Strasberg is available or will be interested in doing your film."

"But we have to know and she has got to do it," blurted out Ergas. "We've got to start shooting in a matter of days. We have to have her. She's the only one who can do it."

Pontecorvo bristled. "You can't say she's the only one. The only one, the only one! You can't say that!"

Hank quickly interrupted. "Gillo, even if by chance she is free and interested, that doesn't mean she comes with her father and mother in her valises and will be forever entrapped by The Method. Strasberg has his Actors Studio, Paula has Marilyn. I can't believe that they're going to come over to tell you how to direct your film, if that's what's worrying you."

Cristaldi, a look of determination on his face, rose from his chair. "I don't think there's much more to be said," he exclaimed. "I just don't think we have a viable alternative."

"But my English…" Pontecorvo broke in. "It's so bad. How do I communicate with an actress like Strasberg? She lives in a world of total articulation. Every motivation is discussed and analyzed. Every action. Every movement. How can I do that?"

Pontecorvo turned to Hank. "Does she speak French? Spanish? Any European language?"

"I told you that I never met Susan," replied Hank gently.

"All we have to surmount, we shall surmount," pronounced Cristaldi. "As Ergas said, we have to start in a matter of days. We have to have our leading actress signed in a maximum of a week. And it has to be Strasberg. I want you to go to New York, Kaufman. You'll know what to do to break down the barriers and to get us an immediate decision. I'll pay your travel expenses and I'll guarantee your office your normal ten percent commission on the deal. I'll give you an English translation of the script and a breakdown of the shooting schedule. Can you get on a plane tomorrow?"

"Out of the question, Franco," responded Hank.

"The day after tomorrow?" asked Cristaldi, as if it were all settled.

Hank stared at the president of Vides before glancing at Ergas and turning towards Pontecorvo. "Gillo, I want to tell you that I'm sure that if Susan agrees to do your film, it will be because she'll feel, sense, realize everything you're trying to say in it. Otherwise, she won't do it."

Pontecorvo looked piercingly at Hank. Is it possible, his eyes seemed to be saying, that this American was a kind of a guarantee? "I'll order your air ticket for Friday, with an open return," said Cristaldi, holding out his hand to Hank. As he and the agent shook hands, the producer said, "I'll phone you as soon

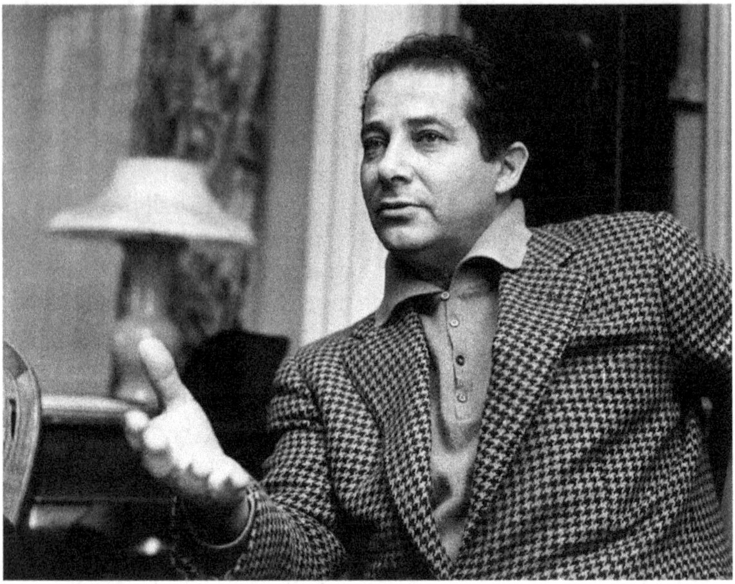

Gillo Pontecorvo

as I have your ticket and we'll talk over all the other things you need to know."

Hank nodded. Pontecorvo walked over and stood looking at him, his eyes half questioning, half hopeful. Smiling, Hank put his hand on Pontecorvo's shoulder. "It's going to be all right," he said. "It's going to be all right."

To Hank's surprise, the Alitalia plane arrived at Idlewild Airport on time that late Friday afternoon, January 29. Though it had been a most comfortable trip, Hank was exhausted from the enormous amount of work he had to finish before departure and the six-hour time difference. He checked into the Madison Hotel, his favorite (unfortunately now extinct).

Awakening late Saturday morning, he sat down to enjoy a leisurely breakfast and luxuriate in *The New York Times*. When he reached the theater page, his eyes fell on the announcement of the final two performances of Tennessee Williams' hit *Sweet Bird of Youth*, starring Geraldine Page. He phoned the box-office immediately and was told that one seat was available for the matinee.

As Hank entered the Martin Beck Theater, Rome seemed to him to be on another planet, dim both in distance and time. His mind became immersed in some of the wonderful theatrical experiences he had had in his earlier years. As he waited for the curtain to rise, he let the pleasures of memory absorb him.

Hank's eye caught a figure moving down the aisle, followed by another. There was a distinct familiarity about them. Suddenly he sat up straight, his whole being transfixed. Could it be? Was it? He shut his eyes tight, shaking his head back and forth forcefully as if to clear it of hallucination. He opened his eyes slowly. There was no doubt. There could be no question.

As the house lights were dimming, Lee Strasberg took his seat.

And taking the seat beside him was…

Susan Strasberg! Susan Strasberg!!!

As effective a performance as Geraldine Page was giving on stage, Hank found himself staring over and over again at the sparkling, petite, dark-tressed girl sitting three rows ahead of him. As hard as he tried to concentrate on the play, he found it less theatrical than the coincidence of his sitting in the same theater with Susan Strasberg the day after his arrival in New York, and less dramatic than the utter futility of all of his cogitation on the Rome-New York flight as to how he was going to find her and persuade her to do *Kapò*.

When the act ended, Hank, not without trepidation, walked down the aisle towards Susan and Lee. When he reached their row, he bent down beside Susan. "Excuse me," he said. "I hope you'll pardon my seeming rudeness in barging in on you like this, Miss Strasberg." Susan quietly turned her head, surprise on her face. "You are Susan Strasberg, aren't you?"

She fixed her enormous, liquid-brown eyes on Hank. "Yes, I am. Who are you?"

"I'm Hank Kaufman, Kaufman-Lerner Associates of Rome. I've just arrived from Rome last night. We're a talent agency there. And I've come on an urgent mission, which happens to be *you*."

"Me?" she replied, startled in her eyes. Lee turned and gave Hank the once-over. "This is my father."

"Yes, I know," said Hank. "I'm very glad to meet you, Mr. Strasberg."

Strasberg nodded, mumbled a greeting, then bent over his program to conceal his interest in the conversation.

"I've brought a film script for you," Hank went on. "I've read it. It's powerful. It's important and the role for you is exceptional. The problem is that I have to have your immediate decision. Will you read it?"

"We can't talk here," Susan said. "Can you come over to the apartment? You can give me more information then and bring me the script."

"I would love that," Hank responded with alacrity.

"Around 5:30," said Susan, as Lee continued to examine his program to hide his seeming disinterest.

"A city of eight million people," said Hank, his voice touched by wonder, "and the one person among all those eight million I traveled from Rome to find happens to come to the same theater I go to and sits herself three rows in front of me. One has got to believe in mysticism. Telepathy. Extrasensory communication. Or destiny. At least one has got to believe."

Susan broke out into a radiant smile. "Yes, I guess at least one has got to believe," she replied, her voice all velvet.

After the performance, Hank rushed back to the Madison, grabbed the precious script and the memorandum he had prepared on the film, hailed a cab and shot off to the Strasberg apartment on Central Park West. All effusion, Paula was at the door to greet him. Chatting away, she led the way to the library, every inch of space bursting with books and manuscripts, the fireplace redolent with the odor of burning pine. Paula immediately asked about theater in Italy. Above all, who were the young, rising talents? Hank spoke of Giancarlo Giannini, Anna Maria Guarnieri, Adrianna Asti, and of KLA's attractive, versatile Umberto Orsini. He spoke in considerable detail of three outstanding artists who had formed their own theater company, and had also become clients of the Agency – the magnificent, Garboesque Rossella Falk, who, he said, could be a first lady of theater in any country in the world; the brilliant character actor and leading man, Romolo Valli; and Giorgio de Lullo, the personable and inventive director-actor. Paula commented on how much she hoped to meet all of them when she eventually came to Italy. The door opened and Susan entered. Expressing her delight over meeting Hank, Paula made her exit.

Hank was alone with Susan.

As he spoke of *Kapò*, the role of Edith, the sensibility of Cristaldi, the solidity of the project, the Jewishness and enthusiasm of Ergas, the profound emotional and spiritual commitment to the project of Pontecorvo and the director's fears over his rapport with Susan, she became progressively more engrossed. She realized that Hank, too, was deeply committed to the film. Soon, she was fingering the script Hank had handed her, as if it had already taken hold of her.

"Can you get back to me by Monday morning?" Hank asked, dubious of any such assurance since he knew about the dilatory reading habit of stars. "I'll try," responded Susan, trying not to show her eagerness. Hank then said his goodbyes to her, and to Lee and Paula, whom he saw before leaving. He walked out into the New York winter and stared at the snow blanketing Central Park, shaking his head in disbelief.

At 10:30 the next morning, a brilliant, crystalline New York Sunday, Hank was awakened by the insistent ringing of the telephone. When he said hello, he had no difficulty in recognizing the voice that responded.

"This is Susan," the voice said. "I read the script last night. I couldn't sleep at all afterwards. I wept. I loved it. Can you come over for coffee right away? I've got so many questions to ask you."

"Weeping, I walked into my father's study holding the script," Susan wrote in her 1980 autobiography, *Bittersweet*. "It's wonderful. There's not much dialogue, but it's so *European*. It's incredibly descriptive visually. When you read it, you can almost see the movie, and the images are so haunting and powerful.

"'I'd like to do it," Susan told her father, 'but mother's going to be busy with Marilyn, so I'd be alone. I don't know what to tell them. They need an answer quickly. The director is a young Italian who's only done one other film. I just can't make up my mind, I can't decide.' Like a young bird, I wanted to fly but I needed someone to push me out of the nest.

"My father closed his book, an unusual gesture for him. He would talk to you and, in between sentences, go back to his book. So this was something important.

"'I think you should do it, Susan. I think you should go. I think you should get away from your mother, be on your own. Get away from... us.'

"'Lee, it's so far. And they're going to be shooting it in five or six different languages. I'll speak English, the French actress will speak French, the German actress will speak German, Yugoslavs will speak Serbo-Croatian.'

"My father nodded. 'Sometimes it can be better that way. It will make you really listen. Besides, you need to be on your own now. It's not good for you here anymore. You can always come home.'

"The relief was incredible. I felt that Europe was the escape hatch I had been seeking. There, alone, I could rise or fall on my own merits, be accepted for myself. I could learn to live my life, I wouldn't have to pretend to be something I wasn't."

Hank's cable to Cristaldi arrived in the Vides offices in Rome on Monday morning. Cristaldi could not believe his eyes when he read its contents.

> HAVE LOCATED STRASBERG STOP SHE READ SCRIPT AND IS READY TO COMMIT STOP HER ASKING TERMS ARE REASONABLE STOP PHIL GERSH OF SAM JAFFE AGENCY IS HER AGENT AND HE HAS AGREED TO KL'S REPRESENTATION OF HER FOR EUROPE SO NO COMMISSION PAYMENT FROM VIDES IS REQUIRED STOP RETURNING ROME WEDNESDAY WITH STRASBERG LETTER OF COMMITMENT STOP AUGURI KAUFMAN.

Cristaldi's gamble paid off. *Kapò* was one of the finest achievements of the Hollywood on the Tiber epoch, effectively forging the diverse talents and styles of Susan and Gillo into a fortunate artistic relationship. At the film's premiere at the 1960 Venice Film Festival, it received a record ovation lasting nine minutes. It brought awards and tributes to Susan from all over the world and pushed Pontecorvo to the forefront as one of Europe's outstanding directors.

Susan, for the first time in her life, found herself in confrontation with herself both as artist and person, Rome being the arena for her painful search for maturity.

And KLA had itself a prestigious new client, thanks to Franco Cristaldi and that precious species of "guardian angel."

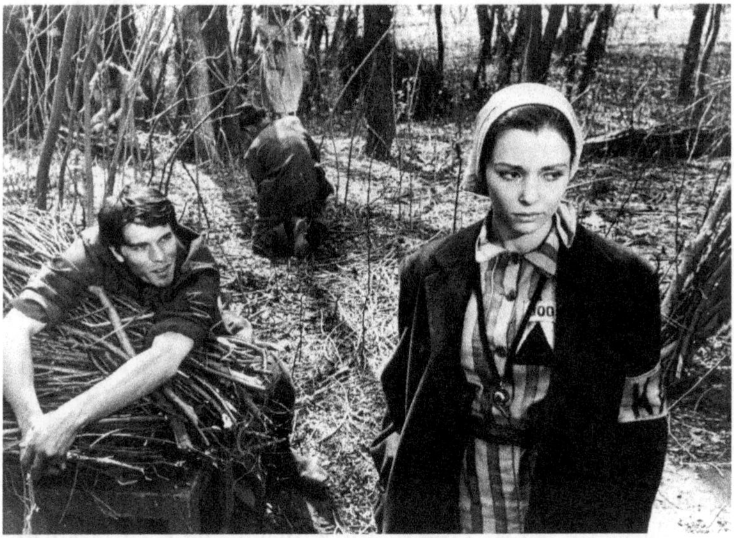

Susan Strasberg in *Kapò.*

In addition, the enchanted incident masterminded by the president of Vides established a landmark first in the relationship between Kaufman-Lerner and the Italian cinema industry.

Cristaldi's recognition of the validity of close collaboration with KLA was by no means shared by a sizable and potent portion of his producing colleagues. Many in the Italian film industry were obsessed with the question of, "How can you tell two Americans to get the hell out of our hair?" These "American assassins" were making far too much progress. Those "Agents of the C.I.A." were not just going to fade away, and as a result, the Italian producer's free-market principle of doing business with actors and directors was being undermined.

The producers had no intention of being forced by "those two anti-capitalists who probably are ruthless undercover spies for the Soviets" to compromise their divine right of dealing face to face with artists, particularly the more vulnerable Italian performers who, in growing numbers, were turning to KLA. Nobody, including the actors themselves, ever believed that the concept of exclusivity between agency and artist would be respected in a nation whose soil was compromise and sun was accommodation.

A number of producers were determined that both the concept of exclusivity and "that Mutt and Jeff team of bloodthirsty bandits" had to be destroyed.

> Gene Lerner of Kaufman-Lerner Associates has filed suit in Rome against producers Ermanno Donati and Luigi Carpentieri following a fistfight in KL's Rome offices said to have been provoked by discussions concerning Geoffrey Horne, a William Morris client, star of a Donati-Carpentieri pic, *Joseph and His Brethren*, and represented by KLA.

That is how Robert Harkins, *Variety*'s Rome correspondent, began his April 22, 1961 story that reported an event, which, were it not for its *opera buffa* elements, might well have had tragic consequences.

March 25, 1961. One of those placid, lazy, early spring Saturday mornings, the air already heavy with the scent of jasmine and hyacinth. On her slightly raised swivel chair, 21-year-old Franca Dalco presided over Via Lisbona 12's bustling reception room and switchboard, all flickering lights and incessant buzzing. Unflappable and luscious, Franca quickly and unmistakingly took care of the stares and comments of every passing male who noted the burgeoning curves in her tightly-packaged body and prayerfully sought favor from her lustrous black eyes.

Franca seemed conscious only of her responsibilities, effectively handling the constant parade of messengers with hand-sent communications; would-be actors desperately clutching their résumés and photos as if they were passports to stardom; clients, usually accompanied by their latest spouse, newest paramour or family counsel; directors with their menagerie of assistants; producers with their coterie of sycophants.

The reception room also contained Marylee Morse, the hearty American secretary, a fixture of the agency virtually since it opened, hopelessly and eternally in love with Italy and everything Italian. The third member of the trio was Paola Scafati, the Italian secretary, squinting through her thick-framed glasses, her serious mien an effective disguise for an obsessive curiosity for juicy gossip.

Saturdays were half-days at KLA. It was near closing time when Hank, in the midst of a long call to London, heard a violent commotion in the reception room which in rapid succession moved from banging doors, heavy footsteps, booming male voices spouting ominous invective, crash of objects against walls, terrified screams from Franca, Marylee and Paola, and then Gene's voice piercing through the tumult, proclaiming as might a Talmudic prophet, "I will not permit this violence! This is a place of peace!"

His words were like kerosene poured on fire, for all they did was enflame the invective and cause even more hysterical crashing, clanging and screaming. As Hank quickly banged down the receiver, he heard a thud, as if a body had fallen. A foreboding silence followed.

With convulsing heart, Hank rushed out of his office to confront an awesome spectacle. Chairs, flowerpots, ashtrays, office supplies were strewn across the room. Eyes closed, immobile, Gene was stretched out on the marble floor. Ermanno Donati (all six feet and 220 pounds of him), Luigi Carpentieri (five foot short) and three horrified secretaries stood hypnotized, fearfully staring down at what seemed to be a corpse.

Hank, and everybody else, to their incalculable relief, realized that Gene was not dead when he weakly lifted himself up by an elbow and said with a wan smile, "I'm all right, I'm all right." Now aware of Hank's presence, Donati and Carpentieri began their lunatic act all over again. Again they threw anything they could lay their hands on and screeched in tandem at an increasingly infuriated Hank, "It's all your fault! You and your criminal partner, pretending he's hurt. We'll fix your wagon. We'll put an end to your illegal activities in *our* Italy. You wait and see."

But Hank wasn't just waiting and seeing. He grabbed massive, ex-soccer player Donati and somehow found the strength to bend him in two, while raining blows on him and trading insult for insult. The Italian army rushed into battle in the person of once-a-soldier, always-a-soldier Barbato, who dashed from his office to tackle all the rubber-blob of Carpentieri while adding colorful Pugliese vulgarities to the verbal fray. Vincenzo Campisi, the dignified, devout and protective *portiere* of the building, and his warm, jolly wife, Vera, came in, their faces showing both horror and anger.

Raising his voice over the battle of invective, Gene shouted at Vicenzo and Vera, "Lock the outside gate and stand guard. Don't let anybody out and nobody in, except Avvocato Ripa di Meana and the police." Vicenzo and Vera nodded. As they hurried out the door, Vera couldn't resist shaking her fist at the two producers and loudly defining them as *disgraziati* and *mascalzoni*. "Marylee, double-lock the door and give me the key," Gene ordered. Knocking over the only remaining vase in her rush to obey, Marylee sidestepped the mêlée to accomplish her task.

Gene then motioned to Franca and Paola to help him up. As they put him on his feet, he felt the pounding ache at the back of his head and shooting streaks of pain through his spine. "Call Meana. Tell him it's vital to get over here immediately," Gene told Paola. "And you get the police to come over right away," he commanded Franca.

As the girls rushed to the phones, Marylee stumbled over to Gene with the key, with which she had double-locked the office door. Everything suddenly came to a halt. "I've called the police and our attorney," Gene said coldly to Donati and Carpentieri. "The *portiere* and his wife, who are dear friends and will do anything to keep us from harm, have locked the gates and are outside standing guard. Neither one of you will leave here until our lawyer and the *carabinieri* arrive."

An oppressive calm fell over the reception room. Donati and Carpentieri, as if spent, stood against the switchboard railing, wordless and waiting. Taking no chances, Barbato moved to the locked entrance and leaned against it with arms akimbo, his eyes fixed on the two culprits. Hank went over to Gene to help his partner to a seat. Only then did Hank realize that he had again damaged the fractured arm that Marlon Brando had so thoughtfully protected years before in the hysteria of the *On the Waterfront* premiere.

Attorney Vittorio Ripa di Meana soon arrived, deeply concerned and no less shocked. Vicenzo ushered in the carabinieri. Then the explanations, followed by shouted denials and charges, and the depositions. Donati and Carpenteri were led away, booked but not arrested. Ripa di Meana urged Gene and Hank to go to the hospital immediately. Barbato drove them to San Camillo Hospital, where both were given emergency treatment. Hank had in fact refractured his arm and had to keep it in a sling for weeks. Gene was x-rayed and ordered to bed under sedation. Damage to his spine was ascertained and several days later a severe sciatica set in, which caused him excruciating pain for more than a year, and which, from time to time, has recurred to the present day.

Gene and Hank were adamant about pressing criminal charges against Donati and Carpentieri. After consultation with Ripa di Meana, they decided to contact the prestigious, internationally known Avvocato Ercole Graziadei. On March 29, 1961, Gene sent the renowned attorney the following letter:

> Avvocato Ercole Graziadei
> Via Veneto 96
> Roma
>
> Dear Ercole:
>
> You perhaps did not hear of the grave incident that took place in our offices on Saturday, March 25, and we feel you should be aware of it.
>
> Signori Ermanno Donati and Luigi Carpentieri, producers of *Joseph and His Brethren*, irate over our insistence that Geoffrey Horne, star of the film, be paid sums past due to him, proceeded to enter our premises against our objections, cause damage, menace our personnel, and violently insult us. In the presence of several witnesses, Donati struck me on the jaw, knocking me on our marble floor. Kaufman, in his effort to restrain them, again injured his once-fractured arm.
>
> We, of course, called the police and our personal attorney whom you well know, Vittorio Ripa di Meana, and Donati and Carpentieri were ousted from the premises. Hank and I immediately went to be examined and treated at San Camillo.
>
> It is likely that in a further effort to intimidate us, Donati and Carpentieri, through their Avvocato Borgognoni, will denounce us to the authorities for our "illegal" activity in Italy. Borgognoni, prior to the incident, had already made threats, and it will by no means surprise us that this plan to harass us is effectuated.
>
> Thus, the incident concerning Geoffrey Horne may have much wider repercussions, of crucial importance to the entire agency situation in Italy.
>
> Sincerely,
> Gene Lerner

The court case was instituted. Donati and Carpentieri offered a sizeable sum in settlement to avoid an eventual prison term. The trial dragged on and on over one technicality after another.

What Hank and Gene had not realized was that with the election of a new president of the Italian Republic, it was customary to amnestize certain categories of crime – and so Donati and Carpentieri were granted amnesty when, in 1962, Antonio Segni was elected Italian president.

An official communication to Hank Kaufman and Gene Lerner from the Ministry of Labor ordered one or the other to appear for a deposition at 11:30 on the morning of January 15, 1962.

Gene's prediction in his March 29, 1961 letter to Ercole Graziadei had only too quickly come true. Italian producers had gone to war.

A law put on the books during the Mussolini regime stated that it was illegal for an intermediary to act between a prospective employer and employee and to receive any remuneration for his intercession. The Fascist law was never repealed when the Republic was established and an office of *collocamento* continued to exist in the Ministry of Labor as a fossil of the past. The antiquated ban was basically applied to the hiring of domestic help.

Anonymously hiding behind the Labor Ministry, a group of bitterly anti-KLA producers had induced the authorities to see the obsolete law in a broader light and to turn it into a legal bastion against the existence of the agency-actor relationship – and a lethal weapon to blow KLA out of existence.

Once Gene was selected to be the victim for the deposition, he spent hour upon hour in preparation in Italian, a language he unfortunately had not yet mastered anywhere near the standard Hank had reached. At 11:30 on the morning of January 16, he appeared at the Ministry of Labor accompanied by legal warrior Ripa di Meana.

For over two ghastly hours, Gene sought in error-laden Italian to make Arturo Gentilo, representative of the Labor Ministry, understand that he and Hank practiced an actual profession that had an accepted and legal function in major entertainment centers throughout the world. Their task was to provide artistic, professional and financial counsel to their clients. The overall purpose of the relationship between Agency and Client was the building of a long-range career, and exclusive contracts were essential to achieve such an end, which took years of concentrated efforts and considerable expenditure.

The ten percent commission, Gene went on in his laborious Italian, was, therefore, only partially related to the particular engagement KLA secured. Moreover, it represented recoupment of agency costs and repayment for innumerable services rendered for the artist-client in the difficult pursuit of greater artistic and material career opportunities.

Gene also pointed out that in addition to all of the responsibilities to its clients, KLA was, in fact, performing a vital liaison service to the Italian picture industry. By putting Italian producers and directors in contact with foreign actors, writers, directors and sometimes distributors, the agency was serving the industry's policy of broadening the international appeal of its productions, for greater revenue and greater prestige.

The Labor Ministry's Arturo Gentile was sympathetic, comprehensive, polite, patient and highly complimentary.

The crisis by no means ended when Gene walked out of the Ministry of Labor with Ripa di Meana. Soon came another fist-to-chin shock. A subpoena issued on January 30, 1962, by Dr. Antonio Di Gennaro, prosecutor of the Italian Republic in Rome, to Henry Kaufman and Eugene Lerner, required them to appear in court at three o'clock on the afternoon of March 16, 1962 to answer formal charges of violation of the laws of the Republic and of involvement in a series of illicit activities!

Once again, Ripa di Meana was called upon to lead the battle. Recognizing the particular danger to Hank and Gene of the subpoena, he turned to criminal lawyer Adolfo Gatti to assist in the Kaufman-Lerner defense. Gatti learned that KLA was to be the major test case and that it was the Ministry of Justice's intention to then move against other agencies.

Ripa di Meana made an effort to unite all existing agencies in common cause, but was rebuffed. Even though they all realized they were also in jeopardy, they were hopeful that KLA would be found guilty and therefore immediately erased from the scene. Hank and Gene also tried to enlist the support of the pitiful actors' unions. One was Communist-led, another Socialist-controlled, a third Catholic-oriented. Only this last one showed any interest in cooperation. It was not only the ridiculous political division that undermined actors' efforts at self-defense, it was also the failure of pride in theirs being an honorable profession entitled to fixed working hours, minimum wages and appropriate working conditions, as well as their morbid fear of offending the god-almighty producer.

Again, as in the Donati and Carpentieri case, there were postponements due to legal technicalities. But it seemed that finally the trial would begin on January 21, 1963.

When the official trial notification from the court came, it listed two principal witnesses against Kaufman and Lerner.

The Labor Ministry's sympathetic, comprehensive, polite, patient and highly complimentary Arturo Gentile was the first of the two.

And a certain Eitel Monaco was the second.

Eitel Monaco! None other than the president of ANICA, the all-powerful association of Italian producers, the equivalent of the Motion Picture Association of America. Whereas Hank and Gene realized that the violent and systematic attacks against them were organized, they never dreamed that ANICA itself would lead the battle against them.

Now that K and L knew the source and strength of "the enemy," they were ready, willing and eager to face trial. They wanted once and for all to establish the legality as well as the value of their activities. And they wanted to put an end to the constant threats of retaliation, boycott and exile from the adherents of Eitel Monaco's ANICA.

On January 16, 1963, Avvocato Gatti advised Ripa di Meana that the trial had been delayed to the next session of the Court, and revealed that the judge in the case had told him, confidentially, that he was not at all convinced that KLA's activities were illegal.

The case never came to trial.

In 1964, Socialist Giuseppe Saragat was elected president of Italy. It was amnesty time again, and the charges against Hank and Gene were erased.

They phoned their friend, Barone Nicola Picella, secretary general to President Saragat, to express their appreciation. And they did not hide their fury.

But they weren't the only ones...

"You tell those bastard bosses of yours that I will not rest night or day until I succeed in freeing the Italian cinema from their filthy clutches and kicking their asses out of Italy forever."

This was the screaming telephone message for Hank and Gene, from Dino Il Primo, Dino Il Grande, otherwise referred to as Dino De Laurentiis, that was taken down carefully, verbatim, on January 9, 1962.

And so began the Dino De Laurentiis boycott against KLA, which was no Sunday picnic for the agency.

Pint-size De Laurentiis was so packed with energy, enthusiasm and gas that he could transform a rubber band into a transatlantic balloon. The greatest producer-showman in Italian cinema history, one of the supreme promoters in the story of films, he combined a gift for sudden improvisation, swiftness of action, and a shrewdness that coursed through his brain as saliva filled the throat of a dog undergoing his Pavlov.

Dino had not only emerged as Italy's most powerful producer, but managed to do it with color and richly piquant seasoning befitting a true Neapolitan. Both literally and figuratively, he became a "studio" in the Hollywood sense. Built to his precise specifications to supersede the long-established Titanus-Farnasina and to compete with Cinecittà, he constructed his own Cinecittà. The mystery of where and how Dino managed to get hold of the land and raise the many billions of lire needed to build the modern and intricate facilities he wanted has never been fully explained. There is no question, however, that Dino had the right instincts, advice and friends, so that much of it was financed by government subsidy through the Cassa di Mezzogiorno, a federal agency whose main purpose was to provide funds for the depressed areas of the South.

Dino was as agile as a champ boxer – dancing, feinting, jabbing, retreating, attacking, carefully covering his face from blows while shifting tactic and style, indifferent as to whether his victory came through points, knockout or a side deal with the referee. Feisty, fiery, indefatigable, stimulating, he unquestionably earned his nickname Dino the Dynamo. He had a distinct and formidable philosophy shared by absolute monarchs, the Mafia, feudal lords, capitalistic robber barons, Communist dictators and well-hung Mediterranean Machos which, in translation, simply meant, "My way is *the* way. I know what I'm doing. I decide. What I said yesterday has nothing to do with what I say today. I brook no interference in getting what I want when I want it."

He did not want to honor a billing clause he was committed to in a deal he had made through KLA with *il duro*, Jack Palance,

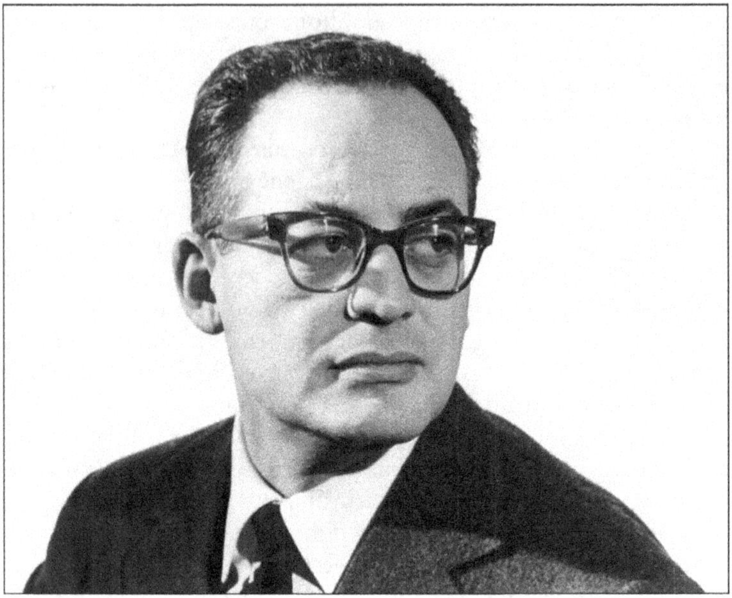

Dino De Laurentiis.

for the film *Barrabas*, and nor did he wish to proceed with the second and third pictures with Palance for which he had contracted. It seemed totally natural to Dino that he simply advise Kaufman-Lerner that he did not wish to proceed with his obligations to Palance. It seemed absolutely normal to him that Kaufman-Lerner would readily accede.

But Kaufman-Lerner did not readily accede, and the battle became more and more heated after Dino's phone call. KLA was determined that Dino fulfill his agreement with Palance. Contracts were contracts, and they had to be respected, unless altered in a spirit of fairness with the client's approval. In all justice to Dino, it was not he but Carlo Ponti who taught Hank and Gene a lesson they never forgot when he walked out on a deal he had made through KLA for Susan Strasberg. For Ponti, a contract, instead of being a commitment to be fulfilled, was often a strategic map for the battle to follow.

Whereas Dino's name either as "Dino De Laurentiis Cinematographica presents" and/or "Distributed by Dino De Laurentiis S.p.A." always appeared in appropriate splendor on-screen, he often hired other producers for films that he either wholly or partially financed, preferably from other sources. Thus, the boycott he instituted against KLA applied to a considerable percentage of annual product shot in Italy.

Hank and Gene were under brutal pressure from almost all their employees to knuckle under. Pressure also came from a number of KLA clients in front of whom Dino and his henchmen dangled glorious opportunities if they abandoned KLA, including some of the foreign agencies with which KLA was affiliated, and producers and directors who worked for Dino and often desperately needed KLA clients. Occasionally, a deal slipped by through the ruse of presumed "direct contact," as certain KLA clients met with De Laurentiis' producers and directors, but this was always done with the full knowledge and counsel of the agency.

Not a single KLA client left as a result of the boycott. The unwavering support and solidarity from KLA's clients and foreign agency partners not only shocked and impressed Dino but also deeply gratified Hank and Gene.

In spite of his penchant for absolutism, Dino was an intelligent realist. Vendetta for him was a tool, not his mission. His mission was to be the first Italian to achieve primacy in the exalted circle of cinema heaven where dwelled such famous and infamous figures as Louis B. Mayer, Harry Cohn, Jack Warner, Alexander Korda, Samuel Goldwyn, Irving Thalberg, David O. Selznick and Darryl Zanuck. He had no qualms about overcoming revenge oaths, declarations of war, personal grudges, or deep-seated prejudices if they stood in the way of his being seated among the aforesaid anointed.

Peace, therefore, was inevitable. It was inevitable because Dino's circumstances and aspirations required it. KLA was in Rome. It was solidly entrenched, at the height of its international fame and not-inconsiderable power. Its agency affiliations covered the globe. Its clients – Italian, French, German, English, American – were of star stature and many were in great demand for films. Dino needed name actors, name directors, and excellent writers to secure American and European financial involvement and distribution, and to develop the personal and professional recognition necessary to merge Hollywood on the Tiber and Hollywood on the Pacific into an enterprise that he could dominate.

London. September 16, 1963.

By coincidence, both Dino and Gene had appointments scheduled with Mike Frankovich, headquartered in the British capital as first vice president in charge of British and Continental Production activities for Columbia Pictures, soon to be transferred to Hollywood to become head of world production for the company.

How can you tell an American? Michael J. Frankovich was hearty, tall, back-slapping, affable and blustering, every foot a man and every inch a boy. Any sophistication he possessed was obscured by steak and potatoes, catsup, Coca-Cola and cigar smoke. He graduated from the University of California as one of the outstanding university football players of his time. His only non-American attribute was his wife, British actress Binnie Barnes, whose English-accented speech never rubbed off on Mike's wide-open, Western American effusion. He had his problems and his faults, but one of the things that made him so likeable was his unadulterated Americanism.

Gene was irritated over being kept waiting. He sat in the private reception room, idly thumbing through years-old magazines, repeatedly looking at his watch. Mike then rumbled out of his office, bear-hugged Gene, put a big arm around him and pulled him quickly into a corner.

"Look, Dino's in my office," Mike whispered, his eyes darting right and left to be sure no one was within hearing distance. "He thinks this thing's gone far enough. I do, too. There are too many important things you guys have got to do to waste your time fighting. I say: smoke the peace pipe. Are you willing?"

"If Dino offers me his hand, of course I'm going to shake it," Gene replied. "But there's one thing, Mike. Dino's got to understand that we're not his slaves or servants. If Dino understands that, the handshake means you're nominated for the Nobel Peace Prize."

"Gotcha," a grinning Mike said with a wink and back-slap. "Gene, you gotta be patient. I still have maybe another twenty minutes with Dino. Okay?" Mike asked. "Okay," said Gene with a smile. Mike quickly rumbled back into his office.

Nearly an hour later, Gene heard Dino's voice, then saw the producer coming towards him, followed by Mike and Guidarino Guidi, De Laurentiis' interpreter, adviser, factotum, court jester. A vast cultural knowledge and an indubitable expertise in cinema accompanied Guidi's wicked tongue, babbling mouth, and five-by-five girth.

There was a dramatic pause as Dino stopped some distance from Gene and turned to say something to Mike, which no one else could hear. Then Dino quickly stepped forward, stuck out his hand, and in English blustered a "How are you?" Immediately sticking out his hand, Gene replied with a "Fine, thanks." The hands touched. The handshake at first was stiff. It then became a clutch. Two hands became four. Then the embrace. The shoulder-pounding followed. Mike beamed with pleasure. Guidarino lifted his eyes towards the ceiling, exasperated.

"What a man, this Lerner, eh?" Dino exhilarated to Mike. "What *balls*!" he cried out, glancing at Guidi, cupping his hands as if they were straining to contain an enviably heavy weight. "I want him to come and work for me," he said to Guidi. "I pay him all the money he want. No limit! Any job he want, he can have. Anything he want to do, he can do!"

Guidi returned his boss' glance with the expression of a mother exasperated by the naughtiness of her child. Straight, loud and clear, he articulated, "But what would he do that *you* don't insist on doing all by yourself?" Guidarino's question dangled in the air like a noose.

It brought a stunned look to Dino's face, wiped away Mike's smile, and brought glints of pleasure to Gene's eyes. "What would he do? Something I don't insist upon doing all by myself?" Dino mumbled, and then in approximately ten seconds, his face all smiles, he had fully recovered his aplomb. With a shrug of his shoulders and a sheep's eye glance at Gene, he threw his arm around Gene's shoulder. His voice warm, he said, "You come see me later at Connaught's. 5:30, okay? We have a drink together and talk, yes?"

Yes. Dino and Gene, Guidarino in attendance, had that drink together. And they talked, but never was Dino's euphoric idea mentioned. It was, however, the beginning of an affectionate relationship between producer and agent and the reopening of the business rapport with KLA. That rapport continued through typhoons and happy landings, tornados and smooth sailings.

A manifestation of positive nature was the seven-year option deal Hank made with Dino for a young American actor Dino thought had a promising future. In 1966, the actor was placed in an Italian "spaghetti Western" entitled *Navajo Joe*, produced and distributed by Dino. The actor's name? Burt Reynolds. Burt, who is part Indian, appeared as... what else? An Indian.

While making the film, Burt was somewhat taciturn, smiling infrequently, immersing himself in his job. *Sans* moustache, bland-faced, he showed little evidence of the raunchy humor and macho sexuality that later was to catapult him into superstardom and the rank of King of the Pin-Up Boys. Dino did not renew the option after *Navajo Joe* and Burt returned to the West Coast to begin his sprint ahead with his spectacular career.

Sophia Loren had an amicable non-client relationship with Gene and Hank for years. When in 1962 the Italian press mercilessly attacked her for her "sinful and blatant concubinage" with Carlo Ponti, who was still legally married to Giuliana Fiastri, Gene wrote Sophia to express his sympathy for her plight. From the chalet in Bürgenstock where she and Ponti were exiled, she replied in a delicious English.

April 24, 1962

Dear Lerner

Thank you very much for your kind letter. Don't worry about your Italian people. I am Italian too. Fortunately there exist the Americans, as you, who can settle the world.

Therefore, we can be tranquil and happy because the Americans look after the justice and the happiness of this low world of ours.

Affectionately
Sophia

How Can You Tell An American?

Through Loren's estimate of the peculiar species that obsesses the world?

If your ancestors, like those of Burt Reynolds, were on American soil to greet the Christopher Columbuses and Amerigo Vespuccis?

If an Italian named Dino De Laurentiis decided to transport family and possessions to the Land of the Free to mount his formidable challenge for supremacy in world cinema?

Four
Cocktailus Romanus

Rome, October 1, 1960.

"Pronto, Kaufman-Lerner Associates," Franca Dalco's clear and inviting voice rang out as she perched on her swivel throne at the switchboard.

"*Chi parla*? Who? I can't hear you I'm very sorry, but you'll have to speak louder. Who? Did you say Anita Ekberg? *Cosa*? Please, Miss Ekberg, please speak up, I just can't hear you. Where are you calling from? Calabria! What town in Calabria? Maratona? Mr. Kaufman is on the phone. So is Mr. Lerner. Yes, I can tell it's an emergency. I'll alert Signor Kaufman immediately."

Franca swiveled towards Bruno Valeri, the lanky 17-year-old office boy. "Bruno, go *subito* to Signor Kaufman and tell him that Anita Ekberg's in some crisis down in Calabria and must talk to him urgently."

Gesturing the shape of a massive bosom, Bruno strode towards Hank's private office as Franca answered another buzz with a flick and a "Pronto, Kaufman-Lerner Associates. Who's calling from London? I'll have to ask Mr. Lerner to call your party back as soon as possible." Flick, shutting off communication. Flick, opening another. "Are you still there, Miss Ekberg? Signor Kaufman will be with you in a moment."

Relentless continuation of buzz and flick. "Pronto, Kaufman-Lerner, *chi parla*? You would like to have a meeting with Ava Gardner?! Are you a producer? I asked you whether you're a producer? Who? Who? I'm sorry, you'll have to speak to Signor Kaufman or Signor Lerner." Flick of her finger, she swiveled towards Marylee and Paola. "What an idiot! He wouldn't tell me his name. He says he wants Ava Gardner to come to his office to discuss a part!"

Marylee let out a howl of laughter. "Ava going to somebody's office? That's a hoot."

"Why didn't you give him Linda Christian's number?" asked Paola, cocking her head suggestively.

Bruno reappeared and gave Franca the sign to put Ekberg through to Kaufman. "Miss Ekberg! Here's Mr. Kaufman!" Intercom to Kaufman. "Signor Kaufman, you'll have speak up. The connection's terrible."

Interruptions from visitors. More flicks in reply to buzzes. The usual salutations from Franca. Then an unusually distinct "One moment, please," followed by a dramatic stage whisper to Marylee, alerting the ever-watchful Paola.

"It's Esther Williams again for Mr. Lerner. He refuses to speak to her. You had better take it, Marylee." "Why don't you just tell her to take a long good swim," said Marylee, a look of martyred resignation creeping over her face. Franca reopened the hold button, speaking with melting sweetness. "I'm so sorry for keeping you waiting, Miss Williams. No, I'm very sorry Mr. Lerner's not available. Yes, I certainly did give him your messages. Let me put you through to Miss Morse... What? WHAT DID YOU SAY, Miss Williams!!??!!" screamed Franca, casting aside all her cool. "Miss Williams!" A pause, as Marylee and Paola leaned forward, one in trepidation, the other in anticipation. Shrugging her shoulders, Franca cut the connection. "She hung up." Franca shook her head, unbelieving. "I never expected such foul language from her! She needs her mouth chlorinated, not her swimming pool."

Paola's eyes were nearly bulging out of their sockets. "Won't somebody please tell me why Mr. Lerner won't speak to her? What did she do?"

"You should know by now that I'm not a gossip, Paola dear," said Marylee. "All I know is that last night Gene took Esther Williams out to dinner with Rossano and Lydia Brazzi."

A triumphant cry from Paola. "Good. Rossano! He'll tell me. He always tells me everything."

In his private office, Hank leaned forward in his desk chair, phone receiver poised in one hand, pen taking notes in the other. With teeth gritted, he listened to the lamentations from one of KLA's more valuable clients, whose stock had risen enormously since Federico Fellini made her a cult figure through the phenomenal international success of his *La Dolce Vita*.

"Yes, I'm here, Anita," Hank shouted, as he listened patiently to Ekberg's husky, little girl voice relating the results of her latest *avventura.* What a sorry little group the Roman press corps would be, he said to himself, without Anita's incredible talent for getting herself into trouble.

"Keep talking slow and LOUD," he added in growing frustration. It was evident from the worried expression on his face that this Ekberg crisis really was a crisis. "You're now in Maratona and it happened where? Castro… what? Castrovillari? Okay, I got it.

"But why did the villagers start slinging rocks at your car? You what? Panicked! But why did you think they would want to hurt you? Tried to turn your Ferrari over? Jesus! Did you get hurt? I said did they hurt you? Good God, what? You think you ran over…! How many?" You stupid, ridiculous, incredible woman, Hank wanted to shout at her. "Jesus Christ, Anita! I said Jesus Christ! Anita, Anita… They wanted to arrest you? No, darling, I can't come down. Now stop crying and listen. Stop crying!" Hank didn't add the "goddamit" that was on the tip of his tongue.

"I'll alert Ripa de Meana and Giorgio Conti right away. Ripa di Meana will take whatever legal steps you need and Giorgio will handle the press. Stay in your hotel room until you hear from Ripa di Meana, Conti or me. And tell the production I said you absolutely have to have police protection until things simmer down. Did you hear me? Did you hear me, Anita?"

The connecting glass door opened and Gene came through. Putting his hand over the receiver, Hank whispered to his partner, "Anita. Jesus, what a mess." Gene shook his head and sat on the edge of Hank's desk, listening.

"Don't forget. Get police protection. Stay in your room until you get further word from us. And keep calm. We'll get you out of this mess, so stop worrying. I'll give you a call tonight. Tonight, yes, darling. I said stop worrying and stop crying."

Hank banged down the receiver and sounded the intercom. "Franca, find Ripa di Meana and Conti for me, wherever they are. It's urgent."

"What happened?" asked Gene.

"I'll tell you at home tonight. Some women should spend their lives in the kitchen!" Hank looked at his watch. "Christ,

I'm late for the Brazzi press conference. I had better run. Then I've got to get over to the Titanus office. Goffredo Lombardo wants to discuss another picture with Ava."

"Remember that Ava has asked us for drinks Sunday," remarked Gene.

"Speaking of Miss G., I haven't been able to locate that damn Walter. I've put his mother, brother, stand-in, barber, masseur and tennis coach on the alert. If they ever do another Houdini picture, Walter Chiari's the ideal one to do it."

The phone on Hank's paper-strewn desk rang. "Mr. Lerner's phone isn't answering," Franca said to Hank. "Is he with you? It's an urgent personal call from Simone Signoret in Paris."

"Simone from Paris – urgent. Everything's urgent today," said Hank.

"So what else is new? It must be about the Montand-Monroe hysteria," Gene said as he took the receiver.

"Give Simone my love," said Hank as he hurried out the door.

"Franca, pass me Madame Signoret," instructed Gene as he settled into Hank's chair.

"Simone, *cherie*, *comment vas-tu*?"

"Gene! I'm so glad I finally got through. Look, I have an awful problem. Yves is going to be in Paris for the premiere. Paris is flooded with rumors that Marilyn is coming, too."

"Is she or isn't she?" asks Gene.

"I wish I knew," an exasperated Simone replied. "Yves swears he doesn't know and you know anything can happen with Marilyn. Listen, I've just got to get out of Paris. Marilyn Monroe and Yves Montand in *Let's Make Love – version originale* at the Ermitage, *version française* at the Max Linder, every goddamn kiosk plastered with the two of them staring into each other's eyes. Those 20th Century Fox bastards! You would think they would have a *soupçon* of consideration. But anything to sell their picture. Gene, I can't be here for that damn premiere. I just can't."

She seemed desperate. "When it is?" asked Gene.

"Saturday."

"That's the fifth..." said Gene.

"The press is calling me a hundred times a day. What do I think of Marilyn? What do I think of my husband's love affair with her? Am I going to ask for a divorce? Will I join my husband and Marilyn..."

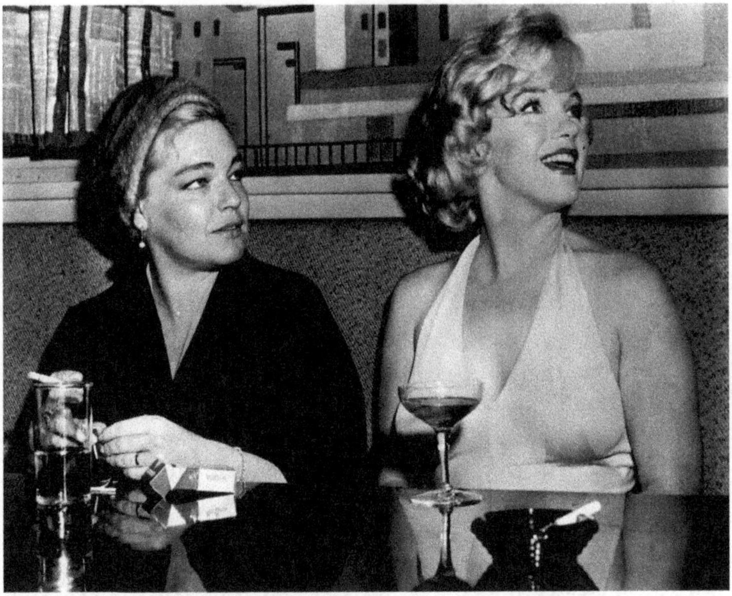

Simone Signoret and Marilyn Monroe

"But is she coming?" Gene interrupted.

"I don't know! They ask when did I last talk to my husband? When I did I last sleep with him? 'When you last talked to him, what did he say to you?' What did I say to him?' I certainly didn't tell those bastards, but I will tell you."

"I don't have to know, Simone," interjected Gene.

"You remember I had to leave for Italy to start my film *Adua and Her Friends* while they were still shooting *Let's Make Love* in Hollywood? Yves would call me from California every evening. More and more I was getting moans and cries like, 'I don't know what to do with her, *cherie.* I really don't know how to handler her, *cherie.* Tell me, what should I do, *cherie.* She finds any excuse to knock on my door. She's driving me crazy, *cherie*. I really don't know how to handle her, *cherie*. Tell me – what should I do, *cherie*?' So I ask him, 'You don't know what to do?' while I'm getting angrier and angrier. 'You want me to tell you what to do?' '*Oui*, *cherie*.' 'You really want me to tell you what to do?' I say, wanting to smash his face with the phone. '*Oui*, *oui*, *cherie*!' 'OK, I'll tell you what to do,' and I screamed out, 'BAISEZ-LA!'"

I really didn't need to know, Gene said himself.

"Gene, *cherie*, find a way to get me out of here for a few days," pleaded Simone.

An idea struck Gene. "When you were doing *Adua* here, remember that I brought you a Bob Aldrich script called *Now We Know*, based on a John O'Hara story?"

"I remember. It was one of the most beautiful love stories I ever read. Why didn't we ever do it?"

"I could choke you, Simone. Do you remember that lunch at L'Escargot on the Appia Antica?"

"We had several lunches there."

"I'm talking about *tha*t lunch when you told me you wouldn't do *Now We Know* because Aldrich wanted to cast it with you and Sidney Poitier to make it the first graphic love story in American film history between a white and a black. That's when you told me you wouldn't do it because you didn't believe a foreigner should be teaching lessons in tolerance to the American people. Even when I accused you of being a coward and a hypocrite about your ideals of equality, you still said you wouldn't do it."

"You don't have to be so damn self-righteous. Besides, career is one thing. What I believe in my private life is another."

"Aldrich happens to be in Rome struggling with *Sodom and Gomorrah.*"

"Bob Aldrich is really doing that kind of *merde*?"

"If he's doing it," said Gene defensively, "he's got his reasons. Anyway, if Bob is agreeable, and I'm sure he will be, Hank and I will give a big splashy cocktail reception at our apartment Thursday to announce that as soon as Robert Aldrich completes *Sodom and Gomorrah*, he and Simone Signoret are going to make *Now We Know.*"

"Fabulous!" Simone cried.

"We'll talk to Bob about it. Today is Tuesday. I suggest you book a flight for tomorrow evening or Thursday morning."

"Okay."

"Hank or I will get to Aldrich immediately. If Bob's *d'accord* for the party, we'll get an announcement out to the wire services tonight. And by having the party Thursday, we'll get you all the press coverage you want on Friday, perfect timing to get a beat on their Saturday premiere."

"Great, *cheri*," Simone responded, her cheerfulness evident.

"I'll be out, so phone Hank at home at midnight. He'll give you Aldrich's answer. Hank will be doing ninety percent of the work anyway."

"I'm afraid I'm putting Hank and you to too much trouble."

"You're one of the few who are worth anything we can do. And I mean *anything*. You're going through an unnecessary hell and I don't think it's fair. We work on a strange theory."

"What's that?"

"Career is not one thing and private life another."

"*Putain*," she hissed, half smiling. A pause, then her very special voice, already husky, trembled slightly when at last she spoke. "*Je t'embrasse très, tres fort*. I kiss you both."

By midnight, as agreed, Simone was on the phone with Hank. "Hank, *cheri*, what did Aldrich say?" she asked immediately.

"He's delighted. But you knew he would be."

"Please thank Bob for me and give him a big kiss. And a big kiss to you and Gene. Thank God everything's all set."

How to prepare a Roman party in 48 hours? Hank's basic guest list numbered 152. With all the "I'm sure you don't mind my bringing…" additions and the occasional gatecrashers, Hank knew it would be wise to prepare for at least fifty more. The order for alcoholic beverages was made accordingly. Whiskeys, gins, vodkas, but also vermouths, Campari, Punt e Mes, white wines Orvieto, Verdicchio Fazi Battaglia and Bolla Soave. More to the taste of a cosmopolitan crowd in an Italian setting, more of a manifestation of Roman "in."

Café Rosati of Piazza del Popolo, undisputed doyen of Roman caterers, was immediately pressed into service. A rich variety of tempting dishes was agreed upon. Hot and cold appetizers and antipasti. Platters of French, Italian and Swiss cheeses. Plates of cold meats, fowl and fish. Bowls of exotic salads in a mélange of colors only Italy could provide. A gluttonous assortment of sweets, starting with zuppa inglese, Mont Blanc, millefoglie, charlot, crostata and individual fruit tarts. Roman cocktail parties could easily stretch out till midnight, and the horde would expect to be overfed.

The everyday agency routine continued, and virtually the entire staff was mobilized on Simone's behalf. Enzo Barbato and Massimo Frosi, co-agents Annalena Limentani and Rossana Pelliccia, in addition to Franca, Marylee and Paola, were on the phone extending invitations. Bruno sped through Roman traffic on the office Vespa to deliver personal notes to a special few and file urgent telegrams at San Silvestro's post office to those who, even for their own funerals, would insist on formalities.

Hank was taking only emergency phone communications, but when Franca told him of incessant "urgent" calls from Angelo Frontoni, he decided to speak. Young, ambitious, shrewd, indefatigable, Frontoni was achieving international fame alongside master photographer Pierluigi Praturlon. Angelo was particularly admired in the world's film capitals and by glossy, prestige magazines for his glamorous and romantic photos of female stars in whom, in his portraiture, he always discovered allure, mystery and sensuality which often was never there.

"*Carissimo mio*, I'm so embarrassed, I don't know quite how to begin," Frontoni started, all in a flap. "I've never made a request like this before."

"You want to photograph me in the nude," Hank spoofed.

"Be serious, will you? Look, I'll say it right out. I've heard rumors of your party and I want to come and photograph it."

"You? Angelo Frontoni, photographing a mere party?" Hank asked in mock horror.

"What will people say?"

"No charge, you understand. All the photos will be your property. And I'll service all outlets for free."

"What's got into you?" asked Hank. "What are you really after?"

"Sincerely, seriously and simply this: I want to do it as homage to Signoret. For me, she's a great among greats, absolutely divine. And I adore Aldrich. But above all, I would like to be part of one of your and Gene's special events, particularly this one. If you let me come, I'll be honored."

Hank quickly realized that Angelo's presence would be useful to Simone.

"Normally I would have to say sorry, no. But seeing that it's the one-and-only Frontoni... I'll make an exception."

"Oh, you're a doll!" exuberated Frontoni. "I couldn't be more thrilled."

"I'll advise Giorgio Conti immediately. You call him in fifteen minutes to coordinate arrangements."

"Whatever the boss says will be done. And thanks, *caro*. A kiss to you and Gene."

Giorgio Conti was not only KLA's press representative but also the correspondent in Italy for the number one public relations agency in world cinema, Hollywood-based Rogers & Cowan. As Italian as he was, Giorgio always seemed uncomfortable with his hereditary genes, like a mutation, as if his Italian blood had been skinned and his manner, speech and cadence cloned in nineteenth-century Victorian England.

It was to Giorgio that the official press release on Simone's arrival and the reception, prepared in Italian, French and English and approved by Hank, was turned over for world dissemination. It was Giorgio who would be picked up at the office by the Ducci-hired limousine and would proceed to the airport to greet Simone, who had given Hank details of her flight. It was Giorgio who had booked her suite at the Hotel de la Ville. Hank, however, personally selected the flowers to be placed there, with a welcome card signed by every employee of KLA, Signora Marion, and even Rosa, the cleaning woman.

Operation Signoret was in full swing.

The moment Franca opened the switchboard at nine o'clock on Thursday morning, it broke out in a rash. News agencies, reporters, the Rome-based correspondents for foreign publications, photographers cajoling, pleading, fencing, weaving. Demands for more information. Insistence on private interviews. Calls for a press conference. Requests for invitations to the party. They showed ostentatious interest in the Aldrich-Signoret film project, but Franca, her radar as oiled as her swivel chair, knew they were wolves out to devour the last morsel of scandal involving France's most famous acting couple and the world's most exciting film star.

"Marilyn Monroe? Wasn't she the wife of an early American president?"

"*Let's Make Love*? And have my fiancé play *Let's Make Murder*?"

"Yves Montand? Moët & Chandon, if you please."

"Monroe-Montand steaming like spaghetti and meat sauce? Don't mention pasta. It's bad for my figure."

"Signoret preparing a crime of passion? She's preparing *Now We Know*."

Rejoinder and repartee could in no way deflect Franca's deft but firm reference of any and all inquiries to Conti, as Hank had ordered. It was poor Giorgio who had the distasteful task of reminding the press that Kaufman-Lerner never permitted a function in their home to become a journalistic orgy, with due respect to each and every member of the newspaper profession.

Whereas itinerant musicians and mournful flower-sellers have privileged status in Italy, their right of invasion is far behind the immunity granted to the genre of homo sapiens classified as photographers. It is the inalienable prerogative of every one of the thousands of Italians who decides he is the greatest picture-taker of all time to record, at any time or place, in whatever state or condition, dead or alive, a human being on camera in any position. The Kaufman-Lerner policy, therefore, was revolution, heresy and insult.

"Yes," Giorgio was forced to admit in response to the whirlpool of questions, pleads and demands, "There will be a few reporters present." Agonizing cries of rage. Vulgar reference to Giorgio's sexual apparatus. Vendettas of unspeakable horror sworn. "But," hastily added Conti, "strictly and only as longtime friends. Like Bob Harkins and Hank Werba of *Variety*, and their wives. Stan Swinton of the Associated Press, and his wife. Curtis Bill Pepper of *Newsweek*, and his wife, Beverly.

"And there will be *one* photographer..." Giorgio was interrupted by protests of favoritism, threats of eternal revenge, pitiful bleats from those bleeding from wounds to their professional pride. "Angelo Frontoni." Derisive whistles. Sardonic hoots of laughter. "Frontoni? Is poor Angelo reduced to doing banquets, weddings and funerals?"

With masterful self-control, his voice raised but dignified, each syllable underlined, Giorgio replied, "Frontoni will make all his material available to all news outlets for morning-paper release. And I will have a press release ready simultaneously."

Mutterings, mumbles, whispered curses, maledictions, vituperations.

All to be forgotten until the next confrontation.

There was another journalist Giorgio did not mention. Asbestos in her veins, she appeared that evening at the door of the Kaufman-Lerner apartment, adamantly refusing to be turned away.

Oriana Fallaci.

At precisely 6:30 on Thursday, Gene arrived at the Hotel de la Ville in the Ducci limousine. The sight of the milling cluster of photographers provoked a smirk of displeasure. Without waiting for the ceremonial assistance of the uniformed chauffeur, Gene opened the car door and moved quickly towards the hotel entrance. His face showed no reaction to the barrage of questions peppered with the names Montand, Monroe and Signoret. As he nodded smilingly and waved at the frustrated members of the fourth estate, he entered the revolving hotel door andwas greeted with a deferential bow by the chief *portiere*, who handed him the house phone and put him straight through to Simone's suite.

Simone had been ready for twenty minutes. Simone was very edgy. Simone would be right down.

Simone Signoret.

Born 1921 as Simone Kaminker.

Half-Jewish.

Though already immortalized by that fanatical breed referred to as "film buffs" for her performances in *Dédee d'Anvers*, *Thérèse Raquin*, *Casque d'Or* and *Les Diaboliques*, she was for years equally well known for involvement in a bitterly controversial series of events: the Rosenbergs, Oppenheimer, Algeria, Hungary, the Stockholm Appeal, Bertrand Russell Peace Tribunal, Vietnam and more recently Poland. Her existentialist and left-wing associations were widely publicized and carefully noted by law-and-order protectors in dossiers on the doubtful. In the political, social and intellectual ferment of the postwar years, any important demonstration of protest, any significant gathering of radical or pacifist opposition to "Western imperialism" attended by a Camus, a Sartre, a de Beauvoir or a Mendès-France, seemed also to mark the presence of Signoret.

She was the star activist among the stars of Europe.

In the McCarthy era, those noble descendants of Pontius Pilate, the Hollywood moguls, frantically sought to cleanse their calloused hands of even the remotest contact with "pinko"-suspected relatives, friends, maids, butlers, chauffeurs and secretaries, and above all, suspected elements of world cinema. It was to be expected, therefore, that Signoret, already much too "special" in looks, much too individual in quality to fit into their mental pigeonholes, spent much of her career under a cloud deep red with suspicion.

If it had not been for Signoret's blazing, Oscar-winning triumph in *Room at the Top* – not, it must be pointed out, a Hollywood product but a creation of British cinema – which won for her a worldwide audience while proving both her talent and adeptness in English, it is almost certain that the brilliance of this French-Jewish "agitator," "fellow traveler" and "Commie sympathizer" would never have had the benediction of the Hollywood studios, a benediction Simone neither rejected nor welcomed.

Sincerity is Signoret's artistic trademark. It is the dough from which she shapes her impressive characterizations. Honesty in Simone is effortless. He frankness is intuitive. But she can wield it like a sword – and cut you to bits. Unpretentiousness is Simone's basic garment. She does not wear it flamboyantly as a rich multi-colored coat to show off or draw attention, yet she can make it shimmer to blind from general view the conflicts that ferment in her. Her so winning, so witty, sometimes so wistful spontaneity does not always flow readily.

No other star seems to have such femininity stem from a quality one associates with the male. It is in her voice, body, carriage, mentality. It is in the look of her. In the look from her. You do not for a moment doubt her womanhood. It is there, persistent, appealing, enveloping. Yet even the pain she is unable to extinguish seems filtered through that curious masculine essence.

Perhaps the pain is the essence.

She is both withdrawn and gregarious, shy and brazen, childlike and sophisticated. She is both amazingly tolerant of weakness and curiously intolerant of strength. Her suspicion is born not from paranoia (no stranger to her) but from her need to test your ability of "mind." She does not consider it her responsibility to put you at your ease, but your own responsibility to be ease with yourself. She puts you on trial and makes you your own judge.

She is rare in that she is driven not by ambition, nor the need for recognition, nor greed. She will talk of her penchant for making shocking misjudgments in her choice of roles, for succumbing to pleas for help from needy directors and producers, and of the disadvantage to objective career-building of having too much money. Yet through the passing years, in spite of endless hours spent in alcoholic compatibility with old or passing friends, her sloth, her added weight and a face of bloated flesh, she retains her fascination and artistic self-respect. The powerful reception in America and elsewhere of her unforgettable portrayal of *Madame Rosa* in the film of the same name proves this beyond a shadow of a doubt.

Signoret is the "people's artist" of France. Self-ravage has not destroyed her capacity for survival nor diminished her art. She reigns supreme, without fanfare, laying no claim to prerogatives or lineage.

The role she plays is Signoret.

Half-smoked cigarette in hand, essential prop in her performance of living, Simone exited from the elevator, her golden-brown hair in a neat coiffure. She strode forward in a skin-hugging, haute couture suit of beige silk in perfect harmony with her incredible sea-green eyes. Smiling wanly, she kissed Gene with a peck-peck on each cheek. The smile disappeared as she looked towards the street.

"Look at them waiting to eat Little Red Riding Hood. *Merde, merde, MERDE!*" She ran her fingers through her hair, a reflex action that revealed her agitation. Gene grabbed the hand, squeezed it tight in his.

"Don't lose your temper," Gene admonished. "Any frown or sign of anger will show up in their photos as just more ammunition. You're in Rome for a very important and very happy occasion. Just try to keep your mind on that."

Simone nodded, inhaled, bit her lip. She took hold of Gene's arm as they started towards the exit. Everyone in the lobby had eyes on her. The chief *portiere* raced over to accompany them. After all, Signoret was an Academy Award-winning star, and there were photographers! Through the revolving door came Simone, Gene and a smiling, solicitous chief *portiere.*

Elbows. Curses. Shouts. Jostles. Snap. Click. Questions.

The photographers and journalists closed in.

Producer-director-writer Robert Aldrich had come early in order to be on hand when Simone arrived. "Any laughs today?" he asked a shower-refreshed Hank, elegantly togged in his newest Italian finery. Aldrich stood at the door, surveying the Lucullian display of abundance aesthetically arranged on silver trays by the Rosati contingent on flower-laden tables.

"*Ammazza*," he finally said, a favorite slang expression he had picked up from his Roman driver. "You guys are really something. Give you a weekend and you could organize the Olympics!"

Heh-heh-heh laugh, hug for Hank, salute to Photographer Frontoni, double scotch from one of the white-coated Rosati waiters.

"C'mon and sit down and give the gab some exercise before the horde takes over," Bob suggested, settling his bulk on a sofa and patting the space next to him in invitation. Holding his drink, Hank plopped down beside Bob. "So what else is new, Hankele? You look like you're in great shape."

"So do you," replied Hank.

"The fat hides that lean and hungry look. Iago in Falstaff's clothing. So tell me."

"Tell you what?"

"Did Esther Williams really pee all over Brazzi's car after getting loaded on too much Italian vino and insulting everybody in your favorite trattoria? Did she really put her legs out the window so she could show off her... talent... *amazza*... to the Via Veneto? And is it true as reported that she forgot the bottom half of her bikini?"

"Not having been present, I'll have to say 'I don't know.'"

"Heh-heh-heh," Bob laughed with satisfaction. "But Rabbi Gene was there. And the whole Via Veneto set is zavazavazavaing all about it. Okay, we'll cut on Esther and whatever she did or did not display. Now we'll dolly in on a three-hour marathon with Signori Lombardo, Franco De Simone and Silvio Clementelli at Titanus this morning. Those Italians sure like to gab. *Zavazavazava*. Are we going to get along, this Lombardo and me?"

"You got charm, he's got charm, maybe the charm will meet."

"You can't take charm to the goddamn bank. What I want to know is does Signor Lombardo pay on time, which means punctual to the split second?"

"Bob, remember what Gene tried to get through your head. Italians don't have the same definition of time that Americans do. And after dealing with it a couple of thousand years longer, they're convinced their way is better."

"There has to be a good reason for being an American. Getting paid *pronto* on due dates may be it."

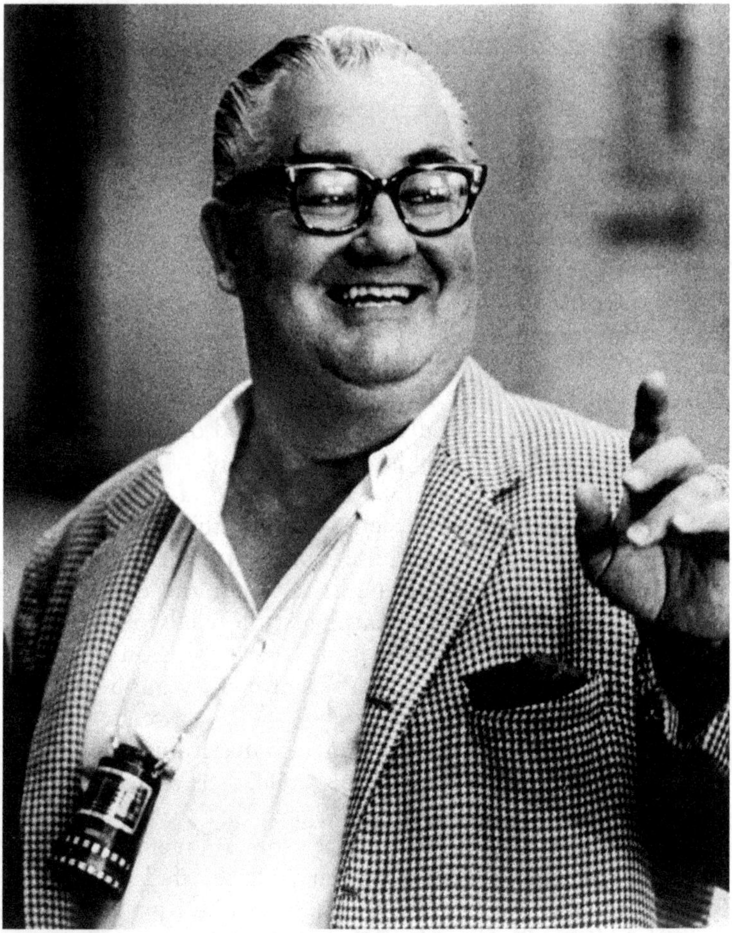

Robert Aldrich

"Titanus is solid, and we've got their accounting office used to a precise, organized way of doing business. We just have to remind them now and then. Sometimes more than once."

"Then remind them, damn it, as often as you have to. The important thing is that I get my salary and reimbursement in full, with no mistakes and on time. Or else I'm leaving. Okay? Okay. And that *farkakte* screenplay!" Aldrich, a WASP, made extensive use of colorful Yiddish terms, such as the aforementioned *farkakte* – meaning "crappy."

"Gene gave you great advice, Bob. Don't try to make *Sodom and Gomorrah* into something more than it is. Don't try turning it into a *Ben-Hur* or another *Gone With the Wind.* It'll never be an art film. The epic poem is not a cinematic concept that Titanus is even remotely capable of tackling. Do the best you can, as the professional you are, and try to be satisfied. Otherwise you'll go crazy, they'll go crazy, we'll all go crazy."

"I smell *tsuris*. That's *trouble* – for those of you who don't understand Yiddish. And I can guarantee you, it isn't Chanel No. 5."

"Don't be so defeatist, Roberto," said Hank, raising his glass for a toast. "Upwards and onwards with the arts. Isn't that your motto?"

Aldrich's laughed loudly. "Upwards and onwards with the arts," he repeated, clinking his glass with Hank's.

Robert Aldrich – as unconventional and unpredictable as they come. For Aldrich, the rain shines, the sun pours. If it were possible to turn his infinite capacity for melancholy into electricity, the world would be lit up night and day. Endless patience and sweetness and inexhaustible wells of kindness. But then, suddenly and inexplicably, an explosion – a burst of frustration, disappointment, resentment, wounded pride. Vulnerability.

A caricaturist might sketch him with that ironic face and big glasses. But when Aldrich smiles his smile, there's overwhelming and irresistible warmth, a carefree spirit, that a portrait painter might be able to capture. If Kafka wrote a novel about Bob's life, he would call it *The Game.* For Aldrich, life is an endless, brutal football game that's rigged against him by a handful of powerful idiots. On the other hand, Aldrich is not one to enjoy an easy victory. Exhausted and humiliated he might be, but Bob somehow always manages to get back on his feet. The final tackle, and defeat, never comes for him. Ignoring the pain, the blows to his dignity, shrieking at his enemies, he starts over, again and again, always aiming for that winning goal, so that the hundred thousand – no, the *two* hundred thousand – fans filling the stadium can celebrate a victory won by him alone, and reporters worldwide finally and triumphantly proclaim him the greatest athlete of the last decade. Of the last century, in fact.

It's hard to name another American director who has poured so much passion, heart and a significant portion of his personal financial resources into his work. For Aldrich, being a filmmaker means total dedication, total commitment. This has been a constant in his life ever since he fell in love with cinema when he worked as an assistant director to Charles Chaplin.

Europeans once made a cult of director Aldrich, who was unconditionally admired by critics and exalted by fans. With films like *The Big Knife* and *Attack!*, both of which won awards at the Venice Film Festival, Aldrich created an aura around himself as the authentic, talented American stepping up to denounce his country's materialism and lament just how polluted is the noble dream it once envisioned for humanity.

Hollywood big shots, troubled by his stubbornness, were reluctant to invest in Aldrich, even though *Vera Cruz* and *Apache* had been hits. He was, they insisted, a *political* risk, a radical nonconformist who couldn't tell the difference between art and commerce. That, in particular, struck them as a mortal sin. Unemployed, overwhelmed by debts, with a wife and four kids, Aldrich went to Rome to find a job – any job, in any kind of film.

Goffredo Lombardo, elegant and well-groomed, ran Titanus with the touch of an amateur from behind a desk the size of a ping-pong table. He had taken a chance on *The Naked Maja*, with Ava Gardner and Anthony Franciosa, directed by Henry Koster, and *The Angel Wore Red*, with Gardner and Dirk Bogarde, written and directed by Nunnally Johnson. Sensing a profit could be wrung from the general inclination for costume spectaculars sweeping the industry, Lombardo, hoping to make a biblical story, landed on *Sodom and Gomorrah*, which became the "any job, in any kind of film" that Bob Aldrich was so desperately seeking. The production was disastrous, the end result was a catastrophe, and Bob was fired by Lombardo during editing. Determined, exhausted, he rose again, this time, instead of holding a football, clinging to a screenplay as if it were his last hope, waving it frantically in front of Gene, getting it into his agent's hands before those dirty bastards dragged him down again to destroy him.

The title of the script was *What Ever Happened to Baby Jane?* And on February 19, 1962, Gene flew to New York with the script and an impossible mission that had to be accomplished in just ten days: (a) get rid of a hysterical, vitriolic Joseph E. Levine, who had a claim on the script and wanted to do the project without Aldrich, (b) secure written commitments on minimal financial conditions from Bette Davis and Joan Crawford to appear in the film, and (c) find the necessary financing to make the picture.

Not a single major company wanted to proceed with Aldrich, nor had any faith in the box office value of those "two has-beens" Davis and Crawford. And there was Levine, salivating like a hungry wolf, certain that Gene could never get the money together to buy him out, and thus could proceed to make the picture without Aldrich. Gene could think of only one thing to do, and he went ahead and did it. He phoned Hank from New York and asked if he would agree to gamble all of KL's savings to pay off Levine. Hank bravely agreed. A wildly-cursing Joe Levine was bought out. Meanwhile, a most cooperative, stateslady-like Joan Crawford and a less cooperative, dubious Bette Davis finally gave Gene the commitment he sought. The one and only hope for financing, after rejection by the major companies, was an important independent producing company, Seven Arts. Gene realized that if Seven Arts didn't come through, all was lost, The Game was over. Not only for Aldrich but for Kaufman-Lerner.

On February 29, 1962, Gene carried his portable typewriter and a sandwich to the Seven Arts offices for final meetings with Eliot Hyman, its president, and David Stillman, its vice-president and legal officer. He was determined to remain there through the night, if necessary, to come out with a signed document which assured the participation of Seven Arts.

The negotiations were so dilatory, unpleasant and onerous that Gene felt more and more that he, too, was caught in The Game. Seven Arts required Aldrich to defer his entire salary. It refused to refund to Kaufman-Lerner more than fifty percent of the amount it had paid to Joe Levine for the script. It took most of the night before Seven Arts finally agreed to proceed with the film.

When *What Ever Happened to Baby Jane?* premiered in November 1962, it was such a hit that Aldrich began to feel that he had, perhaps, at last, made that winning touchdown to give his final victory in The Gang. He got his entire salary from Seven Arts. KLA got a full refund of the money they had paid to Levine, plus a bonus. And Aldrich, Hank, Gene, Davis, Crawford, Seven Arts and the distributor of the picture, Warner Bros., all got a share in the very handsome profits earned by the picture nobody wanted, starring a pair of "has-beens" nobody would pay to see, directed by an outstanding picture-maker nobody wanted to hire.

What Ever Happened to Baby Jane? is noted in cinema history as not only a success but also as a classic of Grand Guignol. Prior to its 1963 European release, Bob had asked Gene to arrange a private screening in Paris for Olga Horstig and several of France's renowned actresses. Sitting on the left in a single row in the projection room were the grande dame of the French theater, Edwige Feuillère, next to Brigitte Bardot and her dog, Michèle Morgan, Annie Girardot, Marie Bell, Simone Signoret and Gene. When the lights went up after the screening, Feuillère was the first to rise. She passed across the row, then turned back and, in silence, looked at the others. With a slight tremor in her voice, she said: "We have just had a remarkable lesson in acting from our American sisters." Without another word, she walked up the aisle and disappeared.

The magnificent performances Bob got out of Davis and Crawford, his masterful directorial and producing job, provided him with a platform to continue his career, with its zooming ups and stomach-twisting downs, until the Eighties. He hasn't yet won The Game, but he sure as hell is still playing it, God bless him, and he sure as hell hasn't lost it. Bitterly cursing those dirty bastards up there plotting against him, he's right in there, trying again, again and then again to make that winning touchdown and to have his final, glorious vindication.

The Cadillac bearing Simone and Gene slowed down in front of the Kaufman-Lerner apartment at Via Salaria 290, situated only a few blocks from KLA's offices at Via Lisbona. The phalanx of press in front of the apartment building was even larger and more unruly than the group waiting at the Hotel de la Ville, and was reinforced by a crowd of curiosity seekers and reserve troops of photographers who had raced after the limousine in their 500 Fiats or Vespas. Giorgio Conti, valiantly trying to hold on to his aplomb, was losing the battle to maintain order.

The uniformed chauffeur stopped out of the car, proceeded to open the rear door with a practiced flourish, and stretched out a helping hand to Gene. As the driver stood beaming, Gene assisted Simone. Upon sight of her, a reverberating moan of blandishments and imprecations arose. Giorgio quickly fought his way to Simone and Gene.

"Grab her other arm, and let's move," Gene ordered Giorgio. As she was pulled towards the building entrance by her two

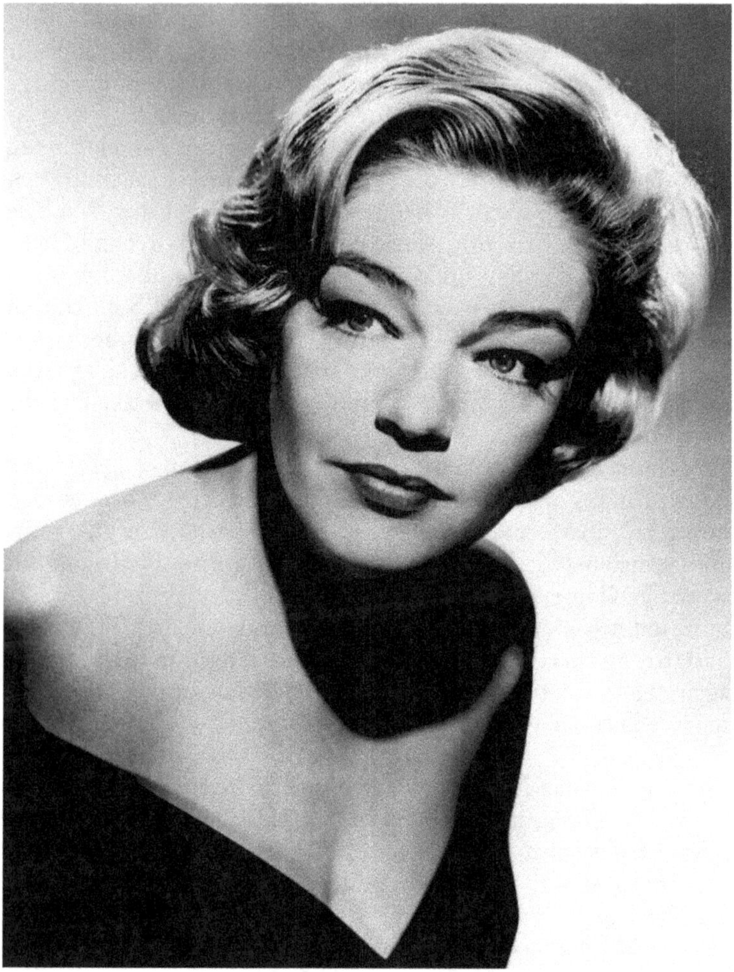

Simone Signoret

chevaliers, Simone was actually smiling. "Madame Signoret, please. Simone, *cherie*, please stop for just one moment! I have children to feed, please, Simone! *Un grande sorriso, per favore! Per favore! Nel nome del Dio*, give us a break! *Per favore!* Please! *Vi prego! S'il vous plait! Je vous prie!*"

Snap, click, push, shove, elbow. Questions. Stupid, ridiculous, banal questions for millions of lustful readers who, in fact, if present, would ask the same stupid, ridiculous banal questions.

"Have you met Miss Monroe? Do you call her Marilyn? Did you talk about men? Did she tell you who her ideal man was? Is it Arthur Miller? Did she talk about her love affairs? Who do you consider more beautiful, Brigitte Bardot? Gina Lollobrigida? Or Marilyn? How would you describe Marilyn's sex appeal? How would your husband describe it? Do you think *Let's Make Love* is the perfect title for a Monroe-Montand film? If you had produced the picture, what title would *you* give it?"

"BAISEZ-LA!" Simone seemed to mutter under her breath in response. And what she was thinking as the smile remained frozen on her countenance was an expression of similar nature directed at the whole lot.

Cocktailus Romanus: a type of social event with its international potpourri of guests only possible in Rome of 1960 A.D. Appropriately referred to by Italians as "the cocktail" (*il coctél*), the adjective twisted into noun. It possesses a distinct but undefinable flavor, sweet but pungent, brewed over centuries. It requires behavioral techniques substantially different from Manhattan, Hollywood or London counterparts, examples of which follow:

Don't expect to be introduced to anyone, sometimes not even to your host.

Don't feel under any obligation to greet the guests of honor, even if they greet you.

If anyone with a title is present (there will always be someone), look upon them as you would survivors of the plague and make servility proof of your superiority.

Don't ever be so gauchely American as to ask what a person does, since so many people do nothing, or will consider your question a reference to sexual habits rather than professional activity.

Don't bother to remember anybody's name, but be sure everybody remembers *yours*, as well as your private telephone number.

If you deign to converse, be sure that what you're saying is loud enough to be overheard, or so whispered that others cease their stinging *repartée* to listen.

If there is background music, sway or dance to it in a trance as if there's no one there to watch.

It is *de rigueur* to exaggerate everything, including oblivion.

Eye all guests indiscriminately as if possessed with an unbearable passion to know them, but once you arouse their interest, turn frigidly away, disgusted by their ill-educated vulgarity.

If you already know someone, be sure your greeting is so thunderous that no one will imagine you had just seen one another in the office (or in bed) just a few hours ago.

If you are talking with a member of the opposite sex, be sure that your intimate posture implies that you are lovers of long duration, or as recent as this afternoon's siesta.

If your interest is excited by someone of your same sex, decide whether circuitous discretion or piquant bluntness will guarantee lascivious acrobatics as soon as you both can indecently get away.

And if you're married, be sure it makes no difference.

Under no circumstances be so vulgar as to use ashtrays. Your hosts have thoughtfully provided you with gleaming marble floors and precious oriental rugs on which to squash your cigarette butts.

The early-bird guests began to arrive, their underlined purpose, carefully camouflaged by an array of excuses, to be the first to attack the food. Hank greeted them, presented them to Aldrich, then moved on to the next arrivals. When Simone, accompanied by Gene and Conti, at last made her entrance, all movement and chatter ceased. Aldrich slapped his thigh, stretched out his arms, bent over as if ready for a huddle, boomed out, "Simone! Upwards and onwards with the arts," simultaneously lifting his arm in a "V for Victory" salute.

"Bob! Dear, dear Bob. Your flowers were so beautiful!" The two Kaufman-Lerner clients embraced warmly. Simone kissed Hank. "And yours and Gene's were absolutely exquisite," she said to him. Aldrich put his arm around Gene and threw a rhetorical "Any laughs today?" at Conti.

"How did it go?" asked Hank.

"No fatalities," replied Giorgio with a weak smile.

"And thank God we're here," Simone added and acknowledged the first guests with a nod and smile before waving at photographer Frontoni, attended by his tight-jeaned macho assistant. Three Rosati waiters, with appropriate bows, surrounded the French star with their trays of drinks. Simone made her selection as Hank lit her cigarette. Simone and Bob at once moved into an animated conversation on life, work and each other, knowing that their opportunity for privacy would be brief.

All eyes were focused on the honored couple, all ears attuned to whispered comments about them. Frontoni, aided by his traveling-eyed assistant, rapidly took several shots of actress and director, while flooding Hank and Gene with a cascade of intimate gossip, accompanied by holy rolling of his huge blue eyes and lascivious gestures, as if what he was recounting to his hosts was so depraved it would drive even the Marquis de Sade to the confessional.

The unique and eclectic potpourri of international party-comers, which could appear only in Rome at that particular moment in its history, were now arriving in greater numbers – a constellation of star-faces seen by millions on the movie screens of the world; Italian nobility of various gradations of blue blood; movie moguls, powerful in fact and powerful by imagination; government officials, gracious and pompous; directors from Hollywood, Italy, France, Greece, England and Sweden; representatives of the jet set; fashion designers, cameramen, doctors, tailors, seers and masseurs, and other fellow travelers of the great and near-great, including spouses, siblings, offspring, lovers, mistresses, gigolos and call-girls, three dogs, one gibbon and a cockatoo.

They came in alone, in twos, in groups. As the minutes passed rapidly, they seemed an unbroken flow. Languages in babble. Movement to and fro. Retreat from here to there. Advance from there to here. Scrutiny. Such affectionate embraces and such superficial kisses. Simone's and Bob's privacy was doomed as a shifting cluster surrounded the two famed refugees, the noted actress from Paris, the important director from Hollywood.

"How exciting. Two such fabulous talents as you, together. Where will you be shooting? Can't you find some way to do it in Rome? What's *Now We Know* about? Who is your co-star? When do you start? Marvelous! Fantastic! Thrilling! Fabulous! Sensational! It'll be a smash. How can you lose with a Signoret-Aldrich combination? Just great! Absolutely unbeatable!" The crowd seeking privileged contact with the guests of honor changed. It was now so large that it was pressed into wall-to-wall tightness, with decibel count to match. What any of the invitees thought or vulturously whispered to one another was insufficiently articulated to be overheard. Whereas Monroe, Montand and *Let's Make Love*, as title both for fiction and fact, hovered over the jabber and the noise, no one was indelicate enough to mention the names or make any reference to the major international scandal which Simone, by her presence, was vicariously sharing with them.

By 9:30, Conti had disappeared with enough notes to prepare his promised press release. Fifteen minutes later, Frontoni exited, leaving behind his assistant, whose new career as an actor was assured by a director noted equally for lechery and impotency.

Kaufman and Lerner left a party moving in high gear. They tried to be everywhere at once. The myriad guests, their tongues and morals more relaxed by alcohol, removed masks and dropped fronts, stimulated by the growing excitement, their self-importance enhanced by contact with importance. The supply of liquor, however, was still ahead of the demand, since per capita consumption at a Roman party is less than a similar "do" in London, Paris, Moscow, Beverly Hills, New York or any average American town. On the other hand, the buffet table looked like the Visigoth sack of Rome.

Shortly after midnight, the last of the guests had drifted off to their various habitats, or on to Roman nightspots to continue their revelry. Plans having been made for the next day, the moment for "good night" between an exhausted Signoret, Aldrich, Kaufman and Lerner had arrived. Simone was relieved, almost radiant, as she hugged and kissed her hosts and agents. And she was moved. "I'm glad it's over. At first, it was an ordeal. Then I found myself enjoying it. And everybody was so unbelievably discreet, weren't they, Bob?"

"But *amazza*, what were they thinking?" countered Bob, his jowls a bowl of Jello as he emphasized his point with vigorous shakes of his head.

"It was a great party. Simply great. I have to hand it to you guys."

"It was," underlined Simone. She squeezed one of Hank's and one of Gene's hands in hers. "*Merci, mes chers amis. Merci mille, mille fois*. And really, we should try to make the picture."

"Do the three of you want to know why we *can't* make *Now We Know*?" asked Aldrich, the expression in his eyes centered between mischief and anger. There was a surprised flutter of "What do you mean?" from Simone, Gene and Hank.

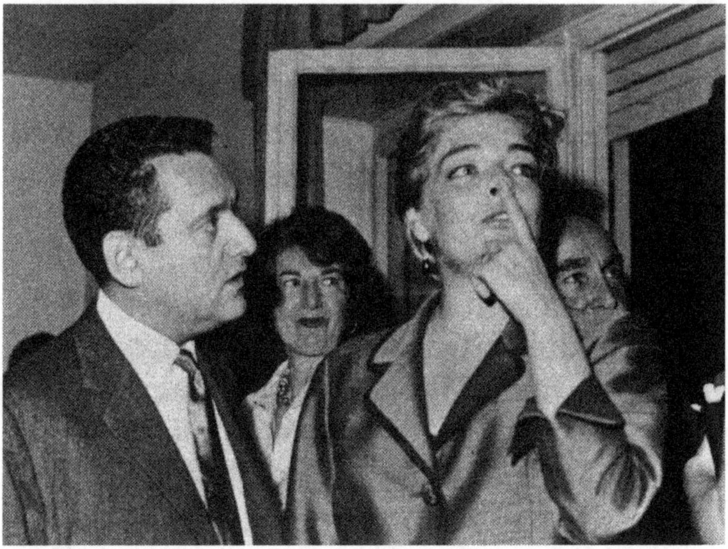

Gene Lerner and Simone Signoret

"*I don't have the rights any more*. That's why!"

"Oh, Bob," Simone responded with distress. "I'm so sorry!" She took the director's hand in hers. "Bob, dear, dear Bob."

Gene and Hank looked at one another, but it was Hank who spoke. Admiration and affection clearly showed in Hank's tone of voice.

"And you went through all this charade, knowing all the time it was just a ruse to help Simone?" he asked, his eyes fixed on Aldrich.

"The ploy worked, didn't it?" And as Bob took Simone's arm and moved towards the door, he lifted his hand in wave. His face was transformed by that smile that turned caricature into portrait as he said, "Anyway, fellas. That's show business!"

Gene, by nature the early bird, had already turned in. Hank sat alone in the salon, smoking his last cigarette before going to bed, his usual habit. He had just finished examining the guest book. Pretty goddamn impressive, he thought. Nearly two hundred and twenty representatives of the entertainment world from nineteen different countries were inscribed. If he started dropping names for Mom and Dad back in Dorchester, they would bounce back glittering with star-dust.

Mom and Dad back in Dorchester, both of them hitting 70. Time was racing. Yes, that's what he would do. He would bring them over and give them the time of their lives. Shuffling from house to house, how many insurance policies had Dad sold for Prudential in his lifetime? And Mom, stuck in stifling routine for more than forty years – home, shopping, cooking, the kids, Dad, the relatives, the synagogue. Did she ever have herself a real holiday? Or real pleasure?

Well, he would give them both a holiday and pleasures they would never forget. And eventually, he would bring over that lovely star of his boyhood revues, sister Estelle and her husband, Bill, and their now 14-year-old Joyce and 7-year-old Lisa.

Hank became euphoric over the idea. Why not bring over everyone he loved, including Gene's family? It had been great to have Jann, Gene's eldest sister, over earlier that year after the agony of her divorce and her problems of adjustment. To see her so revitalized, so joyous over Italy, so delighted at being fussed over by Marion and many of his and Gene's friends, had been heartwarming. Yes, he would tell Gene in the morning. They would bring over every one of the Lerners, too.

He was suddenly suffocated by a profound wave of sadness, feeling the tears accumulating in his eyelids. No, not every one of the Lerners. Not Slavic-faced, light-skinned, blue-eyed Mama Lerner. Not that unbelievable woman, who, at 75, would have become a wondrous child, running and skipping, breathless and wide-eyed, as she absorbed Italy as an ode of incomparable splendor. She would have merged her extraordinary sensibilities with fields and mountains, seas and cities, and above all, with the people, the people, the people. Hank stiffened, entranced by a picture of Mama Lerner with Anna Magnani. How they would have understood one another, the two together a universe encompassing the pain of life.

Every one of the Lerners, but not Mama Lerner. Fleshless, spirit and heart pure and lyric, she had died of cancer four years earlier.

Hank walked out on the terrace to shake off the sorrow. He stood musing in silence as he breathed in the night air. What roads did their assorted guests travel to reach the destination of his and Gene's fifth-floor apartment on Via Salaria 290, Rome, Italy, on that particular evening, he wondered? And how did Gene and he get there?

How could two people be so different? Outside of Gene's and his mutual passion for the arts, their dedication to work and a pleasure in reading, he and Gene pointed in opposite directions on the compass of character.

He was gregarious, greatly interested in clothes and possessions, totally uninterested in sports, had a take-them-or-leave-them attitude towards children and an immense talent for décor. He enjoyed the parties, the visits to the studios, the entire film ambience, had cyclonic tempers that disappeared as swiftly as they came, and had an incessant love affair with the telephone.

On the other hand, Gene was introverted with flashes of extroversion, uninterested in clothes and possessions, had a fanatical interest in sports, an adoration for children, a philosophic, legalistic turn of mind, cared little about ambience, whether home or film, normally avoided partying, hated studio visits, was slow to anger that, when it came, was shooting flame from eyes and icicles dripping from reined-in voice, and looked upon the telephone as an inevitable social disease.

We make a really terrific team – yessireee, we do, Hank pridefully said to himself, a firm shake of his head providing the exclamation point.

The image of Signoret and Aldrich became fixed in his mind. Once again Hank saw Bob take Simone's arm and the two of them moving towards the door. Once again, he saw Bob flashing his irresistible sunrise smile. Once again, he heard Bob saying, "Well, fellas, that's show business."

As Hank stood on his terrace in the middle of the glittering Roman night, he kept remembering and remembering and remembering. In the star-studded distance, he was seeing a parade of events, jumbled like bits and pieces of reels out of sequence. Unconsciously, he began to sing Irving Berlin's "There's No Business Like Show Business."

He was exhilarated by the embrace of recall and the caress of the future and felt both great and grateful.

Five

The Latin Lover: Myth and Matrimony

January 1952. Ilya Lopert, independent producer and foreign film distributor, accompanied by David Lean, the great English director of *Great Expectations*, *Brief Encounter* and *The Bridge on the River Kwai*, had come to Rome to prepare for the shooting of *Summertime*, adapted by Arthur Laurents from his Broadway hit *The Time of the Cuckoo*. Lean and Lopert had decided to film the entire production, exteriors and interiors, in Venice. They envisioned the exotic city as a major protagonist, together with Katharine Hepburn, who had been set for the role that Shirley Booth had so vividly brought to life on the Broadway stage.

A third protagonist was required, the actor to portray Renato, the married Venetian antique dealer. Lean and Lopert felt that the film version required a younger, more attractive actor than the little-known Italian stage actor Dino Di Luca, who had appeared on Broadway opposite Miss Booth. They were anxious to find someone, ideally with an international reputation, with the ability and personality to meet magnificent Kate's histrionic level and, in tandem with her, enhance the romance and power of the love story. The search for a Renato was the principal reason for the Lopert-Lean visit to Rome.

Once knowing of their presence, Gene wasted no opportunity in trying to reach Lopert or Lean to ascertain their casting requirements. They never seemed available for his continual phone calls. Armed with photo albums and KL's precious card catalog of actors, Gene found Lopert in the lobby of the Hotel Excelsior. A burly, gruff, impatient man, Lopert's external characteristics did not overshadow his intuitive artistic sensitivity and mercurial sentimental nature. When Gene cornered the producer, he was not exactly cordial, and nor did he express much affection for agents.

"I never heard of Kaufman-Lerner Associates," he said with a snarl.

"We're new," replied Gene. "But we're the best office here, with the most complete list of English-speaking performers available in this area."

"You know the story?" he asked in his thick, Eastern European accent.

"Of course. I've read the play and I saw it with Hank Kaufman – he's my partner – twice. It's such a beaut. And shooting it all in Venice. It'll be marvelous. You know, I discovered Hepburn..."

Lopert looked at Gene with curled lip. "You... what?"

"In 1933, I was a kid visiting relatives in Des Moines, Iowa. I went to see *Morning Glory.* And there she was! I went back home to Omaha and all I did was think, dream and talk Hepburn, Hepburn, Hepburn."

"Enough bullshit. The story of your life, I don't need to know. What casting problems I have I can put in one word. Renato. You got a Renato for us?"

"We'll get you a Renato," Gene said with an assurance he didn't feel. The faces of all kinds of actors began parading rapidly through his mind. "But can't I read a script, so I know how he's treated in the film version?" Gene asked, his mind frantically at work.

"No scripts, no scripts. Nobody reads a script."

"Then why don't I meet Mr. Lean and hear his ideas on the character?"

"What for you do have to meet Lean? Have you got a Renato? Have you not got a Renato?" Lopert asked gruffly.

All of the racing images in Gene's mind merged into one.

Rossano Brazzi!

Of course, Rossano Brazzi! But before mentioning the name, he had to get a line on Lopert's thinking. "If you would be patient enough to tell me exactly how you see the character it would help me, Mr. Lopert."

"It's easier if I tell you exactly how we *don't* see the character," he replied. "De Sica, out. Too much mannerism and his English stinks. Vittorio Gassman, out. No simplicity, no romance from the gut and he looks too young for Hepburn. Amadeo Nazzari, out. Ham. Old-fashioned. Gino Cervi, out. Too old. Physically wrong. Too much *Cyrano de Bergerac.* Gabriele Ferzetti, out. He's not romantic enough. Hasn't got the spark and here again no speekee di English. There's nobody else here."

Oh, yes there is, dear Lopert, Gene said to himself in excitement. Yes, yes, yes there is! Rossano Brazzi's his name, dear Lopert. But how in hell do I lay my hands on him when he's not a client, Gene asked himself, feeling glum.

"So we've pretty much decided we cast on the coast. Fernando Lamas, maybe. Or Ricardo Montalban. One Latin's as good as another."

"You don't really believe that, sir."

"Listen, Mr. Werner, Lerner, whatever your name is, I got no time to waste. You say you got me a Renato. Lean and me, we've gone over every Italian in the country. So who's your miracle?"

Gene had to get to Brazzi for an authorization of representation. He had to gain time. "Mr. Lopert, Kaufman and I are serious people. You and Mr. Lean have a serious problem. I assure you Hank and I have a solution. Will you kindly see me tonight? Anytime you say."

Just then a bellhop came up to Lopert. Mr. Lean was on the phone. Lopert rose immediately.

"Listen. I haven't got no time for nonsense. You got a Renato? Tell me right now. I'll be back in a minute and I want to know who you got in mind." And with that ultimatum, Lopert went off to take Lean's call.

Gene had several photos of Brazzi in the KLA albums, even though he was not a client. The photos were old and not at all flattering. Hank and he had made incessant efforts to sign Brazzi, but the guy was slippery. Rossano was notorious in his dealings with agents. The principle of exclusivity was anathema to him, as several outfoxed agents and a considerable number of females could have testified. Even when an agent was responsible for opening up a possibility, the actor somehow found a way to avoid paying the justified commission. He always put the blame on his wife, Lidia. It was Lidia who handled all his business. Talk to Lidia, she would straighten everything out. But Lidia then looked at you in surprise. She knew absolutely nothing about anything. It was always very friendly, very civilized, very sympathetic and very futile.

So Gene was stuck. He realized that he would have to take his chances. Knowing the play and the character, he felt certain Brazzi was the ideal choice and would make just the right chemistry with Hepburn. So if Brazzi got the part and then behaved like a shit, there at least would be the satisfaction that

KLA had shown good judgment and instincts, and in the long run that had to pay off. Satisfaction? Hell, that was just face-saving rationalization which put no money in the bank.

As Lopert reappeared and fell back into his chair, Gene had made up his mind. "Well?" Lopert asked, no-nonsense on his face. "Renato or no Renato?"

"He's got everything you want for the part. He'll be sensational. Rossano Brazzi."

Lopert looked at Gene with a Jesus-in-Heaven expression on his face.

"You're maybe the twentieth person who tells me Brazzi. I'm so sick of his name I didn't mention it. And don't *you*! Everybody's selling him. Whose client is he anyway? Anyway, he's wrong. Couldn't be more wrong. Physically? Nothing to brag about. He's too pretty. Too soft. He's got no balls. Hepburn will make pizza pie out of him. Renato's got to make everybody in that audience feel he's got real strength. He's a man! He's got to give you the feeling that he's got what it takes to stay on top of Jane – if you'll excuse the expression."

He shook his head firmly, that lip of his curling. "Brazzi. The poor *schlemiel* can't act. Hopeless. David and I, we've seen film on him. *Vulcano*, *Three Coins in the Fountain*, rushes from *The Barefoot Contessa* that the local United Artists people put together. He hasn't got it. What ain't there, ain't there! Out, out, out, Brazzi, and out, out, out, you!"

The local United Artists people. That said a lot to Gene. As usual, Rossano had been bad-mouthed and ridiculed by the local distributor and, for that matter, almost everybody in Italian cinema. "So effete. Too mannered. So old-fashioned. He's had his day. Times have changed. A ham." These reactions certainly contributed to Lopert's and Lean's prejudicial attitude. It was the same story on *Three Coins in the Fountain* and *The Barefoot Contessa*, and it would be no different in the future. The Italian film industry found the growing international interest in Brazzi totally incomprehensible. Whenever an American major company was to select him for a picture, its Italian distributing arm shuddered. The Rome authority for the Hollywood picture firm claimed he was a kiss of death, the proverbial box office poison.

Anyone with sufficient memory will recall how the American industry tried to kill Katharine Hepburn in the same way. She

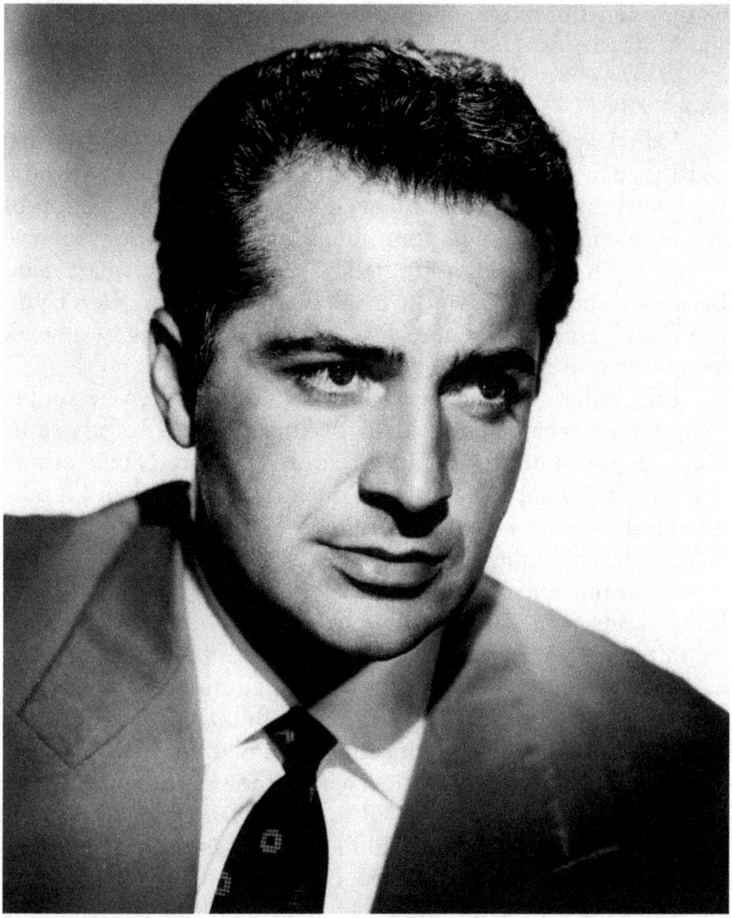

Rossano Brazzi

too was proclaimed the kiss of death years ago, she, too, was, considered box office poison. Yet in the 1950s, there she is, glittering, smiling through her trembling tears, one of the world's greatest stars.

"Okay, Mr. Lopert. You feel that way," Gene said. "But you're in trouble. How can you miss any possibility, no matter how small? Won't you and Mr. Lean at least meet him?"

"You got any photos?"

Gene wished the question had never been asked. "They're no good. The ones I've got are way out of date. I'll get you some better ones. But what good will the photos do? Why don't you and Mr. Lean just meet him?"

"Listen, we didn't come here to socialize. Or waste our time."

"Mr. Lopert, please. Give me a hearing. I know the story and I love it. I know the role. Thanks to you, I now know how you and Lean feel it should be cast. Give me the satisfaction of making a contribution to your film. I know Brazzi. See him face to face. Talk to him. Let him talk to you. You're a smart man. Lean's a director who works magic with his actors. Won't you and he at least see the man? Give him a break. It may be a break for your picture too."

Lopert listened, his eyes slits, pondering. Then he spoke. "I'll tell you what I'll do. I'll waste fifteen minutes of my time, not a second more. But I'm not going to waste David's time. If the miracle happens and I like the man enough, then I'll take it from there with David." Gene kept the expression on his face matter-of-fact, hiding his elation.

"You tell him to come here to the lobby tonight at ten," Lopert continued. "And absolutely no *mishspoche*. Brazzi alone. I don't even want you or your partner, Kaufman – is that the name? No offense, but that's the way it's got to be."

Gene and Hank managed to corral Brazzi by three o'clock that same afternoon. Their meeting took place in the bar of the Hotel de la Ville on Via Sistina, across the street from the tiny flat at Number 87 that belonged to Lidia's father, Signor Pietro, a scholarly gentleman of the old Florentine school, and in which Lidia's brother Roberto also lived. Besides Signor Pietro, Roberto and the Brazzis, the minute-sized apartment housed Irma, the ever-faithful Tuscan cook housekeeper, and Lidia's three toy poodles that, in Lidia's mind, were the three most precious creatures the Lord in his wisdom had over created. Neither Hank nor Gene had ever seen the flat. No one they knew had set foot in it. Brazzi always made a point of holding his meetings in some first-class hotel lobby. He was anxious not to reveal how he and Lidia were forced to live, nor how broke and heavily in debt they were.

When Gene started by explaining to him the encounter with Lopert, Rossano reacted eagerly. Gene then raised the matter of authorized representation, at least on the one picture. Rossano agreed instantaneously. "I give you what you want. Ten percent. Twenty percent. Thirty. What you want. If I get the part, you have me forever," he responded expansively.

"Ten percent, Rossano," Hank said. "That's our fixed policy. But we do have your *absolute* assurance that we're your agents on at least *this* deal?"

Rossano's smile was wide, his eyes sincerity incarnate. "Of course, no question. If you want, we put in in writing. You have my word. I swear on my mother's head." He lifted his hand in oath.

Furtively, Hank and Gene glanced at one another. Could there be anything more binding in Italy than an oath on a mother? Though the suspicion passed through their minds that Brazzi might have crossed the fingers of his invisible hand, Hank and Gene felt they had no choice but to trust the actor.

"What we really want is an exclusive worldwide representational contract with you," said Hank, looking at Rossano as if there was nothing more he wanted in the world.

"Why not? If you get me *Summertime*, I already told you, we sign up for life," replied Brazzi, looking at Hank as if there was nothing more he wanted in the world.

"Okay, Rossano, listen very carefully," commenced Gene. "Everybody's talked against you. Lopert and Lean have seen film on you from *Vulcano* and *Three Coins in the Fountain*. Mankiewicz even showed them some rushes from *The Barefoot Contessa*, and they weren't impressed..."

"Do they know I got more than seventy thousand, eighty thousand fan letters only from America from *Three Coins in the Fountain*?" Brazzi interrupted defensively. "I had to rent the biggest garage in Rome just for those letters. Tell them to come over and see."

"Okay, okay," Gene went on. "Anyway, they were definitely not impressed by what they saw and what people say about you. And I didn't dare show the photos we have of you. They're so outdated. They're not really you anymore. You've got everything against you, except maybe three things. They've got a start-date with Hepburn, so they're desperate. You happen to be Italian, you speak English, and knowing Lean, he'll do everything he can to bring authenticity to the picture. The third thing in your favor is that Hank and I know the play inside out and *we* know you're absolutely the best choice. But let me tell you right now, you're not going to get it unless you prepare yourself for Lopert. You've got to handle yourself perfectly, or you'll lose it."

"What have I got to do?" queried Rossano, mystified.

"I'll tell you," said Hank. "You've got to be as natural, sincere, relaxed and underplayed as you've ever been in your life. Let your strength come out of your quietness. The Gary Cooper touch. Be reserved. Cut the usual charm shit to the bone."

Rossano, while listening to Hank, was clearly not thrilled with the criticism of his personality.

"Let your warmth come through your quiet authority," Hank continued, unperturbed. "No softness. No boyishness. Avoid being ponderous. They haven't seen you in person with that beautiful premature gray at your temples. You've now got some maturity in your face, with very expressive little lines you've never had before. Be your age and be simple. When you walk in, you're just you, natural you, real you, new you. Be a surprise. That's the key: surprise. Let them discover a you they're not expecting. Do you understand?"

Brazzi had concentrated, seemingly more and more impressed by Hank's counsel. He seemed convinced that Hank had really analyzed the situation. "Yes. Very well."

"We should tell him something about the story and the role, don't you think?" Hank asked Gene. "Rossano's got to impress Lopert with his understanding of the role, like he's studied the story and really gets its implications." Gene nodded in agreement. "That's Gene's department," Hank said to Brazzi. Rossano turned towards Gene, the anxious actor concentrating on instructions as if from his director.

"Jane – that's Katharine Hepburn's part – represents the longings of all women who have never experienced love. She aches not just for sex, but for the meaningful sex which only comes through love," began Gene. "She comes to Venice for such love and yet is frightened of it. When or if it comes, will it be real? Will it be false? Will it really be the fulfillment of the dream which torments her? This spinster schoolteacher on holiday thinks about the love she wants. She talks and talks about it. But when she is finally faced with it through Renato, she shrinks from it. It isn't clear. It isn't perfect. It has its complications. She's confused, bewildered. That wasn't the way she dreamt it. You've met many of these American women here in Italy, Rossano."

Brazzi closed his eyes, nodded his head up and down several times, his smile saying, "Have I ever!"

"Renato is a normal Italian man, an ordinary Venetian shopkeeper selling antiques," Gene went on. "He's married. He cares about his wife and dearly loves his son. He and his wife were married young and have lost their passion. There's nothing special which sets him apart from thousands of other Italian men. He's warm by nature. He has his charm which is valuable to him in dealing with customers in his shop. He is both simple and sophisticated, as Latins can be. He's sincere but he's also realistic. He's also missed something in his life. The lightning strikes. The memorable romance. Being realistic, he doesn't ever expect it to happen, especially at his age, but that still doesn't stop his daydreaming.

"So when Jane and Renato meet so casually in the shop, it suddenly isn't casual at all. He's really strongly attracted to her. It's her freshness. That wonderfully candid quality Anglo-Saxon women have which awakens Latin men. She does the unexpected. She's filled with surprises. She's intelligent. She's cultured. She adores Italy and Venice. And you can smell her loneliness clinging to her like a faded fragrance. Renato falls in love with her. Jane falls in love with him."

Gene was being carried away by his summation of the story. Hank was envisioning the scenes on the stage between Shirley Booth and Dino Di Luca. By merely sitting there and absorbing, Brazzi seemed to be turning into the character of Renato.

"Still, Jane can't help but suspect Renato's motives," Gene proceeded. "How can he love her for herself? How can he love a spinster and, in her mind, an unattractive woman like her? Then comes the brutal shock. He is married. He's not free, at least not how her dream would define 'free.' So she is betrayed, the love she feels is betrayed. She's in terrible agony. And so is Renato. He fights with all his romantic instinct, all his acceptance of life's actuality, to make Jane understand that love is love. Whether ideal or mired in realities, love is still love. In passionate anger, he cries out at her, 'Take love, don't talk it!' And she does, and it's absolutely glorious. But it is a situation without solution. Jane's summer holiday is over. She sadly prepares her baggage. She will never see him again. Her heart is broken. And yet, she knows, he knows, that life has given them something more, something unexpected, something for always."

Silence greeted his summary of the basic story of *Summertime.* Rossano seemed to have seen it all, felt it all. He sat looking into space. Both Hank's and Gene's eyes were on him. "Take love, don't talk it! That's very good," he said. He then mouthed the words silently, savoring them. "And that's the theme of the story," he finally said. "The whole point of life is love. There's no other point.

"Love transcends borders, oceans, languages, religion, race, politics." He turned towards Hank and Gene, smiling. "Maybe it's not very original to say, but it's love that keeps the world going round and round. If we must have wars, let there only be battles of the sexes, eh? Ah, if only love and lovers could rule this Earth of ours." He rose, took Hank's and Gene's hands in his own, and shook them in a strong grip. "You're such wonderful people. I feel it here, right here in my heart."

"It's up to you now, Rossano," said Hank. "Call us when you finish. It doesn't matter how late. Any time in the night is okay. We'll be dying to know how it turns out."

"Of course. I'll call you immediately," replied Rossano, still gripping Hank's and Gene's hands. "Now I understand everything. You can be sure I'll do my best."

"*In bocca al lupo!*" Hank called out to Brazzi. "In the mouth of the wolf," an ancient Roman expression of good luck which is simultaneously an entreaty to the fates to get in there and push. Brazzi turned, smiled, waved back. "*In bocca al lupo*," he repeated.

Eleven o'clock. Midnight. Nothing. One o'clock, two o'clock, no telephone ring and no sleep for Hank and Gene. They played records but didn't hear the music. The next morning, they phoned Brazzi's flat. Irma said he and the Signora had gone out early, she didn't know where and didn't know when they would return. They tried Lopert. His secretary at the Excelsior said he was involved with screenings all day and wasn't available. They kept phoning Brazzi, then Lopert, through the day. Neither was available or findable. And all 260-plus pounds of Lidia had vanished.

Hank and Gene were in despair. They tried to make different excuses to one another rather than voice the growing suspicion that Brazzi might after all be getting the part and that Kaufman-Lerner was being bypassed. They decided to take a chance. That night they "happened" to be going by the Excelsior.

They "happened" to walk into the lobby. And in the far corner, they saw a very chummy trio – Ilya Lopert, David Lean and... Rossano. The two partners were too angry at themselves, too humiliated to confront them. Licking their wounds and swearing on their dear mother's head that there would never be an ever again, they left unseen.

Brazzi got the role. Brazzi made the film. His fading career was renewed and an international star was born. What matter if KLA was not permitted to enter the negotiations? What matter if they got cheated out of their rightfully earned compensation?

It mattered. Boy, did it matter.

K and L made deals for Isa Miranda to play the owner of the *pensione* in which Jane was staying and for a Neapolitan youth, Marietto, who was exactly what Lean was looking for to play the Venetian *scugnizzo.* Marietto was later to be seen with Sophia Loren and Clark Gable in *It Happened in Naples.* After that, he was never seen again, having grown out of a movie career.

Hank and Gene had continuous reports on the shooting, centered in the film studios on the Venetian island of Giudecca. The schedule was long. Lean was a meticulous director. Every detail, every take, had to meet his uncompromising standards. He was dazzled by the choice of fairytale location sites in and around Venice.

In interviews Brazzi gave, he spoke of how well he and Hepburn were hitting it off. Upon completion of the film, he declared: "For me, she is the greatest woman I have ever known. Hepburn's beauty is not classic or obvious. It is a glow of womanliness. From every pore, electricity pours out. She has been a wonderful partner and a good friend, a friend one is always in danger of falling in love with. She has all the exciting qualities that set American women apart. I find her irresistible with her sudden bursts of energy, her untiring capacity for work. That drive! That passion for perfection! She has perhaps been my best teacher of acting."

Word was rapidly passing through the fumes of vines and their winey produce that Brazzi had turned in the performance of his life, that he would be hailed as a sensational find, that he would be the new darling of audience ladies and leading ladies, the hot new boy in town. Rossano took no back seat in spreading the plaudits and predictions far and wide. He was great, he was fabulous, he was brilliant, he was sensa… well, all of those adjectives. The rumors, reports and reactions left Hank and Gene with mixed feelings, a churning stew of anger, frustration and depression.

It was late afternoon in early September of '54, not long after the *Summertime* shoot was completed. Hank and Gene were both busily at work at Via Aiaccio. The gate bell rang. Lidia's booming voice and the bark of her adorables announced her arrival long before the all-of-her was in sight. K and L were flabbergasted. Neither she nor Rossano had been seen or heard from for months. She had never set foot in KLA's office. She had made no appointment.

She kissed and embraced her two astonished receivers. She laughed uproariously and screamed commandingly at the poodles to behave. She then came to the point. "Look, Rossano, he waiting in the car. I wanted come in first. I can't stand it no more. I don' want no more responsibility. I can never believe word he say. All the time, he lie. He don' even know he lie, but he lie. Things are happening. Big, important things. He just marrrr-ve-lusss in the picture. Fabuuu-luusss. I don' want he make any more mistake. We make enough mistake for hundred year. You good boys, people can trust, and thassa good. You Americani and thassa good. Everybody say you know your job, you try hard, you honest. Thassa good. I got very good feelin' 'bout you inside. Thassa good. If we don' make good future now, we never have future. I'm no stupid. I know! I ready to put him in your hands. I don' want to do nothin', I don' want know nothin'. I want put him all in your hands. If you agree, you got ta make me one promise and you gotta keep it. You gotta all the time tell me the truth. I got to know all the truth. Now what you say to me?"

Hank spoke first. "Is Rossano ready to sign a contract with us?"

"He do what I say."

"An exclusive, worldwide contract?" Hank added.

"He sign what I say."

"For three years?" Hank continued.

"He sign for how long you want, it you want him. We pay you ten percent, thassa right?"

"That's right," said Gene.

"You want him to come in? He a little embarrassed, I don' know why. If you want him to come in, I go call him," Lidia declared.

"Call him," said Hank as he glanced at Gene.

Her "Rooooooooo-sssss-aaaaa-nnnnn-ooooo" could have been heard as far as Hollywood. The poodles began barking again. "Shurrup! Behave!" Lidia ordered.

In a moment, Rossano appeared, his entrance portraying sheepishness and apology. In a flash, everything changed. He was all booming voice, outspread arms, a smile from sun-up to sun-down, his vocal chords all wonderful baritone vibrato. The hugs and the cheek-to-cheek kisses between him and Gene, him and Hank, Lidia with Gene, Lidia with Hank, were those which could only come from eternal love.

"I wanted Lidia to come in alone. I wanted her to be convinced," he said with steaming sincerity. "I'm so relieved. Thanks to God, I won't have this idiot woman in my hair."

"*You* the idiot," she retorted. She turned to K and L. "You don't know the trouble he give to me. You boys watch him. Every minute, every step. I'm awarnin' you. He got be watched even when he go make peepee."

"Lidia, shut up."

"*You* shurrup."

"You know what this woman does? She takes every lire. She doesn't even give me money for cigarettes. I'm the one who make the money, I tell her."

"And I'm the one who spend it," Lilia interrupted with a burst of laughter.

"She'll kill me. Shut up!"

"Shut up you! He always, talk. Talk, talk, talk," complained Lidia. "You explain something confidential, he gotta keep quiet, he keep so quiet he only call everybody in his phone agenda, from 'A' to 'Zeta.' You tell her somethin' gotta be secret, he swear on his poor mamma's head he tell to nobody. For secret, you can trust him assolutely – to tell it as fast he can on the radio or to all the newspaper." She turned to her husband. "You got to shurrup. You gotta learn not to speak," she said vehemently. She then addressed Hank and Gene. "He don' know how to say no to anybody or to any proposition anybody make to him. He lucky he not a woman. He don' know how say no. He all time

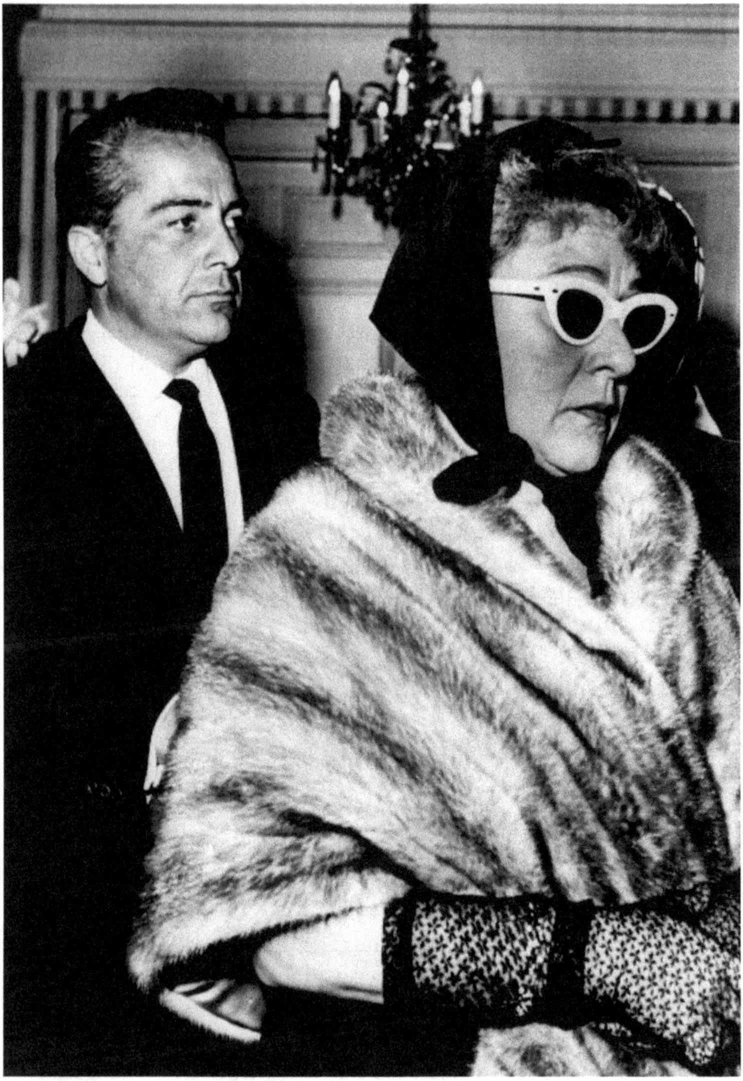

Rossano Brazzi and his wife Lidia

be pregnant. He make more *bambini* than in all the streets of Napoli."

"Shut up, you!" hissed Rossano, as if ready to strike her.

"Shurrup you!" she retorted, turned her back on him, lifted her skirt to show him her ample rear.

Gene leapt into the moment of truce.

"Rossano," he stated, "you're going to have to sign a representational agreement. Exclusive, worldwide, for three years. Automatically renewable for another three years, if neither party cancels."

"Anything you say. Anything you want," was Rossano's reply.

"All your earnings come to our office," said Hank. "We deduct our ten percent and you get the rest. You'll get monthly accountings."

"You give to *me* the money, you give to *him* the accountings," Lidia said.

"Lidia, shut up!" said Rossano, rolling his eyes in disgust.

"Shurrup you."

"Whatever you say," Brazzi repeated to Hank and Gene. "I only want peace! PEACE!" he shouted. "I don't want no worries. I want you boys to handle everything. All I want is to act. I'm an actor. That's my job. I don't want to worry about any other job."

"Rossano, you're sure you understand what we require?" Gene underlined. KLA could not have any more slip-ups.

"I told you anything, anything you want," Rossano answered, his hurt obvious. "I come tomorrow and sign, two o'clock, three o'clock, whenever you say. I swear on my mother's head. You come too, eh, Lidia?"

"Of course."

They arrived at three o'clock the next afternoon, and with Lidia as witness, Brazzi – bless every white hair of his mother's head – signed. And when he married himself to Hank and Gene, a profound personal and professional relationship, one which was to endure for more than fifteen years, was established.

Brazzi was already an important Italian name during the Second World War. Born in Bologna (noted both for its splendid *cucina* as well as certain sexual proclivities) on September 16, 1916, while in his early 20s he had participated in a number of pictures which had their vogue both in Nazi Germany and Fascist Italy, the kind of intensely romantic melodramas which permitted everyone to escape political or party significance. He was never accused of pro-Nazi sympathies, though a number of other Italian actors were. Brazzi was perhaps the most apolitical actor in the business. Abhorring violence and brutality by nature, he shielded himself through every possible psychological device to the horrors he could not bring himself to confront.

He was by no means devoid of acting ability nor of a certain inner strength which would emerge if handed the right role and if working with the right director. Nevertheless, he was seen more as personality than actor, a type rather than an artist, cast as a passionate romantic or as heroic adventurer, a symbol with which housewives, maids, spinsters, sighing adolescents by the millions could identify. His vogue reached a climax in 1946 with *L'Aguila Nera*, which, as *The Black Eagle*, had earlier served Rudolph Valentino as a successful Hollywood vehicle. As a result of his growing popularity, Rossano was able to command fairly high sums for his services.

In 1948, David O. Selznick caught up with the picture. He watched, he raved, he signed. With a seven-year exclusive pact in his pocket, Rossano, 31 years old, accompanied of course by Lidia, sailed across the sea to the glorious new world and to a glorious international career.

The Selznick-Brazzi episode provided another sample of the unparalleled genius of Hollywood. Brazzi sat and sat. He practiced and practiced English. He waited and waited. And at last, in 1949, Selznick came up with the project for Rossano's American film debut. Was it another *Gone With the Wind*? Another *Farewell to Arms*? Another *Grand Hotel*? Selznick's enthusiasm, clout and inspiration unveiled an epic entitled... *Little Women*!

Elizabeth Taylor, Janet Leigh, June Allyson and Margaret O'Brien were the co-stars. And where in the cast was that exciting, handsome matinee idol which Selznick had ranted over as the male discovery of decades and, in a whirlpool of publicity, had imported from Italy? He was buried under a layer of beard, moustache, wig of whitened hair, steel-rimmed glasses, portraying the kind, soft-spoken, ersatz German-accented Professor Behr. Selznick managed to make him totally unrecognizable. To Rossano's credit, he performed the role with admirable technique, but his greatest fan was still his makeup man. After sitting idly for two years, discouraged by *Little Women*, he began to look upon Hollywood as a wasteland. He asked the great David O. to release him from his contract. Selznick agreed.

So in 1949, Rossano and Lidia sailed back across the Atlantic, leaving the glorious new world and the glorious international career behind. Lidia, Tuscan-born like her husband, was camouflaged by the legend of practicality. Her reality was the contrary. Extravagance was her thing and Rossano systematically indulged her. She adored money. She knew the word "gimmee" in every spoken language. She was a serious, dedicated collector of baubles. Diamonds, rubies, sapphires, pearls and other precious little things which were better if they were bigger. She had an addiction for gold and somehow discovered that the heavier the metal, the more fascinating it became.

Even before their departure for America, the Brazzis were living like tomorrow would last forever. In fact, living beyond their means was their way of life from the time they were married when Rossano was still a law student at the University of Firenze. His modest weekly Hollywood salary was always spent weeks before due. So, in his return to Italy, Rossano not only left beard, moustache, wig, glasses behind, but a number of considerable debts as well.

The return *in patria* turned into calamity. In the hope of recapturing his homeland popularity, Rossano, with Lidia's exuberant support, decided to risk everything by producing a film with his brother, Oscar, in which Rossano was of course the star. It was called *The Law's Barrier*, with Piero Costa directing. Debts rose into hundreds of millions of lire. All of Lidia's glittering collection of trinkets, with the exception of her wedding ring, found its way to the Monte de Pieta, the state-owned pawn shop. They had no choice but to return to the tiny overcrowded Via Sistina flat with Signor Pietro, Roberto, Ima and the three poodles, as Rossano tried desperately to find work.

He faced one cruel disappointment after another. The world success of the Italian neorealistic film resulted in a myriad of faded imitations of Vittorio de Sica and Roberto Rossellini. There never had been much interest in Brazzi, who was not considered to have the personality or style for the genre. When it came to pictures of romance or adventure, new names and younger faces had emerged. Older and lacking the body and hair that Italian producers considered "modern," he was no longer looked upon kindly for flashy action or costume movies. Worst of all, he had gone to Hollywood full of boast and bloat and returned in ignominy. Italians were cruelly unforgiving over returning prodigals who overseas hadn't cut the pasta or brought back valises packed with *soldi, soldi, soldi* – heavenly green and of large denomination.

It was brutal for Rossano. He was a proud man who loved his work and felt fulfilled, complete. He hated the morass of debt that became a tighter and tighter noose around his neck. Most of all, he saw no light in the future. With all of his twisting and turning to avoid truth and deny reality, he lived with the desperate feeling that at 33, he was finished. Even when he succeeded in getting sporadic engagements, the salary was small and often as not, he had to run around trying to discount the dubious value of the IOUs with which he was paid.

It was America that gave him new hope. Not the Hollywood of Los Angeles but the Hollywood of Rome, on the verge of exploding into Hollywood on the Tiber. Rossano's sojourn under contract to Selznick had achieved one vital result. He now spoke English effectively. That proved to be as precious an asset as Lidia's hocked jewels.

In 1950, William Dieterle, a Hollywood veteran, had been chosen to direct Anna Magnani in *Vulcano.* Dieterle had a vague idea of doing both an Italian and an English version. He had known Brazzi on the coast, felt he was right for the co-starring role opposite Magnani, and she agreed. The English-language version never became more than a vague idea.

Vulcano was Magnani's challenge to Rossellini and Ingrid Bergman and their film *Stromboli.* All of the sensationalism of the Magnani-Bergman rivalry over the personal and professional possession of Rossellini, all the scandal that surrounded the making of the two competitive films – it was a field day for the press and failed to make either of the two pictures a box office success. Through it all, however, Brazzi managed to prevent bill collectors, creditors and the tax police from putting Lidia and him, and possibly the poodles, behind bars. Brazzi managed this not because of his modest compensation on *Vulcano* but through the prestige of Magnani and the excitement over the fierce competition between the two pictures. He had an apparently valid argument against his creditors. Wasn't he once again moving up towards top earning power, he boasted? What greater prestige could one have than co-starring with Magnani, he boasted further? He happened to have boasted right.

After an agonizing hiatus of two years came 20th Century Fox's *Three Coins in the Fountain.* While his role was not a big one, the film provided Rossano with his first real international exposure as himself – without beard, wig and glasses, and speaking English. He made an impact on world audiences. Then, in 1953, came *The Barefoot Contessa.* Whereas his role was badly conceived by director/producer Joseph L. Mankiewiez, deprived of flesh and blood, the picture was nevertheless a plus for Rossano. He was in a film co-starring Ava Gardner and Humphrey Bogart, both at the height of their box office appeal, produced and directed by an industry idol considered to be incapable of failure.

The battle of economic survival and of fighting off the Italian equivalent of bailiffs continued ceaselessly. Attacked from all sides, the Brazzis fought back with promises, guile, assurances, pleas, *cambiale*-signing at usurious interest rates, and with any other weapon they could wield to stave off ruin. One enraged debtor, sick of Brazzi's fervent promises, fumed: "Brazzi never bothered with the dictionary to learn the definition of truth. Or if he did look, he couldn't find it. Or if he found it, he would have tried to convince me that it was a lie."

By the time *Summertime* had its New York premiere at the end of 1954, the Brazzis were more than $100,000 in debt. They hid their dreadful plight behind an amazingly optimistic front. Hank and Gene only found out the full truth when Rossano was securely placed on the road to world success by his personal triumph in David Lean's unforgettable, bitter-sweet romance.

A solemn pact was made between Brazzi and KLA that he was to do no film, unless of prestige and for greatly increased compensation, until *Summertime* was released in the States and had had its impact on both the public and the picture industry. This meant further tightening of whatever there was left for Rossano and Lidia to tighten.

It also meant the acceptance of Lopert's sacrilegious dictum that Lidia was not to accompany Rossano to New York for the American premiere and the promotional campaign to precede it. This provoked scenes, hysteria, crying. Lidia always traveled with her husband. Rossano at first seemed pleased. Then, as time went on, he became as bereft as she. Even though Lopert had developed an enormous affection for both of them, he remained adamant. Rossano had to project the maximally exciting Latin dream and legend. It was okay for him to have a wife, so long as she was a secret left five thousand miles behind in some kitchen. Lopert insisted that Lidia's presence would jeopardize the projection of the magnificent, sensual male incarnate which he wanted to present. K and L gave their full support to Lopert. It was they who finally brought both Rossano and Lidia to a reluctant acceptance of the producer's position.

The decision was then made that Gene would accompany Rossano and stay close to him during the personal appearance tour. But, Gene asked himself, what about the offers from the Hollywood studios that were sure to come? He felt capable of reading and analyzing scripts and evaluating roles but was insecure about those complex, ultramicroscopic employment contracts of as much as a hundred pages so customary in the American picture industry.

Gene and Hank fortunately had a dear friend in John F. Wharton, co-founder of the renowned New York law firm Paul, Weiss, Rifkind, Wharton & Garrison and one of the most influential lawyers of the era in the entertainment field. Gene wrote to Wharton, explaining his need to study, and asked whether a number of sample employment contracts the law firm had negotiated could be sent to Rome. John was quick to comply but, to protect confidentiality, had his secretary black out all references to the contracting parties in the agreements. Gene's nights and weekends were spent poring over pages and pages of legal tribalisms and fine print.

The personal appearance tour, limited to the eastern half of the United States, was a great success. So were the critical reactions to Hepburn, Lean, Lopert, Venice and, of course, Rossano.

Wherever Brazzi went, so did interviewers, photographers and screeching, hysterical females. In each of the major cities of the tour, Lopert always arranged a gigantic reception that much of the "in" crowd and panting female gatecrashers managed to attend. Everybody wanted to see, meet and, biblically or socially, know the exciting new messiah of cinema. Gene was somewhat surprised by the naked aggression of a number of women, who baldly gave Brazzi telephone numbers or extended late-supper or weekend invitations to him. Gene was positively horrified by the many husbands who turned themselves into pimps, approaching Rossano to hand him their wife's calling card with a "My wife would love you to phone her," or, as they shook hands, said, "I'm so happy to meet you, Mr. Brazzi," quietly sticking their spouse's name and phone number into Rossano's jacket pocket.

There he was, hailed as the most authentic, 24-karat Latin Lover to ignite the silver screen since Valentino. When Jesse Zunser of *Cue* magazine referred to Rossano as the "new Valentino," Brazzi modestly replied: "Thank you for the compliment, but it's also nonsense. Valentino was unique. I would like to think that I am, too. Perhaps it is the fact that we were both born in Italy, or perhaps it is the admiration for women which we both symbolize, which is what causes people to make such a comparison. There is of course no question that I am a ladies' man. I have seldom met a woman I didn't like, and at any age." He played his Latin Lover role onscreen as well as off, as if it were up to him to single-handedly disprove Helen Lawrenson's thesis in her *Esquire* article, "Latins Are Lousy Lovers."

"By profession, inclination and acclamation, Brazzi, the foremost screen lover in Europe, is now busily conquering the United States, at least the distaff side," Zunser continued in his *Cue* interview. "People, women especially, like him on sight. 'I am always falling in love a little. I cannot help it,' Brazzi says. Perhaps he cannot help it, but it has paid off handsomely. Brazzi maintains a reputation and holds the franchise as a Great Lover by advising on – naturally, Love!"

How much wiser Brazzi would have been if he had heeded the advice he so passionately hurled at Hepburn. "Take love, don't talk it!" He should have gone further, as he shaved every morning and put on his nightcap every night: "DON'T TALK!" If there was any star around who had greater talent for sticking his foot into his mouth, he would have been named Rossano Brazzi. Releases would frequently appear in the press of a new Brazzi engagement and phone calls would come into the KLA offices from unheard-of producers, who advised K and L of the preposterous conditions Brazzi had agreed to for some opus. KLA simply adopted a policy of stating that Brazzi had no legal authority to make any verbal or written agreements that were not co-signed personally either by Kaufman or Lerner, of course causing a cyclone of histrionics from the frustrated promotors.

Brazzi's mouth resembled that of a flounder, and the jewels that spewed forth from it were dazzlingly spurious, a heady cocktail of fact, fantasy, invention and off-white lie. He was driven by a compulsion to dispense advice and to regale the press with a stream of imaginative rhetoric. What he disgorged on TV talk shows, press, parties, groups and individuals was so disarming, so sincere and so convincing that he simultaneously convinced himself. He was as full of surprising tidbits as there were coins thrown into the Fontana di Trevi by American ladies, dreaming their secret wish of one night of love with *L'Amante Italiano*.

"I always manage to fall just a little bit in love with each of my leading ladies," Brazzi said in an interview with Wanda Hale, the powerful critic and feature writer of the *New York Daily News*. "First of all, you understand, I am Italian, and I cannot help it. And besides, it makes for much more fun, and realism, when working together. The love scenes take on a greater aura of excitement and authenticity than might otherwise be possible. The audiences sense it, too. They're not stupid or unfeeling out there."

Rossano frequently confused his onscreen passions with off-screen dalliances. It was often impossible to know if he was hallucinating. Over the years, Brazzi had an enviable assortment of beautiful, glamorous, vulnerable or sexually avaricious co-stars. Some were impervious to Rossano's *charme fatale* and kept all amorous play for the set, in front of the camera. But a number of the ladies with whom he might have been sharing a bed on set as the camera rolled succumbed to his appeal, and frequent complications resulted that sometimes required K or L's tactful intervention.

The ladies who did attack or surrender know perfectly well who they are, and quite likely so did Lidia. But she played the game so adroitly that it was often impossible to know if she was hallucinating. Everybody seemed to know about Rossano's endless affairs but Lidia. She laughed, she joked, she shrugged her shoulders as she pasted on her ostrich feathers. "I might be the most blind, most stupid woman in the world," she would always say. "My husband betray me? I don't believe. Sorry, I just don't believe." Blind and stupid, she certainly was not. Secure in her knowledge that her "Roooooooo-sssss-aaaaa-nnnnn-ooooo" would always return to her cornucopian bosom, she was. And he did always return, time after time, for more than forty years.

The triumphant tour ended, and Brazzi, not deigning to give Hollywood sight or sound of him, returned to Rome. Gene was left behind with Rossano's power of attorney to deal with offers, scripts and enthusiastic producers.

Al Daff, Australian-born president of Universal Pictures, wanted to make a three-picture deal with Brazzi, and Gene decided it was the way to go. There were two major advantages important to KLA's strategy: a continuity with Hollywood, which would provide a foundation for the future, and a film suited to Rossano already in preparation: Ross Hunter's *Interlude*, to co-star Jane Wyman, who was eventually replaced by June Allyson.

While Rossano, Lidia and Hank sat impatiently and anxiously in Rome, Gene took the plane for his first trip to the fabled Hollywood. He had no money for glamor hotels like the Beverly Hills, the Bel-Air or the Beverly-Wilshire. When she was making *The Indian Fighter* with Kirk Douglas, Elsa Martinelli had found a small, decent hotel called the Beverly Carlton and recommended it to Gene.

The Beverly Carlton was far off the road of the real big-time, but Al Daff, a true gentleman, was daffy about getting that deal with Brazzi, so he was chauffeured over to the Beverly Carlton in his mile-long black limousine. Mr. Lerner received him in his tiny bedroom, which cost nine dollars a night. Daff sat in the one armchair, Gene on the one bed, and, then and there, the Brazzi deal was struck.

Gene started with $100,000 for an eight-week period on the first picture, a hefty sum in those days. Daff said no problem. Gene then asked for substantial augmentations for the next two films. Daff said okay. Gene said there could be no exclusivity with Universal, that Brazzi had to have the right to make pictures with whomever he wished. Daff said that was all right. Gene said Brazzi would require a number of artistic considerations on script, female co-star, director and billing. With a wave of his hand, Daff said he was sure all of that could be worked out. Gene asked for a specific percentage of each picture's gross. His eyes tightening, Daff nodded agreement after a moment of hesitation. Now the crunch… Gene had to try. He had to bring back money for the Brazzis. Whereas it was a normal practice in Italy for the producer to pay the artist an advance on signing of contracts, Gene knew that Hollywood policy was to commence payment of compensation to the actor only when he began to perform services.

Gene simply had to chance it. He swallowed hard. "And I'll require $50,000 in cash as an advance, payable on the closing of the deal," he said as matter-of-factly as he could. That stopped Daff cold. His mouth moved, but no words came out of it. "In Italy, an advance is always paid," Gene went on hurriedly. "And Universal can take out insurance to protect itself if for some reason Brazzi fails to report."

"Unheard of! Unprecedented!" stammered Universal's president.

"I hate to say this," Gene finally said, his voice quiet and measured, "but the $50,000 advance is an irrevocable condition of the deal,"

It seemed a century before Daff spoke. Daff's face was expressionless, his eyes hard. Gene had a sinking feeling that he had lost the deal. Finally: "If that's the way it has to be, that's the way it has to be." Daff broke into a smile and offered Gene his hand for a firm handshake. After a few minutes of chitchat, an appointment was set for the next day at the Universal Studios, and Daff took his leave.

The next morning, Daff sent his chauffeur and limousine to the Beverly Carlton Hotel to transport Gene for his first visit to Universal Studios. Daff was waiting in the president's office, where Gene was presented to Morris Davis, business manager of the studio, Joseph Dubin, its legal head, and Melvin Sattler, a powerfully-built shorty in his early thirties who was Dubin's associate in the legal department.

When Daff began to outline the terms he had agreed upon, Davis and Dubin maintained an equanimity they certainly did not feel. But Sattler, despite a strong show of deference to Mr. President, made a real college try in defense of good old Universal. He wasn't able to swallow deal points that contradicted his traditional concept of reality. He gestured, got red faced, asked questions while answering them, was really in there pitching or, more accurately, golfing. Golf was his obsession, and as he protested and argued, he seemed to be frantically changing clubs, analyzing the bumps and slopes of the green, driving, slicing and putting in a strenuous effort to at least not come in too much over par. The course set by Daff had already defeated him, but Mel intended to go down fighting.

When Gene finally said that he had to have the complete contract and the $50,000 advance before his departure for Rome two weeks hence, the silence that ensued wasn't dead – it was buried. Normally, Hollywood went ahead with a "deal sheet," which briefly stipulated basic terms and conditions agreed to, and the lawyers on both sides took six months, a year, sometimes never, to complete the full contract. Gene's statement was a real shocker. Everybody sat looking at Gene in horror. Sattler, especially, was dumbfounded. His golf game was over.

"Well, boys, we want Brazzi," Daff eventually drawled in his Australian accent. "We think he'll be a great addition to us. Hunter thinks he'll be sensational in *Interlude*. Gene seems to have some exigencies and I guess we'll have to comply. So Joe, Mel, you both plan to go to New York and meet with the Paul, Weiss people right away and get the contract battened down."

"And pay over the $50,000?" Sattler asked once more as he studied the invader from Italy, convinced he was a full-blooded Mafioso posing as a Nebraska-born innocent.

"And pay over the $50,000," Daff reiterated.

Wharton put Mike Mermin and John C. Taylor III, two of Paul, Weiss' top entertainment lawyers, on the negotiations. For six consecutive days and far into each night, Dubin, Sattler, Taylor, Gene, assistants and secretaries met in one of the law firm's conference rooms to argue out the complicated three-picture agreement.

In spite of heated exchanges and repeated moments of tension, in spite of everyone's frayed nerves, the friendship between Gene, Dubin and Sattler solidified. They often ate together when the supper breaks came in between arduous sessions at Paul, Weiss. One night, at the Pen and Pencil, a journalist eatery on East 45th Street, Wanda Hale of the *Daily News* recognized Gene, whom she had met during the Brazzi tour. Gene introduced the Universal duo and told Wanda off-the-record of the deal being negotiated.

"Are they giving you any trouble?" she asked Gene. "A little," Gene replied jokingly. Wanda shook her finger in their faces. "You had better give him everything he wants. Everything – you get me? He's got the most exciting male star who's worth more than all of Universal combined," she pronounced before tipsily gyrating back to her table.

Eventually the seemingly impossible task was achieved. Dubin signed for Universal. Gene signed for Rossano. The certified check for $50,000 was turned over to Gene by a smiling Sattler. There were champagne toasts, warm goodbyes and promises between Gene, Mel and Dubin to write soon. Gene phoned his thanks to Daff. He phoned his appreciation to Wharton. He phoned Hank to tell him the contract was signed, but didn't reveal the secret of the hard cash he was bringing back.

Gene then raced to the Chase Manhattan branch at 57th and Madison, where his old friend Howard Hassard was manager, then walked out with $50,000 in $50 and $100 bills stuffed in his briefcase, next to the precious contract. He hurried to Woolworth's for Christmas wrappings. Back at his hotel, he quickly wrapped 25 packages, each containing $2,000 in cash, before checking out of his hotel and grabbing a taxi for the airport.

Hank had advised Gene that the Brazzis and he would be at Dawn Addams' pre-Christmas buffet the night the New York-Rome plane was due to land. It was agreed that Gene would come there directly from the airport to surprise Rossano and Lidia, who did not yet know the deal had been signed and that Gene was en route.

Not yet a Principessa, Dawn was having her party at her Via Eleanora Duse apartment in Parioli. It was in full swing when Gene arrived. Rossano and Lidia couldn't believe their eyes. Gene pulled the contract out of the briefcase and waved it for all to see. There was a pandemonium of cheers, kisses and hugs. Winking at Hank, gesturing that Hank follow, Gene excused himself, saying he just simply had to freshen up a bit to survive. He instead tiptoed into Dawn's bedroom, followed by Hank, signaling Hank to lock the door. Gene reopened the briefcase, and one by one, as Hank looked at him in bewilderment, his face a question of what's-this-all about, Gene laid out the twenty-five Christmas-decorated packets on Dawn's bed. "Don't ask me anything, please," Gene said as he filled the bed with the booty. "Just call Rossano and Lidia. Only them and you. Nobody else can come."

In a moment, Rossano and Lidia appeared, led by Hank. Hank again locked the door. The couple had not yet seen the packages spread out on Dawn's bed. Theatrically pointing to the bed, Gene said "I brought you a little something for Christmas." Rossano and Lidia looked down, then at each other, stunned. Lidia reached down and began to open the first packet. She saw the green. She dropped it, tore open the second. She picked up the third. Rossano just kept staring. Then he, too, began to open one package after another. As Hank and Gene watched with pride and delight, they began to shout, they began to scream, they began to jump with joy, they began to dance. Then they sat down on the bed, spent. His voice hoarse with emotion, Rossano finally asked, "How much?"

Gene turned and smiled at Hank, who was waiting open-mouthed to hear the answer. Gene looked back at the Brazzis. "$50,000," he said quietly. Rossano and Lidia didn't seem to understand. Then clapping his hands with unrestrained glee, he bent over them and as if making a public announcement, repeated, "$50,000!"

Lidia burst out crying in at-long-last relief. Rossano, too, was no longer able to resist the tears he hidden for so many years. They sat on the bed and sobbed for a long time. Hank moved over to Gene, put his arm around his partner.

It may have been Christmas, but it was really Easter. It was a moment of resurrection.

Two years later, Lidia and Rossano had a surprise for Hank and Gene. The Brazzis were still living in the tight confines of their Via Sistina flat, to which their adored agents now had open-door access as well as many magnificent samples of Tuscan cooking that Lidia had concocted.

Lidia had phoned to say that she and Rossano had to talk to the boys on a very serious matter and it had to be in person. Could they please come by that evening at eight, after which they would all go out somewhere to dine?

There was no sign of Lidia when Hank and Gene arrived. Rossano was at his most affable. As he offered his friends and business collaborators – he disliked referring to them as his "agents" – the Campari sodas they had requested, he was beaming. "There is something we want to share with the dearest friends we have in the world, the ones who saved our lives," he pronounced senatorially. "Lidia's dressing. You know Lidia, always late – but what can you do?" The sharp-cutting instrument with jagged edges that was Lidia's voice was suddenly heard from the bedroom. "Darlings! Close your eyes! I'm coming out!"

K and L did as instructed. They heard the swish of skirt that marked her entry into the small salon. "Now open your eyes and look!" she commanded. Hank and Gene opened their eyes. They didn't look. They couldn't... The spectacle before them was so dazzling that they were momentarily blinded. An ecstatic expression on her face, her arm outstretched, Lidia posed, bedecked head to foot in a sparkling array of jewelry. From the gem-encrusted tiara on her honey-hued hair to the diamond buckles on her spike-heeled shoes, she was 260 pounds of flashing ostentation, a baubled, blinking Christmas tree.

She and Rossano had succeeded finally in amassing sufficient funds to redeem her precious horde. Lean days could always crop up again in the transitory life and career of a star, but Lydia vowed that never again would she be parted from her jewels. She had no intention of being without security and insurance against the transitory life and career of a star's wife.

The affluence began to sprout like springtime. Rossano and Lidia found a triplex penthouse off the Via Paiesello overlooking the Villa Borghese with a terrace big enough to land a jet. A half-million dollars went into its purchase, remodeling and decor, which included splendid paintings, authenticated museum pieces and a special bedroom for the poodles. Guests, dinners, parties, cars, more servants, trips – anything and everything to show how glorious success could be.

The KLA campaign for Brazzi to portray the role of the French planter, Emile de Becque, in the film version of *South Pacific* – so memorably played on Broadway by Italian opera star Ezio Pinza – began even prior to the release of *Summertime*. It was a campaign that was only successfully concluded after three years of arduous long-range planning.

As Gene and Hank saw it, the development of Rossano's new career had to be based on a parlay from the Renato of *Summertime* to the de Becque of *South Pacific*, the creation of Richard Rodgers and Oscar Hammerstein II and the most successful theatrical musical in Broadway history. The role of de Becque was one of the most coveted in Hollywood annals. Everyone in the picture industry, everyone on Broadway, was certain that the actor fortunate enough to be chosen to play the part in the film would not only find himself a superstar but could not help but be the favorite to win the Oscar.

Gene and Hank decided that whereas any film between *Summertime* and the eventual *South Pacific* should, if possible, consolidate Rossano's position, none would warrant interference with his being selected by Rodgers & Hammerstein when they transferred their Broadway masterwork to the screen.

K and L decided on two basic things to implement their strategy.

The first was to do what would normally seem to anyone in the industry to be not merely ridiculous, but utterly insane. Gene got a clause in that endless Universal agreement stipulating that not only did Universal have no exclusivity over Brazzi, but also gave *South Pacific* preemptive rights whenever it was scheduled for filming. A *South Pacific* priority clause also went into agreements concerning other pictures starring Brazzi. The result was that whenever *South Pacific* was to be shot, Rossano Brazzi would be ready, willing and legally able to portray Emile de Becque. Since R&H had never heard of Brazzi, had made no deal for the motion picture rights, hadn't the slightest idea of the year or decade in which the film would be made, it would seem in 1954 that the odds for KL's getting the de Becque role for Brazzi were something like one in a million.

The second of the two fundamental elements in KLA's campaign was to get a letter off to Messrs. R&H. It was sent prior to Brazzi's departure with Gene for the USA promotional tour of *Summertime.*

Rome, Italy, October 11, 1954

Dear Richard Rodgers and Oscar Hammerstein,

You perhaps or perhaps not will remember me as executive secretary of the New Dramatists until the summer of 1952. We had a number of occasions to meet during my two years of service and membership in the group. As you will note from this letterhead, I am now living in Rome and am co-founder with Hank Kaufman of the Kaufman-Lerner Associates talent agency

However, I do not today write you moved by nostalgia, unless it is a nostalgia for the emotion felt at the last preview of *South Pacific,* to which you were kind enough to invite all of the New Dramatists as well as Hank.

It is actually about *South Pacific* the film that I am writing you. Fully aware of your exacting standards,

Hank and I have great pleasure in advising you that you can put your minds at ease. We have your Emile de Becque.

I am aware that you may not be doing the picture version for years and years. From the grosses I see listed in *Variety*, it seems like the play will run on Broadway forever. Nevertheless, the time will come to do the film, and it is never too early for you to know that one of your two major casting problems has been resolved.

He is the one actor on this Earth who can fulfill the role on the screen. He was born to play it. All his life seems to have been a preparation to portray it. Everybody in the world will believe Nellie Forbush's falling in love with him, because everyone in the world will fall in love with him.

His name is Rossano Brazzi. Hank and I strongly recommend that you see him in David Lean's *Summertime*, which has just been completed, and in which he co-stars with Katharine Hepburn. You can arrange to screen it through Ilya Lopert or United Artists.

I will be coming to New York with Brazzi for a promotional tour in connection with the picture's release. I would be most happy to meet with you not only to talk of Rossano but to say hello after more than two years. In the meantime, while awaiting some word back from you, Hank and I join in sending you both our very best wishes.

Sincerely,
Gene Lerner

The reply from Rodgers was brief and formal. But it was a reply. He expressed his thanks for the letter. He said it was much too early to consider casting. They had formulated no plans as to when the film would be made. He had never seen Brazzi, but had vaguely heard of him. When Gene came to New York, he might telephone and possibly they could meet. They did meet briefly in New York that November '54, together with big-beared, pock-faced and far more affable Hammerstein. They said they would eventually get around to seeing *Summertime*, and that if they were sufficiently impressed, they would be in touch at the appropriate time.

Joshua Logan, director of both stage and screen versions of the musical, said in a 1957 interview that he and R&H, independently of each other, all picked Brazzi for the de Becque role after seeing him in *Summertime*. Rossano never lost his conviction that he could do justice to Rodgers' songs. Though not a trained singer, he had a baritone that was rich, sensual and attractive. He argued that the screen Emile should not have an operatic image. He was convinced that a more naturalistic approach was vital. Good singing, *certamente*, to do full justice to the Rodgers melodies. But wasn't the ultimate end, aided by the wonderful songs, the effective delineation of his character and the communication to every heart the touching love story between Emile de Becque and that lovely United States Army nurse, Nellie Forbush?

Gene and Hank agreed it was imperative that Rossano not only perform Emile but also sing his music. This, they reasoned, was important both for the maximum fulfillment of the character Rossano sought, and for career purposes, to demonstrate yet another facet of Brazzi's capabilities. When, a year before the picture was scheduled to commence, Gene began negotiations with Howard E. Reinheimer, the R&H attorney, he fought strenuously to prevent a contractual provision which permitted the production to dub Emile's songs with a voice other than Brazzi's. Gene decided to take the matter up directly with Rodgers.

The composer finally agreed to give Rossano a chance, and once other issues were resolved the deal was set and the contracts signed. There were approximately eight months left before the picture was to start with prerecording of the songs. Four months prior to prerecording, Brazzi was to submit a recording of his songs, which would then be adjudicated by Rodgers, Hammerstein and Logan. Gene was determined that Brazzi was going to pass the test. Hank was no less determined.

Hank contacted Maestro Vitale, head of the Rome Opera. While still managing to protect his bachelorhood from Vitale's nubile daughter Milly, Hank asked her father for help in finding the best available vocal coach in Italy, and persuading him or her of the imperative of a relentless, crash course with Brazzi. They needed to develop his voice to its max in the brief period available. Rossano talked discipline and dedication, advised everyone that the Rodgers music was as difficult to master as *Tristan and Isolde*, *Turandot* and *Don Giovanni* combined, and that he, like a monk, was going into retreat to worship Lord God Richard Rodgers and his heavenly compositions.

He managed six desultory visits to his Maestro. Gene and Hank ranted, raved, pleaded, threatened – to no avail. Didn't everybody, at a trattoria or at home, everywhere, in fact, around town, always tell him he had a wonderful voice whenever he burst forth with "Scuri, Sciuri" or "Three Coins in the Fountain"? Didn't Lidia just adore him when he sang? When he lifted his arms and opened his mouth before his bathroom mirror, weren't the tones that emerged the most glorious anyone had ever heard?

No, said Joshua Logan when he heard the recording, which a discouraged and reluctant Hank finally sent to New York. No, said Oscar Hammerstein II. No, no, and no, said Maestro Richard Rodgers. Brazzi was shocked, and now desperate. They had betrayed him. They were trying to crucify him. But no Brazzi was going to die on the cross.

Though enraged at Brazzi for his sloth and overconfidence, Gene jumped back into battle. Would Rodgers et al., before making a final, final decision, at least let Rossano prerecord his songs on the Coast, with the advantage of the complex recording facilities and the personal guidance of the Great Richard himself? Rodgers pondered, then ultimately agreed. For the last ten days before his and Lidia's departure, Brazzi spent every waking hour with his vocal teacher.

He left the exhausted Maestro tone deaf and with an undying hatred for "Some Enchanted Evening."

Another instance of the KLA *Cocktailus Romanus* at Via Salaria. The June 15, 1957 evening was steaming. So were the more than two hundred guests who had come to honor Rossano and Lidia, who were to leave the following day for prerecordings and preparations in Hollywood, then for Hawaii, where most of *South Pacific* was to be filmed. Pan American's public relations chief in Rome, George Seabury, just a bit under seven feet tall and just a bit over 300 pounds in weight, had arranged to have exquisite white orchid leis and Hawaiian delicacies flown in from Honolulu.

There was an undercurrent of excitement in the crowd, awaiting some climax. It was scheduled to have been Brazzi, draped with orchids, in concert. It wasn't. Signora Marion upstaged him. Without any advance warning, she collapsed in a heap center stage of the salon, causing consternation among all present. With Hank rushing to the phone for a doctor, Gene frantically giving orders, Marion was quickly picked up by Brazzi, Alain Delon and Rock Hudson. Followed by Lidia and several others, Marion was carried into her bedroom and immediately stretched out on the bed.

All watched as Gene leaned over her, holding her hand, repeating her name over and over again. Everybody shouted different suggestions as to what to do. Her arms and legs were massaged, cold compresses laid on her forehead. Hank carried in a cognac and forced it down her throat.

After two or three minutes, she moved. Everybody held their breath. She opened her eyes. Everybody stood still, waiting. She looked unsteadily at the faces around her. Was it Rossano Brazzi? Alain Delon? Rock Hudson?! Her eyes brightened and proceeded to smile. What a way to go! And she fainted a second time. When the doctor came, he diagnosed the collapse as a mild epileptic fit, brought on by heat, exhaustion and emotion.

Marion never missed an occasion to be photographed with one of her favorites – Gardner, Bardot, Magnani, Brazzi, Delon, Chiari, Ekberg, Loren, Romy Schneider, Belinda Lee. Her personal collection of photos, with affectionate inscriptions from her stars, was her dearest possession. She willed it to Hank and Gene, her "Comandante" Kaufman and her "Baby" Lerner, when she died in Monza on June 19, 1978.

That June, twenty-one years earlier, *Cocktailus Romanus* was the most enchanted of her enchanted evenings.

"Some enchanted evening, you will meet a strrrannngggerrrr, acrossss a crow-deeeed room," boomed the bass-baritone voice of Metropolitan Opera singer Giorgio Tozzi from the 70mm blown-up splendors of *South Pacific*.

Brazzi's mouth quivered in synchronization as convincingly as possible, but his heart just wasn't in it. "I wanted to sing 'Some Enchanted Evening' with my own voice, which is plenty good enough," he confided to columnist Bob Thomas of the *Los Angeles Times* in 1960. "I would have done it gently, convincingly. Instead, the voice of an operatic basso was dubbed in histrionic style, which only weakened the impact of the character. I feel that Emile de Becque should have been played much stronger. The film should have more fully developed the character of this man, who after all had once committed murder."

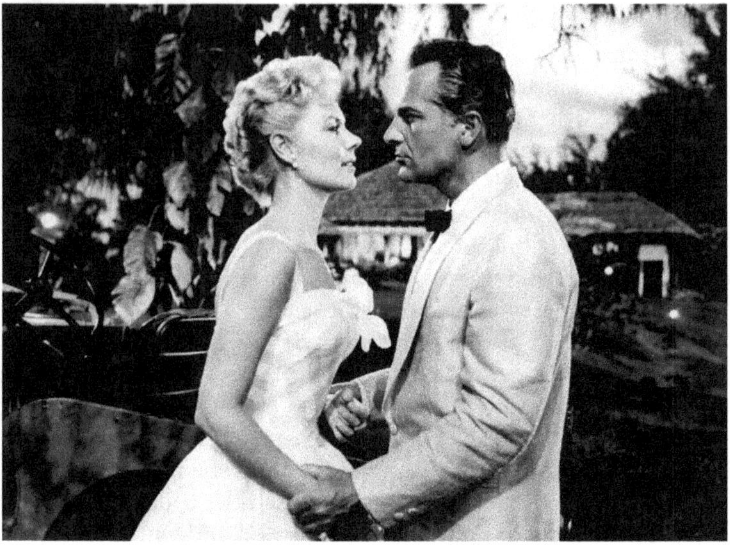

Rossano Brazzi and Mitzi Gaynor in *South Pacific*

The rapport between Joshua Logan and Brazzi was not always Mary and Jesus. In a moment of pique when the troupe, including John Kerr as Joe Cable, was still on location on the Island of Oahu, Rossano blurted out, "I need more help, but Josh is too busy spending time adjusting the light on John Kerr's tits."

South Pacific was not a box office success. Nor was it an artistic one. Its unexpected and probably unnecessary failure was a bitter disappointment to Rossano. Dreams of an Oscar nomination and universal acclaim faded. Perhaps more than anyone, it was he who suffered the consequences, and unfairly. Instead of *South Pacific* becoming *Summertime*'s subsequent platform for further development and greater opportunities, it marked the beginning of the end of his international charisma. The dissolution of his Latin Lover mystique over the following years coincided with the slow decline of Hollywood on the Tiber.

The *Summertime-South Pacific* parlay, on which KLA worked so assiduously and in which Hank and Gene believed so fervently, had not achieved its end. The other films in between, and those that followed, were generally of good caliber in co-stars, directors, authors and budgets. In almost every department, they were definitely "Class A." But, in total, they were insufficient to sustain Rossano's world standing and his high earning power.

Interlude, the first of the Universal pictures, was old-fashioned and banal. *Loser Takes All*, a British product, was a Grahame Greene story directed by Ken Annakin, and co-starred one of Britain's biggest draws, Glynis Johns. It ended up with its promise broken. *Legend of the Lost* was full of great expectations. It was directed by expert, eye-patched Henry Hathaway and co-starred Rossano with John Wayne and Sophia Loren – on paper an unbeatable money combination. The film was shot on superb locations that resembled the depths of Hell, an archeological relic in the middle of the Sahara called Leptus Magna, a city that had died centuries ago. There was considerable excitement during the shooting. Sophia had a narrow escape from a tarantula and Brazzi had a harrowing fright when, in an angry scene he was playing with Loren, things got overly realistic. Sophia was supposed to kick. Accidentally or not so accidentally, she kicked Rossano right smack in his prized territory. Screaming and moaning, he fell to the ground, doubled up in excruciating pain. An alert stills photographer caught the dramatic moment, and the photo is proof of what otherwise might have sounded like "one of those stories."

Thank God there was no funeral necessary for Rossano's most precious possession, but the Hathaway pacing of his picture was so slow that the box office was like a hearse.

In his interview with Bob Thomas, Brazzi complained about his roles. "Hollywood can see me only as a lover. I hate it! Love scenes are the worst of all to make convincing. Why? Because when you make love to a woman you say things that already sound silly to someone listening at the keyhole. When you say them in front of everyone on a giant screen, you risk being laughed at." Maybe a change of image would jolt his fans, he added, but in his opinion, an actor sometimes had to take chances.

So Brazzi took a calculated risk on *The Story of Esther Costello*, which co-starred Joan Crawford and was based on a gruesome story by Nicholas Monsarrat, directed by David Miller. As Crawford's slimy husband, Rossano was required to rape his lovely, deaf-mute stepdaughter, played by Heather Sears.

By that time, Rossano had proliferating fan clubs around the world: Tokyo, London, Buenos Aires, Melbourne, Glasgow, Rio de Janeiro, New York, Cleveland, Chicago, Los Angeles, Dallas. His fans were horrified at how he had betrayed their image of him. In their letters, several even threatened him with castration.

Rossano got the point. The film was a disaster and he turned back to more sophisticated continental-type stories and to his stereotype, never again being seen in a part as cruel and inhuman as the one in *Esther Costello.*

There was 20th Century Fox's *A Certain Smile*, based on Françoise Sagan's best-seller, in which Brazzi had two leading ladies: the young, innocent French actress, Christine Carère, and the lovely, maturing Joan Fontaine. Good friend Jean Negulesco, with whom Rossano had worked so well in *Three Coins in the Fountain*, was the director. The picture did modestly well.

There was also Metro-Goldwyn-Mayer's *Count Your Blessings*, a bright comedy with a top-line cast of Brazzi with Deborah Kerr and Maurice Chevalier. The public did not respond with fervor to its combined blessings. Nor to the Warner Bros. production of *Light in the Piazza*, co-starring Olivia de Havilland, nor Universal's *Lovers Must Learn* with Angie Dickinson, nor *The Bobo* with Peter Sellers and Britt Ekland, nor *Woman Seven Times* with Shirley MacLaine.

The Brazzi decline as Latin Lover Numero Uno came after slightly more than a decade of preeminence in the field and earnings considerably in excess of three million dollars. His two major successors to sprout from Italian soil were Marcello Mastroianni and Giancarlo Giannini. Neither ever succeeded in making the transfer from Rome to Hollywood. Thus, in the 60-year chronicle of the Latin Lover as a symbol of Hollywood's struggle to command world audiences, in the end only two Italians were entitled to a special place: Rudolph Valentino and Rossano Brazzi.

How did he achieve it?

His figure was toady, his head and neck massive, his height short, his mouth fishlike, his torso too heavy in proportion to the remainder of his body. He wore built-up shoes, walking preciously and slightly pigeon-toed, as if heading for a pratfall.

He was a profile, his chin pulled tight, then angled upwards. He moved with tortoise deliberation. He poised his inner expressions to fit his outer sculpture. Spontaneity, gesture and movement were all emanations of his peacock iridescence. In his youth, he must have had some sense of rhythm, but by the time he reached international stardom, it was clear that if he was required to dance, it was wise to keep the choreography to a basic one-two-three and the camera trained on his Tuscan-blue eyes. His hair was a nemesis. It was getting thinner. Wigs, toupees and hairpieces were all experimented with, as were various hair colorings and rinses. He needed ample hair to minimize the disproportion of his head and neck.

Yet none of it robbed him of his magnetic attraction.

So how *did* he achieve it?

Indubitably, KLA played a part in his growth and emergence on the international scene. It strategically planned and made a career – out of wood and sand, many have sneeringly said. The personal relationship that developed between the Brazzis and KLA resulted in a greater concentration on Rossano's welfare than even major star clients had the right to expect. But as important as it was, the KLA role did not explain the Brazzi phenomenon.

Commencing with the 1950s, masses from all parts of the world discovered Italy, with all its physical beauty, mystic appeal and refreshing live-and-let-live naturalness. "The charm of Italy is akin to that of being in love," wrote Stendhal, something that tourists well understood. Brazzi was the nation's dream as he was its fairytale. He was its fantasy and its nostalgia. He was charming, winning, warm, courtly, gentle. He possessed sensuality. He embodied sentimentality, shyly, like a child. He made a woman feel like... a woman. He made friends with men through his unreserved acceptance of the view that they, too, were entitled to admire the female and to have her admiration. His eyes, however marvelous, were perennially sad. Each of his glances was a plea or a need, a hope or a promise. He was capable of such intimacy of speech that it seemed his vocal chords had fallen into his heart. His voice was rich in range and timbre and he was versatile enough to make recitative of recital, recital of recitative.

It happened to be the moment. It happened to be the right moment. In his mid-thirties, English-speaking, it happened to be the Brazzi moment, simultaneously the moment that Italy herself was proving to be sensational worldwide box office. What was more sound, what more logical, than to get on the ground floor with a valuable and exciting Italian export?

As Stendhal might have envisioned, Brazzi seemed the perfect export. The great French writer easily could have written, "The charm of Brazzi is akin to that of being in love."

There were millions of dreaming romantics and fairytale believers who would have agreed.

*

September 1963, on the massive Brazzi terrace overlooking the Via Paiesello and the Villa Borghese. What an afternoon that was! Roger Vadim and Rossano were waxing eloquently on the subject of Love for Women. Hour after hour, whiskey after whiskey, they sat, stood, paced, postured and gesticulated as they wove their spellbinding monologues. Each was a formidable actor striding the stage of female bodies, projecting to the other his greatest moments, his most refined techniques, his most naked feelings for Womankind of the World. These two noted Casanovas of the epoch, the Gallic who numbered Annette Stroyberg, Brigitte Bardot, Catherine Deneuve and Jane Fonda among his amorous companions, and the Tuscan who numbered whatever number that happened to come to his head – with all their gentlemanly solicitude, their array of courtesies – had not the slightest intention of being overshadowed by the other.

What poets they were! What chevaliers! What worshippers of Female Glory! What humble and longing pilgrims they were, prostrated before the altar of Eve, groveling for the favors of the most glorious of all of Heaven's creations!

Caressing, touching, embracing, eye-drinking, soul-stirring were gerunds repeated in rising exaltation. Hair, earlobes, back of neck; eyelashes and eyebrows in an infinity of colors, expressions and eyes sizes; nostrils, noses and lips; cheek structure, arms and armpits, shoulders; breasts – their rise, their fall, their texture, size and nipples; fingers and fingernails; waist, navel, stomach curve; vaginal size, shape, particularized characteristics; the back, shape of spine, spread and shape of buttocks; the special secrets of the between-the-leg area; thigh, knee, calf, ankle; top of foot and bottom, the toe, from small to large, and skin, skin, skin, SKIN! All were lengthily extolled, just as personality, intelligence, sense of humor, soul, heart, the significance of beauty were exactingly and enthusiastically praised.

No pornographic imagery was evoked. No cheap or vulgar titillation to arouse desire. None of that. A paean to The Female, her summation and her symbol, the exquisite object that was their air, food, drink and life, and their privilege, honor and joy to love.

It was a stunning exhibition as each sought to demonstrate his sensitivity, his gentleness, his tenderness, his awareness of the meaning of Woman. It was an awesome spectacle of unselfishness, abnegation, sacrifice to the Ideal of Ideals. Man was merely instrument, means. He was nothing more than donor and giver, at the service of all those Superior Creatures who had to live in such painful unfulfillment because they had never been transfigured through the self-immolation of Roger Vadim and Rossano Brazzi.

Perhaps five hours later came the surprising climax to the afternoon of worship. There was a third male present, who sat speechless in amazement at the extraordinary demonstration to which he was accidentally privy. It was Vadim who asked him the question. "Do you prefer love of a woman? Or love of a man?" Taken aback by the query, the guest hesitated in his answer as the two Great Lovers waited for his response, not knowing what his frank reply would provoke, he finally said, "I prefer the love of a man."

"Ahhhh," said Vadim, closing his eyes, lifting his head, barely able to control his emotion. "Ahhhhhh, love for a man. Yes, yes, that is really love! What could be more profound than to love a man?" He opened his eyes, turned to Brazzi for an endorsement. Rossano sat in a trance of ecstasy, as, deeply moved, he listened approvingly to Vadim's reflections. "You can cry over the love of a woman," Vadim continued. "You can weep and weep until your heart breaks. But to cry over the love of a man! Ahhhh!!!"

And why, for forty years, were Rossano and Lidia such an excitingly unique couple? She was four years older than he and people who didn't know better asked whether she was Rossano's mother. On first acquaintance, at first glance, they just didn't fit. Each was a caricature. They seemed hopelessly miscast. Lidia resembled a whale. She flaunted her fatness outrageously. Her bathing suits were shockingly skimpy. Her miniskirts were a joke for her figure. It was sometimes hard to tell the difference between décolletage and topless in the dresses she wore.

Spontaneous gift-giving was not one of the Brazzis' traits. One Christmas, they sent a package over to Via Salaria for Gene. It contained a custom-tailored beige shirt of expensive silk. Pleased and surprised, Gene immediately showed it to Hank. Examining it more closely, Hank commented, "It's got an 'RB' monogram over the pocket." The partners fell into gales of laughter, which increased when Gene, short and slight, tried the shirt on, to find himself a ridiculous double for a scarecrow. Rossano's old shirt was the one and only gift K or L ever received from the Brazzis in all their years of association and friendship.

So *why*, for forty years, were Rossano and Lidia such an excitingly unique couple?

The caricature of each was self-drawn, sketched with a robust sense of humor. The couple shared a rare human virtue. They knew how to laugh. Brazzi at and with himself. At and with each other. At and with the world. Lidia's remarks, Rossano's retorts, her winged rejoinder were repartee spiced with wit and seasoned with love, and their public and private battles, all hot peppers and undiluted garlic, were marvelous cures for indigestion.

The more you were exposed to that phenomenal female who looked like she was Brazzi's mother, the younger both she and you became, and you then realized that all the *avoirdupois* was deceptive. Lidia had such grace that she seemed a bird in flight. To dance with her was to learn that one did not have to be a tightly muscled, sylph-like ballerina to achieve such delicacy of movement and such lightness of foot. What energy! The vitality, jollity, boisterousness – it was all uniquely Lidia.

The Brazzis were also synonym for home, hearth and hospitality. Lydia was a magnificent practitioner of Italian cuisine. But it was not her plentiful table with its variety of wines that caused salivation. It was the cheer, the open, loud, everybody-talking-at-once infectiousness with which you were embraced and the wholehearted laughter that made you think it came from them, until you realized it was also pouring out of you. As hostess, Lidia made Pearl Mesta seem a Wimpy waitress.

What fun when during one of those dinners at home in Rome or in Hollywood, or in a crowded trattoria like Rome's Angelino, Lidia would suddenly raise her leg, remove her shoe and, her eyes a dance of mischief, command: "Rossano, kiss my foot!" With exasperation in his eyes, mixed with a smiling wink, he did just that. It was one way they had to show the world that in spirt of everything, theirs was a marriage that nothing and no one could destroy.

Rossano and Lidia became friendly with Judy Garland from the time of her marriage to Vincente Minnelli. It was through the Brazzis that Minnelli met Denise Brigante, an ambitious, voluptuous Yugoslav refugee who became his second wife. In

1970, the Brazzis invited Judy to be their houseguest for a brief Roman stay in their penthouse. However, a family crisis among Lidia's relatives in Florence obliged them to leave Rome before Judy's arrival. Hank, who had never met the singer-actress, agreed to meet her at the airport, explain the situation, accompany her to the Brazzi residence, and try to make her feel as much at home as possible.

Judy was in physical and mental deterioration. When she stepped off the plane, she was almost unrecognizable – obese, bloated, no makeup, hair cropped close to her head. There were no press or photographers awaiting her. Hank made his presence known to the slightly bewildered Judy and whisked her and her baggage off to the Brazzi abode, where housekeeper Irma was waiting.

Irma, as instructed, led Judy to the best room in the guest quarters, which was exquisitely appointed and had a splendid view of Rome. Judy looked it over silently. "May I see the master bedroom, please," she asked in a somewhat superior tone. Hank was at a loss. Irma flushed with embarrassment. But they were helpless. Once in the Brazzi bed chamber, she announced that really, she would be so much happier there, and immediately took possession.

The next day, Judy appeared at Via Lisbona and gave Hank a list of errands, chores and shopping requirements. She asked if the office would kindly place a number of transatlantic phone calls for her because she just got lost with the Italian telephone system. Looking at the great Judy with sadness, Hank agreed to all the requests and, together with the Brazzis, covered her unpaid bills. It was for Hank a grateful restitution for all the joy and sometimes tears she had brought to him across footlights and from the silver screen.

A star is born.
A star is dead.
The pattern too often seemed inevitable.

Rossano and Lidia ended up having to sell that penthouse at a heavy loss. They lived for years quietly in Rome at the modest Pensione Porpora, less than a block away from the magnificence they were forced to leave behind. In partnership with his loyal, hardworking brother Oscar, Rossano managed to keep afloat throughout the 1970s. Oscar and he put together several low-budget exploitation films for European television and cinema, in which Rossano performed and that Oscar produced and sometimes directed. From time to time, there have been guest appearances on American television and in American movies.

Just prior to Christmas of 1979, Gene happened to be in Rome. He noted that there would be a presentation that night on Italian television of a dramatization of Friedrich Dürrenmatt's *The Pledge*. Brazzi was listed as star, so Gene decided to watch it. The next morning, it was reviewed in *Il Messaggero* by critic Paolo Zaccagnini, who wrote:

> Let's say at once that if a Rossano Brazzi so intense, committed and remarkable had not been found, the television adaptation would not have been so effective. The old ex-Latin Lover knew how to throw away decades of his legendary attractiveness, was able to erase his facile smiles and put himself totally into the demeaned character of Commissario Mattai.
>
> The final image of the three-hour film was a long close-up of the dried-up face of Brazzi, paralyzed by rain and cold, as he sat with his face void of any expression of life, awaiting the appearance of a ferocious murderer of children. The close-up on his face was the key to the remarkable achievement of director Alberto Negrin. Brazzi was a revelation and gave us a performance on TV which had rarely been equalled for a very long time.

Gene was intensely moved by Brazzi's extraordinary characterization. Not for a second did Rossano reveal a single one of the mannerisms that had afflicted him throughout his career. No muscle, no gesture, no expression called attention to itself. His control was as amazing as it was heartwarming.

Then a realization struck Gene. That final close-up, which focused for a full minute on Rossano's face, was of a man buried under a layer of beard, moustached, wigged with white hair, peering through heavy steel-rimmed glasses. Thirty years before! *Little Women*! Rossano as Professor Bhaer. Back then it had been nearly fatal to his career, but now it was an unmitigated triumph. At 63, he had travelled full circle, returning, gloriously, to where had begun. Rossano at last seemed to accept the validities inside himself and recognize that the distillation of personality could also be art.

Wanting to congratulate Rossano on his performance, Gene phoned the Pensione Porpora the next morning. He soon heard Rossano's "pronto" for the first time in nearly five years. When Brazzi heard Gene's voice, recognized instantaneously, he could barely control his emotion. Lidia's "Who is it, who is it?" was heard shaking the background. "It's Gene," Rossano told her. Lidia grabbed the phone and cannon-boomed, "Gene!" Over and over again, moving from Italian to English and to a sauce of both, she repeated how happy the phone call made her. Over and over again she commented on how much she had missed Hank and him. What wonderful years they had had together! Why had there been a drifting apart? Why so much time lost in separation? Thanks to God, contact between them had been reestablished.

On April 23, 1981, exactly sixteen months later, the funeral services attended by Hank and Gene for Lidia Bertolini Brazzi took place in Rome's Chiesa di Santa Teresa del Bambino Gesù, which she and Rossano had for years admired from the splendid terrace of the penthouse they once so proudly owned.

Through the entire service, Brazzi leaned stiffly forward, his eyes fixed on the unbelievably small, seemingly weightless coffin containing the remains of the woman to whom he had been bound for two-score years. His concentration was unbearably intense, as if through it he could arouse her to speak boisterously and move with the lightness of foot and grace which made her seem a bird in flight.

She did not speak. She did not move. There was not the "Shurrup you" he seemed to expect, or her turning of her back on him, or the lifting of her skirt to show him her rear. There was not the sudden raising of her leg, the removal of her shoe, and the mischievous command of "Rossano, come kiss my foot." There were no winged rejoinders, spiced with wit and seasoned with love, flung out at him so that he could, all hot peppers and undiluted garlic, respond with fiercely adoring outrage.

"You have given to me the best Christmas present I had in my life," were the last words she had spoken to Gene before she passed the receiver back to Rossano when Gene had telephoned the Pensione Porpora in December 1979.

But Lidia had forgotten another Christmas. It was a Christmas a quarter of a century before, with twenty-five packets of green lying on the bed in the home of Dawn Addams, Rossano and she both sobbing with joy as Hank and Gene, holding back their tears, stood together, watching.

Once asked to describe his favorite woman, Rossano replied: "She should combine the intellect and sense of humor of Katharine Hepburn, the allure of Ara Gardner, the enticing charms of Marilyn Monroe, the verve of Mitzi Gaynor, the good sense and practicality of Lidia, the sophistication of Deborah Kerr, the sincerity of Sophia Loren and the earthiness of Anna Magnani."

How Monroe got on his list, there is no way of knowing, and his comment on Lidia was just one of those Brazzisissmi. The others he referred to had all been his leading ladies. But then, now, tomorrow and forever, Lidia was the real star, the co-star and the life in the Life Story of Rossano Brazzi.

Six

The Janus Face of Beauty

On February 16, 1965, Henry Miller, one of America's revolutionary writers, author of *Tropic of Capricorn* and *Tropic of Cancer*, wrote the first of a series of letters to Ava Gardner. In it, he asked whether Gardner was "running from something or towards something." He spoke of her "perpetual flights" and lack of concern with "happy landings," of "confrontation with oneself at the most unexpected moments and in the most absurd places," and of her giving "the illusion of having visited realms unknown, undreamed of, by us."

For many years of Ava Gardner's "running from something or towards something," Rome was the destination for her "perpetual flights" and focal point of her unconcern with "happy landings." In Rome, as in innumerable villages, countrysides, towns, cities, metropoli, states and various nations of all of the Earth's continents, she descended in "confrontation with oneself" as exotic vagabond, alienated vagrant, sensational film star, melancholic, extraordinary woman, frenetic ballerina of the night and nightclub, boozed-up flotsam, nurse for the emotionally wounded, nun in habit of blouse, skirt, low-heeled shoes, scarf covering her swept-back hair.

In all of Ava's disguises, Rome never failed to recognize or to accept her, and during those years, the endless dodges, shifts and wanderings in her disparity of life roles took her all over the globe: Madrid, London, Paris, New York, Hollywood, Buenos Aires, Rio de Janeiro, Melbourne, Mexico City, Puerto Vallarta, Tokyo, hidden islands and snow-laden mountains, low roads and high seas. Rome, with its atavistic recall of Empire, accepted the inevitability of co-existence with the Empire of Ava.

In writing of Gardner, one is unable to escape that inevitability. One travels the inner and outer empire of her wherever it leads. One crosses borders that exist, boundaries that do not, labyrinths real or imagined, already aware that the most analytical poring through the dictionary of her will fail to reveal her definition. One makes the voyage accompanied by the illusion of visiting realms unknown and undreamed of.

Ava Lavinia Gardner was born in North Carolina on December 24, 1922. No unholy trio of talent scout, agent and studio executive traveled from afar to hail the infant. Nor did black sharecroppers in the area gather to kneel in homage to the babe who would wander the Earth and be worshipped by millions on all of its continents.

By the time Ava was 17, she was branded – cattle-style – a Hollywood starlet. While attempting to get rid of her drawl with the aid of drama coaches, she twisted and turned in the dizzyland of flimflam, trying to figure out all that tinsel and tawdriness. Nobody told her that in the Movie Capital of Mammon's Earth, the basic concept of *home* was deranged, as was the significance of *love*.

Soon after her arrival in Flicker Kingdom, Ava (the Lavinia having disappeared from view) started a series of nondescript film appearances. In 1946, she was loaned out to Universal by Metro-Goldwyn-Mayer, with whom she had signed an exclusive, seven-year option contract, to appear with Burt Lancaster in Ernest Hemingway's *The Killers*, and soon afterwards made Frederic Wakeman's *The Hucksters* with Clark Gable and Deborah Kerr. She found herself on the merry-go-round of success.

Driving ambition was never Ava's thing. When she stretched her hand towards the brass ring of stardom, it was part involuntary, part curiosity, part child's play, part a jarring push from the make-or-break pharaohs of the business. "Sanity was more important than stardom to me," she has said. She got the latter while hazarding the former.

At 26, she made the Ogden Nash-Kurt Weill musical fantasy *One Touch of Venus* for Universal. She was, as Venus incarnate, one hell of a statue. There were a series of other pictures, some Metro-produced, others on loan-out for Metro profit. Some were better, some less than better, but none slowed the pace of the merry-go-round. Then came *Show Boat*, the Jerome Kern-Oscar Hammerstein II masterpiece. It was 1951. Ava was 29. As the tragic mulatto Julie, she made half the world weep. The painful

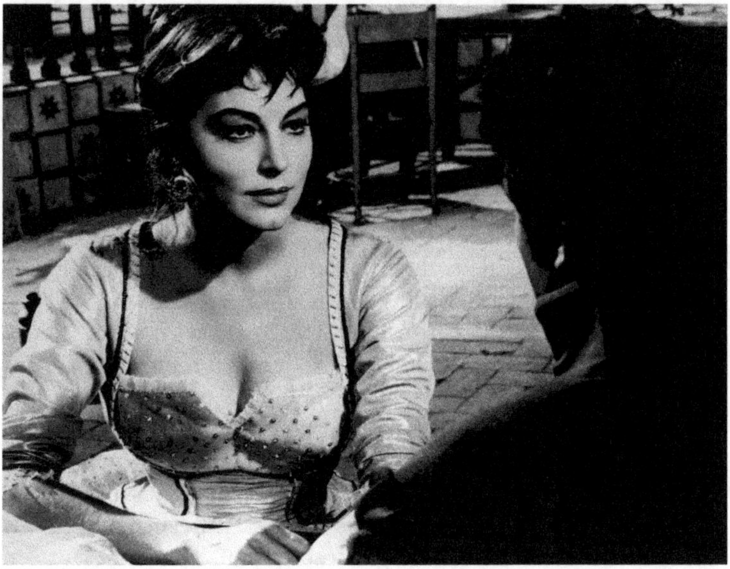

Ava Gardner in *The Naked Maja*

intensity and indelible reality of her performance contributed to the whispers, winks and gossip that she, like Julie, was "colored."

London. January 1965.

The Berkeley Hotel.

"Do you think I can do it?" Ava asked a troubled Gene. She was referring to the offer she had received to film the life story of Billie Holiday, America's Lady Day of song, whose tortured life was destroyed by drugs and jail, the heartlessness of men, and the poison of racism.

"You know I think you can do anything, so I'm the wrong guy to ask," Gene replied, trying to bring order to his thoughts.

"Okay. Do you think I *should* do it?" Ava's question came with her swift twist of the neck and the pasted stare which imprisoned the most infinitesimal change in expression in anyone she might be talking to.

"Tough," said Gene, shaking his head. "Billie is a flag at half-mast, saluted night and day by millions of blacks who blame her death on our white society. A white woman doing Billie... It's tough, Ava. But I really think you can do it." Gene looked at

Ava, into her. "I really believe you understand in your gut all the agony and convulsion that was inside her."

"Remember her on 52nd Street?" Ava asked. Her eyes seemed to be seeing Lady Day and her ears hearing Billie's cries for love and life.

"And that Carnegie Hall show when she got out of prison," Gene added. "I was there with Hank. I never cried so much or so loud in my life."

"Jesus," Ava said softly. "But would I dare? I don't give a good goddamn how the whites take it. And you know as well as I do a lot of people think I'm a secret n****r anyway. What's really important is, how will the blacks take it? Will *they* accept me as Billie?"

"If this were ten years ago, I would say yes," was Gene's reply. "And I would say, let's go ahead. It's a risk, but it's worth it. It's a hell of a different ball game today. The civil rights movement. The struggle for black identification. Black is beautiful, white is exploitation. The blacks have got to buy you. That's the bottom line – underlined, followed by a hundred exclamation points."

"How are we going to know if the blacks will buy me? Do we just go out and take a poll?"

"No." Gene suddenly clapped his hands. "We ask Jimmy Baldwin!"

Ava's face jerked towards Gene, her eyes eager.

"Honey, that's a great idea. Where is Jimmy?"

"Istanbul. At least that's where he was a couple of weeks ago. In that goddamn haunted house of his."

"Call him, honey. Call him now."

"Calling that crazy asylum of his might take the rest of my life," replied Gene. "Most of the time the phone doesn't work. If it does, nobody answers it. If by some miracle somebody happens to answer, you can't hear a word. No, honey, I'm going to write."

"Okay, hon. But get him to phone or to answer pronto. And ask him to come to London. We'll have a ball."

"That's just what I'll do."

But James Baldwin couldn't come to London to have a ball and it seemed for a while that he was no longer able to write. Finally, the letter came from the South of France.

"The question of Ava playing Billie Holiday really threw me," wrote Jimmy, "and caused me to put off answering your letter. It's a very loaded question. I know Ava a little, I admire

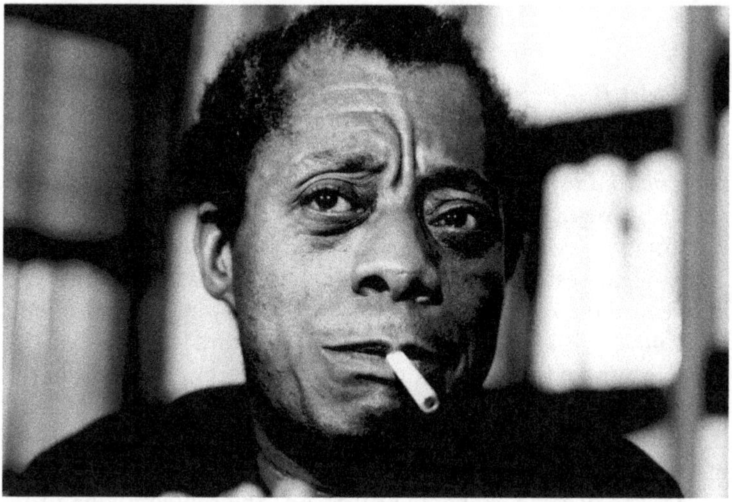

James Baldwin

her very much, and I'm very fond of her. She's very honest, and she knows the score, and she certainly wouldn't cheat on old Billie. But we come up against, on the hideous other hand, the deadly question of race. It is widely rumored – and this may sound like a joke, but it isn't – that Ava Gardner is white."

And yet, explained Jimmy, "It is too bad, and it certainly shows up the nature and the depth of our trouble: because, in fact, the stories of a girl like Billie and a girl like Ava are not, when you examine them, so very different and Ava knows this and Billie certainly would have known it. But most of the people in our country are still persuaded that what happens to a black girl cannot happen to a white girl, and vice versa. In this particular case, I don't quite see how we could hope to get around this problem."

Baldwin's reply was read, re-read and re-read by Ava and Gene. They pondered it all day before rejecting it.

As the world knows, Ava never did the life story of Billie Holiday. Diana Ross did and should have won the Academy Award for it. It is Diana's major identification with the great mass of filmgoers.

But through Ava, Billie would also have been reborn. Ava would have merged the white with the black, the black with the white in overwhelming transfiguration.

*

The brass ring of stardom (those cheap bastards of Hollywood could at least have made it gold) toppled into Ava's hands through a group of pictures, including a loan-out to 20th Century Fox for *The Snows of Kilimanjaro*, another Hemingway opus, co-starring Gregory Peck and Susan Hayward; *Mogambo*, a Metro presentation, co-starring Ava with Clark Gable and Grace Kelly, marking the establishment of the warm and lasting friendship between the two women; and Metro's *Pandora and the Flying Dutchman* with James Mason, shot entirely in Spain.

With these films, Ava consolidated a preeminent place in the glittering constellation of cinema. With them, she actually marked the end of her "Hollywood period" as well as the end of the marriage institution in her lifetime. Confused, unhappy, restless, bored, she became enchanted by Spain. She rented a villa in La Moraleja, some forty minutes west of Madrid, a red-painted, vine-laden, sprawling, decrepit, typically Spanish villa. La Moraleja served as a hideout as well as point of reference for her wayfaring, but never grew roots that meant home.

She had reached 30 and was an enormous world star. From that time on, she began to play the role of Hollywood refugee, the role which has endured now for half her life. Her "European period" was simultaneous with the opening of the gates of Via Aiaccio 12-bis to mark the commencement of Kaufman-Lerner's Roman Adventure.

At that moment, Ava seemed a magnetic creature swirling on top of the world. She was so glamorous, so exciting, so beautiful, so stimulating for the "hard-on" dreams of American marines, so thrilling for the addictive masturbation of the Italian *maschio* and all of their moaning and panting brethren on the five continents. And she was oh, such a succulent household word in palaces to igloos. Perched and swirling she might well have been, but she always had too much taste to wear brass as bracelet, and brutal facts rattle romantic ideas to death. And the brutal facts, not necessarily in order of importance, were perched and went swirling with her.

No financial security.
No emotional security.
No psychic security.
No home security.

No woman-man security.

No professional liberty.

Three failed marriages, to Mickey Rooney, Artie Shaw and Frank Sinatra, to haunt her through her "perpetual flights" and to mock her unconcern with "happy landings."

The Barefoot Contessa established the significance of Rome in Ava's European period. Metro loaned her out to United Artists for the fantasy-drama, concocted and directed by Hollywood's kaiser, Joseph L. Mankiewicz, the co-stars including Humphrey Bogart, Edmund O'Brien, Valentina Cortese and, as Ava's impotent husband, that self-advertised cocksman of cocksmen, Rossano Brazzi. In contrast to *One Touch of Venus*, where Ava began as a statue, Mankiewicz had Ava end as one. Statues apart, any resemblance between the two films was non-existent.

The shooting of *Contessa* in Rome in 1953/54 coincided with the final breakdown of the marriage with Sinatra, then officially referred to as a "separation." Whereas the incessant transatlantic phone calls from Frank to Ava and from Ava to Frank continued, and the impetuous flying visits full of ardor and argument went on, and intimate contact was threaded through years to come, the marriage was now definitely over.

The actual divorce, for which Ava neither requested nor received alimony, took place quietly in 1957. It seemed matter-of-fact, routine, a mere formality, a signature to scrawl on a document. But when it was placed right there, it became a blur, indecipherable. Because of the tidal flow of memory. Because of the scorch of mascara in eyes. Because of the series of Sinatra records heard softly in the background.

"We expect too damned much from life, particularly from men," Ava is quoted as having said in a 1953 fan magazine interview she gave in Rome on the set of *The Barefoot Contessa*. "There's much too much romance, too many illusions. It all looks so rosy and beautiful, so heavenly from a distance. Then, in close-up, you're in it, but good. You wonder, how did it happen? Why didn't somebody prepare you? Why did nobody have the courage to tell you the truth? Why didn't anybody explain just what you were really up against, and what you could do to make a sensible life for yourself?

"Some people asked me the other day what advice I would give on marriage." (Ava's eyes went wide with amazement.)

"Asked *me*!" (Ava shook her head in disbelief.) "I thought they were joking! Now I ask you, what do I know about marriage? What could I possibly advise anybody else on the subject? The only thing I've ever learned about men is they don't know how to put drops in their eyes."

The interview byline read "Gene Morris." This guy's last image of Ava that day was of a wild-eyed Democrat, pupils dilated, arms akimbo, staring down at him in mock affront when, kidding her, he said, "I understand you're a great fan of Eisenhower."

It was the first time he had met Miss Gardner. In his disguise of *Silver Screen* reporter, Gene Morris was Gene Lerner.

Rome was also Metro's *The Little Hut* in 1956, a pitiful attempt at farce co-starring Ava with David Niven and Stewart Granger, shot entirely on the sound stages of Cinecittà. It need only be remembered for three reasons. One, it was the last of Ava's pictures actually produced by M-G-M under her exclusive contract to that increasingly mangy studio. Two, it marked the height of her flaming, obsessive relationship with an Italian actor in the film, Walter Chiari. Three, it marked Kaufman-Lerner's official representation of the great star through its William Morris connection.

Rome was also the site for preparations and costume fittings by the Fontana sisters for another Hemingway work, 20th Century Fox's *The Sun Also Rises*, co-starring Tyrone Power and Errol Flynn. It was Metro's final loan-out of Ava to another studio and was of landmark importance to her since it erased every obligation to M-G-M. It marked the end of seventeen consecutive years of bondage at piddling compensation when judged by Hollywood star standards. Ava earned countless millions of dollars for Metro in her studio-produced movies and countless millions more through its loan-out of her name and talents to other studios. But at the termination by her of perhaps the longest exclusive contract in Hollywood history, she was comparatively poverty-stricken.

The Naked Maja, which Ava signed to do for Titanus Films of Rome to commence the summer of 1958, was a milestone in Ava's professional life. It was the beginning of a new career for her. It was the first picture Ava was to make free of the shackles of Metro. She was for the first time on her own, independent, at last able to ask and to get the kind of compensation her world standing merited – all of it, to the last penny, hers. At last, some economic security for her future years entered the realm of possibility.

When Ava signed her "contract of freedom" in 1958 to do *The Naked Maja*, she was 36 years old.

London, January 3, 1958. *Bulletin of the Associated Press.*

> A *Daily Express* columnist said today Ava Gardner damaged her beautiful face in an accident in a private Spanish bullring last autumn and now needs an operation before she can make another movie.
>
> William Hickey, the columnist, gave no source for his story but said: "Ava has been told she must have an operation, possibly followed by plastic surgery. But she is terrified of undergoing the operation and so far has refused to do so."
>
> The accident was said to have occurred when the screen star fell from a horse during a visit to the private bull ring of Angel Peralta, a leading Spanish horseback bullfighter.
>
> Ava made a sudden mysterious trip from Madrid to London last October 29. She arrived at the airport with her face hidden in a scarf. The actress went at once to a hotel and stayed there, not visiting any of London's night spots. A friend insisted at the time she had "just a touch of Asian flu."
>
> Hickey claimed the wound has never healed and that in December she flew to New York to see a prominent American surgeon. Frank Sinatra, her divorced husband, also came to New York to urge her to have the operation, Hickey went on. He said she first agreed to surgery, then backed out and fled back to Spain.
>
> "Now with her face still numb and bruised, she is hoping time alone will effect a cure," Hickey said.

May 19, 1958. One of those unmatchable Roman days, the sun not yet stoked for summer overheating. Bathed in sensuous sunglow, flowers, trees, brush and bushes gracefully, gently swayed in a chorus of colors to enhance the ochres, yellows and pinks that paint the Eternal City.

Mario, the chauffeur Titanus had assigned to Ava, was driving Ava and Gene to the Titanus-Farnesina studios for a makeup test Ava was to undergo for her Duchess of Alba role. Rags, Ava's Corgi dog-of-dogs, aroused by both springtime and the ride, was with her. Nervously, Ava kept caressing the wound on her left cheek. Gene kept watching her from the corner of his eye. Mario was continually glancing at her through his rearview mirror as the black Cadillac crawled along the deep-yellow Tiber.

Suddenly, Ava turned to Gene. "Why don't we get out and walk a while?" Without waiting for an answer, she ordered Mario to stop. He quickly came around to open the rear door. A delirious Rags tumbled out. As Ava and Gene got out, the actress ordered Mario to drive at a pace just fast enough to keep up.

Rags raced like a banshee, stopped, turned back to stare at his mistress for approval. Though she did not respond, he continued his wild gambol. Ava and Gene walked along the Tiber towards Ponte Milvio, in silence. Ava lit a cigarette, barely managing with her heavily shaking hands. After a single puff, she angrily tossed it away. Over and over again as the two sauntered, the left hand moved nervously up to the left cheek. She said nothing. Gene said nothing. The Cadillac kept its funereal pace. A bewildered Rags pattered back to Ava.

Gene slipped his hand through Ava's right arm as the slow promenade continued. Rags, now trekking beside Ava, looked up at her, furious and puzzled. Why wasn't she bending over and shouting, "Go, Rags, honey, goooooooooo." Why wasn't she trying to outrace him? Why weren't they playing their very own brand of hide-and-seek?

Ava stopped. Gene stopped. Rags stopped. The Cadillac stopped. Like a somnambulist, Ava thrust her hands forward. Shaking her head in disbelief, she stared at them trembling, uncontrollably.

"Look at them," she said to Gene. "Just look! Can you believe it? Like I've got the palsy. Me, in this shitty business for nearly twenty years. Twenty lousy years and you would think I had never been to a goddamn studio before. And all I have to do is a makeup test. A goddamn makeup test! And I feel so scared, like it's the first I'm taking in my life. Honey, why am I so scared?"

Why am I so scared? indeed.

Beauty is Janus-created. It has two faces. Two faces forevermore turned away from one another, forevermore staring into timeless space and spaceless time in irreconcilable dichotomy between feeling beautiful and being beautiful. Each face has its mirror distorting true reflection and confusing clear image. It is a dreadful and cunning curse devised in ancient times by mischievous gods to punish women willing or unable to renounce their subjugation as objects or accept their annihilation as human beings.

Ava's beauty was the only membership card Hollywood was willing to give her. It was the only equity she was told she had in womanhood. She was made to believe that she had no other saleable resource in the bank of herself. She was made to accept the lie that she had no other capital, no alternate line of credit sufficient to give her value. She was forced to think that if her beauty did not exist, she did not exist, that without it she was no more than a defaulted mortgage or a bankrupt business.

Over and over again, Ava has tried to clamber across the chasm between feeling beautiful and being beautiful. Clutched by anxiety, gnawed by dissatisfaction, stung by delusion, she has made strenuous efforts ranging from poignant to desperate to grim to bitter to ridiculous to laughable. "My hands are repulsive. My hair unmanageable. My feet too big. My thighs too short and too thick. My proportions out of whack."

As she fingered her beads of self-pity, she muttered her appalling litany of self-depreciation, self-debasement, self-mutilation. "When will I ever learn from experience? When will I absorb some lesson from life? I never learned to spell. I never learned to write. I can't even read." Repeated lamentations of "I can't act, I can't act, I never could act," driving everybody out of their cotton-pickin' minds with her unbearable dirge which was not without the shrewdness of an abandoned child seeking approval or emotional sustenance.

December 12, 1959.

Hank and Gene were in the United Artists private projection room in Rome. Together with a dozen others, they were watching *On the Beach*, Stanley Kramer's production, Gregory Peck and Fred Astaire as Ava's partners, the one-and-only Giuseppe Rotunno as cinematographer, costumes by The Fontana Sisters. Ava herself had arranged the projection.

Gene was on Ava's left, Hank on her right in the last row of the projection room. Each of them held one of Ava's hands. When her scene with Astaire in front of her house started, her hands started trembling. Caught by Ava's acting mastery and the power of the scene, Hank's and Gene's hands gripped Ava's tighter. By the time the scene finished, the hand-clutching was mutual. Ava's fingernails dug so deeply into Gene's and Hank's skin that blood marked the scratches.

Ava released her hands and leaned over to Hank to whisper, "Honey, I've got to go to the little girl's room. I'll be right back."

She didn't come right back. She didn't come back at all. When Hank, Gene and the others Ava had invited to the screening, all deeply moved by Ava's performance, went over to her rented villa off the Via Po for the buffet she had prepared for them, she never showed.

Ava left because she was unable to cope with the authentic appreciation of her own friends. She had to twist her merited pride into unmerited humiliation. She could not bring herself to lay claim to the true talent she had displayed, nor the emotional distillation she had so effectively achieved. Her performance was heartrending. It was painful in its realism. Nevertheless, she ran away to finger her beads of self-pity while repeating her lamentations of, "I can't act, I can't act, I never could act," adding, "I hate this work. I despise the whole goddamn bit. There's only one reason why I keep doing it. The loot, honey. That's right, hon, the loot."

London. July 1965.

Maria Callas was all front-page headlines. She had announced that at the order of her physicians, she was cancelling all of her Covent Garden performances of *Tosca*, with the exception of the Command Performance on the night of July 5 for Queen Elizabeth II and the Queen Mother.

Kaufman-Lerner client Franco Zeffirelli, director of the production, had providentially offered Gene two seats for the performance. Gene immediately phoned Ava in Madrid. Did she want to fly up to London for the event? Did she indeed!

The next day she was at the Berkeley Hotel. That evening, Gene, in the tuxedo especially designed for him in Rome by Aldo Uggeri of Angelo's high-fashion man's shop, went in the hired limousine to fetch Ava.

When he entered her apartment at the hotel, she was nowhere to be seen. "Hi, hon," Ava shouted from the bedroom. "Don't come in. Just grab yourself a drink and make yourself comfortable."

"Let's not be late, Ava," Gene shouted back. "Respect for the Queen and the Queen Mother, and all that."

"I know, sweetie. I'll be ready in a min."

As he passed the full-length mirror en route to the bar, Gene glanced at himself. Aldo had really done a great job with that tuxedo. The filigreed black braid on the lapels was really special and the lines even made him look smart. Then, without warning, Gene began to laugh and laugh. He couldn't stop laughing. "Hon? What's so funny?" called out an unseen Ava. "Hon? Did you hear me? Will you for Christ's sake tell me what's so damn funny?"

"It just came back to me," spluttered Gene.

"What just came back to you?" asked Ava.

"Well, I was 14. The Ballet Russe was making its first visit to Omaha. I already told you about my selling newspapers after school…"

"Only a hundred times, honey," answered Ava.

"I managed to eke out enough dough to buy the two cheapest seats for the performance. Well, in my adolescent mind, I felt that art required obeisance…"

"You bet your sweet life it does. Especially the ballet."

"So I persuaded my 16-year-old sister Lil that we simply had to go formally dressed. Lil rummaged through every secondhand shop in Omaha. Finally, she found a heavy, brown velvet gown. It so overwhelmed her that the only way she could walk was to alternate between mincing quarter-steps and waddling like an elephant. You know, like Garbo in that eighteen-ton velvet train in *Mata Hari*."

"You should have seen some of the ridiculous contraptions they tried out on me. You wouldn't've believed it," interjected Ava.

"Well, I was five-foot-two and weighed less than a hundred pounds. The only solution I had was to borrow the tuxedo owned by sister Jann's brother-in-law. He was only five inches taller and forty-three pounds heavier than me."

"It sounds like Halloween," said Ava, laughing.

"It was ghastly. When we made our entrance that night, there was a shocked reaction through the crowd, titters, whispers, you know. We acted like we didn't notice, and as majestically as we could we walked towards our seats, which seemed to us to be no less than thirty miles away. Poor Lil, with her sweet, delicate frame in that gown. I clutched her as tight as I could to keep her on her feet and we kept our heads so high that we both had stiff necks for days. Anyway, we finally reached our destination. And do you know where that was?"

"Where?"

"The last two seats on the left side of the last row of the second balcony."

"Oh, no. How awful. You poor darlings, you must have wanted to die," commiserated Ava.

"Honey, I was raised on Karl Marx. And I can tell you right now that that man was a complete ignoramus. He didn't know that formal dress and second balcony were bitter enemies in the class struggle."

There was no comment from Ava. Puzzled by the silence, Gene turned towards the bedroom. His mouth fell open in astonishment at the apparition before him.

Ava had stealthily entered the living room and was standing there.

She was superlative. No, absolute. So glorious that she could only be acknowledged with awe. So majestic that everyone, as if magnetized, would be forced to lift their head to stare. Her ankle-length Balanciaga was in rich, brocaded, deep-green velvet. Her splendid shoulders and breasts in draped *décolletage* would have impassioned a Raphael or a da Vinci. Embracing her neck was a dazzling emerald pendant. Dangling from her ears were long earrings in matching emeralds. Her black hair was pulled back severely, held in place at the back of her neck by an emerald-and-pearl clip. Her mouth was luscious strawberry cream. Framed by meticulously plucked, slanted brows and mascaraed lashes, her brown eyes seemed to flicker with starlight.

Gene slowly walked over to her and kissed her. "Unbelievable," was the only word he managed to say. Clearly pleased over the effect she had made, Ava smiled, then quickly said, "Christ, we're running late," in order to break the spell. "Hon, we've got to run."

"So let's go," said Gene, grabbing Ava's hand. Moving swiftly, they left the apartment, raced down the corridor, grabbed the elevator and jumped into the waiting limousine.

On that delirious night of July 5, Ava and Gene walked hurriedly down the aisle of Covent Garden, breaching protocol by appearing at the theater after the arrival of the Royal Family. Fortunately, the Queen, Queen Mother and their party had not yet appeared in the Royal Box.

Ava and Gene quickly slipped into their seats, immediately to be engulfed in a nerve-wracking hubbub of anticipation. One could easily have imagined that the event was not opera, but a world-heavyweight championship bout. The touts, gamblers and *appassionati* were simply of a different breed – notables, celebrities, until-death devotees of the singer, jet-setters gathered from all parts of the world to witness the dramatic occasion.

The bets were many, the stakes enormous, the odds in constant flux. Would it be the last time that Callas would perform *Tosca*? Could, would the night mark the ultimate appearance of the Diva of Divas to opera? Would she reach the difficult high note that preceded her first entrance? Would she manage the challenge of *Vissi d'Arte*? At what point would her voice give out? Would she stagger through to the final curtain or suffer the terrible humiliation of a knockout?

A tailed-and-white-tied balding gentleman on Ava's right was speaking to her. She permitted him an ear but nary a glance. After a moment, she leaned over to Gene and whispered: "That creep says we've met before, but I sure as hell don't remember."

"I know his face but can't place it," said Gene. "Who is he?"

"King Umberto of Italy," Ava responded, rolling her eyes with a Christ-why-does-he-have-to-sit-next-to-me expression in them.

Just then, Queen Elizabeth and the Queen Mother, followed by their entourage, entered the Royal Box. As they nodded and smiled, the entire audience rose and turned towards them. The orchestra burst into "God Save The Queen."

As the anthem of Britain blared forth, the eyes of Elizabeth II passed slowly through the crowd below. As they reached the commanding, sublime figure of Ava, they stopped as if gripped in a vise. For what seemed an eternity, the gaze of England's monarch and Ava Gardner locked. It was Elizabeth II, having acknowledged the presence of another sovereign, who broke the stare. Ava accepted the tribute because, for that magical moment, she felt herself a queen.

At Covent Garden the night of July 5, 1965, which indeed marked Maria Callas' farewell to opera, Ava achieved her miracle. By successfully clambering across the chasm between being beautiful and feeling beautiful, she had defied the Janus curse.

And it was a beautiful sight to see.

"Whenever I have to make a public appearance, I'm terrified. I've been that way all my life," she has said. And Sydney Guilaroff, her favorite hair stylist, who had worked with Ava on many films over a thirty-year period, said, "Ava is a cripple of shyness. She was never born to be exposed."

Why am I so scared?

Honey, Mary Wollstonecraft wrote you an answer nearly two hundred years ago:

> Taught from infancy that beauty is woman's scepter, the mind shapes itself to the body, and roaming round its gilt cage, only seeks to adorn its prison.

July 16, 1958. Late afternoon.

Ava in her Grand Hotel suite in Rome. She sat like an immovable object, staring with fixed jaw, her eyes burning, her hands fidgeting between cigarette and booze. Occasionally, the left hand caressed the minute indentation on her cheek that was the only apparent evidence of the accident on Angel Peralta's ranch in October.

Oscar Saul, a Hollywood screenwriter of modest achievement, was reading aloud new scenes he had been hired to write between the Duchess of Alba and Francisco Goya for *The Naked Maja*. Tense as he evidently was, Saul seemed surprisingly oblivious to Ava's ill-concealed exasperation, but Gene could feel it.

The writer was in the midst of one of the Duchess' lines when Ava precipitously rose. Barely able to control her ire, she blurted out, "Why don't you just leave the script? I'll try to read it tonight and we'll talk about it tomorrow."

Fumblingly, Saul also stood. "What do you think so far?" he asked anxiously.

"I'll tell you when I finish," Ava replied curtly. "I've got to get dressed for dinner now." She turned and swiftly disappeared into the bedroom.

Having no comprehension of what had gone wrong, Saul stuttered goodbyes to a figure no longer there. He looked helplessly at Gene, shrugged his shoulders and left. The moment Ava heard the door close, she reappeared.

"What the hell does that motherfucking bastard think?" was her opener as she paced in a 100-degree snit. "That I can't read? Does he think I'm retarded? I've been in this business all my life and this is the first time some half-assed writer thought I was so damned illiterate that I couldn't read a script. You don't have to be a Vassar graduate to know what he wrote is shit! I don't want that stupid asshole near me again!"

If a seminar on "The Woman's Propensity for Language That Is Foul" had been organized during the lifetime of Emily Post, the most powerful arbiter of social propriety in American history, she would have thought it had something to do with squawking chickens and egg-laying.

Miss Post-Toasties had a mentality similar to that of Queen Victoria who, while demanding criminal punishment for men caught in homosexual acts, saw absolutely no basis for similar treatment for women. How was it possible for two women to indulge in lovemaking, the British Empress asked? How was it possible for women so beautiful, so chic and so glamorous to need Lifebuoy soap stuffed into their mouths, the American Queen of Suitable Behavior would have asked? How could she have realized, as did Elizabeth Taylor, Joan Crawford, Anna Magnani, Esther Williams, Ava and a host of other silver-screen ladies, that "trooper" in the expression "to swear like a…." was a computer error and should have come out as "trouper"?

Among the underthings of intimate nature that a pretty, decent Southern gal like Ava packed in her luggage for the Hollywood of once-upon-a-time, unmentionables like basic innocence and pain-lovely fantasies of forever as better-to-be-forgotten examples, she also brought along pithy homegrown expressions, which, while not exclusive to Dixie, still carried the aroma of magnolia, cottonseed and black ghetto. As the years passed, her speech became more and more hot-peppered with expletive, until it became a case of "doin' what comes naturally."

Dirty speech adds no charm to a woman's appeal. Nor, for that matter, to a man's. Nor does it mark the dividing line between class and no class, nor shift the weight between good and evil, decency and indecency, dignity and indignity, sexual morality and sexual depravity.

The scum spewed by Ava simply contributed to her self-deprecation and self-debasement. It sullied her beauty without contradicting it. Through familiarity with her and with her addiction to foul language, distaste eventually turned to acceptance of its being just another facet of Ava.

Anthony Franciosa in the role of Francisco Goya was Ava's co-star in *The Naked Maja*. The Titanus production's director was Hollywood's champion crybaby Henry Koster. All three were WHA-KLA clients.

It was with *The Naked Maja* that Ava formed a strong friendship with the Rembrandt of cinematographers, another client of KLA, Giuseppe "Peppino" Rotunno. Among his list of creations, Rotunno numbers Federico Fellini's *La Dolce Vita*, *8½*, *Amarcord* and *City of Women*, Luchino Visconti's *Rocco and His Brothers* and *The Leopard*, Stanley Kramer's *On the Beach*, Bob Fosse's *All That Jazz* and Robert Altman's *Popeye.*

"Cinema for me is light, light for me is everything," is a Fellini maxim. "Images can't be expressed, can't live without light. Rotunno is the bestower of light." And it was this "bestower of light," soft-spoken, gentle, empathic, who saved Ava for herself and for the screen. On that horrendous May day in 1958, with Ava in trauma over facing her first makeup test after the horse-throwing incident in Spain, it was this dark-faced, intensely relaxed, tender Italian who was able to put a trembling somnambulist in front of a camera and find a way to mask the injury that blemished Ava's face and spirit, transforming it into another attribute of her beauty.

"Such a dear, talented and sensitive human being," is how Ava referred to Rotunno in a 1975 letter to Gene. "I'll always be grateful to him."

But poor Henry Koster. All those tears. Leading man Franciosa spitting in his face. Tears. Franciosa in screaming fits. Tears. Franciosa in a furniture-breaking spree on the set. Tears. Franciosa rushing off to his room at the Excelsior Hotel to pack his bags never to return, madly throwing shirts, ties, socks and underwear into his valise, while Gene and Hank, just as madly, removed them, accompanied by melodramatic gesture and dialogue of, "I'm going!" Socks and underwear tossed in. "You can't!" Socks and underwear pulled out. "I'm leaving!" Shirts and ties thrust in. "You can't!" Shirts and ties in angry tug-of- war.

Franciosa contrite, sending Koster affectionate missives of apology. Tears, tears, more tears.

Ava showed considerable patience for her insecure co-star, and Koster had every reason to be grateful for her professionalism under what seemed a permanent state of guerrilla warfare. She generally suffered Tony's tantrums with equanimity. When furniture flew, she either ducked or, shrugging her shoulders, slowly walked off the set. In order for Franciosa to get into the necessary dramatic mood, he spent hours in ghostly self-communion, Actors Studio techniques and sticking his finger way down his throat, choking and gagging. Ava sat and watched, usually controlling her feelings. She was not always undisturbed and undemanding, particularly when Tony's emotion came out in spit. After all, *she* was the star of the picture.

She demanded that the shooting schedule begin at night, commencing when the blazing heat of Rome subsided, at eight in the evening. True, the Titanus studios were not air-conditioned. True, Rome was undergoing a dreadful heat wave in July. True, Ava's magnificent costumes were velvet, brocade and weighed a ton. Ava got her way. Scenes of folk-dancing and costumed crowds were shot way into the night and Ava was a willing participant. They became stopping-off places for "Rome-by-Night" tourist buses. Her achievement in turning day into night, night into day, suited her admirably. She was, after all, a creature of the night.

When an Ava Night happened, it would take a while for you to recover.

The companions on an Ava Night might have been labeled acquaintance, friend, chum, sister, favorite of the moment – or might have had no label at all. The city might have been Rome, Madrid, New York – any city. The restaurant might have been the Cabala, Ranieri, the Jockey Club, Valentin, Mario's, Romeo Salta, Chasen's – any restaurant. The nightclubs might have been Il Pipistrello, Number One, the Florida, the Chateau Madrid – any nightclub. The dives might have been a Trastevere cave, a flamenco spot on the outskirts of Madrid, the Champagne Club stuck in an Eighth Avenue cellar – any dive where gigolos, hookers, pimps, gays, transvestites and gypsies mixed with the famed, the rich and the slummers who paid for excitement and anonymity.

As an Ava Night commenced, she was imposingly lovely. She and her companions had themselves a couple of drinks before starting on their "let's have a ball" adventure. Off they went to dinner. Afterwards the improvised, impetuous chase through the night began, one club after another, one dive after another. As the hours passed, Ava went through a metamorphosis, as if a magnificent, swift-winged butterfly had turned itself into a still-born cocoon.

She might have been hanging on to a companion's arm, expressing affection and showing pleasure. She might have been conversing with ease and wit, her throaty laughter rich and contagious. She might have fallen silent, playing nervously with her food. She might for no apparent reason have turned on someone, vicious, vituperative, plunging him into mental anarchy. She might have sunk deeper and deeper into alcoholic mists, devoid of contact. She might have suddenly said, "I've got to go to the john," never returning, thus driving everybody frantic with concern. She might have risen from the table to announce, "I hate this dump, let's get the hell out of here," and everybody would have put down his forkful of food, closed his mouth and followed.

She might have left her seat and her companions at one of the dives to dance alone, pirouetting, stamping her feet, snaking her hands over her head, snapping her fingers, clapping her hands, shutting everybody out of her fenced-in existence. She might or might not have noticed that the joint had emptied, that everybody had vamoosed, that only she and some cadaverous companions were left.

She might or might not have realized that the weary musicians were still going through their paces long past schedule so she could doggedly go on with her voodoo of booze, bare feet and boogie, to exorcise her terror of lying alone in darkness, waiting for the sleep that would not come. Her face flushed, her eyes bleary, her hair slovenly, she seemed in her frenzy to try to conjure up the dawn, to force morning into the night, to find someone to hum her a soft lullaby. At three in the morning, at five, at seven, through boredom, exhaustion or lack of anywhere else to go, the Ava Night might have finished.

Or it might not. There might be a visit to her hotel, any hotel, like for example the St. Regis in New York at six o'clock in the morning. From her suite's refrigerator, she might bring out a five-pound tin of Beluga Caviar, vintage champagne and other gourmet goodies. She might serve Hank and her other companions, all reeling with fatigue, the most sumptuous Sunday breakfast of their lives. She might be, could be, would be gracious, delightful, sweet and together, again the butterfly broken out of the cocoon.

Another Ava Night had passed.

She was at last ready for sleep.

It was approximately the time that Ava was shooting *The Little Hut* in Rome that she really began to formulate what seemed to be a decisive decision to live permanently in Europe, not in a rented villa such as the one at La Moraleja, but in a home of her own. The word "decision" when applied to Ava must always be used with caution. The state of "living abroad" was never a hundred percent countersigned in her mind. It was constantly subject to shift in mood, political events, economic trends; the recognition that Internal Revenue and Santa Claus didn't celebrate the same holiday; all kinds of conflicting advice from numerous wise men and wise guys, out of sincere interest in her welfare, or in sincere self-interest.

Throughout much of the 1950s, Rome was a strong candidate. Ava got considerable pleasure from its life, its psychology and attitude towards work, and through the William Morris connection she became closer to Hank and Gene.

She gathered unto her some "chums." A "chum" had a special significance to Ava, and it was she who made the selection and designation. You could be a chum whether you were male or female. You were not quite the same as a "friend" and not quite "family," but you hovered in between. You were a kind of throwback to the deep, meaningful, heart-touched relationship one sometimes formed in childhood. A chum had prerogatives and a chum had obligations, and they were not always equal. You were special, you were precious, you were on occasion permitted to share in privacy, but you were not immortal. You could be a chum today and be gone tomorrow, and *paparazzi* and chum were mutually exclusive. As she gathered chums unto her, she found herself in vicious warfare with the roaming band of photographers that relentlessly hounded her wherever she went and whatever she did. They adored her, not only because they found her fascinating, but also because they knew they

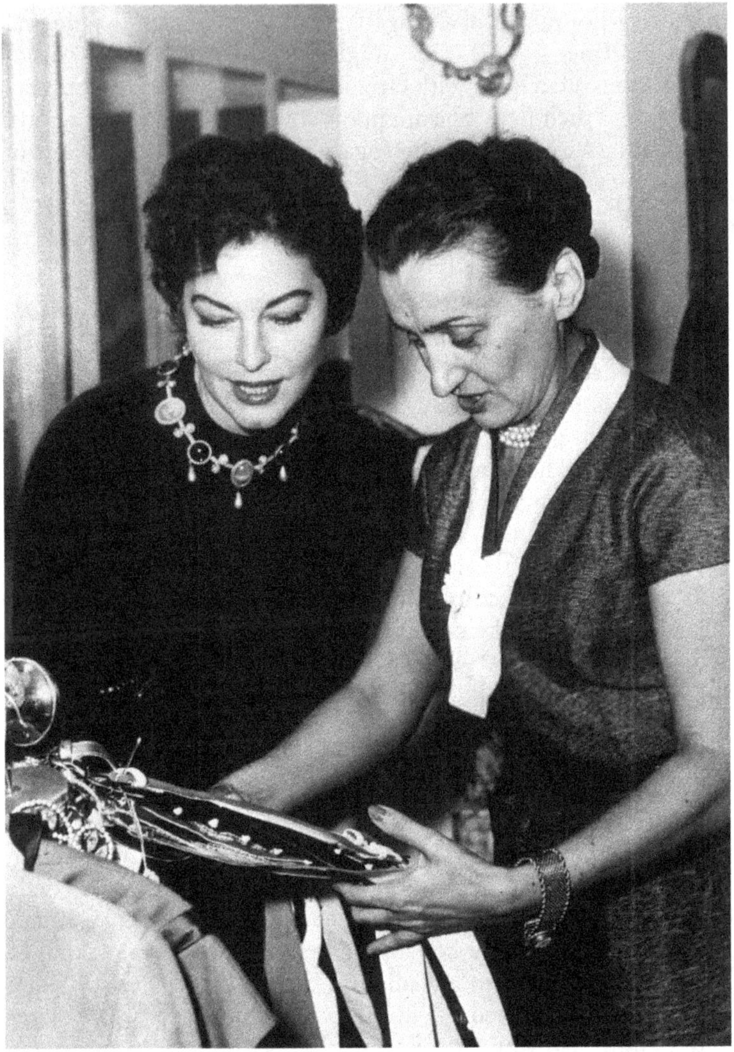

Ava Gardner and Micol Fontana

could provoke her, and thus get from her the unflattering kind of photos that sell. As far as Ava was concerned, neither rat poison nor chemical gas was adequate to give them the kind of violent death they deserved. So Rome, which somehow manages to provide everything, offered both scum and chum for her to consider in any decisive decision as to where home was to be.

Chums included Hank and Gene; Robert Edwards, Titanus' head of publicity, later European head of Embassy Pictures, and Edwards' charming and emotionally generous Italian wife, Luisa; the Lee Kamerns of Metro-Goldwyn-Mayer of Italy; Micol Fontana, all business and all woman, as devoted to Ava as one hopes a blood sister would be; David Hanna, press representative on *The Barefoot Contessa*, who later became Ava's personal publicity agent, and whose fall from grace outdistanced Lucifer's.

Other chums were Mario Russo, the multilingual assistant director to Koster who, a competent director himself, was by far one of the most capable and dedicated directorial assistants to the American and British directors who found themselves floundering in the morass of Italian picture-making; Doctor Frank Silvestri, American medicine man for Rome's foreign colony and world stars; Angelo Vitucci, handsome, chic and gracious protégé of the mentor of Italian high fashion for men, Brioni; and of course Peppino, *the* Peppino, Rotunno, *the* Rotunno.

Last and never least was that Southern-bred gentleman, the loving, loveable and delicious Nunnally Johnson, who wrote and directed *The Angel Wore Red* for Titanus in 1959, which co-starred Ava and Dirk Bogarde (Dirk, too, being something of a chum) and was photographed by Rotunno. Deep chummery also developed between Ava and Nunnally's wife, Dorris. A natural worrier, Dorris had a stiffness that one associates with pioneer women. She was often uncomfortable with Nunnally's agility with words and the whipped cream that topped his Southern charm. With time, her own warm personality appeared to enhance an indominable sense of duty. In her own way, she became as delicious as that unforgettable man.

And, of course, there was Walter.

Walter Chiari.

Compagno straordinario to the female of the species.

Reincarnated *cavaliere*, dashing, charming, poetic, deft, dexterously thrusting lances right and left at vile *paparazzi.*

Psychic radar permanently trained upon the feminine sensibility.

Blind and crippled if unable to dedicate himself to someone. A female someone, to be more precise.

Horizons seemingly limitless. Adored by the Italian public. Fame being gained throughout the continent, strides being made in international films.

Swift and inventive brain, shown off as others might display an elegantly-cut cashmere sweater, or new swimming trunks carefully tailored to ultimate smugness. Good looks unblessed by tradition. A smile with teeth in it. Tall, lithe body. Excellent athlete – tennis, swimming, skiing, running and racing, racing and running, all perpetual motion, as if every human activity had to be the 100-meter dash. An extraordinary affinity for children. It was with them that he had his most passionate love affair. With the slightest encouragement, droves of them would have left their homes, mothers and fathers, to run and race, frantic, frenetic, wherever they were to be led by their adored *Walterino*.

Why didn't Ava have children? This is a question Walter says he repeatedly asked her, and that he certainly asked others close to her. She expressed her love for them at every possible occasion. So, why? Having a child was a monumental decision. She feared decision. Having a child meant putting herself on the line, no flagellation of self and no blame fastened on others. "All in woman is an enigma and all in woman has a single solution," wrote Friedrich Nietzsche in *Thus Spake Zarathustra.* And it is the pregnancy that frightened Ava most of all. Her hypochondriac panic would increase as the fetus in her womb grew. She could not summon up the will as potential mother or the faith in herself as woman.

Even Porfirio Rubirosa, Roger Vadim and Rossano Brazzi envied Walter's conquest of women, including three of the most remarkable to grace the Hollywood on the Tiber era: Lucia Bosé, later to become the wife of Luis Dominguín; Elsa Martinelli, who matched presidents, prime ministers and war criminals by three times making the cover of *Life*.

And Ava.

These relationships were not only for an afternoon quickie. Or for a night. They were real *fidanzamenti*, lasting for years. The one with Ava went on longer than any of her marriages.

How did Walter do it, jealous-maddened Casanovas asked one another?

How could Walter do it, if there was truth in statements from his green-eyed rivals that his sexual organ was no bigger than a snail's horn?

But Walter did it. The physical attraction between Ava and him was magnetic storm. While they were shooting *The Little Hut*, an irate production manager on many mornings forced

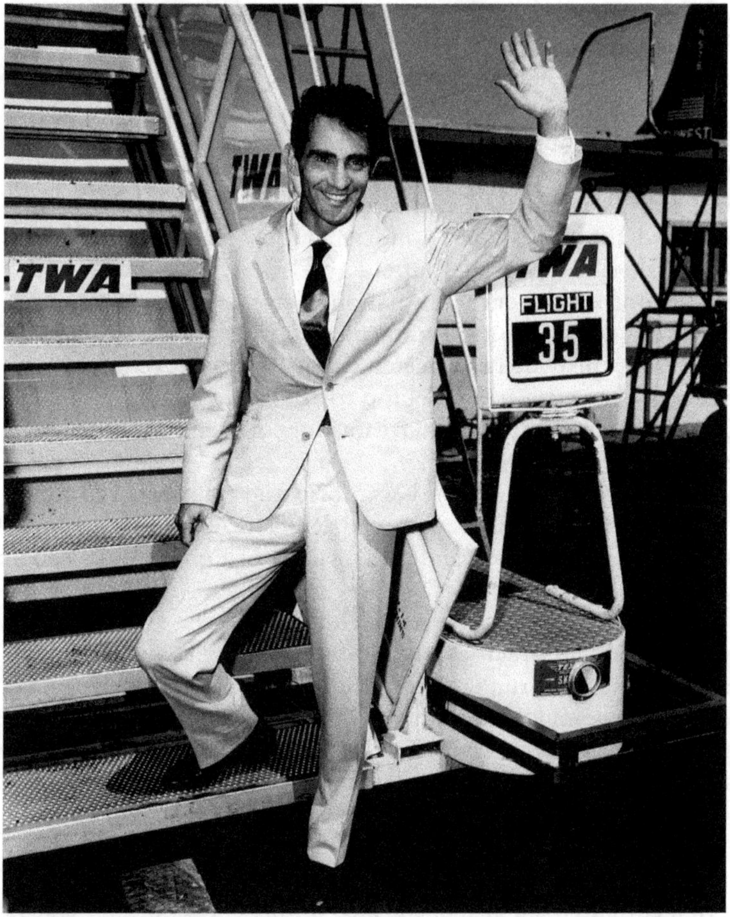

Walter Chiari

Hank to go to Ava's Planza di Spagna apartment, where he almost had to break down the door to get Ava and Walter up and out to the set to commence shooting.

There was also meanness in Walter, corrosive and stinking. And sudden resentments that shriveled his tenderness. There were struggles for supremacy and bouts of jealousy, juicy and vulgar. And That Ol' Devil Suspicion came to pay Ava a visit and wasn't about to leave. He began to dance his serious *pas de deux*, which had her swirling like a dervish. Walter was in a secret plot with journalists and photographers to get publicity at her expense, she alleged. She was being used, used, used to enhance Walter's career, she charged. She was being made a fool of by his fucking around, she accused.

One witness to their rows was one of show business' most extraordinary personalities, who Hank recently went to visit in New York: 87-year-old Bricktop, retired, ailing, but still glowing. Real name Ada DuCongé, Bricktop is still referred to as the world's most famous "saloonkeeper." She established the most elegant club of 1920s Paris, the *de rigeur* night spot for the era's international jetset. Anybody who was anybody, including the Prince of Wales, made it a point to be seen there, provided the selective Bricktop approved. It was to the more sophisticated Bricktop to whom the young Josephine Baker, the toast of Paris, often came for counsel, confidences and solace.

After the Second World War, Bricktop transferred to Rome to reign over the Via Veneto, particularly at the height of the dolce vita. As Bricktop and Hank talked of Rome and its epoch of glory, she began to speak of Ava and Walter.

"They used to come to my club often," she recalled. "Ava was usually so gracious and so well-behaved. Sweet, lovely, affectionate, not drunk or boisterous at all. However, I remember one night she and Walter came in. Walter showed me some photos of orphan girls. You know how he was mad for children, and he knew that one of my most important charities dealt with poor creatures without mother or father.

"For some strange reason, Ava became convinced that Walter was showing off pictures of other women. She got drunker and drunker, started cursing. She kicked off her shoes, like she enjoys doing. She went into a tizzy, screaming at Walter to leave. I kept my temper and walked over to her. I told her that I didn't tolerate that kind of behavior or that kind of language from anyone, even a good friend like her, and that she had better get out of my place quick!

"Ava got up, really burning," Bricktop continued. "She shouted, 'You're not going to throw me out of this dump.' I told her I was. Ty Power's chauffeur was there, so I got him over to Ava and asked him to escort her out. She went, still screaming even out on the Via Veneto. I really got mad. 'Don't you dare come back in here again,' I shouted back. Poor Walter didn't know what to do. He just sat there looking at the floor, like all his nerves had fallen out of his body and were spread out in front of him.

"Ava phoned me. I believe it was the next day, or the day after. She apologized and went on apologizing. She came in later that day and began to cry on my shoulder, telling me over and over how sorry she was, swearing she would never behave like that again, how much she cared about me.... You know – the whole bit.

"I loved that woman. You could see her in broad daylight without a stitch of makeup on, and she was breathtaking. She was the most beautiful creature I've ever seen. No, that's not right. She's not past tense. She is the most beautiful creature I'll ever see," concluded Bricktop, her far-away look seemingly envisioning Ava as her hand gripped Hank's.

With all of Walter's strengths, he came to realize that the gravity of his weaknesses outweighed them and was pulling him down and down. Ava pleaded with him to protect the potential international career she astutely recognized in him. She raged at him to cut his ties with "friends" who knew how to wreak advantage from his good-natured lack of will. She was saddened and disgusted by the way his talent, the sharpness of mind he possessed, his natural sensibilities, were slowly being sapped.

The ghoulish specter of drugs insinuated its presence in the Ava-Walter relationship. When she began to suspect that he might be on something, she threw snits that would put any epileptic to shame. Walter, who had a remarkable facility for denial, denied and denied and denied, and Ava was unable to pin down irrefutable evidence.

When it comes to drugs, Ava was a puritan, female Cotton Mather. She would have no truck with drugs or anyone addicted to them. She detested, despised and abhorred the drug scene. Whatever permissiveness she was prepared to accept, definitely and specifically did not include *that* shit.

In 1957, there was a dramatic scene in the Chiari-Gardner suite at the Principe di Piemonte hotel in Turin, where Walter was performing to standing-room crowds in his new revue. Ava was going out of her cotton-pickin' mind trying to convince Hank and Gene that Walter was hooked. Neither could bring himself to believe her.

Ava was dressed for the evening, ready to go to the theater when Hank and Gene arrived from Rome. She had been waiting for them in increased agitation. As soon as they entered the door of the suite, she pulled them into the bedroom.

"You've got to talk to him. I've tried. Jesus, how I've tried! Maybe he'll listen to you two. Maybe you'll get through to him."

"What's happened? What's he done?" were Hank's and Gene's puzzled questions.

Ava looked surreptitiously around her, went to the bedroom door, surveyed the living room. She then turned back towards K and L, closing the door behind her. She came close to them, her eyes dilated.

"He's taking dope," she whispered, waiting for the shock to sink in.

Hank and Gene looked speechlessly at one another, then looked back at Ava.

"I'm telling you. He's on drugs." She was riled by the lack of response. "For Christ's sake, have you gone deaf and dumb? Drugs! DRUGS! Do something!"

"Honey, don't get so hysterical," Gene said.

"Goddamit, I am hysterical," Ava retorted.

"How do you know?" asked Hank.

"How do I know?"

"Yes, just tell us how you know," Hank repeated.

"I know. I see him every day. I watch him. I see the creeps fasten on him like leeches. I'm telling you, he's hooked."

"On what, Ava?" queried Gene.

"Cocaine, that's what. I swear that he sniffs the stuff. He might be on something worse but I won't swear to that. But I *will* swear to the cocaine."

Shocked but unconvinced, Hank and Gene realized they could not ignore Ava's charges. She was too certain, too upset. That night, back in the suite after Walter's show, they decided to confront him. Ava diplomatically said she was tired and was going to bed. Now alone with the accused, Hank and Gene asked Walter some rather blunt questions. Walter laughed. He made delightful jokes. Soon his two agents found themselves caught up in a delightful Chiari performance. He went through improvisations of diverse methods of sniffing cocaine, and they were funny. And he did his routines loud enough for Ava to hear every last word in the bedroom. Walter indeed had a remarkable facility for denial, and he denied and denied and denied so disarmingly.

On May 22, 1970, the dreaded banner headlines, as black as death, appeared on the front pages of every Italian newspaper. "Chiari Imprisoned on Drug Charges!" "Walterino Confesses

Drug Use!" "Italian Public in Shock Over Chiari Arrest"! "Chiari, Another Tragic Victim of Drug Addiction, Confined to Regina Coeli Prison!"

It was one of Italy's biggest postwar scandals. Walter festered in Rome's Regina Coeli prison while his son, Simone, was born to Alida Chelli, whom Walter had married in Australia a year earlier. Only on August 28, nearly fifteen weeks after his arrest, was Walter released to stand trial, the legal process dragging on and on until May 1972. The next time Ava saw Gene, she expressed her concern over Walter's plight, but knew that she was helpless. "I tried to tell you and Hank. I tried so hard. But you wouldn't believe me," Ava said. Even though the prosecutor asked for a two-year, six-month prison sentence, Walter was instead convicted on a minor charge and not required to return to prison.

The Chiari who emerged from a ghoulish nightmare lasting more than two years was a sad shadow of the Chiari who might have been. Now 50, he still functions, still works in theater, in television, does one-night stands in clubs or arenas, occasionally is seen in film cameo roles. He is still always "on," always in perpetual motion, but there is no sound and the silences grow longer and deeper. He still adores children, but they're all grown up now, and the magic they and Walter shared is but a trembling echo of recollection.

In the summer of 1961, years before the drug scandal broke, years after Ava had sounded her warning, Walter went to New York to work on voice and English in preparation for his starring role in *The Gay Life*, based on Arthur Schnitzler's *Anatol*. With a book written by the praiseworthy husband-and-wife team Fay and Michael Kanin, it was the last Broadway show ever done by one of Broadway's outstanding teams of lyricist and composer, Howard Dietz and Arthur Schwartz.

Oriana Fallaci came to Detroit in October of that year for the Italian magazine *L'Europeo* to do an article on Walter in conjunction with the show's world premiere at the Fisher Theater.

"Ava is a name, whether spoken or unspoken, that constantly hovered over the two days I spent with Walter in Detroit," wrote Fallaci. "Ava who helped Walter learn English, Ava who had encouraged him to confront the challenge of Broadway, Ava who kept pushing him and pushing him to do only good things, Ava who no longer existed as Ava but as a memory of love nestled in renewed wisdom."

"I wrote a poem about a spiderweb I found in a corner," Walter confided. "I recounted all my dreams to it, dreams that before were so numerous and so big there was no space for them stacked from celling to floor. But here was a spiderweb in a corner and I found it sufficient to hold all my dreams, because now my dreams are so few and so fragile," Fallaci quoted him as saying.

Goodbyes are endless among Italians. Chiari's sign-off gesture after all his performances was a meaningful trademark known to millions. He lifted his hands over his head and waved over and over again. But his wave was not towards them but towards himself, not a goodbye but "come back." Many of Ava's and his months together were really a series of goodbyes, but they didn't always realize it because the goodbyes were also "come back."

In all disparity, in every contradiction, there is or seems to be some point of contact. Both Ava and Walter knew that love once given and received was the clutching grip of a handshake that one day would have to be broken. No matter the distance in miles or years, no matter the gyrations of life, they both also knew that the handshake would permanently remain in outstretched finger-to-finger touch.

Seven
The Human Voice of the She-Wolf

May 14, 1959.

Gene's hand reached out in the night shadows and flicked on his bedside lamp. A quick look at his watch revealed that it was 4:20 a.m. He picked up the receiver to halt the ringing phone that, at such an ungodly hour, sounded like a fire alarm.

The voice was unmistakable.

Magnani, her voice rising in a crescendo of irritation.

"Gene! *Pronto! Pronto! Pronto!*"

"What happened, Anna?" Gene asked.

"I had a terrible dream. I'm still in a sweat. It was so real. Too real! I'm sorry I had to wake you."

"So tell me."

"Ingrid Bergman was in some hotel room with Brando and Sidney Lumet. Martin Jurow was there, too. Bergman was whispering something to them she didn't want me to hear. Then Tennessee Williams came in carrying a big poster lettered like a Florentine scroll. With that Southern dialect of his, he read: 'Anna Magnani, Marlon Brando, Joanne Woodward in *The Fugitive Kind* by Tennessee Williams, directed by Sidney Lumet, Produced by Martin Jurow.' Bergman's face turned to ice. She got up, walked over to Tennessee, and without a word tore the poster to pieces." Anna's words came faster and faster as she recalled the dream.

"Tennessee didn't try to stop her. Lumet and Jurow just sat there. They just stared at her like they were dead. Then a hard smile came to her face. She waved her arms and suddenly there was a new poster in her hands. And *her* name was there not mine, Ingrid Bergman, not Anna Magnani! Gene, I warn you. If you try to tell me it's just a dream, I'll… Dreams are warnings. You don't tempt fate by ignoring them when they're as clear as this one."

"Anna, there's nothing Bergman can do. You have a confirmed deal," Gene tried to reassure her, but Magnani wasn't listening.

"What does that woman want from me? Hasn't she done enough to my life?"

"Anna, I said…"

"Now she wants to take away my roles. My livelihood!"

"Anna, please hold it, will you? Anna…"

"Call Jurow right away. Or Lumet. Tennessee. Somebody! Anybody! I want you to…"

"ANNA! Let me get a word in. I said there's nothing Ingrid can do. You have a confirmed deal!"

"What does that *strega* care about a confirmed deal? And people squirm out of firm deals a hundred times a day in this sordid business."

"Tennessee wrote the part for *you*. Jurow left his big job at William Morris so he could make the picture with *you*. Brando was only persuaded to do it because *you're* in it. Anyway, it's ludicrous to think of Ingrid in that part. No one could be more wrong for it and she would be the first to say so."

"She doesn't *care* if she's wrong for it, don't you understand? She just doesn't care! You're my agent. You have to do something to calm me down."

"If only I knew how to calm you down, Anna."

"Ever since they stole *Two Women* from me, there's no peace inside me. Quicksand or earthquakes is all I feel. I get crazy."

"Do you want me to come over?"

"No. I'm okay now. Go back to sleep."

There was a pause. Gene realized that Anna needed to talk. The telephone was her connection with a world she mistrusted more and more. Night and day it provided her with communication of sudden fears, sudden joys, ideas, impressions, reactions, impetuous fits of anger or anguish she felt compelled to share with the few who still retained her confidence.

"You're sure you don't want me to come over, Anna? I don't mind." Another pause. When she spoke, it was more to herself than to Gene.

"I'll never get over it," she said. "Never."

"I'll never get over it either," he replied.

"Loren playing my Cesira in *Two Women*… Loren! When Moravia wrote the book, he knew he was writing the role of my life. He knew! But he sold himself to Ponti for money.

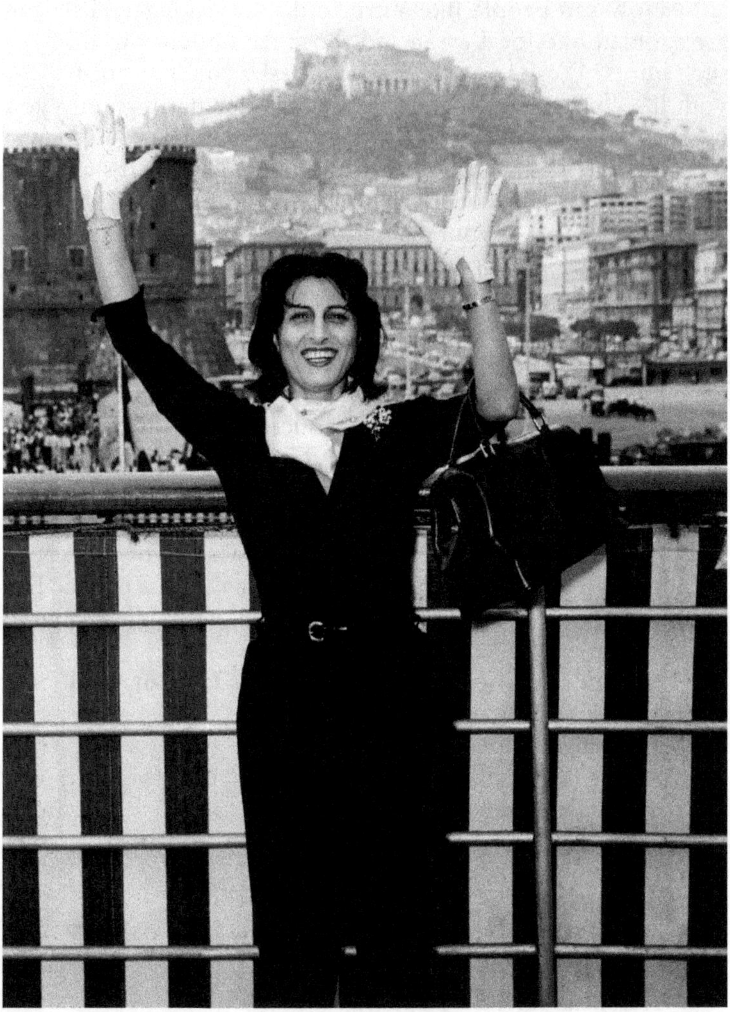

Anna Magnani

To be Judas Iscariot to Christ is bad enough, but to be your own Judas...

"If God had decided to give a name to the serpent in the Garden of Eden, do you know what it would've been? Carlo Ponti! Carlo Ponti... ugh! And poor De Sica. His gambling has rotted away his soul, poor man. Now he's just a whore who will accept anything to pay his debts.

"How can people like Vittorio do such things? How can grown men like Joe Levine and those Paramount big shots be such idiots? 'Yes, Anna darling, the Cesira role was created for you. It's your role, Anna, darling. Yes, Anna darling, only you in this whole world can play it. Yes, Anna darling, you'll be the sensation of all time. No question, Anna darling, it's another Oscar in the bag for you. Won't it be sensational with you as the mother and Loren as your daughter? Won't it just be stupendous, Anna darling?'

"Stupendous, for sure. Sensational, no doubt. With those two balloons of hers the same height as my face? What was I supposed to do? Play soccer with them? They would have to put me on a ladder. Or cut off her legs. Stupendous, hah! How can anybody in his right mind make me such a proposition? Making a farce out of a pain and tragedy! *Two Women* is no fantasy. It's about the cruel experience of living people! About children hiding in caves from bombs and bayonets, living in terror and starving. How could they even have asked me to be a party to such a thing? Me the mother and Loren my little Rosetta. The audience would expect her to rape the Moroccan soldiers, not the other way around. Gene, are you there?"

"All you're doing is getting yourself and me angry all over again, Anna. What's the point? The picture's going ahead with Sophia playing Cesira."

"You're right, you're right. We must try to forget it. You swear to me Bergman can do nothing?"

"I swear, Anna."

"You're one hundred percent sure?"

"Two hundred percent."

"How much did they offer me as a bribe to accept their proposition?"

"You mean for *Two Women*?"

"What else are we talking about?"

"Two hundred and fifty thousand dollars," replied Gene.

"They could have offered me a million dollars and I would have spit in their faces. How could I cheat the people that way? How could I cheat *myself*? I could have said yes. The Cesira role belonged to me and nobody else. Even Sophia agreed. But the public could never believe me as the mother and Loren as my Rosetta. How could I ever believe it? When I die, Gene, when

I die, when people think of me, they must know that Magnani never lied to them. They must be sure that Magnani never betrayed them. And that Magnani never betrayed herself."

On September 10, 1973, when it was announced that Anna Magnani was entering the Clinica Mater Dei for a possible exploratory operation, hundreds came to the clinic for information and thousands went to churches to light candles for her recovery.

When, at 6:35 Wednesday evening, September 26, 1973, Italian radio broke in with a bulletin to announce her death from cancer of the pancreas, the people of Rome converged on the clinic, stood or kneeled in its gardens or against its walls, whispering to strangers wedged beside them what they knew, all they felt, whatever they could recall of their *Nannarella*.

When the radio and television networks and newspapers announced that her body would lie in state through the night of September 27, 1973, people came in masses to take their last look at her. Even in death, in her long, black shroud, even in the putrefying stillness of the flower-adorned chapel of the clinic, her suppressed inquietude seemed to be alive in her. It was as if the tranquility she beseeched and that had only fleetingly held her in its arms had not yet come to claim her.

"Inquietude simmers in me, like a kettle of water on a burning stove," she told Hank and Gene the first time they met, twenty years before, for a *Silver Screen* interview. "I'm full of violence. If it weren't for Rome, I don't know how I could survive. Rome doesn't resist me when I'm angry or in torment. It doesn't inflict itself on my moods. It soothes me. It never tries to force me to be something I don't feel or can never be."

She spoke of death during that first encounter.

"Suddenly, I crave to go somewhere at fantastic speed. I climb into my Ferrari in the middle of the night, and, as if I have a fever, drive to the sea. I'm too excited to think of the danger. But when I reach the sea, I'm horrified. I tell myself, 'Anna, Anna, you're insane. You must go slower next time. You must be more careful.' Who knows? Someday you'll open your newspaper or turn on the radio and you'll learn that somewhere on the road between Rome and the sea, Anna Magnani killed herself."

*

On the Friday morning of September 28, 1973, the people of Rome – from Trastevere, Testaccio, Salario, Tiburtina, Appia, Prenestino, Centocelle, Suburra – came in trams and buses hours before the time scheduled for the funeral service to be held in the Church of Santa Maria della Minerva, dedicated to the pagan goddess of wisdom as well as the Mother of Jesus. How many thousands of times, pensive and convulsed, at dawns and sunsets, under clouds and stars, in wind and rain, had Magnani looked upon its dome from the terrace of her penthouse apartment that topped the nearby Palazzo Altieri?

They, and others from all parts of Italy, from other nations and continents, came in tens of thousands, forcing all traffic in the heart of Rome to grind to a halt. Men, women, children, great grandparents to babes-in-arms, from all social strata. Those unable to crowd into the huge church spread through the Piazza della Minerva. They surrounded and hung from the obelisk in its center. They passed in the crooked streets of centuries all the way to the Pantheon.

Many who came were famous in Italy or throughout the world, but they were unimportant. The truly famed and important were the nameless crowds of Romans and other Italians in whom, in a miracle of transfusion, the blood of Magnani seemed to flow. They came to bear witness to the fact that for more than thirty years, both in the character she was in life and the roles she played, she was the incarnation of the comedy-drama of their daily lives, the instrument of their customs, attitudes, experiences and emotions. They came to testify that in the gamut of her films, ranging from Roberto Rossellini's *Open City* through the three she made for Italian television in 1970, their *Nannarella* was the personification of an epoch that time, men and history first glorified, then shattered.

They crowded into the Church of Santa Maria della Minerva that blistering autumn morning, their clothing and faces wet with sweat, breath and air stifled.

They stared at the bier placed not on the customary base but directly on the floor of the church, the signal honor of *more nobilium*. The tribute was traditionally reserved for nobility, granted to her both for the majesty of her art and the majesty she had given to ordinary men and women.

They stared at the two elongated pews at the left of the bier blocked off by the horde of uniformed carabinieri, on which her few living relatives and intimate friends sat, stood or kneeled.

They stared at her only son, 30-year-old Luca, child of a liaison between her and actor Massimo Serrato, the Luca who refused to accept his father's name, preferring to live the remainder of his life bearing the name Magnani, as if she alone had created him. Impassive, proud, the face sharp, strong and uncompromising, his eyes a distillation of grief, bitterness, delusion, Luca stood there on crutches watching no one, seeing no one, his legs chained by the heavy steel braces of infantile paralysis.

"When my son was born it was a glorious day for me," Magnani recounted not long before she died. "I was afraid. Lying in my hospital bed waiting, I was afraid of all I had suffered for the child I didn't yet know. I perspired and kept on perspiring. My throat burned so, I thought I would go mad. I desperately held on to the operating table, feeling the sweat run down my thighs and I screamed like an eagle. Then everything became normal and I began to feel wonderful. I asked to see my baby. When I saw Luca, I no longer remembered the pain.

"I didn't have a lira, but I couldn't care less. I had Luca and Luca seemed always to be laughing. I went back to work immediately. I was happy. Luca was happy. Then, then, it happened. With the malady of a child, you can cry out your grief, you can scream with anger. You *want* to suffer. You *want* to die. You try to delude yourself with hope. You tell yourself, 'It'll all pass.' Why couldn't my one baby, my one child, my son be *normal*? Why? Why? Why? The injustice of life is unspeakable.

"I had to leave him in Switzerland. There was nothing else I could do. He was only a few years old. He was twisted by that terrible infantile paralysis and I had to leave him alone. I couldn't sleep night after night. That poor child. So sick. So bewildered. To be separated like that. Horrible, horrible. But they told me I had to leave him.

"Today, my Luca is a handsome young man. Luca, believe me. I didn't want to leave you. I didn't want to abandon you. I didn't want to let you go. Perhaps one day you'll understand. I'm afraid of your silences as I'm afraid of my own. I'm afraid of your solitude as I'm afraid of my own. I only want to be able to live near you. The thought of one day my being deprived of that hope makes me tremble."

The people stared at all the faces of the occupants of the two elongated pews, searching for the one man she had married. Goffredo Alessandrini was not there. Nearly seventy, he sat quietly in his modest apartment in Ostia, where he lived with his dog, "the only companion I have left." Married in 1935, separated seven years later, divorced two years before she died, they remained friends. It was her monthly check that helped him survive until he departed on May 16, 1978.

"It happened in Milan," Magnani recalls. "I was performing at the Arcimboldi, an unpretentious experimental theater. He invited me to a sumptuous restaurant where I had often dreamed of going. He was so elegant. And spoke with such refinement. He told me he was to direct the dubbing of a picture into English. He had studied at Cambridge! Later, when he asked me to marry him, I said yes like the puppet of a ventriloquist. I would have said yes just as quickly if he had asked me to jump with him into the Tiber.

"We were together for seven years of happiness, jealousy, suspicion and fights. I knew that before we were married, he had other women and I was able to forgive that. But I couldn't once we were man and wife. All my threats, screams, tears and scenes didn't stop him. I had no choice but separation.

"In all honesty, in spite of his infidelity, I have to say that Goffredo was a good husband. Could I hate him because he sometimes preferred other women to me? No. I could have closed my eyes. I could have acted as if I knew nothing. But I couldn't. It was not my nature.

"When a man has offered you happiness, when he has told you, 'You are you and you must have faith in yourself,' when he has given you the joy of love, you can't forget or hate him. And if he needs you one day, you have to be there beside him. Years later, when I was much better known, he asked me to play the lead in a film he was directing. The producer didn't have money to pay me. I accepted all the same. Goffredo had been my husband. The least I could do was to help him, no?

"We weren't drowned in sadness when we separated. We knew we had cemented a friendship that would endure forever. The day we parted, Goffredo gave me a horse as a farewell present.

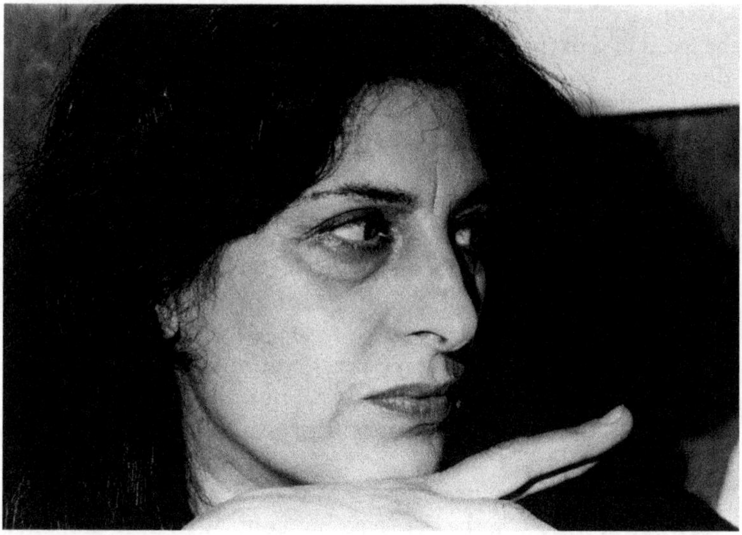

Anna Magnani

He said, 'I bought her for you because she resembles you. You see, it has a wide back and thin, bow legs.' What a lovely horse she was! I called it *Via dell'Impero.* I never succeeded in dominating her. She would take off like she was insane, virtually tearing my arms and hands apart. 'You daughter of the devil you,' I would shout at her. 'Maybe you don't realize I'm the devil, too! You'll exhaust yourself, I'll exhaust myself. But in the end, it's going to be me who will win.'"

The crowds stared at Silvana Pini, the private secretary who had suffered Magnani's temper and mercurial moods with love and loyalty for so many years. They stared at 83-year-old Francesco, caretaker of her retreat on the sea of San Felice Circeo, bewildered and unbelieving, repeatedly muttering to Hank, "She always called me my old one, my old tree, my shade. How can she have gone before me? How could she go before me? She always called *me vecchio mio, sei mio vecchio...*"

They stared as one of Italy's great anti-fascists and heroes of the Resistance, Sandro Pertini, then presiding officer of the House of Representatives, now the President of the Italian Republic, walked over to Luca, wordlessly grasped the youth's hand, then disappeared among the masses. They stared at the pocked and haggard face of the great Neapolitan actor and dramatist Eduardo de Filippo. They stared at Giulietta Masina and searched in vain for the face of her husband, Federico Fellini. They stared at a kneeling, head-bowed Audrey Hepburn, her red eyes hidden behind oversized dark glasses. They stared at the huge crown of flowers sent by Elizabeth Taylor. And they stared at Franco Zeffirelli, Vittorio Gassman, Alberto Sordi and Amedeo Nazzari.

They stared at Roberto Rossellini, who had returned to be at her side in recent months, demonstrating an affection and steadfastness that somewhat assuaged the heart he had so ruthlessly violated twenty-five years before. Affable, charming, agile, warm, swift in action and reaction, he moved through the pews, taking a hand in his and pressing it, kissing a cheek tenderly, offering an embrace or a caress, bending over to listen to someone's grief, murmuring words of comfort as if he were her rightful widower, the bereaved but controlled husband, once again the world-renowned talent directing a great production after years of faltering career.

With the consent of Luca, he had arranged the ironic but just denouement to her final drama, which was to place her body in the family chapel of Roberto Rossellini in Verano until the City of Rome decided where to place her tomb and build her monument.

March 21, 1949. London.

"Anna Magnani's rapport with Rossellini was in a dramatic phase," recounts Fabrizio Sarazani, a patrician Roman author and one of her cherished friends. "We were off to London, Anna and me. She had been invited to the London premiere of *The Honorable Angelina*, the picture she had done for Luigi Zampa. Roberto Rossellini came to the train station in Rome to see us off. The atmosphere was so heavy it seemed like any moment a cyclone would burst.

"We stayed at the Dorchester. Every morning I went out to buy the papers. My eyes almost fell out of their sockets when I saw enormous photographs of Ingrid Bergman arriving at the airport in Rome and Rossellini there to greet her. I was overcome by a nervous seizure. Anna knew I always went out for the papers and waited for me to bring them to her. How could I face her? Still, I knew I had to.

"I stuck the papers under my coat and went up to her room. She was having breakfast. She took one look at me and knew something was amiss. She continued eating, casting glances at me without saying a word. Then the bolt of lightning came, her peremptory command of 'Give me the papers!'

"I decided I couldn't tell her the truth. 'I didn't get them,' I said as matter-of-factly as I could."

"'Give me the papers!' she demanded. 'And don't you ever again try to lie to me!' She stretched her hand towards me. I slowly pulled the papers from under my coat. Flashes of pain coursed through my stomach.

"Her angry eyes still fixed on me, she slowly unfolded the first paper, *Le Figaro*. There it was in front of her. Bergman smiling, Rossellini so adoring. She stared, riveted, her expression impassive. Then, like a pond caught by rising winds, her face became sore and contorted. She made an incredible effort to suppress her emotion. She failed. The agony that poured out of her. In all the years I knew her, I had never seen her so beside herself. She didn't touch food for three days. I didn't dare leave her alone for fear that she would do something fatal."

Magnani on the telephone. 1948. Jean Cocteau's *The Human Voice*, directed by Rossellini at the height of his relationship with Magnani, just the time that Ingrid Bergman had quietly opened the door to a scandal that, a year later, rocked the world.

Magnani is waiting for the phone call of the lover who has betrayed her. It finally comes. The lover is never seen. The film is without cuts or dissolves. The camera never moves from the rejected woman's bedroom. Forty-five minutes of Magnani on the telephone in an uninterrupted flow of movement, as life blood flows through arteries to the heart, registering every gradation of emotion a woman confronts in the collapse of her life.

Even inanimate objects take on life. The telephone is friend and confidante, lover's arms and phallus, armor of defense, weapon against enemy. The telephone wire as umbilical cord, chain of slavery, fetter of torture, tantalizing instrument of excitement, serpent, tourniquet for bleeding heart. The bed, cradle of grief, lap of tenderness, of sexual ecstasy, bier of suicide. The walls circumscribe a garden of euphoric delight, courtroom of accusation, claustrophobic prison, casket.

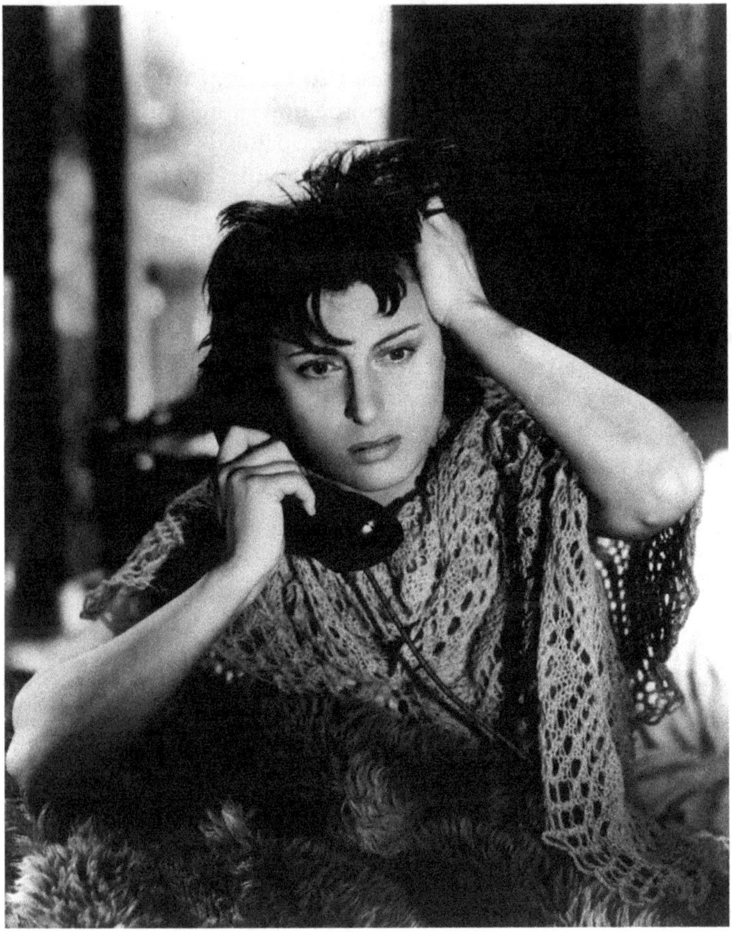

Anna Magnani in *The Human Voice*

There is no other solo performance in film history to equal it. Any human being who has longed for, or experienced love, should see it.

"Love? Take everything away from me. The Oscar, my house, money – *everything*," Magnani said the year she died. "But don't try to take love away. Love is rain and wind, sun and stars. It's breath, and I know, I know – it's poison. You can't know how many times I say to myself, 'Anna, open your eyes, this madness of yours will only send you to the crazy house.' Look, I admit my character is not noted for restraint or moderation. I'm a car with no brakes. Every time I love, I commit myself to the roots of my hair. What torment! How do I come out alive? What tragedy trying to escape! Then one morning you wake up drained of all your blood. But you start again and it's… fabulous.

"It's bad luck to look back. It's like dying twice. Rossellini? Maybe I'm mistaken, but he seems so feeble now. There's more the pleasure of business in him rather than a passion for art. When we started to work together in 1944, it was an exceptional collaboration. Unbelievable. He was able to materialize in a flash what I felt. A small gesture from him, a quick glance of his was enough for me to understand and go ahead. But that magical comprehension between us was limited to our work. In our private life, communication was blocked. Bankrupt. I spoke *romano*, he spoke what could have been Chinese. I was frank, direct. He was evasive, equivocal. I was loyal. He was, well, what he was. I would say to him, 'Roberto, when I finish my play at night or my day's work on a film, I want to come home a woman, the woman I am. But will you please explain to me why you have to perform all the time?'

"I believed in Rossellini. I shared maybe the most important years of my life with him. I thought there would be no limit to what we could do together, or be together. I looked at the heavens and gazed at the horizons and believed that nothing would be impossible for us. I was wrong.

"Why I never married him? First of all, let me tell you that when I hear the word 'marriage' my stomach turns. And then, Rossellini? Him – married? No. Roberto shouldn't be, *can't* be, a husband. Any serious country would deprive him of the right to a marriage license. Oh, as a friend, absolutely. He can be the most delicious, the most entertaining companion imaginable. The problem comes when you have to add up accounts. It's always you who has to make up what's missing. To put it bluntly, you're better off if you have nothing to share."

The funeral hordes listened to the words of Anna's friend and confessor, Father Virgilio Rotondi, when he said: "In that casket lies an inanimate body, a body without soul, a body destined to disintegrate into ashes while the soul is destined to live in eternity.

Anna Magnani has not left us. In spirit, she's here with us, here among you. Her life has not ended but is transformed."

A loud murmur of agreement rose among the throng. Heads turned in all directions expecting her to push her way through to greet them, joking in her piquant Romanesque dialect, shrugging her shoulders, constantly pushing her hair out of her eyes, throwing her head backwards in abandoned laughter, gesticulating her colorful vocabulary of gestures.

"One night several years ago," Fabrizio Sarazani recounts, "Anna decided to take me home in her car. She brusquely stopped when she saw a young prostitute walking her beat along the Tiber River bank. It was raining and very cold. As Anna got out of the car, every trace of good humor disappeared from her face.

"'Do you know who I am?'" she asked the girl, her voice hard.

"'You're *Nannarella*,'" was the reply.

"'I'm a woman first, *Nannarella* second. Don't you feel cold?!"

"'Sure I feel cold. But what choice have I got?'"

"Anna opened her purse and without counting the money, gave the girl a number of 10,000 Lire bills. 'Get yourself to bed now, *alone*,' Anna ordered.

"The girl didn't thank Anna. She just stood there, stunned, as Anna and I walked back to the car. 'Christ in Heaven, how cold life can be,' Anna exclaimed, and without another word, started the car and drove away."

The animals she loved with such intensity had not come to the funeral. However, no one would have been surprised if her menage of house cats, ranging from splendid thoroughbreds to refugees of the Roman streets, had appeared. Or if a procession of all races and classes of dogs slithered through the crowd of mourners to say goodbye forever to their Pied Piper.

Over many years, thousands of Romans had seen her come to Piazza Argentina late at night or before dawn to distribute rations of food to the host of voracious cats huddled among the ruins. Magnani's tears came rarely. But when once she read that fifty homeless cats had been exterminated by Roman authorities and that they were planning to murder others, she sobbed. Her tears were of short duration. While never on friendly terms with most journalists, she immediately phoned the editors of all the newspapers, passionately appealing to them to join her crusade against any further inhumane acts against animals and begging them to arouse their readers to battle on behalf of God's creatures.

She was no less zealous or protective of the dignity of artists.

November 3, 1969. Nina Simone was giving a concert at the Sistina Theater, which was only one-third full. Magnani, who rarely missed any theater performance or jazz concert in Rome, was conspicuously present. She kept looking at the empty seats in growing concern. Over and over again, she turned towards the entrance, expecting that at the last moment a vast crowd would pour in to fill the house. Only a few more straggled in as the time came for the concert to begin.

The house lights remained undimmed. After a moment, to a burst of applause, Nina Simone walked regally onto the stage. She looked over the empty house. Making no effort to hide her anger, she addressed the public. "I want to thank the few of you for being here tonight. I didn't realize this is the way Rome treats artists. If I had known I wouldn't have come. I want all of you to know, I want all of you to tell your friends, that if I ever come back to Rome again, it'll only be when I'm advised every seat in the theater has been sold. If not, Rome is never going to see Nina Simone again."

The audience squirmed. It didn't know how to react or what to do. But Magnani knew. She quickly rose to her feet. "You are right, Nina," she shouted. "Shame, shame, shame!" she apostrophized as she shook her fist at the empty seats. Then she turned to the audience. "On your feet, everybody. Let's applaud this great American artist like each one of us is ten!"

Anna on the telephone. 1958. "For me, Josephine Baker is the greatest," she exclaimed enthusiastically to Hank. "And do you know why? Because no matter what, she never compromises the truth of herself. They try to tell me that she's finished. An artist like Josephine is never finished. All those hypocrites will be there cheering their heads off when she's back on top."

"You don't have to sell me," replied Hank. "All I want to know is, am I going to meet her?"

"Of course you're going to meet her. We'll have a drink or supper with her after the show."

"I was a boy the first time I saw Josephine. Jesus, nearly twenty years ago. The Ziegfeld Follies of 1936. The show came to Boston for a tryout. You know she was a flop."

"Josephine? No..."

"It was her first return to America after she left for Paris in 1925. She was black, of course. But she didn't look black or act black or dance black or sing black. You know how it was in America those days. They didn't know how to handle her. The critics and the public didn't know how to take her. She was bitterly disillusioned and left the show as soon as she could go back to Paris."

"Josephine never told me. I guess she didn't want to talk about it. Her own country treating her like that! Terrible!"

Still today Hank recalled that first time he was exposed to Josephine Baker, how she had mesmerized him. Her way of moving. Her gestures. That voice. It still sent chills. It was a flute. Bells tinkling. And that body! "Anna, I think seeing Josephine had as much to do with my deciding to go into show business as anything else that ever happened to me. Oh, I forgot. There was another artist who maybe had a little effect on me."

"Who?"

"I doubt you ever heard of her."

"C'mon, tell me who." Magnani insists in mock irritation.

"She made some picture.... Was it called *Open City*?"

"*Stronzo. Va fa in culo*. C'mon, c'mon, I want to know everything... me and Josephine Baker... mmm!'

"Not now, Anna. I'll tell you in the car. I'll pick you up at eleven."

"Okay. But don't forget to tell me."

That night in a cab on its way to the Josephine Baker opening at the Rupe Tarpea, a nightclub on the lower part of the Via Veneto near Piazza Barberini, Anna turned towards Hank, intently scrutinizing his face, listening.

"Gene and I had just met in New York. All Gene could talk about was you and *Open City*. He had seen the picture five times. My birthday was coming up, so Gene said, 'I'll take you to *Open City* for your birthday.' This was in 1946.

"In all my life, I had never experienced anything like it. I could barely walk out of the theater. Gene knew I couldn't talk, so he didn't make me try. But when I started talking, he couldn't stop me. Words and expressions I never knew were in me came tumbling out. Violent urgencies of life. Depth of human sacrifice. The passion of love. The tenderness of love. Emotions that burned like fire. On and on and on... Nothing I had experienced in life prepared me for the impact."

"*Mio caro, caro* Kaufman," said Anna, deeply moved, taking his hand in hers and pressing it tight. Hank looked at her, then quickly turned away.

"Anna, I just can't look at you."

"Oh, I'm not that ugly."

"I'm afraid if I look at you, I'll cry all over again, remembering. Anna, you opened my heart to feelings I never knew existed in me. Don't you dare make fun of me if I tell you that to be here sitting beside you, well, I just can't really believe it's all real," Hank said, now looking at her.

"I only wish Rossellini were here this minute so he could hear you," said Anna after leaning over and kissing Hank on the cheek and squeezing his hand even tighter. "He gave an interview not very long ago renouncing all his best films, including *Open City*. I felt he had slapped me in the face." Anna shook her head in admonishment. When she spoke, it was as if she were addressing the absent Rossellini. "You insult me, Robé. Why don't you keep your mouth shut? Don't you know it's the same as throwing a child into the sea to drown? Or destroying something precious you can never have again? Like youth."

Arm-in-arm, Anna and Hank started down the stairs to the club. Anna was humming Josephine Baker's theme song, "*J'ai deux amours*," and Hank was joining in. As they entered, they looked at the scene in shock. There were no more than twenty-five people.

"This shit of a city!" exploded Anna. "Twenty, twenty-five people for a Josephine Baker opening! And she has twelve children to support!"

She addressed a humiliated *maître d'hôtel*. "How much time before she goes on?" "A half hour, maybe forty-five minutes," he replied.

Magnani turned back to Hank.

"Maybe we have time to do something."

"Let me dash up to Doney's and the Cafe de Paris and round up some people," said Hank.

"No. I have a better idea. Did you bring your phone book with you?"

Hank, nodding, patted his breast pocket.

"Good. Get fifty, a hundred tokens. We'll both get on the telephone. We'll call everybody we know. Josephine's a trouper. She would come out for two people and give them the greatest show of her life. But I'm not going to let her be insulted this way. I'm not going to be insulted this way. Let's get moving."

Anna followed Hank as he hurried over to the hat-check girl. The girl looked at him as if he was crazy when he asked for a hundred phone tokens. "Start calling all your friends," Anna ordered. "Tell them you're with me. Tell them they'll be my guests. Tell them to bring as many others as they want. Tell them I'm giving a party for Josephine afterwards and they're all invited. Tell them any damn thing you want, but get them here."

Hank handed Magnani a pile of tokens. As he raced to a telephone booth, Anna grabbed his arm, grinning. "Big-shot agent, eh? I'll show you! We're going to give Josephine an opening she'll never forget," she boomed, making gestures like a cheerleader. Then, her agenda of phone numbers in hand, she banged her booth door shut and began to dial.

Anna, dear, crazy Anna on the telephone.

Rome. April 16, 1958.

Several times over the years, Magnani had spoken of her admiration for Ava Gardner. Several times over the years, Ava Gardner had spoken of her admiration for Magnani. Hank and Gene decided that the time had come for their two prestigious clients to know one another.

The scene: the Kaufman-Lerner apartment on Via Salaria 290. All preparations were left in the secure hands of Signora Marion. There was no extensive guest list, only a select thirty, all of whom already knew Magnani or Gardner, or both.

Arm-in-arm with two swains, Ava arrived first. Splendidly dressed and perfectly made up, she was as incandescent as she was nervous. Her laugh was a tone too high, her reactions a bit too fitful as she kissed and embraced Hank and Gene. She was led to an armchair centered on the far wall of the living room. As Hank got her a drink, she nodded and smiled at several recognized faces. Gene sat beside her. He, Hank and her two hovering escorts joined her in ill-at-ease nibbles of small talk. The atmosphere was desultory.

Without advance fanfare, and unaccompanied, Magnani soon arrived. Modestly dressed, makeup at minimum, her hair in usual disarray, it seemed she had deliberately sought to place herself at her worst possible disadvantage. Hank quickly crossed the room to embrace her. One glance and he knew she was in foul humor.

"Where is she?" she whispered, squinting.

Hank nodded towards the far wall. "Over there. She arrived no more than ten minutes ago."

"I didn't have a second to get to the beauty parlor or get changed. What a day. Everything happened, and you can be sure none of it was good. I look like hell, don't I?"

"You always say that, Anna," replied Hank. "Stop worrying and come and meet Ava." He gripped Anna's arm firmly, hoping she would sense his support.

"Let me catch my breath," she hissed impatiently, furtively glancing over at Ava.

"Do you want a drink?"

"No, no. C'mon, let's get it over with."

As they started across the room, all conversation stopped. Everyone was caught by the drama. Two of the great personalities of our era, two fabulous stars of cinema, two women of fiery temperament about to meet for the first time.

Gene came forward to kiss Magnani, grabbing her by the other arm. Oppressive silence, mouths half open, lips dry, breath held, eyes fixed as the guests watched the hosts lead Magnani to Ava. Ava and Anna were now face to face. After what seemed an eternal pause, Ava extended her hand, a nervous smile ever-so-slightly edging her lips. Without rising, she said politely, "I'm very glad to meet you."

"I'm very glad to meet *you*," replied Anna, with an attempt at a similar smile. She took the extended hand, gave it a firm but brief hand-shake, and let it fall.

The two women looked at and past one another, attempting to sustain their smiles. It was awkward, ridiculous. K and L sensed they must not intervene. Ava and Anna were the protagonists. It was their stage. It was they who had to perform the scene. And neither knew how! Each was blocked by imagined or actual limitations, each one's talent as actress, each one's naturalness as woman hopelessly obstructed. Each too envious of a quality she lacked and the other possessed, each too fearful of making a bad impression on the other, they just looked at one another impotently, unable to find means to open the channel of communication.

The climactic scene anticipated by all was over. And it was a catastrophe.

In order to break the impasse, Gene quickly guided Magnani to the armchair on the other side of the room. Marion followed to hand Anna a drink. Ava was once again chatting away with Hank and the attentive swains. From time to time, she paused to examine Magnani as unobtrusively as she could.

Gene lit Anna's cigarette. The conversation he tried to make with her was clearly of no interest to her. Magnani was too busy studying Ava. So great was her concentration, she was unaware that Gene had her under his intense scrutiny. Magnani's eyes were first on Ava's face. They measured the proportions between nose and lips, then lips to chin. They fixed on Ava's fabled dimple. They searched for the injury that had caused Ava such terror. They noted the size of forehead, curve of cheeks, sweep and drape of the black hair.

Magnani's eyes then dissected Ava's body. They observed the shape and slope of her shoulders, the outline and firmness of her marvelous breasts, the tapering to the waist, the arms and hands both in stillness and movement. The more the eyes absorbed, the more Magnani sank into her self-inflicted tomb of inferiority.

A curious ritual began. The invitees began to move around the room. One focal point of deference was Ava, the other, Anna. By the time the procession ended, every person in the room had spoken to each of the two. The improvised march was not obsequious, the conversation not loquacious. It was a stately minuet of homage, an instinctive effort to turn wreckage into retake. In their own ritual, Hank moved from Ava to Anna, Gene from Anna to Ava, then back again.

As Gene once again sat beside her, Magnani leaned towards him. Her eyes still on Ava, she whispered, "I must go." Startled, Gene began to interrupt. The hard grip of Anna's hand silenced him.

"I'm going to leave quietly. You go and hold the elevator. Then I'll sneak out."

"You can't do that," said Gene. "Let me get rid of everybody. Then you and Ava will..."

"No! I said I have to go."

"You have to say goodbye to Ava. She'll feel insulted if you don't. And she'll be right."

"I have to go, *capisci*? You'll give her a message."

"I'll bring Ava over and you can give her your own message," retorted Gene.

The red light flashed in Anna's eyes. "I told you I had to go," she repeated, biting each word. "I'll give you the message when we're outside. Now will you go and get the elevator?"

Barely keeping his temper, Gene rose. He glanced over at Ava and Hank, then walked out of the living room.

Magnani appeared in the hallway as the lift arrived. She avoided Gene's eyes as he opened its door, held it, waiting for her to speak. She didn't.

"You wanted to meet her. Isn't that what you said a million times?" Gene said, his irritation evident. "She wanted to meet you, too. And what do we get? Disaster. Total disaster. It didn't have to be that way, Anna."

"Don't be so angry. And don't be sorry. It was all right. I'm glad I came. Really, I swear! *Ciao, ciao*. Give Kaufman a kiss. And give Ava this message..."

She lowered her eyes. When she spoke, her voice was drained. "Tell Ava..." Pause, as Anna struggled. "Tell Ava... she's the most beautiful woman I've ever seen in my life." She raised her eyes, looked straight at Gene, and said it again: "She's the most beautiful woman I've ever seen."

Gene felt the stab of Magnani's pain. "I wish you had said it to her yourself," he murmured.

Magnani looked at him in amazement, her hands in articulated gesture.

"How could I? How could I? Are you crazy?" Her eyes still blazing, she entered the lift. When again she glanced at Gene, they had softened.

"You won't forget?" she asked in a whisper.

"I won't forget."

At the end of the funeral service, the bier was lifted to be carried out into the brightness of the Roman morning, to pass through the ancient streets of the capital and be placed in the Rossellini family chapel. As the phalanx of carabinieri struggled to clear a path, people surged forward to touch the bier as it slowly passed and throw her favorite red roses towards it.

Then a crackling sound was heard, as if the Church had started to crumble. It was applause. Applause of the people of Rome rising in recurring echoes against the centuries-old walls of stone.

And then voices. Neither wails of grief nor keening of the bereaved. Voices, choral and convoluting, in up lifting crescendo. "*Brava*, Anna! *Viva*, Nannarella! *Brava, Brava, Brava!*"

The cosmopolitan, celebrity-filled audience that came to Paris from all of Europe to attend the annual Théâtre des Nations Festival was on its feet the night of June 8, 1965, fervently cheering and applauding Anna Magnani's portrayal of the title role in *The She-Wolf*, an adaptation of Giovanni Verga's short story, directed by Franco Zeffirelli. From orchestra, boxes and balcony, red roses were thrown onto the stage of the Sarah Bernhardt Theater, trod half a century before by Eleanora Duse, with whom Magnani as woman so totally identified.

The cheers and applause were no less fervent when *The She-Wolf* had its world premiere on October 18, 1964 at the Teatro Pergola in Florence, or its subsequent openings at the Teatro Nuovo in Milan and the Teatro Valle in Rome. Magnani's return to the theater after a decade was greeted with an exuberance and enthusiasm of sensational proportion.

Few knew of the trauma of suffering that accompanied the homeward voyage back to the stage.

"In my many years in films," Magnani recounted, "rarely have I succeeded in being more than a diligent artisan. Cinema gives security. If a scene doesn't work, you repeat it. Two, three, four, even ten times. You feel more at ease. The public isn't there as your co-performer. The theater is totally different. Every night when the curtain goes up, you're there, you and the public face-to-face, eye-to-eye, emotion-to-emotion. You have no choice but to give what you have, be what you are, then and there. You stretch your arms out for an embrace. If it comes, you know you are not alone. If the embrace isn't there, well... you have committed suicide."

"Magnani was a woman of extreme fragility," recalled Zeffirelli. "Her bones were like crystal, her nerves always at the breaking point. She lived in unrelieved trepidation. She seemed just as afraid before a failure as she was after a triumph.

"I believe her fear was born from an excess of self-criticism – so strong, it seemed a compulsion to self-destruction. What was

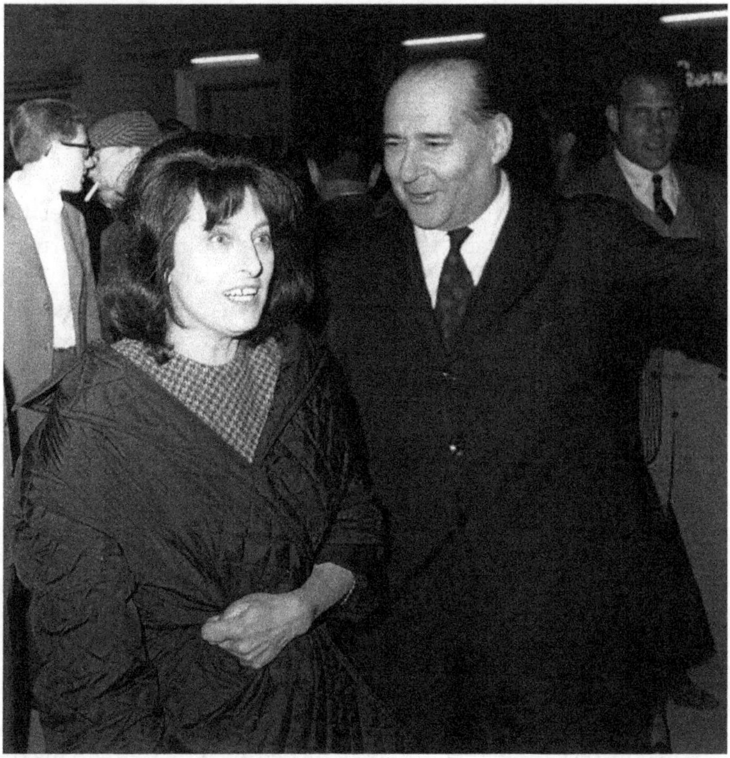

Anna Magnani and Roberto Rossellini

astonishing was the contrast between her security in performance and her capacity to dominate the stage with such authority against those agonizing moods of doubt and inquietude that afflicted her between one performance and another.

"Thank God Magnani was able to have confidence in me, for she had so little in herself. She seemed to me a frightened child who needed to be protected, but above all, needed to trust. There were so many times I desperately felt I lacked the capacity to help her. There were moments I had to go beyond the limits of my own strength and understanding. The problems we had never stemmed from her lack of discipline, scenes of temperament, failure at professionalism, or any limitation in her art. They came from her obsessive fear, that incurable malady of self-doubt.

"*The She-Wolf* was conceived and shaped for Magnani. In an amazing way, she was the author both of herself and of the piece.

It was an incredible experience for me, as if Titian or Raphael in the process of creating their masterpieces, were also giving birth to themselves. Sometimes I think that artists like Magnani have to live in desperate fear. Their greatness is so close to madness. What an awesome responsibility they bear."

Magnani stood on the stage of the Sarah Bernhardt Theater to acknowledge the acclaim that exploded the moment the curtain descended. She stood there in her long peasant costume, her pallid makeup a ghostlike contrast to her kohl-darkened eyes and the intense blackness of her hair. There was no smile on her face as she, the she-wolf, bowed again and again, still possessed by the tragic role she had played and lived.

Gene arrived in Paris, invited by Magnani and Zeffirelli. Neither knew that he had decided to surprise Anna before that opening performance. Unannounced, he headed backstage to the dressing room once occupied by Bernhardt and Duse, and silently opened the door. To his surprise, the room seemed empty. He started to back out when he became conscious of a slight movement, then saw Magnani rise from the chaise longue and walk slowly towards the dressing table. His face immediately flushed with embarrassment.

Magnani was nude.

In consternation, Gene quickly turned away. Careful to make no sound, he started to close the door behind him, but a strange emotion gripped him. He stopped moving and found himself turning back, gripped by some force he couldn't understand, watching as Magnani moved, wearily, her energy seemingly drained. He saw her sit at the dressing table, lift her face, and stare at herself in the mirror. Fifty-seven years old, her breasts heavy, her short body softened by flesh, she leaned forward and began to scrutinize her face in the mirror, searching it for some surprise or discovery, a miracle never to come. The expression in her phosphorescent eyes warned hard, the recurring ache of illusion concealed.

Embarrassment gave way to wonderment as he watched Magnani put on her makeup and slowly transform herself into her she-wolf personage. Occasionally, in creating life, Gene mused to himself, God errs. Primeval forces of nature intertwined with hereditary genes and an earth-woman seethes into being. They live with such fever, wrestling with drives distilled through generations and over ages, driven as cyclones and torrents are driven and yet seem permanently stillborn in terrifying emotional insecurity. Yearning for the total surrender they rarely or ever seem to accomplish. Dreaming for the romance of which they feel themselves so unjustly deprived.

Anger suddenly surged through him. Goddamn all those middle-, upper- and no-class Italian women who delight in ridiculing you. Goddamn those aseptic snobs who take pride in their sneers at you, those rectum-blocked intellectuals who make you fodder for satire and butt for their tasteless jibes. Goddamn them all for moaning their misfortune that with so many exquisite females to choose from to demonstrate the splendor and grace of Italy's feminine glory, the mantle had to fall on the then, now and always commonwoman of the marketplace who seemed so out of place in elegant drawing rooms. Goddamn them all.

And above all, goddamn you, Anna. Because what *they* feel, *you* feel.

Eight
Discovery of Realms Unknown

Rome. September 1959.

As Ava entered the door of Via Lisbona 12 and mounted the three steps from the entrance to the reception area, Franca, Marylee, Paola and Bruno rose slowly as if in hypnotic trance. They thought they were seeing an apparition.

It was the first and only time Ava ever set foot in the KLA offices. She graciously introduced herself to each of the incredulous four, commenting that she happened to be in the neighborhood and wanted to meet the Kaufman-Lerner personnel who had been so nice and helpful to her. She asked if Gene and Hank were in.

Gene was. Franca quickly flipped and buzzed to advise him of Ava's presence. An astonished Gene hurried from his office to embrace her.

"What a wonderful surprise," he said.

"Honey, if you're busy..." Ava started.

"C'mon, Ava," Gene immediately interrupted. "Your first visit to KLA? We'll stop everything."

"I was in the neighborhood. I only have a minute but I wanted to see the offices and meet everybody," she said nervously.

"You met the girls and Bruno."

"Yes, I have." She turned to smile at the still-standing, open-mouthed quartet.

"Okay now. Everybody at ease. At ease, everybody," Gene called out. Stiff and staring, the four slowly sat. "And Franca, no calls. Not for anything or from anybody." Gene took Ava's arm. "C'mon, I'll take you through," he said, as she let herself be led.

He took Ava from office to office. As she passed through the corridors, she glanced at the mounted photos of renowned KLA clients on the walls.

She said hello to Sandy Lieberson, the able, affable young agent who had come from Hollywood to work with Hank and Gene. She greeted Annalena Limontani and Rossana Pelliccia, and warmly shook hands with Enzo Barbato, who saw to it that her weekly living expenses due from her Italian-shot films were promptly paid on contracted days. A pleasantry with Massimo Frosi. A smile to Giorgio Conti. A wry comment on her generally negative estimate of lawyers to Vittorio Ripa di Meana. Then Gene led her into Hank's office. She examined its decor, nodding approvingly.

"Hank will be furious to miss you," Gene said.

"You tell him I think the offices are beautiful."

"He'll be pleased."

They then entered Gene's office. "Honey, I really can't stay. I just wanted to come by and say hello."

"Sit a minute, sweetie," replied Gene, sensing there was some purpose in this sudden "coming by." "We should be drinking champagne to commemorate this historic occasion. Should I send out for some?"

"No, darling, I really haven't got time." She walked over to the window. "You've got such a lovely view from here."

"Yes, it's very pleasant," commented Gene as he came beside her and put her arm through hers.

"Plenty of light," Ava went on. "You need it for all the reading you have to do. And you always see green. And kids playing. Look at the dogs having themselves a ball."

"Every time I look out, nerves stop screaming," answered Gene. The small talk was camouflage for something of import, he said to himself. But what?

"Honey, I've really got to go. I'm sorry as hell I missed Hank, but give him a big kiss from me."

Ava was already moving back into the reception room as she spoke. She glanced at the large framed photograph hung just outside of Gene's door. It was of Rossano Brazzi. She then turned towards the three girls and Bruno, all of whom rose once more as she came near. "I'm glad that at last I've seen you all in the flesh," she said to them, then walked down the trio of steps to the main office door.

She turned to Gene, who followed just behind. There was a pause. And when she finally spoke, her voice was low. There was a slight smile on her lips and her eyes were warm.

"Honey," she said, "I hope that when my photo goes up as a Kaufman-Lerner client, it's going to be as big as Rossano's. Or bigger!" Mischief glinted in her pupils. "Goodbye, honey, give me a holler later."

Stunned, Gene followed her out into the lobby, where the *portiere* Vincenzo, and Vera and their daughter, Pinuccia, were standing and staring. "Ava, what…"

"Don't you want me as your exclusive client for all this world?" she asked, the mischief still giving glint to her eyes, the smile still shaping her lips.

"Oh, dear God, Ava," Gene said, his stomach convulsed in flip-flops. The smile disappeared. The mischief died. "What's the matter?" she asked in darkened voice.

"Our agreement with William Morris…"

"What do those bastards have to do with it?" Her mouth became tight.

"We're not allowed to sign a client who came from William Morris as one of our own. We got you through them. We can't steal you."

"You mean… if I leave them and want to come to you, you won't take me?" The stare at Gene was hard.

"Not *won't*, Ava. *Can't*. It would be a breach of our agreement. We can't take on one of their clients and they can't take on one of ours. We just can't."

Gene felt the churn of vomit rise inside him but he knew that what was happening inside Ava wasn't any less painful. Ava had come that day after long reflection. She had come to offer herself to Hank and him. For Ava to do that of her own volition, submerging her fears and vulnerabilities, was an extraordinary act of faith and love. It merited a response no less meaningful – and Gene couldn't deliver. It was as if Ava had trustfully closed her eyes, lifted her head and waited expectantly for his tender kiss but instead felt a brutal slap across her face.

"Don't worry about it, honey," Ava managed to say without looking at Gene. "It was only an idea." She quickly started to walk away.

"I'll take you to the car," Gene called after her.

"You don't have to bother," she said, not turning back. Gene knew from the swing of her walk and the way she had stiffened her body that the hurt he had caused was rapidly spiraling into fury. His impulse was to go after her. To say what? To hell with the William Morris agreement, we'll take you anyway? To do what? Advise the WA hierarchy to go stick it, that Ava was more important? She really was – but no, he couldn't do that. It was impossible. So there was nothing to say, nothing to do.

Gene stood watching as Mario opened the rear door of the limousine and Ava hurried in to the car. As it started to pull away from the curb, Ava did not wave as she usually did. Nor did she look at Gene. Gene, however, lifted his hand and waved as the Cadillac turned and disappeared up Via Panama towards the Piazza Ungheria.

Vicero, Vera and Pinuccia, who knew not a word of English, nevertheless understood that something was wrong. They glanced at Gene as if to say, "Is there anything we can do?" Too torn even to look at them, Gene, head down, his step heavy, started back to the office.

It was one of the worst moments of his life.

If, as and when Ava decided to cut herself off, she had a treatment that had no classification under fun-and-games. She became untouchable, unreachable, unspeakable. Her face became a mask, her stare as effective as tear gas in forcing one to keep a distance. She slammed the door in your face, locked it carefully, then tossed the key into the garbage.

In response to the inevitable stream of your phone calls, she had prepared her staff in an ornate routine of responses of she's-having-her-bath, she's-sleeping, she's-not-in, she's-gone-away-for-a-few-days, we-don't-know-where-she-is, she-can't-come-to-the-phone-because (please fill in any of the score of different excuses that end up deranging your mind). With childish glee, she participated in the torture by sometimes answering the phone herself disguised as a secretary or maid in a series of incomprehensible accents. And the bouquets of flowers you send her could be found in the same garbage in which she had thrown the key. The estrangement might have a run of a couple of days, a week, a month, then suddenly come to an end in glorious reconciliation.

It might also turn into forever, a tribute to Ava's exceptional capacity at erasure. And in the Roman winter of 1959, Phil Kellogg, who on Bert Allenberg's lamented death became the head of the WMA motion picture department, found himself mercilessly humiliated by that exceptional capacity.

Already fighting a flu bug, weak and feverish, he flew to Rome from the West Coast to confront cold, rain and humidity for the single purpose of seeing Ava. Kellogg was the clean-cut, blond, blue-eyed WASP pride of William Morris, but Ava's estimation of him was that "He doesn't know his ass from a hole-in-the-ground."

Like a schoolboy with his books, he carried several scripts under his arm with which he hoped to entice her. His incessant phone calls were certainly no medicines for his flu, and the treatment he got from Dr. Ava only increased his fever and frustration. For hours on successive days, he camped on the rain-damp doorway of her rented villa off the Via Po. He was never admitted. Physically exhausted, emotionally distraught, prestige punctured, he finally left the scripts with Hank and Gene, returning to California to recoup his strength and severely damaged morale.

Shortly thereafter, Ava left the agency she had been involved with virtually her entire career, but wasted not a tear in lament. Rejected by Kaufman-Lerner, Ava decided in 1960 to go her own way, "a freelancer," as show business parlance would phrase it. All legitimate agents on a non-exclusive basis could subject projects for her through her business manager in Hollywood, Jess Morgan, and she would pay her ten percent commission on any project she accepted.

Fortunately, Ava did not permanently exercise her capacity for erasure on Hank and Gene after her one and only visit to the KLA offices. After a ten-day period of "the treatment" that caused them untold anguish, communications between her and "the boys" returned to what seemed to be a normal level. But in the more than score of years to follow, Ava never once mentioned her visit to the KLA offices, nor the conversation she'd had with a remorseful, tormented Gene.

And the ingrained camaraderie between Hank and Gene persisted.

Hotel Richmond, Madrid
January 9, 1961

Dear old Hank and Gene,

Just think. All that pretty paper you gave me for my birthday to write letters to you, and look here I am writing on this crappy hotel stationery. But everything in my house is in such a mess now, I couldn't find a damn thing. We'll be able to start painting. The Spanish workers are only two weeks late in finishing – which is a record.

George Stacey is decorating for me, and I have found almost all the furniture. All the drapes and rugs have been started and I hope to be moving in about the middle of February – which *really* is a record for this crazy, adorable country. I'm so happy with my house and have never had such fun. I won't tell you anything about it, so you'll be surprised when you get here. Can you come about the end of February?

It's such a shame we couldn't have had Xmas together there. We didn't even have a turkey! But we drank a lot of Xmas booze and had fun. Bappie and Art left on the 29th, so George and I had a ball on New Year's right here in this *triste* hotel room, just the two of us and many bottles.

Got to get over to my house and see how many walls are torn down and how many doors are holed up and how many bathtubs have been put in. Write me soon, love to you both. Hope to see you *pronto*!

Ava

So Madrid, not Rome, finally became the capital of the Empire of Ava. After eight years of living in hired apartments, hotel suites, *residenzas* and rented villas, mostly in the Eternal City, she had made a "decision." In one of the most charming residential areas of Madrid, she bought a spacious, though not over-luxurious apartment at Avenida Dr. Arce 11, an address coincidentally shared by Juan Perón, exiled dictator of Argentina. She made it an unmistakable point to have no truck with the deposed despot of Argentina and loudly expressed her resentment over the presence of his goons in the building. Ava also made little effort to hide her contempt for Franco or Fascism, in spite of her choice of Spain as her country of residence.

By the time Ava moved in to Avenida Dr. Arce, she had turned 39.

On March 7, 1961, the following telegram from Madrid was delivered to Hank and Gene at Via Lisbona 12:

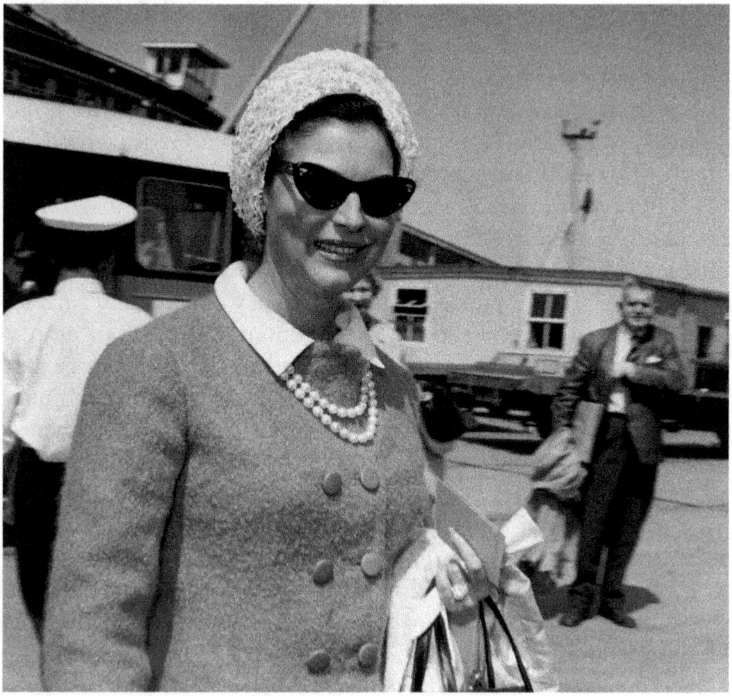

Ava Gardner

PLEASE BRING SIX CANS EACH SASSO OIL AND ITALIAN COFFEE STOP ALSO PARMESAN CHEESE, FETTUCINI AND ASSORTED PASTAS, GRAPPA, FINOCCHI AND PROSCIUTTO STOP TWO COTECHINO ZAMPONE AND TRADITIONAL NEW YEAR STUFFED PIGS LEGS STOP SIX PAIR SIZE SIX AND HALF GLOVES TWO BLACK SUEDE TWO WHITE KID REGULAR TWO WHITE KID EIGHT BUTTON LENGTH LOVE, AVA.

Madrid might have won but clearly the magnificent specialties of Italy never lost.

On March 8, she welcomed, as her first official house guests, two heavily-laden delivery men from Rome.

Dear old Hank and Gene, no longer her agents, but still wearing the decoration of their special rank of chum.

There was overeating and overdrinking, and Gene had to hobble around because of an attack of gout. There were *corridas*, one fought by Dominguín, who had not yet lost his *primo assoluto* status to the rising El Cordobés, and a photo of an intensely watching Ava, flanked by Hank and Gene, which hit the front pages of newspapers and magazines across the world.

There were dinners in, Ava sometimes making her lip-smacking Southern fried chicken, and dinners out, lunches in, lunches out. There was one vivid "Ava" night in a flamenco joint on the outskirts of Madrid where only gypsy dancers and singers, Ava, Hank and Gene and an unaccountable number of empty wine bottles remained until dawn. And as the sun was rising, there was Ava driving her Facel Vega as if she were a stunt woman, scaring the bejesus out of her visitors and decimating a number of Spanish chickens who foolishly got in the way.

Ava's house *was* beautiful. Warm. A woman's affectionate hand stretched out in welcome. Soft. Colors: cream, satin silver-grey, shaded white, canary yellow. Luminous, as if Peppino Rotunno had come there to light it. Graceful. It had heart. It gave shelter. It seemed a lovely, sweet peace pact between Ava and her lifetime longing for home.

Ava's "European period" was simultaneous with the opening of the gates of Via Aiaccio 12-bis to mark the commencement of Kaufman-Lerner's Roman Adventure. Similarly, while she was moving into her first "home of her own" on Avenida Dr. Arce in Madrid, Hank and Gene were buying land sixty miles south of Rome to build their first home together.

Villa Casa Bianca, designed by Hank in collaboration with local architect Alberto Pedini, was completed in May 1963. Equidistant between the villages of Sabaudia and San Felice Circeo, it was built Mediterranean-style in a series of graceful arches on four levels, offering a unique panorama of Lake Paola, woods sloping down from the back of the villa to the lakefront, hills and valleys of sand dunes in every direction, and at Casa Bianca's front, stretching to meet horizons far in the distance, the Tyrrhenian Sea in marvelous blue expanse. Jutting out into the azure waters of the limpid sea that, through centuries of tidal ebb and flow, sculptured mysterious grottos, Mount Circe rose a mere hallf-mile to the southwest. It was there where Circe's bower lay, there where the Goddess slept forever. The magical influence of Circe and Nature had woven unique enchantment over the land, through the vista, into the air. It is no wonder that the legend of Ulysses seemed more reality than fantasy there, and that Casa Bianca seemed to possess such charm and such curative capacity for unsettled nerves.

A cablegram dated September 29, 1963, from Mexico City, addressed to Hank Kaufman, Via Lisbona 12, Rome, read as follows:

> SAW PHOTOS YOUR HOUSE STOP BABY, AREN'T YOU IN THE WRONG BUSINESS STOP AFTER FIGHTING IGUANAS FOR THREE MONTHS, WILL BE STRONG ENOUGH FOR THE PAPARAZZI, SO HAVE YOURSELF MY ROOM, TERRACE AND VIEW READY LOVE YOU. AVA

Approximately six months later, Ava finally arrived in Italy. She was definitely *not* strong enough to cope with the *paparazzi*. Her arrival was a shambles. Her several days in Rome were maddening for her and no less maddening for her chums like Micol Fontana, Walter Chiari, hairstylist Frederic Jones, secretary Ed Schaefer and, of course, "good-ol' Hank." (Gene, working in London, was unable to get away for the occasion.)

In one of her fouler moods, Ava left Rome soon thereafter for Naples to start a Sicilian cruise with a party including her longtime, Madrid-living friends, the Sicres, and two-time Democratic Party presidential candidate Adlai E. Stevenson. Not finding the cruise sufficiently stimulating, finding it, in fact, downright boring, Ava found some adequate reason to leave it and hurry back to Rome. She now wanted to have her long-awaited weekend in "her" room at Casa Bianca.

So together with Hank, Ed and Fred, they fought off the *paparazzi* and managed to make it to Sabaudia, where Signora Marion, groomed with particular care, awaited her beloved Ava.

Ava adored the villa. Ava adored her room. Ava adored "her" terrace, which opened off her quarters, overlooking the shimmering silver of Lake Paola. She adored the area. She adored the sea and its sunset spectaculars. She adored seeing what seemed to be the form of Circe stretched out, hair flowing, on top of the Mount. She was relaxed, loving, full of conversation, wistful in silence. She willingly posed with Hank, Ed, Fred, Marion and the Casa Bianca staff in numerous Polaroids.

And she willingly took a walk. A walk that might have made her the patroness of the Italian Olympic rowing squad.

Accompanied by Hank, Ed and Fred, she happily descended to Lake Paola through the dunes and woods of the Casa Bianca property. Ava wore a bandana over her hair, huge dark sunglasses over her eyes. Her face was devoid of makeup, and she wore a simple T-shirt, brief cotton shorts and sandals. Ava, of course, needed very little outside help to project her extraordinary facial and physical qualities. As the group reached the dock, an eight-man racing boat suddenly shot into the scene, Coach shouting out a back-breaking rhythm to a swarthy and handsome octet rowing with all the strength they possessed.

Playfully, Ava waved at them. As if a hunting dog had suddenly seen his quarry, the muscular, torso-nude group altered the course of the boat, and to the shock of Coach, headed straight for the Casa Bianca dock. There Ava was, confronting a hefty cargo of healthy Italian males, whose average age could not have exceeded 21.

They were very shy, but their eyes, ranging from piercing blue to pools of dark brown, were all obsessively concentrated on that splendid woman who seemed to them a species of mermaid who had decided to give legs a try and see what dry land had to offer.

"Unfortunately, the Lady knows only a few words in Italian," Hank said in Italian to ease the embarrassment of the youths. Ava at that point made it clear through spatterings of Italian and precise gestures that she would love to take a spin in their boat. What the Lady would love, the gracious Italian crew would love. Hank, Ed, Fred and Coach notwithstanding, off went Ava on a cruise that went nowhere near Sicily or Adlai E. Stevenson, guided by a crew that Hank later discovered was made up of Naval cadets handpicked to prepare for the Italian Olympic team.

After a couple of miles of being rhythmically rowed on Lake Paola by sixteen muscled arms of Italian youth, Ava was proudly delivered to Hank, Ed, Fred and Coach at the Casa Bianca dock. Graciously thanking each of her escorts, Ava courteously suggested that all of them come up to the villa for a drink. Beside themselves with frustration, the poor lads reluctantly declined.

They absolutely could not break training miles, they ruefully explained. But might they accept the Lady's invitation at one o'clock tomorrow, after the important trial race they had in the morning? Of course, with pleasure, beamed Ava.

At one o'clock the next day, a boat docked at Casa Bianca. It contained eight youths flushed from their early morning victory as well as from their eagerly anticipated appointment with the Lady. They were all immaculately dressed, giving definitive proof that they were indeed an exceptional hand picked group of Italian male sexuality. They were as well equipped for an Olympic competition in masculine beauty as they were in eight-man rowing.

They waited for the Lady, who regretfully never appeared. She had been up much of the night and was still asleep in "her" room of the villa, shutters closed on "her" terrace overlooking Lake Paola. Hank had to go down to explain to the bitterly disappointed lads that, unfortunately, the Lady had returned to Rome on an urgent matter. He suggested they all come up for a drink anyway, an invitation that was politely refused. Hank realized it would be no fun for them without the presence of Ava. And so, the eight stalwarts of Italian sport and maledom clambered back into their boat, and in a rhythm that wouldn't have won a race with a somnolent snail, started back to their base. Lifting their oars in salute, they vanished around a bend of Lake Paola, never to know that their boat had been struck by a star and their powerful oars were the escort of none other but the one and only Ava Gardner.

May 10, 1964

Hank and Gene, I'm not the first guest. But I'll make you a bet. I'm about the happiest. Love and thanks to you both, and dear Gene, I'm sorry you weren't with us.

Ava

That was the message Ava wrote in the Casa Bianca guest book as she, Hank, Fred and Ed left for Rome the next day.

Late afternoon, August 23, 1965.

The Madrid sun was losing its heat and the burn of the day had diminished.

In the living room of Avenida Dr. Arce, Ava sat with unusual quietness on the sofa, listening. As she listened, her eyes were sometimes closed, sometimes opened to secrets she shared only with the distance, sometimes fixed on Gene.

The black hair severely swept back and knotted with a rubber band at the back of her neck, her face without makeup, each individual feature fixed in proportion, a classic ballet in tableau: her white blouse following the natural curve of her breasts; her brown skirt hovering over crossed knees; her feet bare, a drink, a cigarette held aimlessly in her hand.

Gene was reading aloud from Antoine de Saint-Exupéry's *The Little Prince*, a book he had brought with him as a gift for Ava. He was on the episode in which the Little Prince, looking for friends, meets the Fox and asks him to play.

"I cannot play with you," the Fox said. "I am not tamed."

The Prince asks the Fox what "tamed" means.

"It is an act too often neglected," said the Fox. "It means to establish ties." And then: "To me, you are still nothing more than a little boy who is just like a hundred thousand other little boys. And I have no need of you. And you, on your part, have no need of me. To you, I am nothing more than a fox like a hundred thousand other foxes. But if you tame me, then we shall need each other. To me, you will be unique in all the world. To you, I shall be unique in all the world..."

The episode finished, instead of continuing to read more of the extraordinary fairytale of the French poet, Gene slowly closed the book. He glanced at Ava. She seemed caught by communion, her listening so intense, so encompassing, that neither the story, nor characters, nor the moving sequence of Prince and Fox, wheat-fields and taming, could have existed if she had not been there to absorb it.

Gene did not then know that the very next afternoon, Rags, whom Ava had tamed as the Little Prince had tamed the Fox, and who had tamed her as, in a profound sense, the Fox had tamed the Little Prince, would be put to sleep forever. He was not then aware that at the age of 16, Rags, her "fox" since the time she had been not only Ava Gardner but also Mrs. Frank Sinatra, would be buried the next afternoon at La Moraleja. The only living creature to whom, without reserve, she was able to give all her trust and reveal all her vulnerability, on the morrow, would be placed under earth in final rest.

The threshold of Dr. Arce 11 was often crossed by men. The door to Ava's first home remained open and ready, but the love hoped for but almost never mentioned by Ava did not appear to give it its fundamental *raison d'être*. Her home had music and sometimes dance, but the ultimate dance of dances – man and woman cadenced in kissing embrace, consecrated as husband and wife – never took place.

The burial of Rags had a significance that at the time Ava herself was perhaps not fully aware of. Though it would be years before the final transition was made, it marked the beginning of the end of her Spanish period.

London was calling. Actually, London – which also had an affinity for Empire – had never really been ousted in the where-will-I-make-my-home dilemma, as Rome was not or a place in the Caribbean or the Pacific or a return to the States or somewhere else or anywhere else "in confrontation with oneself at the most unexpected moments and in the most absurd places."

London had always had its charm for Ava. She adored the English sense of privacy and genuinely loved the opera, the ballet, the concerts. All of it felt like the city was quietly opening its arms to her. She had no objection to an environment that she could handle in her native tongue and she had a number of chums there, including Nunnally and Dorris Johnson.

After tax and residency consultations with Jess Morgan and Milton A. Rudin (Hollywood's powerful attorney, Sinatra's trusted counselor and associate, Gene and Hank's lawyer and close friend), Ava made a decision. By October 1, 1965, less than five years from the time she had moved in, Dr. Arce 11 was sold. After a brief sojourn at the Hotel Richmond in Madrid, restless wanderings to Jamaica, a visit to her sister Bappie in Hollywood, a stay in New York and another in London, Ava returned to Madrid and moved into what was nothing more than an interim residence on the Calle Jenner. She rid herself of Calle Jenner in 1967 and soon afterwards made the move to London, eventually buying a house at 9 Alexander Square, South Kensington. Then, as she was nearing the age of fifty, Ava rid herself of the Alexander Square residence and bought her Ennismore Gardens townhouse, which very much became the "home of her own."

November 1964. A pearl of a day for an English autumn. The sun was in full splendor, the air pure and invigorating, touched by the wand of spring. Birds chirped, swooping through the trees that seemed to tingle with a gentle breeze. What a magnificent day for a drive from London to Oxford! And what did it matter that Ava's left wrist was sprained and that she had to wear her arm in a sling?

For a change, she was ready, even impatient, when the Bentley and its liveried chauffeur arrived. As she had so often done before, and so often would later, Ava cracked hackneyed jokes about her miserable lack of education. This time, however, her comments lacked their usual self-bite. As the limousine sped towards its destination of higher learning, she seemed more and more like the girl going to her first date with the Campus Hero who she never dreamed could possibly notice such a poor little ol' thing like her.

"Oxford. Christ! How am I supposed to act? What am I supposed to say? They're not going to ask me to make a speech, are they? I mean, I'm not going to have to stand up there and talk?"

Gene kept his expression serious. "They might. After all, you're the guest of honor. That means a certain protocol. They might want to hear your opinion on the works of William Wordsworth."

"Oh, no, honey. They've got the wrong gal. We'll just head right back. If they think... Honey, they wouldn't do a thing like that to me. Would they?" She turned her head with that inimitable jerk of jaw and stared hard at Gene. Gene stared back, but couldn't hold back the laughter. It broke out in a fit.

"Sir!" Ava paused for effect, her eyes dilated. "You are a bastard," each word enunciated like an exercise in elocution. "If I knew some quote from William Wordsworth or anybody else to cut you down to size, I would use it." Then rising peals of church bells poured out of Ava, and for a long time, she and Gene laughed. And laughed. And laughed.

"Whew! I need to breathe," said Ava, closing her eyes, rhythmically inhaling the fresh autumn air deep into her lungs. Suddenly, she straightened up and looked out at the exquisite panorama of the English countryside. "I'm going to Oxford. I'm the guest of honor at a poetry lecture on William Wordsworth. Me!" she whispered to the trees, the rolling green and the distant church spires. And then, proud and delighted: "What do you think of *that*, Mister Smart-Ass Artie Shaw?"

Capped-and-gowned Robert Graves was waiting as the Bentley arrived. Untapped poet laureate of England, Graves was ignored when the monarchs of the Sceptred Isle were passing out titles. Poet, critic, classic novelist, literary commentator, dissector of ancient times and assembler of mankind's myths, Graves was now occupant of Oxford's honored chair of Professor of Poetry.

Ava took Graves' arm, and together, poet and actress entered the lecture hall, stiflingly packed by hundreds of students and professors. There seemed to be more dons in caps-and-gowns than priests and nuns at the Pope's Christmas appearance at St. Peter's Square. As Gardner and Graves mounted the stage with its rows of seats left and right of the podium, trailed by Gene and a number of dons waddling like penguins, the ancient structure shook in a burst of spontaneous applause. In enviable control of herself, the self-proclaimed semi-illiterate North Carolinian was in instantaneous command of the eight-hundred-year-old bastion of intellect and snobbery which, in all of its centuries, had perhaps never seen the likes of her, except in sexual fantasies.

Graves motioned Ava to the first seat at the right of the podium, and Gene next to her. The Penguins squatted in the remaining seats. The applause mounted. Tall, sturdy, his gray-white hair long and disordered, his nearly 70-year-old face ruddy, his eyes mischief and wisdom, Graves stood at the podium, looking out at the applauding audience. Ava encased herself in her sculptured posture, slowly turning her head, her eyes warm and happy in acknowledgement of the excited reception being given to her.

As the applause reached ovation level, Graves turned towards Ava, his face bobbing up and down, illuminated with pleasure. They caught each other's eye. For a moment, it seemed that Ava would rise from her seat and, in front of that sardine-packed mass of intellect, forget her shyness and her shield of inferiority, and embrace the renowned poet.

Graves motioned for quiet. The applause diminished, soon replaced by a suffocating silence. The poet-lecturer surveyed the hall, his face mockingly serious. He leaned over to the microphone, then with a flourish said, "I never thought William Wordsworth could be so popular."

The lecture hall broke out into a delirium of applause and laughter. Ava enthusiastically joined in. Then the performance began. Master of spectacle, caustic, brilliantly sarcastic, body, hands, face, eyes, even hair a symphony of gesture, Graves gave poor Wordsworth, two centuries earlier poet laureate of England, a critical deflation that relegated him far below the level of Edgar Guest, America's so-called "People's Poet."

Graves was undoubtedly the star of the show, but not for one moment was he unaware of his co-star. Like all consummate actors, he played both to his co-performer, even if she had no dialogue, and to his audience. The instrumentation was perfect, electric. He knew he had never before participated in quite such marvelous theater. Its uniqueness and fascination were not merely in Ava's presence on that stage, or in his merciless pummeling of the over-lofty poet that England worshipped. All ears were tuned in to Graves, all eyes fixed on Ava, and the dichotomy of sensory concentration was simply astonishing. In the ninety minutes of the lecture, Ava sat listening in her own incredibly communicative stillness, her body slightly turned towards the poet. Her gaze was unflaggingly on him, the expression on her face active and consuming, sometimes crossed by a smile, often broken with laughter, but always in concentrated repose. In no way did it reveal the secret that England's master of poetry was in love with her.

In his fine, labored hand, Graves had written Ava poems of adoration, introspection and pain. They are precious, profoundly moving assets of his and her patrimony.

> She speaks always in her own voice
> Even to strangers; but those other women
> Exercise their borrowed, or false, voices
> Even on sons and daughters.
>
> She can walk invisibly at noon
> Along the high road; but those other women
> Gleam phosphorescent – broad hips and gross fingers –
> Down every lampless alley.
>
> She is wild and innocent, pledged to love
> Through all disaster; but those other women
> Decry her for a witch or a common drab
> And glare back when she greets them.

Here is her portrait, gazing sidelight at me,
The hair in disarray, the young eyes pleading:
"And you, love? As unlike those other men
As I those other women?"

Hank and Gene ended their relationship with William Morris in March 1961, but all their efforts to reestablish an exclusive agency-client relationship with Ava foundered. She nevertheless maintained a de facto professional rapport with then, occasionally asking their counsel on a number of career matters and not hesitating to ask KLA assistance in arranging trips and hotels for some of her "perpetual flights."

Then came 1964.

Gene was living in London, working in conjunction with The Grade Organisation but still partnered with Hank in KLA. Ava, then 41 years old, was again back in Rome to shoot her fiftieth motion picture, the Dino De Laurentiis production of *The Bible*. The deal was made directly between Dino and Jess Morgan, with no agency involved. Its director was John Huston, with whom Ava felt comfortable. Rotunno was once again her cinematographer

Her co-star?

George C. Scott.

Rome. September 1964.

Gardner and Scott were on strike. They had refused to continue their roles of Sarah and Abraham in *The Bible* to protest Dino De Laurentiis' allegations concerning their public and private behavior. That the two stars were seriously in love was clear, and that they were contemplating marriage, more than a suspicion. Scott was ready to divorce Coleen Dewhurst. Ava, seven years after she and Sinatra had terminated their marriage, was tuning herself to the clang of wedding bells.

The relationship had become more and more tempestuous. It erupted into ugly rows and physical violence, animal and primitive. Alcohol, which did Ava no good and was psychic poison to Scott, was poured on the already perilous fire. Dino had specified times and places where Scott had purportedly struck Ava. He referred to damage to her face and even a broken clavicle. The producer stated that he would hold them liable for delays in shooting, taking the position that if their personal relationship caused him losses, he would not hesitate to take them to court to seek punitive damages.

Gene came to Rome from London for several weeks of work with Hank on a number of complicated deals. Gene asked his partner for confirmation of the rumors that were all over London. Hank told him all he knew, which was a considerable amount. Gene phoned Ava at the Grand Hotel to say hello. Ava begged him to resolve the impasse with De Laurentiis. After conferring with Hank, Gene agreed to do so.

The sun focused all its heat on the windows of the ground-floor apartment of the Grand. Ava, in her usual blouse-and-skirt and shoeless, sat in a stuffed armchair, nervously smoking cigarette after cigarette. She was on the edge of explosion. Sprawled on a sofa, Scott sat quietly, as if empty of all vital organs. Mearene Jordan, always referred to as Rene, Ava's companion, maid, adviser, hairstylist, confidante and butt of the actress' variations in humor, sat in an imitation Louis XV chair, her lips biting one another as if she was trying to avoid an epileptic fit.

That was the scene as Gene entered carrying his briefcase.

Ava's face jerked towards him.

"What did that pygmy Mussolini say?" she asked.

"He said it's all for your benefit."

"My benefit! MYYYYYYY benefit!"

"He said you're in serious danger and he has to take tough measures to avoid tragedy."

Ava's scream interrupted. "Who the hell is he to interfere in my private life?" she demanded as she jumped up from the armchair. "He had better keep his cotton-pickin' hands out of it. My private life is mine, and nobody but nobody had better stick his nose in it."

Gene ignored the outburst.

"He said he can't afford to stop the picture or recast if anything happens to you. He insisted that he has hocked everything he owned, every last thing he had in this world. He said his life's at stake. He..."

"He's a fucking fascist bastard, that's what he is. Did you get hold of Mickey Rudin?"

"I left Mickey three urgent messages. We're lucky as hell he happens to be in London. I know he'll get back to me the moment he can."

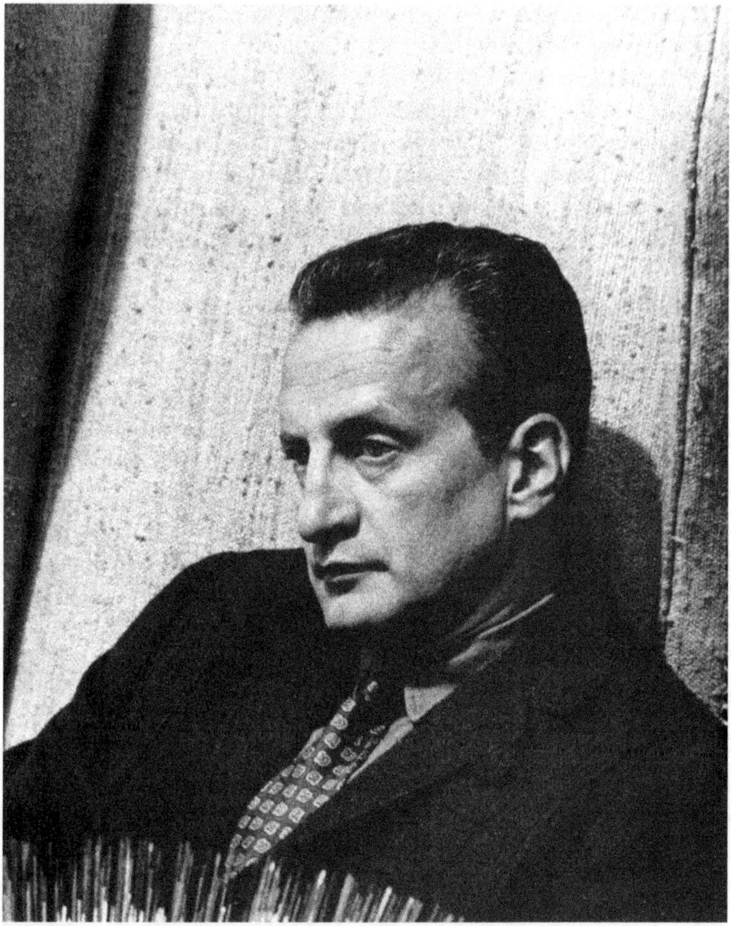

George C. Scott

"Honey, I can't keep this up. I CAN NOT KEEP THIS UP!"

After pouring herself a drink, Ava began to pace. Neither George nor Rene changed posture or expression. Ava stopped in front of Gene, looked at him, her eyes a plea for help.

"We'll work it out, sweetheart. I'm sure we will."

Ava's voice was low and anxious. "But no legal hassles, honey. I don't want any of that. I just want to get this mess settled and finish the picture before I'm as old as Sarah."

Gene had been waiting for the right time and place to put a point across. He knew this was the moment.

"Listen, sweetie, all on your own, you decide on a course of action. You don't ask Hank, who's been here all the time, ready and willing to help. You don't ask me. You don't ask anybody. You decided you didn't need an agent. Don't you remember, honey? You decided to go your own way four years ago. Okay, KLA didn't make this deal. Okay, I'm not your agent. But I was and am your chum and always will be. So as your chum, who happens to be a pretty good agent around town, I'll tell it to you straight. All you can do now is stick to your guns. You can't negotiate because there's nothing to negotiate. Dino has got to withdraw his charges and you've got to have it in black-and-white, that past, present or future he has absolutely no claim for damages, otherwise he'll always have something hanging over your heads and you'll go to work every day feeling like you've got the curse."

"Shit! Shit! SHIT!!" growled Ava, her eyes flaring as she threw herself deep into the armchair.

"You have no recourse but to sit tight," Gene said, his voice cold.

"What the hell do you *think* we've been doing?" a blazing Ava demanded, resenting the tone in Gene's voice. "We're stuck in this cell like criminals. We can't go out because those lousy reporters and scum of *paparazzi* are waiting. We can't sneak out of town because that will give Dino the grist for his goddam-whatever-it-is..."

"Mill," Rene broke in as if out of a dream.

"I know what grist is for, honey. I don't need you around to tell me," said Ava, who turned back to Gene. "And Rene's afraid to answer the phone. She never knows who the hell she's really talking to." Ava furtively looked around her, then whispered stealthily. "I'm sure the phone's being tapped. And everybody in this lousy hotel's a spy out to make himself a few bucks." Horror dilated Ava's eyes. "Honey!" She grabbed Gene's arm. "Honey... you don't think... you don't believe... that Dino can get us *arrested*?" She clutched Gene, hard. "Christ, can he?"

"Ava, will you for Christ's sake wipe that thought right out of your head?" Gene replied, releasing himself. "Dino doesn't want you in jail. He wants you on set. The last thing he wants is to have you arrested."

Gene sat on the sofa, put his briefcase on his knees, weary and waiting. He concentrated on London, hoping Rudin would feel the telepathy and call.

Uneven whir of the malfunctioning air conditioner.

Ava sitting back, eyes closed.

Scott still staring into his abyss.

Rene's eyes darting in rhythm to sone unheard melody.

Suddenly. No rhyme. No reason. Gene turned to George.

"Did you ever read any Peretz, George?" Gene asked.

A stir. Summoning up all his powers of concentration, Scott managed to focus on Gene. Ava's eyes opened and she looked over at George.

"What?" he managed to say.

"Isaac Peretz. He wrote fantastic short stories about Polish Jews at the turn of the century. Something like Sholom Aleichem."

"I know about Sholom Aleichem," said Ava, the country gal who didn't know a thing about literature.

"All of Peretz's stories are great," said Gene. "But there's one that's my favorite." He fumbled with his briefcase, pulled out a paperback, started to turn the pages. "I reread it last night. Tremendous."

"Peretz," repeated George, pondering the name.

"What's it about?" asked Rene.

"Well, it's about a man named…"

Ava interrupted. "Why don't you just read it, honey?"

Gene looked at Ava warily. He hadn't forgotten the Oscar Saul fiasco when the writer tried to read Ava new scenes for *The Naked Maja*. Was this some kind of trap? Gene quickly glanced over the room. My God, it was the same suite.

"Yeah, read it," said Scott.

Gene looked at Ava, not hiding his skepticism. Watching her carefully, he asked, "You really want me to?" She was lighting another cigarette. "You're sure you want me to, Ava?" he repeated. Ava put the lighter down on the end table beside her and then spoke. "Yeah, honey, I would like you to." She sank back into her chair, pulled her legs under her thighs, picked up her drink. She was waiting. Saliva began to block Gene's throat and his hands slightly trembled.

Good Christ, he thought. Here I am about to perform for two of the world's biggest stars. How the hell did I get myself into a bind like that? Is this what it means to be an agent? I guess

I've got to go through with it. Something's got to melt down the tension, or it's going to be stretcher-and-asylum time. Anomaly, insanity, whatever… what else is available but this Yiddish writer who has been lying in his grave for fifty years? It was crazy. End of the world. Oy vey and Jesus and Mary.

And so, shakily, he began reading the story of *Bontsha, The Silent*.

Bontsha was a human being. He lived unknown in silence, and in silence, he died. He passed through our world like a shadow. When Bontsha was born, no one took a drink of wine. There was no sound of glasses clinking. When he was confirmed, he made no speech of celebration. He existed like a grain of sand at the rim of a vast ocean, amid millions of other grains of sand exactly alike, and when, at last, the wind lifted him up and carried him across to the other shore of that ocean, no one noticed. No one at all. In silence he was born, in silence he lived, in silence he died, and in an even vaster silence he was placed in the ground.

Ah, but in the other world it was not so! No! In Paradise, the death of Bontsha was an overwhelming event. The great trumpet of the Messiah announced through the seven heavens: Bontsha the Silent is dead! The most exalted angels, with the most imposing wings, hurried, flew, to tell one another, "Do you know who has died? Bontsha! Bontsha the Silent!"

When the young, singing angels encircled Bontsha with love, when Abraham our Father embraced him again and again as an old friend, when Bontsha heard that a throne and a crown for his head awaited him, and that when he stood trial in the court of Heaven, no one would say a word against him. When he heard all this, Bontsha, exactly as in the other world, was silent. He was silent with fear. His heart shook, in his veins ran ice, and he knew this must all be a dream, or simply a mistake.

"He never complained" began the defending angel, "not against God, not against man. His eye never grew red with hatred. He never raised a protest against Heaven. He never had a friend, never was sent to school, never was given a new suit of clothes, never knew one moment of freedom.

"He was silent even when his wife ran off and left him with her helpless infant. He was silent when, fifteen years later, that same infant, now grown up, became strong enough to throw him out of the house.

"He even remained silent when he was run over by a coachman, carriage and horses. In the hospital, where everyone is allowed to scream, he remained silent. He lay abandoned by the doctor, by the nurse, by everyone, uttering not a sound. He was silent in that awful moment just before he was about to die, and he was silent in that very moment when he did die. There was never one murmur of protest against man, never one murmur of protest against God."

The prosecutor rose. "Gentlemen!" he began in a harsh and bitter voice, before stopping. "Gentlemen – " he began again, but now his voice was less harsh, and once again he stopped. Finally, in a soft voice, that same prosecutor said, "Gentlemen, he was always silent – and now I, too, will be silent."

The great court of justice grew very still, and at last from the judge's chair a new voice, loving and tender, was heard. "Bontsha my child, Bontsha!" – the voice swelled a great harp – "my heart's child…"

"There, in the other world, no one understood you. You never understood yourself. You never understood that you need not have been silent, that you could have cried out and that your outcries would have brought down the world itself and ended it. You never understood your sleeping strength. There in that other world, that world of lies, your silence was never rewarded. But Paradise is the world of truth. Here in Paradise you will be rewarded. For you, there is not only one little portion of Paradise, one little share. No! For you there is everything. Whatever you want. Everything is yours!"

For the first time, Bontsha lifted his eyes. He was blinded by light. The splendor of light lay everywhere – upon the walls, upon the vast ceiling. The angels blazed with light. The judge dropped his weary eyes.

"Really?" asked Bontsha, doubtful, and a little embarrassed.

"Really!" the judge answered. "Really! I tell you, everything is yours. Everything in Paradise is yours. Choose. Take. Whatever you want."

"Well then" – and now Bontsha smiled for the first time – "well then, what I would like, Your Excellency, is to have every morning a hot roll with fresh butter."

The silence that fell upon the great hall was more terrible than Bontsha's had ever been. Slowly the judge and the angels bent their heads in shame at this unending meekness they had created on Earth.

Then the silence was shattered. The prosecutor laughed aloud, a bitter laugh.*

The silence that had fallen upon that Grand Hotel suite in Rome was no less terrible than Bontsha's had ever been, and the heads of Ava, George and Rene were bent as if to honor the unending meekness the judge and angels had created on Earth. Gene looked over at Ava. The realization struck him in the gut that from the very beginning, Ava had really meant to listen, had really wanted to listen, that she had longed for nothing more than to lose herself among Peretz's poor Jews of other times and of other places and to take solace in them. Gene wanted to embrace her, hold her tight to him.

Suddenly, as if drawn by a magnet, all sadness was pulled out of the suite. Euphoria rose to replace it. Gene felt capable of levitation. He had an overwhelming desire to jump up and dance all over the place and shout out, "Everything's great. No more Dino problem. No more troubles. Hallelujah and *Gott sum deinken*, this Peretz has made us a miracle!"

Miracle, schmiracle, so long as things got worked out.

Within twenty-four hours, they were.

Mickey Rudin arrived. Ava, who had known him from her Sinatra days, greeted him like the Angels of Heaven greeted Bontsha the Silent. When Mickey and Gene met to discuss the matter, Mickey suggested that Gene do all the talking and that he, Mickey, to batter things down solidly, limit himself to a single, solitary, one-liner. Gene was perplexed by Rudin's strategy but knew he could have full confidence in the attorney's judgment.

So Mickey and Gene went out to see Dino at the De Laurentiis film studios.

Gene made an impassioned plea to Dino. He recalled the glorious Neapolitan tradition of chivalry towards women. A great Neapolitan patriot like Dino, devout and faithful believer in the Madonna, should give that ancient and splendid tradition precedence over everything else, whether in business or life. Gene went on in rising emotion.

* This is an abridged version of Hilde Abel's translation, published in *Selected Stories* by I.L. Peretz (ed. Irving Howe and Eliezer Greenberg), Schocken, 1974.

Neapolitan to the corpuscle, Dino seemed genuinely carried away by Gene's paean. But Dino wanted to be carried away, off the hook on which he had been wiggling in the crisis. Even before Gene and Rudin had made the appointment, he had come to realize that he had boxed himself into a corner, both for the picture and for himself. By the time Rudin quietly spoke his one line, it was apparent that Dino was seeking both a way out and a saved face.

"I believe we have a mutual friend named ________," the attorney said. The pause that followed contained lightning. The name made such an impression on De Laurentiis that Gene, so taken aback by its effect, has never been able to recall it. His face sparkling, Dino jumped up to express his heartfelt desire for an immediate, peaceful resolution of the problem. Explaining to the producer that he had to leave that to Gene and, pleading an urgent appointment, Mickey made his exit.

Dino then turned over to Gene his massive desk and his faithful, able secretary-assistant, Lilliana Matthews. In a grandiose, florid English appropriate for a passionate Neapolitan like De Laurentiis writing to a fabulous star like Gardner, Gene dictated a letter to Ava for Dino's signature. It told of Dino's undying respect for womanhood, particularly as ravishing as hers. In order to demonstrate his dedication to this lofty ideal, he was immediately and unilaterally withdrawing all charges and claims against her and Scott, ghostwrote Gene, and would be overjoyed to once again see them both back at work. Dino signed the letter with masterful flourish, delighted with Gene's subsequent suggestion that it be accompanied by two dozen roses.

In late afternoon, the hand-delivered letter arrived at the Grand Hotel. Roses accompanied it, but, small in stature as he was, Dino was virtuoso of the magnificent gesture. Not two dozen roses, but *four* dozen!

And so ended the strike.

But not the roses.

On September 18, 1964, eighteen long-stem red roses were delivered to Gene. They came from Ava. Accompanying the flowers was perhaps the most unusual representational agreement in the annals of cinema. Dated the same day, written in Ava's own special scrawl, witnessed by Rene "with love," it read:

Gene dear, I don't believe in contracts but by God I do believe in you, so, if I ever do another cotton pickin' picture, would you please take ten percent?

Love you.

Ava

On October 22, the Screen Actors Guild was officially advised by Ava that her worldwide exclusive representation had been turned over to Gene, and Jess Morgan, in his November 9 letter to Gene, expressed delight and added his endorsement.

And thus, what did not come to pass when Ava paid her one and only visit to the offices of KLA in 1959 did come to pass five years later through Bontsha the Silent and Isaac Peretz, with an assist from Milton A. Rudin.

Miracle, schmiracle, so long as things got worked out.

London, December 1964. Approximately 9:30 p.m.

Rene on the telephone to Gene at 16 Cowley Street, Sir John Gielgud's townhouse, which Gene had rented during Gielgud's engagement to star on Broadway in Edward Albee's *Tiny Alice.*

"He's trying to kill her!" she cried hysterically. "Get over here right away. You've got to get over here right away!"

Alarmed, Gene immediately phoned for a cab to pick him up at the great actor's house near Westminster Abbey. He told the driver to get him to the Savoy immediately. "It's an emergency!" The cabbie obliged, screeching to a halt at the entrance. Gene ran to the elevator. Once it reached the fifth floor, he dashed down the corridor leading to Ava's apartment. As he ran, he noted three house detectives lounging in the corridors.

Gene's head was pounding as he knocked at the suite door. No sound. As the house detectives eyed him without moving, he knocked even harder. No sound. Saliva seeped into his throat. He started to knock once more when suddenly the door was opened. Not by Ava or Rene but by a ghost with twisted face, bloodied from head to foot, clothes torn and disheveled. Before Gene could to say a word, George C. Scott gripped him in a strong vise and wrenched him into the living room of the suite.

It looked as if it had been struck by an earthquake. Furniture had been battered and overturned. The drapes pulled down. The television set a mangle of wires. Blood splattered over walls. And no sign of Ava. Was she in the bedroom? The bathroom?

Was she unconscious? Christ, was she dead? From where had Rene placed the frantic call? All the dire questions raced through Gene's aching brain.

George gave Gene no time to ask any of the questions flying around his head. Instantly, Scott flung a long bath towel, elegantly emblemed as "Property of the Savoy," around Gene's neck. Tauntingly, Scott began to pull it tight, then tighter. "I'm going to kill you," he hissed between his teeth, the noose tightening, his eyes peering intently into Gene's, searching for the fear in them. In sadistic litany, as he tightened and tightened, he chanted, "I'm going to kill you, I'm going to kill you, I'M GOING TO KILL YOU." Like a heavy weight, instinct pressed down ruthlessly to hold down Gene's rising panic. It kept any sign of hysteria from distorting his face. Gene realized that under no circumstances must he demonstrate fear, for fear is what Scott seemed to need to compel him to fulfill his threat of murder.

"Where is she? Where did you hide her?" Scott snapped viciously.

A joy of relief surged through Gene. If George didn't know where Ava was then at least she was alive. But the joy was quickly truncated by the thought that George himself might not remember that he had killed her. Or that, diabolically, his demons freed by alcohol, George was slowly leading Gene to the horror of discovering her body.

The towel was pulled roughly, nearly suffocating Gene.

"You know where she is," Scott continued. "You know goddamn well where she is. I'm going to kill you if you don't tell me."

The towel was slightly loosened so Gene could speak. "I don't know, George. All I know is that we had a half-assed date to go to see the Nunnally Johnsons after dinner and I came by to see if she wanted to go," Gene added in spontaneous invention.

A tight jerk. "You're lying. Liar! LIAR!" Scott screamed in his hoarse voice, which seemed to stem from only one vocal cord. The towel was pulled tight again, choking, choking. George's eyes were now no more than an inch away from Gene's, staring deep into them, searching for the fear. George was right, of course. It was a lie. But how could Gene tell him of Rene's desperate phone call?

"George," Gene managed to eke out, as he also tried to come up with a semblance of a smile. He tried to loosen his bondage by very gently twisting his neck. "George, I've had a bitch of a day. I need a drink." The words came out in a strangled gasp, but they had their impact. The cry for alcohol was a cry Scott understood. As perilous as he knew it was for him, he could still recognize it as a logical, sensible cry, as a compelling absolute. If a guy needed a drink, he needed a drink. George bought Gene's ploy outright, not remembering that Gene rarely touched the stuff.

"Go on, get yourself a drink," he replied, gesturing towards the side table heavy with bottles. Gene walked the few steps to the table, George right behind him, still gripping the towel around Gene's neck. As Gene poured himself a vodka tonic, his mind was racing. What to say? What to do? Could he get to the door, unlock it, and escape? And if he could, would those goddamn house detectives take some action? Who could he call?

Gene took a sip of his drink, then, as matter-as-factly as he could, said to George: "You don't know where Ava is. I don't know where Ava is. So why don't we call Nunnally and Dorris? Maybe Ava's there. Or they'll know where she is."

A long suspicious stare from George as Gene gulped down more of the vodka-tonic. Finally, sound from the one-corded voice. "Yeah. Call Nunnally and Dorris." Momentary reprieve. Putting his drink down, Gene walked over to the phone, George right there behind him, snaking the towel around Gene's neck. Gene put the call through to the Savoy operator. "Grosvenor 2951, please," a number Gene fortunately knew by heart. The rings seemed to go on forever. Panic again rising, it kept on ringing. At last, a voice!

"Dorris, dear. Is Ava there?"

"No honey. We're not expecting her."

"I'm here at the Savoy." Gene was measuring his words as much as he dared, hoping Dorris would realize something wasn't right. "Ava told me to come by. She said we might drop by to see you and Nunnally after dinner. And she's not here. I thought maybe I had misunderstood and that I was supposed to meet her *chez vous*."

Silence. Dorris was clearly puzzled. "She's bound to turn up sooner or later," she said at last. "Why don't you come over and wait for her?"

"No, thanks," Gene replied, the frustration maddening. "I'll wait here with George. He doesn't know where Ava is either and he's pretty upset. In fact, he's *very* upset."

That's a signal Dorris will pick up, Gene said to himself. Dorris will get that. But Dorris didn't. "I don't know what to say," Dorris replied. Gene's stomach flip-flopped. "But you're both welcome to come over, honey."

"Thanks, but we'll wait in Ava's suite. If you hear anything, anything at all, will you please call? I'm really worried."

"All right, dear."

Gene hung up the phone. Keep up the action, he kept thinking. The bedroom. The bathroom. Quickly, momentarily catching George off balance, he jerked himself towards the bathroom, the towel partially slipping from Gene's neck. Gene dashed towards the bedroom, George racing after him, hissing, "You're not getting away. You won't get away. I'm going to kill you." The towel again slithered around Gene's neck, but Gene kept moving.

"We've got to look everywhere, George. She might have come in without your realizing it. There's a bedroom entrance too, remember."

"No tricks, you little bastard. She's not in there. You're trying to get away, and you won't ever get away, I'll see to that!"

"We have to look, George," Gene repeated. By then, Gene had surveyed the bedroom and staggered into the bathroom with an image of a bloodied Ava dead in the tub. An increasingly angered George was on top of him. The towel was tightening. Keep moving, moving, moving, Gene kept repeating to himself. He managed to open the closet door. No Ava there either. Ignoring the pain ripping through the right side of his neck after a vicious jerk of the towel, Gene bent down to look under the mangled bed. Elation swirled through him. Ava was somewhere else! Ava was safe!

George grabbed him, now shaking with rage. The actuality of murder seemed to Gene ominously near. George pulled Gene back into the salon. The towel loosened, slowly tightened, slithered back and forth, jerked mercilessly. How much longer was he going to be able to resist? Those goddamn house dicks. They knew goddamn well what was going on. Why in the name of Christ don't they do something? The dignity of the Savoy to be preserved at all costs, that's why. The sons-of-bitches were not going to intervene unless violence spilled out into the corridors to compromise the reputation of the Savoy, that's why.

Then it happened.

Why it happened, how it happened, Gene neither knew, understood nor cared. But it happened.

Scott was on his knees, sobbing, gripping Gene's thighs. Gene looked down at him, totally bewildered.

"Don't ever leave her," he sobbed. "You're the only one she trusts. She needs you. She loves you. Don't leave her, ever. Help her. Promise me you'll help her. Promise me you'll never ever leave her."

Confused, wary but moved, Gene caressed the blood-matted head that George himself had wounded in his siege of auto-destruction. "Yes, George. I promise, George. Yes, George, yes, I promise." Gene knew the denouement had come. "You go back to your apartment and rest. I'll go try and find her," Gene said gently as he helped George to his feet. Gene wanted to get the towel out of George's hands but decided not to break the spell by grabbing for it.

As George was back on his feet, Gene released himself, speedily unbolted the door, and hurried towards the detectives, who suddenly became alert. George stood at the door, helpless. The towel slowly slipped from what seemed beseeching hands.

Gene knew there was no time for a diatribe with the house guards. "Mr. Scott will go quietly if you treat him gently... very gently," Gene whispered to them. "Once you get him to his suite, lock him in. Get Peter Stafford to stay with him. Mr. Scott likes Stafford." Stafford was the Savoy's attractive, charming assistant manager, and an admirer and chum of Ava's.

Scott, disoriented, meandered into the corridor. Ready for anything, two of the detectives moved towards him. Gene grabbed the arm of the third.

"Now tell me where Miss Gardner is."

"We've got strict orders not to tell anyone."

Gene watched Scott being led down the corridor to his suite. Once Scott had entered and the door shut after him, Gene blew his top.

"You're goddamn well going to tell me! And you're goddamn well going to have a tough time, you and your buddies, explaining why you kept your distance while George Scott was playing murder with me. Now, once again: *Where is Miss Gardner*?"

A hard look from the detective. "Okay," he finally said. "She's in her maid's room. It's number..."

"I know the number," Gene interrupted, racing down a second corridor to Rene's room. Frantically he knocked at the door, repeating, "It's Gene, open up." A crack of the door, held by a distraught Rene. As Gene pushed it free, Rene whispered, her eyes raised to Heaven.

"Thank you, Jesus, thank you, Jesus."

The sight Gene saw was something out of Bette Davis in her last scene of *Of Human Bondage*. He tried not to see Ava sitting there on Rene's bed, her arms hugging her legs, a terrible effigy of humiliation. As she slowly rocked back and forth, she gradually lifted her eyes towards Gene.

She then stretched out her hand, the fist closed. Like a bud opening to the morning sun, she tremblingly opened her fingers as, finally, she spoke. "He tore half the hair from my head." Gene looked down at the ball of strands in her hand, shook his head in disbelief, then looked at that face blotted with sweat, puffed by insomnia, booze and blows.

"Are you okay, honey?" Gene managed to ask, forcing the tremble out of his voice.

"He tore half the hair from my head," repeated Ava.

Quietly, she began to weep. "Is she all right?" Gene asked Rene. Rene just stared, her face shaking uncontrollably. She repeatedly nodded, murmuring brokenly, "Okay, she's okay, she'll be okay."

Tears burning his eyes, Gene sat on the edge of the bed and put his arms around Ava.

"Where is he?" she asked in an Ophelia voice.

"Back in his suite. I asked Peter Stafford to stay with him. Honey, we can't let this go on. It's got to end. I think it's best if you stay here until I give the all clear. There's no way of predicting if we're in a calm before another storm. Try to rest. Just lie down and rest. Anything you need? Anything you want?"

Ava didn't answer.

"Rene, don't leave her, even for a second. Okay? And keep her here, you understand? Don't open the door for anybody but me. You got it?" Rene nodded as Gene gave her a quick kiss. He turned once more to Ava. She was huddled in another world.

"I'll be back as soon as I know everything's under control," he said. He didn't know whether she had heard him. He leaned over and kissed her on the cheek, trying to catch her eye. She continued to stare into some distance. Gene left the room.

The hours passed. Peter Stafford kept his vigil over Scott. At Gene's request, he finally located a doctor to give George a shot to knock him out. Tall, heavyset, the physician could have doubled for a wrestler, but it took him and four others to hold George down for the injection.

It was nearly five o'clock in the morning by the time Gene once again knocked at Rene's door. No Ava. Gene was furious, Rene beside herself. "She insisted on going back to her suite," Rene explained. "I did everything I could to stop her, but I couldn't. And she wouldn't let me come with her."

Gene rushed to Ava's suite. After knocking and shouting his name over and over, the door opened.

The expression on Ava's face was brewed in trouble.

"What did you do to him?" she asked combatively. Gene realized that Ava had neither intention nor capacity to control her rage. "Why the hell did you call a doctor? Who told you to order an injection? Who do you think you are? I'm the one who knows what to do with him when he gets like that. I'm the only one who can help him. Now you better tell me where he is!"

"I told you in Rene's room hours ago. He's in his own suite. And he's out. Really out."

"I'm going to him."

"No, you're not, Ava. "

"I said I'm going to him."

"I said you're not."

"For Christ's sake, he needs me. Don't you understand?"

"Okay, Ava. If you really want to be killed, go ahead. Go on. I'm not going to stop you. Nobody's going to stop you."

The confrontation of eyes was violent. The battle was joined. For a moment it really seemed that Ava would go after Gene with her fists. Then she began to pace – wild, ugly.

"Why doesn't anybody come running?" was the start of her tirade. "Where the fuck is everybody?" she went on. "Is everybody dead? Or are they all over there with George? If getting attention is what you're after, George Scott's the man to teach you how. He's the champ! Doctors. Detectives. Peter Stafford. You. Anybody he wants!" She gestured towards the wreckage of the living room. "Carry on like he does and everybody comes running. *Everybody!* Good ol' George, he sure knows what to do. And goddamit, I know what to do."

She grabbed the cloth from under the bottles of liquor on the side table. She jerked with all her strength. Off came the cloth. Crash went all the bottles, splintering on the floor. The rug and nearby furniture became a crazed cocktail, and the stench of alcohol quickly permeated the room. Breathing hard, Ava looked at Gene defiantly, waiting for him to react, daring him to react.

Gene let a few seconds pass before he spoke. "I've had it, Ava," he said, not keeping the ice from his voice. "I'm going home. If you have any sense, you'll go to sleep. You know you're due to leave for New York tomorrow... today."

Ava just stared at him. Her hand was running nervously through the remains of her hair. She then jerked her head down to look at the confusion of broken bottles and alcohol around her. Gene's disgust for her seemed part of the pounding ache in his head.

"Do you want me to come and see you off?" he asked, expecting, hoping like hell that she would say no.

She looked at him hard, hatred in her regard. "Do that, honey." And without another word, Ava turned and disappeared into the bedroom.

Back at Cowley Street, at six in the morning, Gene staggered to the bathroom, vomiting out his guts.

Later that same morning, through cautious planning between the Savoy management, the London police and the airlines, George C. Scott was quietly transported from the Savoy and just as quietly put on a plane for New York. His departure marked the end of the Ava Gardner-George C. Scott love affair that came so close to being Ava's fourth marriage.

That same day, Gene, feeling ghastly and looking worse, appeared at the entrance of the hotel to see Ava off, also to New York but on a different airline. She and Rene were already on their way down. As Ava, followed by Rene, walked out of the elevator, Gene looked at her in both astonishment and anger.

Her transformation in a brief lapse of hours was beyond belief. After all she had been through, she was utterly fabulous, incredibly vibrant. Made-up with care, spectacularly dressed, not a sign of torn hair in her meticulous coiffure, she came towards Gene with a radiant smile.

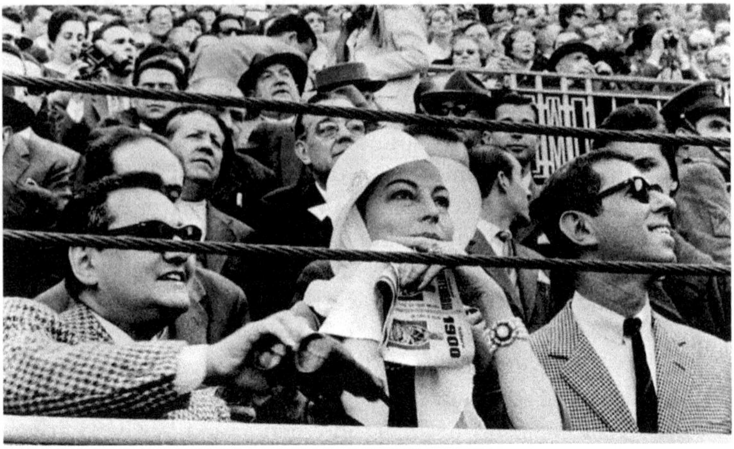

Hank Kaufman, Ava Gardner and Gene Lerner

Ava kissed him on the cheek, took his hand, as she and Rene moved rapidly to the waiting car. "I'm running late, honey. I'll call you from New York."

The chauffeur opened the car door. Laden with packages and carry-on bags, Rene staggered in. The motor started. Ava jumped into the back seat beside Rene. The car started moving, Ava leaned out of the window and waved, as did Rene.

"See you soon, honey," Ava shouted, throwing Gene a kiss.

As Gene watched the limousine pick up speed, his fury twisted every organ in his body.

The involuntary or deliberate toll Ava has taken on others is, in human terms, massive. Virtually no one in her life has been able to bring consistency to the volatile swing of her pendulum. In her ever-changing Imperial State Council, paranoia has struggled to keep a permanent seat. Ava has had such a turnover in servants, secretaries, acquaintances, friends, enemies and chums, that the comings-and-goings often resembled a Feydeau farce.

Some who at one time or another have been involved with her viciously indict her, condemning her for a series of crimes, such as…

Emotional rapacity.

Cannibalistic boredom.

Maddening unpredictability.

Cruel behavior.

Outright prevarication.

Unmitigated selfishness.

Pleasure in punishment.

Shameful exploitation of good will, friendship, even love.

But have these plaintiffs really known Ava? Have they really watched Ava listening? Or listened to her listening? This facet of her is crucial to the understanding of her. When Ava listens, the fire of her fades to embers. The earth of her ceases to feed the maggots that gnaw at her soul. The air and water of her gush forth to refresh both the other and herself. She becomes an attuned ear of empathy. She is transformed into a chalice of comprehension for unappeasable needs of the birth-wronged. The listening Ava. Infinitely patient nurse. Compassionate priest. Even if hurt, even when betrayed, she has the force to metamorphose environment into chapel. A particularly meaningful demonstration of her resurrective powers took place in Madrid at Eastertime, March 1964. By listening for interminable hours, from evening through night, from morning through day, she salvaged Gene's life.

And have her accusers given appropriate weight or realized the fundamental importance of another, even more precious gift possessed by Ava? In their anger, bitterness or envy, have they failed to see this second incandescent jewel sewn into her inner matrix?

Her *simplicity.*

There will never be an Ava equivalent of Arthur Miller's Marilyn-by-another-name play, *After the Fall*, authored by a presumptuous intellectual, for the power and veracity of Ava simplicity would shatter both him and his dramatist pen.

Her simplicity is physical, tangible, instinctual.

It is there in Rome, when emotion and peace mingle as the story of *Bontsha the Silent* is told. It is there, lullabying, healing, when she listens to Gene in her Dr. Arce bedroom during Easter of 1964. It is there in Madrid in August 1965, when she sits envisioning foxes as they emerge from *The Little Prince*. It is there when she races through the gardens and parks of the world with Rags, or his companion, Cara.

It is there, anguished and honest, when she speaks to Gene of herself, of life and the future, throughout the August night, after Rags is laid to rest in La Moraleja. It is there in the nobility that flows between her and the Queen of England on July 5, 1965. It is there when she sits on the stage at Oxford University in November

1964 to hear Robert Graves propound on the worthiness of Wordsworth. It is there on May 19, 1974, in an afternoon of gymnastics and yoga at her sister Bappie's house perched on the edge of the Hollywood Hills.

It is there on June 19, 1971, in the playground of Alexander Square in London, when at nearly fifty years of age she rushes to a swing to hoist herself high over the trees, laughing and giggling like an innocent child. It is there in May 1964, at Casa Bianca in Sabaudia, when she poses with chums and servants for a series of Polaroid informals and goes on her boating venture with eight Italian lads. It is there in her posture, in that splendid synthesis of self, space and nature, which is a miracle of inner choreography. It is there in her presence when, in those rare, delineated moments, she feels complete within herself and, above all, is able to be herself. It is there when she sits in her pilgrim's habit of blouse-and-skirt, her feet bare, bandana over hair. It is there when she suddenly drops the mask that shrouds her vulnerability and finds herself able to look at you with love.

Perhaps only in recent years has Ava herself begun to realize the puissance, the invincibility, of her simplicity. Perhaps only now, as she nears sixty years of age, has she understood that above all else – learning, wealth, sophistication, wit, sexual coupling, physical beauty – it is her simplicity that is her guarantee for survival, and even, if one dare say it, her step towards the threshold of serenity.

In her restorative capacity for listening…

In her ability for transforming environment into chapel…

In the simplicity sewn into her inner matrix…

Is where we discover the realms unknown and undreamed of, to which Henry Miller once referred.

Rome, December 24, 1959

Dearest Ava:

I feel that with this 37th birthday, you have reached a critical moment in your life. The fact of your growing older is of course involved. But what really is at stake is what you do with your maturity, what you achieve as woman and actress through the coming years.

The time has come for you to clarify your own goals. You cannot stumble about without self-direction, failing to recognize your responsibility to yourself and, as so movingly evidenced by your brilliance in *On the Beach*, to the enrichened talent that can emerge with even greater profundity, if it is carefully nurtured. The capacity to love and to accept love has a direct relationship to self-respect and inner security. These can come to you through work well done, and such work is a crucial key to your potential for contentment as a person, as a woman.

The mystery of self is so complex that one rightfully trembles in fear, taking refuge in anger or defiance. But the grandeur of the human spirit is so vast that, when faced with the choice between living in Life or dying in Life, we choose to live. I know that inevitably you will, you must choose to live and thus, to achieve through work.

Happy Birthday, dearest Ava, and all our love, Hank's and mine.

Gene

No reply came from Ava… then. But more than fifteen years later, when Ava had passed her 53rd birthday, it finally arrived.

London. May 22, 1976. Cocktail hour at Ava's Ennismore Gardens home.

George Pan Cosmatos, the stocky, exuberant, young director who had just completed *Cassandra's Crossing* in Rome with Ava, Sophia Loren and Richard Harris, was saying his goodbyes to Ava in endless retakes.

"Would you do another picture with me again?" he asked Ava.

"I sure would, honey," she replied. She jerked her head towards Gene. "George is a good man and a hell of a director. Gobs of talent. And a chum." Gripping both of the Greek's hands, she looked into his eyes. "Find something good and we'll do it. I want to work. It's about the only thing that keeps me from going batty."

Suddenly Ava became her amazing posture, standing silent, caught by once-upon-a-time. She seemed to feel Gene's eyes upon her. Slowly, she turned towards him, her face not yet a smile, not really a tear. "You wrote me something like that a hundred years ago, didn't you, hon?"

Not trusting himself to speak, Gene simply nodded. For years, he had no longer been Ava's agent. For years, he had no longer been anybody's agent. All that was packed away and stored in the past. Ava pursed her lips and smacked him a kiss. He just stood there, looking at her, trying to control the tremble on his lips. How he loved that woman!

Ava turned back to Cosmatos, took him by the arm, and, chattering away, disappeared into the hallway to see him off.

"So my face looks lived in," she has said. "I don't resent a thing. Not a thing. You won't find me standing in front of a mirror, weeping. Ageing is the great equalizer, whether you're rich, poor, young, old, beautiful or ugly. Sooner or later, it robs you. Only it isn't really stealing a thing because what you had was only a loan to begin with. Eventually, you have to pay it all back."

> She is no liar, yet she will wash away
> Honey from her lips, blood from her shadowy hand,
> And, dressed at dawn in clean white robes will say,
> Trusting the ignorant world to understand:
> "Such things no longer are; this is today."
>
> Robert Graves

Nine
Art and Life: Simile and Metaphor

Approximately ten minutes before eight in the morning. March 23, 1956.

Anna on the telephone.

"Can you believe it, crazy boy? We won! We won!"

The news had just been flashed from Hollywood that Anna Magnani had won the Oscar for the best female performance of the year in *The Rose Tattoo.*

"I know, I heard it on the radio," replied an excited Gene. "I kept trying to get through to you, but everybody must be trying to call you or you're trying to call everybody. I always knew you would win."

"You Americans and your fetish of optimism. I know one thing. If I would have gone to Hollywood like everybody wanted, I wouldn't have won. And me getting on a plane? Who are they kidding?"

"You and your silly superstitions."

"So I'm superstitious and I still won the Oscar! I wouldn't let myself believe I could win. I thought you Americans would give it to one of your own. It would be natural, no? You Americans may be crazy, but I have to say it… You're fair and you're democratic. And, sometimes, even wonderful! Listen – has Paramount called you?"

"Anna, it's only eight o'clock in the morning."

"You wait… That nice Viero Nicoli will call you about some reception or ceremony. Anyway, enough! I can't take any more time talking to you. My phone's got to be free for congratulations from all those kiss-my-ass bigshots and all those dear friends and lifetime admirers, all those hypocritical *stronzi* who never before wanted to hear my name."

"Anna, it's great to see you so happy."

"Happy? I'm delirious, hysterical! Are you happy?"

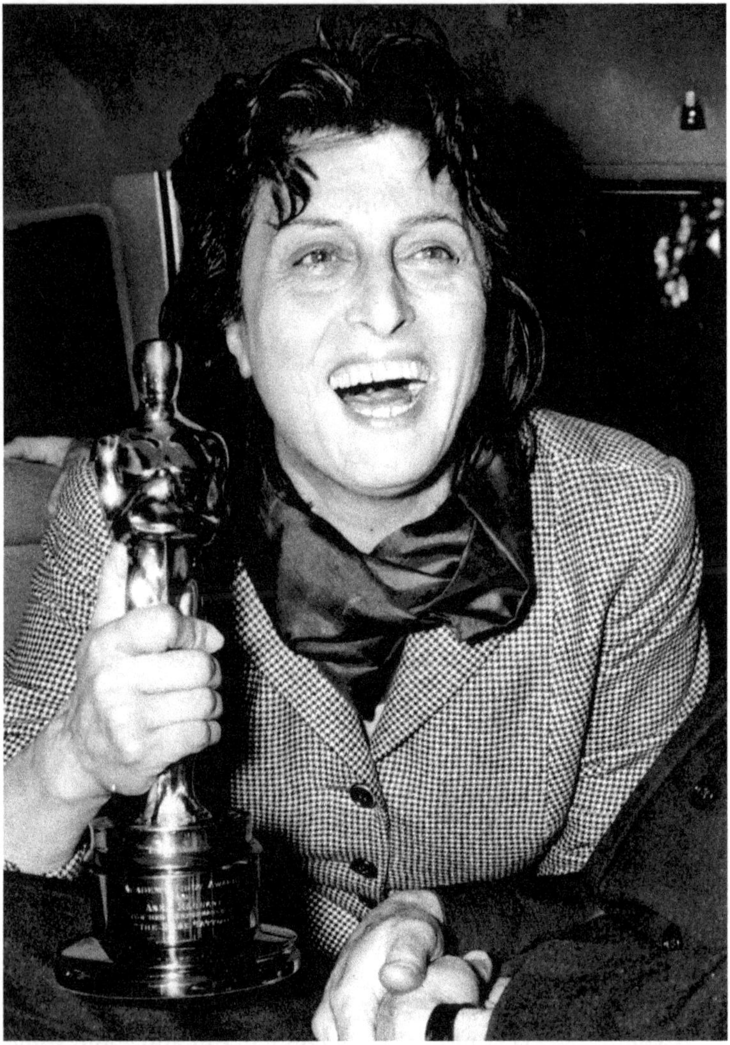

Anna Magnani

"It's one of the happiest days of my life."

"Ah-hah! Maybe you're going to cry! How many times in life can you cry from joy, eh? Why don't you come over right now and kiss me? We'll both cry. And let's pray that there will be other times in our life that our tears will taste so sweet."

March 18, 1960. Anna on the telephone.

"It's Magnani. Mr. Lerner, please."

"I'm sorry, Signora, Signor Lerner is out," said Franca.

"Mr. Kaufman – is *he* out?"

Flick. Buzz. Phone ringing in Hank's office.

"Anna Magnani," Franca announced.

Another problem, Hank wonders? Some new crisis? "Put her through," replied Hank, wondering what was coming.

"*Ciao*, Anna."

"Kaufman. Did you see *Suddenly Last Summer*?"

"I sure did, Anna. Why?"

"That Hepburn. Unbelievable, no? Did you ever see such an actress in your life? My eyes popped out of my head, staring at her. I watched the screen like a drooling idiot, like a person possessed. How could one solitary woman seem to be a thousand butterflies flying through the air in a hundred different directions, all at once? Unbelievable. Just unbelievable!"

Click. Hank shook his head as he put the receiver back in place. He broke out in a broad smile. Unbelievable, just unbelievable, that Anna on the telephone.

January 1959. Magnani, Kaufman and Lerner were in the first row of the Eliseo Theater for the Rome premiere of *Irma La Douce*, directed by Vittorio Gassman for his mistress, Anna Maria Ferrero, who five years earlier had cost Shelley Winters tears, screams and broken mirrors during *Mambo* days.

Anna was wearing a long, deep-blue gown, her lips and eyes carefully made up and her hair rigidly amassed on top of her head in the Empire hairstyle, which was all the rage. She seemed as delighted with her unusual coiffure as she was by the prospects of the evening. Her adoration for theater neared obsession, her passion for perfection in stage performance legendary and understandably unpopular. If a production was not up to her expectations, she became impatient and found it entirely impossible to maintain decorous behavior. She was, after all, *romana*, and for centuries Romans have been blatantly vocal in their approval or disapproval.

Anna was already at the edge of her seat when the overture started. The music pleased her and she beat out the rhythm with her feet. But as soon as the curtain rose and Ferrero appeared,

Anna's stage whispers began and reverberated through half the theater. Hank and Gene had a hard time keeping her quiet.

"Anna Maria, idiot! You're in a musical, not in a dirge. *Bambina mia*, what are you *doing*? Child, child, no, no, no! For the love of God, Vittorio, didn't you teach her *anything*?" Some forceful, blunt "shut-ups" from members in the audience helped keep her under control.

The bar at intermission was crowded with tall, willowy ladies whose height was vastly increased by their gigantic layer cakes of twisted hair. Magnani stopped to look at the women on her left, then those on her right. She stared into the mirror at her reflection. Suddenly she burst out into her cascade of laughter. The towering skyscrapers turned towards her in shock. She looked at her escorts and, still laughing, shrugged her shoulders. Then, as everyone watched, she gripped her coiffure roughly with both hands. "What's the use?" she said with a grin. She swept her fingers through the lacquered labyrinth and tossed her head vigorously to bring her hair back to its natural disorder. The Empire was forever destroyed.

She gave the astonished pillars of the temple of chic a radiant smile, as if to say, "I may look ridiculous, I may not be as piss-elegant as you, but whether you like it or not, you bitches, at least I'm *me*."

"Let's have some champagne," Hank suggested, putting his arm tightly around her.

"Why not?" she replied, hugging him, and, taking Gene's arm, the three pushed their way through the crowd.

Rome. December 19, 1959. Two o'clock in the morning.

Anna on the telephone to Gene.

"I have a piece of unfinished business to take up with you," she started in, her voice a threat. Gene stifled the "Christ, what's this all about?" that he almost said.

"At this hour, Anna?" Gene asked warily. "Can't it wait?"

"Why should it wait? Because I'm disturbing your sleep?" The sarcasm was meant to be a provocation. Anna was angry. She was a dog who was not going to give up its bone.

"Okay, Anna. What's this all about?"

"I just finished a shit of an evening for those 'David of Donatello' awards. A visit to the zoo would be more fun. President Gronchi himself was there."

Oh, Christ, this is about Ava, Gene realized. Ava was set to be there to be, honored as the best foreign actress of the year. Something God awful must have happened between them, thought Gene. He had better take the bull by the horns.

"Did you see Ava there?" he asked with an effort at lightness.

"Yes," Magnani replied with her unique brand of darkness. "We exchanged a few stupid words when Gronchi was receiving us. I don't even remember what they were. By the way, did you give that message to Ava?"

Electric shock. More than a year had passed since the Gardner-Magnani Via Salaria fiasco, which seemed to Gene a permanent rock in his stomach. "Yes," he finally said, choking on the word.

"What did she say?" Magnani demanded. "I want to know *exactly* what she said." The voice was granite hard.

"Anna, look. I don't know what happened between the two of you tonight, but you have to know Ava to understand."

"*Nothing* happened tonight," she replied in a half-scream. "I just want you to tell me what she said when you gave her my message," biting out the words.

"She said… she said…" Gene was squirming.

"What?"

"She said, 'Why don't you ask her…?" Gene began. He couldn't force himself to go on.

"Go on, go on. What don't you ask me *what*?"

Magnani's third-degreeing was upsetting Gene. "You really have to know, don't you? Why didn't you ask you yourself tonight? All right, Anna. I'll tell you. She said, 'Why don't you ask her why she never combs her hair?'" Gene blurted out as if it was all a single word. "Now that you know, are you satisfied?" he finished, angrily.

"Why… I *never*…. comb… my hair," Magnani whispered to herself, incredulous. Gene's remorse over Anna's reaction thrust away all vestiges of his anger. Clutching the receiver tight, he began to speak rapidly, intensely. Sleep, exhaustion, the night – all was forgotten.

"Ava doesn't know how to handle compliments, particularly from somebody she admires, like you. She said the first ridiculous thing that popped into her head, that's all. It wasn't meant to be offensive or cute. It wasn't a put down. Believe me, Anna, what you said in your message was very important to her. Last night certainly wasn't the occasion for her to tell you how much she appreciated it, but I can tell you that for months she told friends what you said about her. She was very proud. Believe that, Anna. I had always hoped the two of you would meet again. Why didn't you make the effort tonight? You certainly know how to open your mouth. I guarantee you, she would have met you more than halfway. Goddamit it, the two of you have so much in common and you should hit it off."

There was only silence on the other end of the receiver.

"Have you understood anything I've said?" Gene asked, his voice reined tight with frustration. "Have you *tried* to understand anything I've said?"

Silence. The dressing room scene at the Sarah Bernhardt six years before flashed through Gene's mind. He could no longer restrain his rage.

"You're such an idiot. They should give you the Oscar for stupidity. Your head is just a slab of marble," he spit out at her.

Silence.

"Can't you get it through your thick, *romana* skull that you are beautiful, too? Beau-ti-ful," he repeated, underlining each syllable. "Anna, did you hear me say that you are beautiful too?" he asked pleadingly.

Silence. A click of the receiver. Magnani was gone.

The debate among critics and fans of the world as to who should be enshrined on the greatest screen actress list will never be resolved. Four in the august group of women stars in cinema history worthy of selection are Greta Garbo, Bette Davis, Katharine Hepburn and Anna Magnani.

Garbo, Davis, Hepburn, Magnani. Personalities so extraordinary, so unique, that fundamentally, with only slight variation, they appear on the screen as mirrors of themselves. Magnani, however, was the exception among the four. With Garbo, Davis and Hepburn, it's the actress who is imposed on the woman. In Magnani, it's the woman imposed on the actress. The former three fulfill the myth of a bourgeois culture and are creatures of literature – good, bad or indifferent. Magnani personified the mass and was the graph of the oscillations of life.

Merely to classify Magnani with Italian neorealism is misleading. Her professional and artistic roots grew in much different soil and under diverse influences. She was no personality taken from the streets, as was so often the practice of neorealistic directors. Before she became the indubitable mistress of her medium, she served years as apprentice and journeywoman. By the time she was selected by Rossellini to appear in *Open City* in 1945, she had had a long, distinguished and successful career as tragedienne, comedienne, soubrette, buffoon, mimer, singer, dancer and burlesque star, already noted both on stage and screen. Because of what she was as a woman, what she possessed as an artist, she leapt out of any defined category to create her own.

While she accepted a socialist political view of life, it never inflicted itself upon her characterizations. They were never rooted in ideology. They sprang from wells she dug deep into the earth, and her vision of the future was riveted in the past. Neither the class struggle nor social idealism formed the structure of her interpretations. The unanswerable relationship between life and death, mother and child, man and woman, did.

Although she played variations of *romana*, she was, in reality, closer to classic Greek theater than Italian cinema. When she tossed her Medusa-like hair or expressed laughter, pain, love, tenderness, joy, hate, defiance, contempt or fury in her Medea-like eyes, it was Euripides, not Rossellini, who came to mind. It was not a face but a tragic mask that filled and totally dominated the screen.

The contrast with neorealism was evident. Neorealism chronicled the events of daily life. Magnani transformed them into essence of drama. Neorealism was documentation, Magnani art. Neorealism represented its particular times. Magnani's characters were beyond time.

There was no role she had played that did not deal with the liberation or fulfillment of women. There was no rapport she had with men or society that did not show her struggling against domination or diminution of woman, or fighting for the dignity of person and the totality of personality of woman or the unprotected. She, more than any other actress, has sharply delineated the spiritual, emotional and psychological disparity between woman and female, and in her portraiture of mothers, never submerged nor compromised the persona of woman.

As is generally known, *The Rose Tattoo* was offered to Magnani by author Tennessee Williams as a Broadway vehicle.

Even though Williams had written it with her in mind, it was reluctantly rejected by Magnani. She felt she could not handle the English in a theater. When Paramount bought the film rights, it was again submitted to Magnani, who this time warmly accepted it. Directed by Daniel Mann, co-starring Burt Lancaster and featuring Marisa Pavan as Maria, the daughter, it won Magnani not only the Oscar but also resulted in such critical paeans as "a Vesuvian temperament never before seen on the screen" and "a grandeur of personality we are privileged to see only once in a generation." *The Rose Tattoo* resulted in an international mass popularity Magnani had never before achieved. The homage of her noted Hollywood colleagues, and the enormous and respectful attention of the world's journalists based in Los Angeles, gratified her.

Unnatural protectiveness of a beloved adolescent daughter, mystic rapport with the dead, refutation of life and of love that lives, morbid religiosity, obsession, guilt, sexuality suppressed then exploded, tragedy bordering on the ludicrous. These are the variety of primary colors she slashed on the canvas of her characterization of Serafina in *The Rose Tattoo.* The resulting portrait was the amalgamation of two essences, one of woman, the other of mother. Her mastery was so great, her instincts so profound, that she achieved the fusion of the two without diminishing the shape, force or purity of either.

In Luchino Visconti's *Bellissima*, filmed in 1951, Magnani portrayed Maddalena, prototype of the fiercely protective *romana* mother. The story was simple. A little girl was being sought to play an important role in a film, and an open screen test was announced. Maddalena, envisioning a life of fame, wealth and glamor for her golden-curled Maria, was determined that nothing would stand in the way of getting the part for her adored child.

Magnani's characterization of Maddalena was of tragic stature, inspired by a union of technique, discipline, instinct and emotional depth. She was brazen, aggressive, supplicatory, coquettish, tender, infuriated, frightened and bewildered. Then, once struck by the shock of betrayal, she became animal in her desperation. In the use of her voice, she shifted from notes to half-notes, sharps to flats, octaves in waterfall. It shrieked like an orchestra in cymbal-like climax, then fell dumb in tormented pause or shaken silence. Those who saw *Bellissima* have never forgotten the pain, horror and humiliation scratched deeply into her face when, in watching her child's hopeless screen test, she realized that her own flesh and blood, her own daughter, was merely the cruel butt of malicious laughter. Her gesture of sudden dignity and defiance when she quickly covered the eyes of her Maria, so that the child at least was shielded from their mutual degradation, was, to say the least, memorable.

Sophia Loren's Cesira in *Two Women* won her the Academy Award of 1960. When audiences saw Loren's splendid portrayal, they saw an Italian mother of the provinces trying to protect her innocent Italian daughter and herself from the terrible desecration of war in the Italy of 1943. It would be an experiment of exceptional interest to all film lovers to see Magnani's Maddelena in *Bellissima* and her Serafina in *The Rose Tattoo* on the one hand and Loren's Cesira in *Two Women* on the other.

Had Magnani portrayed the *Two Women* role that rightfully belonged to her, the world, in her Cesira, would have seen, no, would have *participated* in, the superhuman struggle of mother, beyond nationality, boundary, race, color or epoch, mother of *all* children in whatever part of the world endangered by starvation, violence, mortification and death.

As mother of them all, Magnani would have merged actress and woman, art and reality, celluloid and audience. It would be as if, bodily, she carried every person in the audience into the screen so that together they would endure what all mankind was forced to endure, and, like her, join the struggle against evil no matter how terrible the price or sacrifice.

It is no wonder that so many strenuous efforts were made over the years to get Magnani to come to Broadway or London to appear as Bertolt Brecht's *Mother Courage*. She epitomized the role like no other living actress. The temptation for Magnani was great. She loved the play and understood its value and international repute. She empathized deeply with and felt all the pulsations of the character. She was in complete harmony with the drama's theme. She would have loved nothing more than to have had a success in America and England, two countries she admired.

But the fear of performing in English, of having her art and personality sieved through a language not her own, was too deeply embedded. For every reason that pointed to acceptance And so, Mother Courage never appeared in *Mother Courage*, and the theater could not record in its playbill of history a great, memorable and legendary event.

The people of Rome at Magnani's funeral did not stare at Maurizio Burratini, even though he stood together with Hank and Gene among her family and friends to the left of her bier. They had no knowledge of, or interest in, the short, black-haired brown-eyed 27-year-old Roman.

Burratini had made an impact in the final months of Magnani's life by writing the story and collaborating on the screenplay of the film she had planned to make in the 1974 spring she was not destined to see. If she had lived, the billboards in the Roman winter of 1974-75 would have read, "ANNA MAGNANI in *Any Resemblance to Any Person Living or Dead is Purely Coincidental.*"

"Every film Magnani did is in a special binder, placed in sequence in her library," her secretary Silvana told the distraught young author soon after the funeral. "She so looked forward to doing yours that we decided to put it with all the others, as if she had made it."

Burratini was undergoing his military service in Sicily when, in 1971, he wrote the screen story and sent it to Gene. It recounted the love relationship of two Roman youths: Andrea from the upper bourgeoisie and Massimo from a working-class family, and what ensues when Andrea fully accepts the implications of homosexual love and Massimo finally turns from it and him to embrace society's definition of normalcy.

Gene noted the still undefined character of Renata, Massimo's mother. He recommended to Maurizio that the role be developed for Magnani and that a new character of Margherita, Andrea's sophisticated and delightful grandmother, be created for eventual submission to Bette Davis. Thus, through the eyes and reactions of the mother of Massimo and the grandmother of Andrea, two women of totally dissimilar backgrounds and experiences, the audience could more readily identify with the love story of the two youths. While finishing his military service, Burratini worked night and day to complete a new version of his story. Lerner felt that at last it was of sufficient quality to present first to Magnani, and then, when translated, to Davis. The appointment to see Anna was the night of June 23, 1972.

Gene had last seen Magnani in November 1971 when she was shooting the third of her films for RAI-TV. He was no longer an agent. The faithful Silvana was waiting for him that June '72 night as he entered the penthouse apartment of Palazzo Altieri for his appointment with Magnani. Greeting him warmly, she ushered him into Anna's salon. The haunting portrait of Eleanora Dusa, as if the patron saint of the household, was still there. The huge montage in which Magnani was the focal figure still covered the wall behind the divan. All the other portraits of Magnani that Gene remembered were still in their place. The small painting by Aldo Pagliacci that had obsessed him the first time he and Kaufman had come to see Anna nearly twenty years before was also there. Its four figures lay prone in a never-ending twilight, their faces turned towards the earth in speechless grief. In the distance, a pitiful, desolate sun fights to bring warmth to the scene, but is doomed to failure. The painting never failed to fill Gene full of sadness.

Anna was standing beside her grand piano, provocatively posed, her right hand pressed against the piano top. She was wearing a flowing diaphanous gown of white, under which a fitted body-stocking was evident. Her arms were bare.

"Well, how do I look?" she asked without breaking her pose.

"Fabulous," Gene replied. She *did* look fabulous. Her black trenches were perhaps slightly more pronounced, but they seemed to Gene only a stage set for the variety of expressions in her translucent eyes.

Gene approached her for the customary embrace. As he touched her arm, his own broke out in goose bumps. The miracle of that sixty-four years of skin! So fresh and sweet, without age. Satin and velvet and innocent, vulnerable girl in bloom, forgotten by time. As he examined that tragic mask of life and art that awed and haunted and aroused and thrilled, he realized that it, too, had neither time nor age.

"That's what *she* said. 'I think you're beautiful,' is also what she said," Anna replied with a haughtiness that was almost a sneer.

"Who are you talking about?" asked a mystified Gene.

"What do *you* know about opera? All you're interested in is deals and, how you say, *moolah*! No culture. But what can you expect from somebody born in Nebraska."

"You've gone nuts, Anna. You're not making any sense," Gene replied, now somewhat irritated. "What are you talking about?"

"Ha, ha!" Magnani shouted, clapping her hands. "You don't know anything, crazy boy. You don't know your ass from a hole in the ground." And she went into crescendos of raucous laughter, as Gene, the burn of his curiosity increasing, studied her. The laughter diminished into titter and ended in a smiling silence and a carefully timed stare.

"Ava!" bellowed Magnani, her eyes shining in merriment. "The woman you *love.* We saw each other at La Scala in Milan for the premiere of that opera John Huston directed. The opera stank, but what can you expect when the title is *The Mines of Sulphur*! And your Richard Rodney Bennett is no Puccini."

Gene had known from Ava that she was going from Madrid to Milan for the world premiere of the Bennett opera, but Ava had never told him afterwards about any encounter with Magnani.

"But that was four or five years ago, Anna. And you've waited to tell ne *now* when you had twenty chances before? You are really the end!"

"I don't pick up the phone for just anything or anybody..."

"Anna, *not* on the telephone?" interrupted Gene. "The end of the world. Please don't make me laugh."

Anna glared, ready to retort. Instead she broke out in a grin.

"Well," she started. "We saw each other during intermission. The message I asked you to give her that day in the elevator, I gave to her myself. And that's when she said... what she said. 'I think you're very beautiful.' So sincere. So generous." Anna seemed to be reliving the scene, which actually took place on February 26, 1966.

Quickly shaking herself out of her mood, Magnani took Gene by the hand and started to lead him to her studio. "You're jealous, eh?" she teased, her eyes scrutinizing his face. "You wished you had been there to arrange it all, no?"

"Stop it, Anna," Gene answered impatiently. That bitch, Ava. Why hadn't she told him about it, he thought to himself. He and Ava had been on the phone four or five times the week after the premiere. She could have at least mentioned it.

Swaggering with pleasure over the effect of her revelation on Gene, Anna sat behind her oak desk heavy with manuscripts, notes, letters, files, flea market paraphernalia and souvenirs.

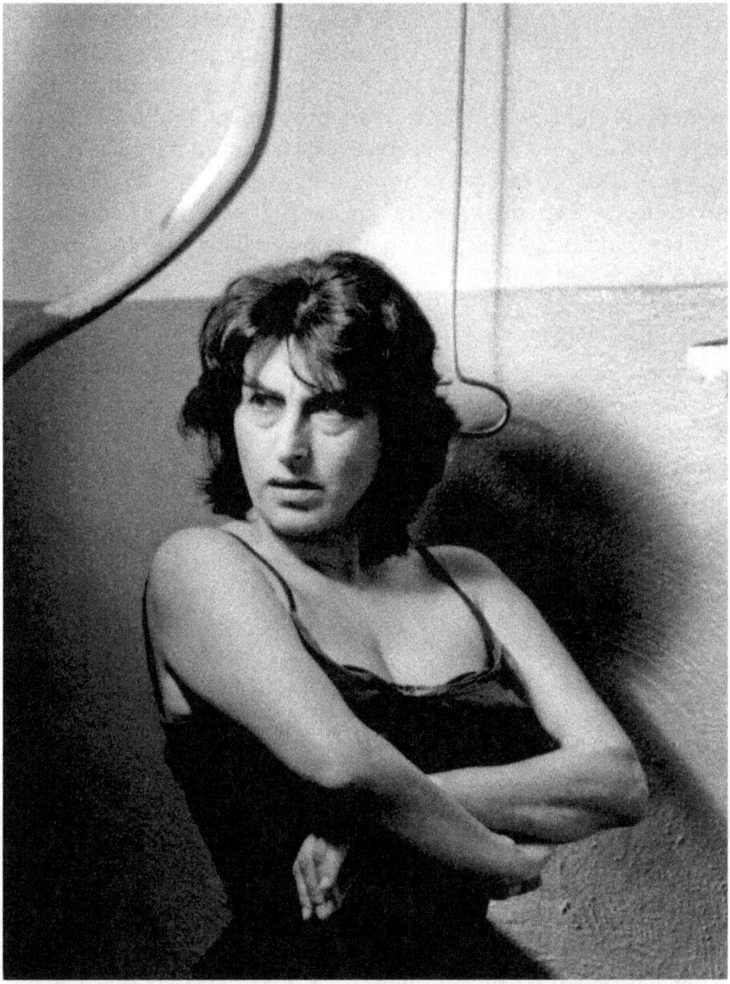

Anna Magnani

Anna smiled at him warmly. Gene, sitting in front of the desk, smiled back. "You're happy, aren't you?" Anna asked him quietly, her eyes now embracing him

"You know I am, Anna. It makes up for that horrible afternoon at Via Salaria. Anna, God Almighty, that was almost fifteen years ago. You were both so awful!" Gene eyes were now sharing the pleasure in Magnani's. "I sure wish I had been in Milano for your and Ava's great love scene."

"All you every talk about is Ava, Ava, Ava! Can we get down to *our* business? Okay? But I haven't offered you refreshment, have I? What an idiot I am. My apologies. I'll get hold of somebody right away." Buzz-buzz-buzz-buzz. Nobody answers the call. Rising ire. "I have secretaries," Magnani mutters. "I have servants. But when I want something, I have nobody!" Buzz-buzz-buzz-buzz-buzz, more and more insistent. Then shouts. Curses. Pounding. The pattern had never changed in the score of years Gene had known her.

("Silvana! Oo, Silva! *Strega! Scema! Cretina!* Where is this? And where is that? And where are you? Where did you hide such and such? And why? Did I tell you to put it there? Why isn't this or that where I want it? Why don't you ever do what I tell you? Nothing is ever in order and I can't live without order! How can I go on like this? I live in an asylum. This is a crazy house! I go mad! Sil… vaaa… nnnaaaa!")

She took the Burratini story Gene handed her and thumbed through the pages. "Okay, I will read it. Maybe this week. You're sure you'll produce it if I decide to do it, right?"

"If you do it, I do it," Gene replied. "Maybe with Kaufman as co-producer."

"Good. We can work together. You both understand all my craziness." She looked at Gene intently. "And you have the stomach to tell me the truth."

"Well, I'm going to tell you the truth right now. It's going to be hell getting the financing for the film. The subject is very controversial. And you know what distributors are saying about you."

"Jesus Christ! Not that again! I'm finished! I have no market. The public won't pay a lira to go and see me. Ask them what happened to their cinemas the night those films I made for television were shown. Go on, ask them. They were empty, that's what. Not even the projectionist came to work! There was nobody in the streets, not even the whores! These distributors of yours are all pygmies. They should go to their jungles and die eating each other."

"We're going to have to make the budget as tight as possible, Anna. Everybody will have to make sacrifices."

"*Caro mio*. Crazy boy. Let me tell you something. I don't work for nothing. I have to eat. Luca has to eat. My secretaries and servants, even if they never do anything, have to eat. And more than anybody, my animals have to eat. But why are we discussing finances? That's not my job. That's what the agent is supposed to do, remember? If the role's right for me and the story is really strong, why should we have problems, you and me? I know you won't take advantage. And you know if you try, I'll cut your balls off."

They both burst out laughing.

"Boy, am I afraid of the big, bad she-wolf," said Gene as the laughter subsided.

Gene had to leave Rome to work on a New York theatrical production based on the life and music of Kurt Weill, which he and Hank were co-producing. In his absence, plans for *Any Resemblance* advanced. After reading the Burratini story that Gene had given her, Anna conferred at length with the young writer. Maurizio then went to work on his screenplay, which took months of night and day work. After Magnani had read it, she discussed it thoroughly not only with Burratini himself but by mail and phone with Gene and Hank. She advised Carol Levi, Rome head of the William Morris agency who represented Anna, that she was ready to proceed with the picture. The question of a director came up. After careful consideration of a number of "name" candidates among Italians, there was joint agreement on a rising young director named Giancarlo Mingozzi.

As elements of *Any Resemblance* began to fall into place, the search for a financing-distribution deal continued. The insidious but still undiscovered cancer was steadily sapping Anna's strength. Delusions and betrayals, a no less treacherous malady, now ravaged her.

After finally having agreed to do a film with Carlo Ponti, she found that he had replaced her with Florinda Bolkan, a young Brazilian actress enjoying a certain vogue in Italy. Harold Pinter had asked Anna to do his latest play, *Old Times*, in its Italian version. When Luchino Visconti agreed to direct, Anna eagerly looked forward to her return to the theater alter the years of interval following *The She-Wolf*. With shocking disregard for professional decency, Franco Enriquez, self-inflated administrator of the theater, publicly opposed Pinter's choice. With Visconti's incomprehensible compliance, only explicable by his exhaustion in his own struggle with death, Enriquez handed the role to Valentina Cortese. As Pinter was disowning the entire project, Anna decided that she was not taking Enriquez's crude slap-in-the-face in silence, and called a press conference. Through an open letter, she at least got the satisfaction of slicing Enriquez to shreds.

Any Resemblance became more and more a symbol of her future and vindication. She grew increasingly impatient for the return of her producers from the States with assurances that the picture would be moving forward, her anxieties unconsciously inflated by the cancer growing inside.

In August of 1973, Gene finally returned from the States. Hank remained in New York to oversee the theatrical production of their Weill show, *Berlin to Broadway*. From Silvana, from Burratini, from others, Gene had constant news of Magnani's worrisome illness. Gene's informers described Anna's sudden weaknesses, her severe loss of energy, the abdominal pains so strong she was robbed of breath. A battery of doctors and specialists could not come up with a consensus diagnosis. If any of them suspected cancer, they maintained an ironclad conspiracy of silence. Hypochondriac Anna, ready to believe that the slightest malfunction in her system or body was certitude of doom, continued to exist in pain and doubt.

Gene phoned Silvana immediately upon his arrival in Rome. Emotionally and physically battered, Silvana broke down on the phone. "They say it's her liver. They say it's her kidneys. Something not working in her intestines. They say so many things. She seems to get better, then she has a relapse. We often have to keep her under sedation. I wish I know what it was. I wish I knew. Gene, we must pray. We must pray. I'm so afraid. You must tell her good news about the picture. She knows you're having difficulties, but make her believe that you're going to make it happen, no matter what."

"I *am* going to make it happen no matter what, Silvana. It *is* going to happen. Whatever Anna has, she's going to get well, Silvana. She has to get well." All this Gene said with conviction, for he believed what he was saying.

Magnani was not standing by the piano in provocative pose when Gene came to Palazzo Altieri this time. She was already seated at her desk, her mouth set like a thermostat to measure her discomfort. She was dabbing the perspiration from her face and neck with a handkerchief. She neither rose nor smiled, but there was clearly no shrinkage in her powers of observation, nor in her insatiable curiosity. She gave Gene's new USA finery the once-over, noting the huge bow tie on white shirt, navy blue blazer, white trousers and high-heeled black boots. Her mouth broke out into a smile as Gene came behind the desk. She stared at him mockingly.

"You little bastard. How dare you look so young?" Gene bent over to kiss her. "No, no, don't touch me. Can't you see how I'm perspiring?"

As Gene took his customary seat, he immediately queried Anna about her health. "I don't want to talk about it," she replied impatiently. "I'm so tired. I'm weak. I've got some problem with my stomach, my liver, or whatever the doctors decide. I'm just exhausted. With people. With this business. With this dishonest world we live in. I need rest. A long, long rest. I'm going to my villa at Circeo. And I'll talk only to my animals and take care of the trees and look only at the sea. Do Kaufman and you still have your Casa Bianca at Sabaudia?"

"Yes, but it's running down. We can't seem to find people who will take care of it properly."

"Idiot. Your Casa Bianca is a dream. And it's so beautiful there between the lake and the sea. And Mount Circe right beside it. You should take care of it. You don't leave a child to die, you don't leave a home to die. You and Kaufman go spend a month or two there. I'll be in Circeo. We'll be five minutes away. We can see each other every day."

"Are you strong enough to...?"

"We'll do the film, if that's what worries you."

"Of course we'll do the film. There's no film without you, you know that. You've just got to get your strength back."

"That's what I want to tell you. We shouldn't try for November. April or May next year I'll be ready."

"When you're ready, we're ready," Gene assured her.

"Good. Then that's settled. Listen, between you and me, we have to do more work on the script. Remember we're telling a story of pederasts."

"Anna, Andrea and Massimo aren't pederasts."

"What are you saying? Andrea, Massimo, they, well, they... have sex, don't they? They make love, no?"

"Don't you know there's a difference between pederasts and homosexuals?"

"Oh? What difference?"

"Pederasts make love only with very young boys, eleven, twelve, thirteen, even younger. Homosexuals relate to other men. They can be twenty or eighty. You've been in show business all your life, Anna. Where have you been hiding?"

"I'm an actress, not a spy. Oh, I know plenty. I can give you a long list, famous, in high places. They're artists, you understand. But boys from the streets! Normal boys from normal homes, with normal mothers and fathers! Bartenders. Mechanics. Athletes. Anybody! It never entered my head. You're sure Burratini knows what he's talking about? I mean, this is no exaggeration, this story of Massimo and Andrea?"

"Anna, I can't believe this! I just can't believe it."

"Don't make me out to be such an ignoramus. I didn't have to go out on the streets to sell my body so I could play the whore in *Behind Closed Shutters* for Comencini, did I? Or spend a year in jail so I could do those scenes with Giulietta Masina? Some imagination I have, *caro mio.* Here's some part of life I never really knew. I never really understood it, so what's the big deal? So I'm learning. Since when is it a crime to learn? One of the things wrong with the script is that Renata is too innocent. She should know that something's going on between her son and Andrea much earlier. After all, he's her son. He's her own flesh and blood. Renata's not stupid, even if you think I am. The public would expect Renata to be more aware, not so naïve."

"Who in the world could have been more naïve than your Maddelena in *Bellissima*?"

"You're talking about twenty years ago. And this is different! Maddelena is not Renata. Renata's more modern. She knows something about life. She talks to people. She has a job in a pharmacy. She reads. She and Massimo are very close. He's already 20. How could he hide such a thing from her for very long? Her one and only son."

"Luca's nearly 30, Anna. He's your only son. Do you think you know all his secrets?"

Magnani clenched her fists, looked at Gone with shock.

"What are you implying? Are you saying that...? Have you gone out of your mind? How dare you insinuate Luca is queer."

"You completely misunderstand me, Anna. I'm sure Luca isn't gay. I'm only making a point. The idea that parents know what's deep inside their children is about the biggest illusion of life. That's one of the key things about *Any Resemblance*. And

Renata really does face a situation as traumatic as Maddalena's. The shock of discovery is what brings on your guilt and humiliation. In each case, it's your child in a circumstance that tears you to pieces. If you learned about it gradually, the terrible impact would be lost.

"Remember," continued Gene, "everything between Andrea and Massimo seems too normal. They take wild trips on Andrea's motorcycle. They go to the movies. They go to Andrea's home. Andrea comes to your home. They listen to records. They discuss. They argue. They laugh. To all appearances, their relationship seems no different than any other. They're both masculine. Nothing could seem more normal."

"My Massimo *has* to be normal. He *has* to live a normal life," added Anna in a low voice. "He *has* to get married and have children, and be a good husband and father. I can't let my son be a homosexual. For me, his relationship with Andrea is impossible and it *has* to be destroyed. And when the break comes between them forever, I feel like God has freed me from a terrible burden,"

"You've hit the character exactly, Anna," declared Gene. "Still, you can't forget Andrea. Andrea's not your son, we know that. He's really nothing to you. Yet you don't want him destroyed. How to look upon him, what to do about him, is even more of a crisis for Renata."

"Yes, yes, I understand," Anna rushed to say, stimulated by the discussion. "And it's right. It's a shock for me to realize that Andrea's homosexual love for Massimo is normal the way Andrea looks at it. It's even more of a shock to me when I find myself actually respecting him and his love. When I embrace him as he goes away and I know that I'll never see him again, I forget that he's homosexual. I forgot that his love threatened the normal life my son had to have. I want Andrea to fulfill his own life. I want him to be happy. Because I've come to understand that he's no less a person, no less a man than my Massimo." And then, after a moment of reflection, Anna added: "Andrea might even have been my own son."

Gene thought in silence, then felt his way when he finally spoke. "You, Renata, and hopefully the public that identifies with Renata, learn that the contradiction between appearance and reality exists and that, at the same time, the unity between appearance and reality also exists."

A sharp look at Gene darted from Anna's eyes. "That's very deep. But not too deep. This is a world of misfits struggling to put the pieces of themselves together. 'I have always depended on the kindness of strangers,' Blanche DuBois says in Tennessee's *Streetcar.* Animals who don't have to depend on the kindness of human beings are better off."

The room was silent, Anna lost in thought, staring into space, Gene watching, absorbing her. Finally, she said. "It's a good story. A strong story. I think we'll have a very good film, if I live long enough to do it." She turned to Gene. "So what about Bette? Is she going to be Margherita?"

"No."

"What? Such a wonderful part and she won't play it?"

"I wouldn't have her now even if she wanted to."

"Why? What happened? Did you tell her I was going to play Renata?"

"Of course I told her."

"She told me a dozen times how much she would love to do a picture with me. From the first time I met her in New York." Anna lifted herself from her chair, walked heavily over to the fireplace mantle. She picked a photo of Bette Davis out from among many and looked at the back of the picture. "Yes, 1953. The year we met."

Gene walked over and took the photo from Magnani.

"To Magnani the Magnificent," he read. As he put the photograph of Davis back in place, he noted Anna wiping her forehead and wearily sinking back into her chair.

"Maybe I should go, Anna. We can meet again tomorrow."

"No, no. You must tell me about Bette."

"Well, I kept trying to reach her from Los Angeles and never seemed to find her. I finally got her at her home in Connecticut. 'I don't know why you sent me such a script,' she said. 'Oh, don't get me wrong. I think the script's very good and so is the role of Margherita. And Anna's role is simply marvelous. And I really do adore Anna. But who cares about homosexuals? I'm sick and tired of hearing about them and reading about them. I don't give a damn what they do in private. But I don't have to know about it and I don't want to know about it. You said it was a love story. In my book, a love story is between a male and a female. There's friendship between two men but no such thing as a love story. And what's more, homosexuals don't play their part in society like normal people do. They don't marry. They don't care about children. Why, they shouldn't even be in contact with children. They're dangerous for children. I'm sick and tired of the whole damn subject. And I'm sick and tired of finding out that virtually every eligible man over 50 I find attractive and who could interest me turns out to be homosexual. No, darling, I don't want anything to do with it.'"

Anna, her lips puckered, was shaking her head in disbelief. More to herself than to Gene, she kept repeating, "I'm very surprised, I'm very surprised."

"Bette Davis, Anna! I was at a friend's house when I finally reached her. I was so furious over her tirade, I signaled him to listen in on the extension."

"Did you tell her how you felt?"

"I certainly did. When she finished, I said, 'All right, Bette. You've done all the talking. Now are we going to have a democratic discussion or just a one-sided diatribe?' All sweet and sugar, she said, 'A democratic discussion of course, darling. And then I started. Boy, did I let her have it. But I don't want to go into all that now."

"Who will you try for now?" Anna asked, wracking her brain for ideas.

"Guess."

"Who?"

"I said guess."

"I'm already sick. I don't need games. C'mon, tell me," she said with impatience.

"Ingrid Bergman."

Gene waited for the reverberations of shock.

"You want to kill me. YOU WANT TO KILL ME! That one. Get out of my house and never come back!" Suddenly Magnani broke out in refreshing waves of laughter, as full and deep that it seemed an antiseptic powerful enough to destroy any malady languishing in her. Her delight was marvelous to watch.

"Why not, that old bitch? She's decrepit enough. And what would be sweeter? I'm... well, a year or two older than she, and she would have to play 65 and me only 50. Let's do it! Go ask her. Ask her! Just for the fun of it. Let's see what she says."

Once more she burst into laughter, shaking her head back and forth. The laughter faded into a diminuendo of silence before she had a fit of coughing and began dabbing her mouth, then her face, with her handkerchief. Gene watched with growing concern, feeling his helplessness.

"Have you seen the woman you love?" finally asked Anna, mocking jealousy.

"Yes, I've seen the woman I love. And I'm seeing another one right now."

"The most beautiful woman in the world," Magnani said, her eyes unmistakingly seeing a vision of Ava.

"I think she's the *second* most beautiful woman in the world," Gene replied lovingly.

"Of course. Sure. Magnani, Miss Italy! Why not Miss America? Or Miss Universe? Don't make me laugh. I'm too sick." She dabbed her face with her handkerchief, partially to camouflage her pleasure at Gene's statement.

She looked at her watch. "Oh! You've been here an hour and a half. Out with you! Call me in a few days, here or in Circeo. And see what that Swedish trollop has to say about playing Margherita. But let's not have any misunderstandings, eh? I didn't say I would ever do it with her."

"But you didn't say you never would, either," said Gene.

Anna looked hard at him. He knew he wasn't going to get either a yea or a nay out of her at the moment.

"You ask her. I can't wait to find out what she'll say. We should organize a meeting with Kaufman, Burratini and Mingozzi, maybe at my villa, maybe in Sabaudia. I'll ask Carol Levi to come out too. I'm very fond of Carol. That William Morris is very lucky to have her."

"I agree," replied Gene. "Carol's very good. Be sure to ask her."

"Look how I'm perspiring. Enough to fill the Tiber. Doctors, doctors. What can you do with them? They're all ignoramuses or hypocrites. They dare call medicine a science. Hah! They know nothing, tell you nothing, do nothing. They just experiment. Go, go now. I have to rest. And when you talk to Kaufman, give him my love."

Gene started around the desk to kiss her.

"No, you crazy boy. Can't you see I'm all wet?"

"Who gives a damn? I want to embrace you."

Anna didn't resist. Gently, he brushed his lips over her perspiring cheeks. He then bent over and kissed her neck. Magnani then took his hand in hers, tightening her grip fiercely, as if simultaneously to show and to seek contact. She looked up at him, a glorious smile illuminating her face. Then slowly, she shook her head.

"Crazy boy, you. You crazy boy. And after *Any Resemblance*, you know what we're going to do? *One Hundred Years of Solitude*. You'll go to Madrid and talk to Gabriel Márquez. I've already written to him. I *have* to play Ursula. That old woman of all time, of all visions, of all truth, the forever of life. Ursula's me. You go and convince him and you'll produce it for me."

It was the last time Gene saw Anna Magnani alive.

Anna on the telephone. Early afternoon of September 17, 1973.

"Anna wants to speak to you," Silvana said.

Gene's heart shriveled as he heard that unmistakable voice.

"*Caro, mio caro,*" it said. "Thank you and Hank with all my heart for all the flowers. And for your beautiful letters. You are very dear, both of you. Especially you. You are very, very dear."

"You know we love you, don't you, Anna?" Gene managed to say.

"I know, I know. I love you too. *Vi voglio tanto bene.*"

Ten days later…

That woman of all time, of all visions, of all truth, the forever of life…

Anna Magnani…

Was dead.

Any Resemblance to Any Person Living or Dead is Purely Coincidental.

Or Wholly Encompassing.

When before has a people recognized in an actress its own heart? Its own soul? Its own conscience?

When before has a city seen in an artist its personification?

Anna Magnani was the first actress, the first artist, to be recorded by history who, in dying, was commemorated as if she were a head of state. She was the summation of a people and symbol of a great and ancient site that, like Jerusalem, has for centuries obsessed the minds and spirits of the world.

She made no conscious effort whatsoever to achieve what no other actress or artist has ever achieved. She had no political power, nor the influence of economic empire. She possessed neither the blood nor the wealth of centuries-old aristocracy. She had no publicity machine to cultivate her image. She had no press representative to propagandize such an effect. She was no party to clever manipulation of public opinion.

Her art was enough. And she was enough. All the daily newspapers of Rome ran banner headlines and some devoted five full pages to her death, and again to her funeral.

FAREWELL, NANNARELLA.

NANNARELLA IS DEAD.

MAMMA ROMA HAS GONE TO GOD.

A TOO GREAT WOMAN IS GONE.

OUR GREATEST ACTRESS HAS PERISHED.

MORE THAN AN ACTRESS DIES WITH ANNA MAGNANI.

AN UNPARALLELED WOMAN IS NO MORE.

NANNARELLA, INTERPRETER OF THE PEOPLE'S SPIRIT, DIES.

THE ESSENCE OF ROME DIES WITH ANNA MAGNANI.

In an eight-column streamer, *Il Messaggero*, Rome's *New York Times*, declared: "CARA POPOLANA, the mythical star of neorealism and the symbol of humanity, passion, protest, magic and inspiration a people rediscovers in moments of grace and truth, has disappeared."

In similar fashion, *Paese Sera*, Italy's foremost left-wing daily, headed an entire page dedicated to her: "PROUD SYMBOL OF THE PEOPLE OF ROME, you gave nobility to the hidden aspirations and profound grief of The Woman through the extraordinary instinct and rare intelligence with which you forged your characters."

Pier Paolo Pasolini, who directed Magnani in his *Mamma Roma* in 1962, and was to be brutally murdered in 1975, wrote:

As her disordered hair taunts the shifting winds,
And her silent eyes of fire ignite eternity,
Her cry resounds through the desperate panorama of
  time,
Emblem forever of the surging torrent of human tragedy.

The great and the powerful sought to rob her of the forum of her art. They flagellated her resurrective aspirations. They shredded the fragile sensibilities of her pride. They punished her because they could not control her, could not bend her to their way or to their will, could not abide the simplicity of her grandeur.

"Grief was her cancer," sobbed Silvana as she sank into Gene's and Hank's arms the night the body lay in state at the Clinica Mater Dei.

The year before she died, or was left to die, or was spiritually murdered in a conspiracy of disdain and indifference, Anna made her final appearance on film. Hers was a 60-second apparition, like a spirit that suddenly appears among men to render judgment or reveal destiny. *Roma* was the title of the picture.

It is night.

A figure of a woman walks through the Via Degli Astalli. She nears the Palazzo Altieri. A man follows her – the same man who, in Rossellini's *The Miracle* of 1948, played the sheepherder that Magnani, in religious trance, mistook for a saint and to whom she succumbed.

"Anna," the man cries out. Magnani doesn't stop.

"Anna," the man repeats. Magnani halts without turning.

"Will you make some comment on Rome?" he asks. "You know you're almost a symbol..."

She turns to stare at the man. Then she who knows everything asks, "What do *I* know?"

"She-wolf and vestal..."

"Don't give me that stuff," she interrupts.

"In what way would you say you resemble Rome?" the man persists. Tentative and uncomfortable, he awaits her reply.

"Go home and go to bed. Away with you," she says, before turning abruptly and entering the huge portals.

"But listen...!" the man shouts, taking several quick steps towards her. She turns back to face him. He stops, waiting. She now speaks the final words she is ever to utter in a film.

"I don't trust you."

And she disappears through the portals forever. Uncertain, confused, the man stands a moment.

The man is Federico Fellini.

Life.

La Vita.

The *Sweet* Life.

La *Dolce* Vita.

An adjective modifies. It also can murder.

In the ancient Via Degli Astalli, the reincarnation of the She-Wolf, who, in suckling Romulus and Remus, gave birth to Rome, stood staring at this master magician, this incomparable juggler of truth and lie, to tell him:

"I don't trust you."

In place of the She-Wolf, Fellini, prestigious peddler of magical wares, created another symbol of Rome. He had her rise from the waters of the Fontana di Trevi, a statuesque and solitary figure draped in black velvet, her splendid breasts pushed forward in succulent temptation, her long blonde hair falling loosely to accentuate the sensuality of her naked white shoulders, her exquisite childlike face in a euphoric trance of abandon, her arms lifted to exalt satiation as the new faith to be worshipped by the excited populace of Rome and a Titillated World.

Anita Ekberg.

Anna Magnani.

Anitona.

Nannarella.

When the City of Rome finally builds its monument to honor Magnani, she will not rise from the waters of the Fontana di Trevi. She will be no statuesque, solitary figure conjured up by Federico Fellini. She will emerge from the burning fissures of the Earth. She will eagerly bend forward to confront life, fierce and proud, uncompromising in her love and hate, "her disordered hair taunting the shifting winds," the anguish in her eyes on the verge of cascading pearls of laughter, her face invoking the triumph of spirit over grief.

Her arms outstretched, she will be surrounded by a pulling, pushing, shouting, living melee of men, women, children and animals she has forever ennobled and her genius deified.

Applause.

Applause of the people rising in recurring echoes.

Voices.

Voices, choral and convoluting, in uplifting crescendo.

"Brava, Anna. Viva, Nannarella. Brava, brava, brava!"

"If Death still frightens me a bit, it's because I'm like Don Quixote and would like that each and every one of us be himself so that he will be able to die in peace," she has said. "What frightens me is suddenly to disappear without having discovered who Magnani was, or better, who the child Anna was.

"But I know who she was," Magnani continued. "She was a little liar who lived in dreams to avoid confronting reality. No mother, no father, I tried to transform myself. I played the part of aggressor, without being one inside. As a result, storms of rage. I played the part of a coward when I felt a lion's strength. Upshot, scenes of wrath. I played the part of the brave when in truth I was a trembling lamb. Again, fits of anger. Poor crazy thing. If today I should die, I want people to know that I die rich because I've finally realized that all my rage, wrath and anger were really vented on the lie of myself.

"I've also understood that I was not born to be an actress. I only decided to become one in the cradle, between one tear too many and one caress too little. All my life I've screamed with all my strength for someone to stem that tear. All my life I have humiliated myself with imploring for that one caress. It's taken me so many years and forced me into so many mistakes, but at last I no longer scream and implore.

"I worked so hard to prepare myself. I struggled. I shouted at Life. Today I can smile at Death. At the end, I won't kneel before the Crucified, I'll stand and look upon Him as another self who dies, so that on this Earth, no one can ever again live to lie to one another."

Grief was not her cancer, dear Silvana.

The *truth* was.

Ten
The Viking Love Goddess

A me m'ha rovinata Fellini – Fellini ruined me – screamed the headline of the Italian magazine *Gente* on January 7, 1978.

The scream came from a terrified, disillusioned Anita Ekberg following the second robbery in a year of her modest house in Mentana, a hamlet one hour outside of Rome, where the once-reigning Empress of Roman Nightlife was living among vegetables, chickens, pigs and countryfolk. Three bandits with drawn pistols tied and gagged her, then made off with the few treasures and personal belongings she still possessed – the last souvenirs of a career and lifestyle now passed.

In 1960, Federico Fellini added a new expression to the lexicons of the world: *La Dolce Vita*. For some critics, intellectuals and filmgoers, his film was the most exciting mass seduction of a city, people and era ever achieved in cinema. It was for them a stupendous hallucination stage-managed by an astute purveyor of art, a master juggler of truth and lie, a great poet of the motion picture who turned his genius into sleight-of-hand metaphor. They saw it as truth in sensational counterfeit – counterfeit romance, counterfeit sensuality, counterfeit pain, counterfeit pity, counterfeit surfeit, counterfeit intellectualism, counterfeit faith.

For other critics, intellectuals and viewers, *La Dolce Vita* was a paean to the Rome that Fellini loved, but that he felt had perilously neared the zenith of hedonism, sensuality and debauchery, a Rome in which mysticism and paganism were each corrupted by its fascination for the other. Yet, with typical Felliniesque optimism, while portraying decay and depravity, he, in their minds, permitted the infiltration of light in the darkness, admitted a ray of innocence, left open the hope of redemption. They saw in his film a masterpiece that paralleled the rise and decline of *Roma antica* with that of *Roma moderna*.

"Fellini made me the symbol of everything that seemed so wonderful about Italy," Ekberg said. She did not exaggerate. Throughout the world, she was identified with the film through a towering photographic blow-up, Anita Ekberg, the Viking sex goddess in her prime, her blonde tresses caressed by the Roman breeze, her unbelievable 40-22-37 measurements sculpted into a black-velvet sheathe to reveal more of her mammoth mammary equipment than it covered, her pose a joyful liberation from inhibition. The tremendous success of the picture made transference from celluloid to life inevitable for Anita, or "Anitona" – Big Anita – as Fellini affectionately christened her. Anitona became the most noted celebrant of the sweet life, that sugar-coated, slow-acting poison corroding society and debilitating its participants.

"*Tu sei tutto*. You are everything. You are the first woman of the first day on Earth. You are Eve. You are mother, sister, *sei l'amante*, *la femmina*, woman, angel, devil. You are *la terra*, *la casa*," murmurs an overwhelmed Marcello Mastroianni to Anita as they dance in a Roman nightclub in a scene from the film.

As he watched an inspired, barefoot Anita leading the horde in a parade of undiluted joy in the famous Caracalla dance sequence, Fellini remarked to Hank, "She's the absolute personification of unrestrained gaiety, the essence of pagan innocence. She has exactly achieved the quality I have envisioned for this film and never quite believed I would get. But doesn't it frighten you, the idea that one day she must grow old?"

Archer Winsten, in his review of the film for the *New York Post*, wrote: "The emblazoned messages of *La Dolce Vita* are namely, that publicity is the order of the day; that newspapermen and photographers are the common carriers, the bloodstream of that society where titled aristocrats mix without embarrassment with muscle men, homosexuals; that there are beautiful women, well-dressed men, sleek luxury cars everywhere, and that this rushing stream of life is *totally pointless*!"

Whether totally pointless or not, millions of goggle-eyed people converged on the new Sodom, in search for the seemingly endless party-going, scandalous orgies and round-and-round, upside-down fun for fun's sake, which Fellini portrayed as being Rome.

"When I began *La Dolce Vita*, I really knew nothing of Rome," declared Anita to a journalist in 1972. "Federico said that

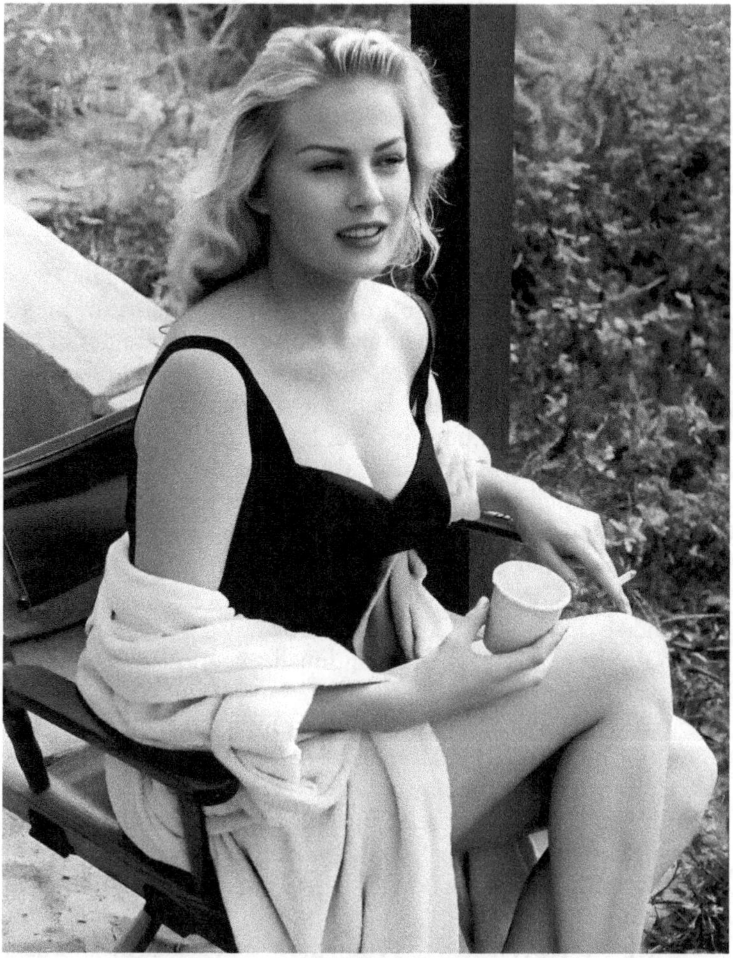

Anita Ekberg

what we were filming was a representation of what had been going on in Rome for a long time – spiritual seances at the various *castelli* of the nobility, dancing and drinking till dawn in Roman nightspots, and all the rest we now know so well. I reacted positively because I liked that kind of life instinctively. To me it seemed wonderfully liberated, the way I always dreamed of living. I didn't yet understand the rottenness of it. The apple seemed so fresh, so juicy, that I didn't realize how fermented it was at the core."

In her very early Hollywood days, noted photographer André de Dienes commented, "Anita Ekberg could be the greatest glamor girl of them all. She is strong and intelligent. She has the most beautiful breasts in the world, firm and large. But Anita loves to enjoy herself. She stays up all night and sleeps all day." People of the night are not destined for tranquility or the preservation of the gifts God has given them. They are bewitched and in the darkness are strangers to themselves.

"Better a night in good company than sleeping the night away in boredom," was Anita's motto. "It was no big drama for me to go to work at six in the morning after having spent most of the night having fun," Anita mused in retrospect. "Fun, something natural, spur of the moment, behaving like crazy kids, laughing like mad fools over nothing, is dead. It's all artificial now. Fake. It comes out of boredom, not out of the sudden desire to take a deep breath or running towards a star you know you can never catch, something spontaneous like that. People are so serious now, so grim and sad. They're more tied and gagged than I was by those horrible thieves. Everything has changed."

And so, indeed, had Anita. Gone was the famous figure, the freshness, the naturalness, that continually astonished Fellini. But she never seemed to tire. She abounded in such good health and wonderful energy. Even though her contract specified that she could not be required to do close-ups in the afternoon, Fellini frequently prevailed on her to do so. Incredible as it seems now, though she might have been up half the night and had been working since eight o'clock in the morning, hours later she still seemed fresh as a rose. As though she had just awakened, beautiful, resplendent, sparkling.

Then, she represented to Fellini the female sexual ideal. Then, through *La Dolce Vita* and the immense publicity plastered throughout the world about her, her image everywhere, she was also the exaltation of the sensual dreams of untold millions of males whose idea of Heaven was to regress into breast-suckling infants.

The statuesque former Miss Sweden of 1951 was born Kerstin Anita Marianne Ekberg in Malmo on September 29, 1930. A photographers' model in her birthland, Anita decided she was just what Hollywood needed. She arrived there in 1952 and clearly made an immediate impression. She instantaneously excited press and photographers and never escaped the double-take notice of men. Shortly after her arrival, she told columnist Sidney Skolsky, "I want to get married to an American and have lots of babies."

There were husbands, there were men, but somehow the lots of babies never got born.

When she was asked how she thought she had succeeded in winning the Miss Sweden competition, she replied, "I just drank more milk than the other girls."

Publicity was unquestionably the springboard for her Hollywood career. The movie writers began to refer to her as "that Swedish iceberg." Later, in Italy, she was dubbed *ghiaccio bollente* (boiling ice) to describe her upright, diffident, almost haughty manner that contradicted the promise of her voluptuous body. Her years in Hollywood made her better known to avid readers of fan magazines and gossip columns than to the mass picturegoing public.

Not a single male star, producer or director could help being astounded by her physique, which she generously offered to share. She seemed also to have an abounding capacity for "friendships," which she often confused with "romances" or "affairs," so that it was not always possible to ascertain the line of demarcation.

There was her friendship with Bing Crosby, between wives. There was her friendship with Howard Hughes, whose contract she rejected, even though she was still a nobody. There was a friendship with "wonderful" Gary Cooper. There was a friendship with John Wayne who, in partnership with Robert Fellows, had an independent production company named Batjac. When Wayne offered her an exclusive contract at a measly $150 a week to begin with, she accepted, and the picture-making of sorts began. In typical and inexplicable Hollywood fashion, everything possible was done to cover up her pulchritude and the sweet loveliness of her face by casting her as a khaki-clad, half-caste Oriental missionary in her first Batjac film, entitled *Blood Alley*, in which Wayne starred. Batjac then made it a business of lending Anita out to independent producers and major studios for a series of undistinguished roles in various states of dress and undress in such films as *Artists and Models* with Jerry Lewis and

Dean Martin, *Paris Holiday* with Bob Hope, *Zarak* with Victor Mature, *The Man Inside* with Jack Palance, and *Mississippi Gambler* with Tyrone Power.

There was a friendship with Frank Sinatra, who considered her great fun at parties and on dates "until," according to Anita, "a big fight brought about by Frank's Sicilian jealousy put an end to our relationship."

Both on and off screen, Anita seemed to be holding her considerable own in the bigtime. The admiration for her super anatomical proportions never flagged, but the public never turned her into a big box office idol *à la* Gardner, Hayworth or Monroe. Her roles were too one-dimensional. She seemed always to be the butt of the jokes of the comics with whom she co-starred. She was treated as a sort of overstuffed piece of female furniture. No one ever bothered to provide her with a role that required animation or the projection of her real personality. If anyone was treated as a sex object, it was Anita, and it made her seem either sullen and wooden or ridiculously overglamorized. Yet she somehow always managed to avoid being vulgar, which in itself was an impressive accomplishment.

Fortunately, Hollywood on the Tiber was calling, and Anita, through Batjac's loan-out, answered the call. When Arlene Dahl was forced to withdraw from Dino De Laurentiis' production of Leo Tolstoy's *War and Peace* in 1955, Anita was hastily substituted. No medium nor soothsayer would have predicted that she would live virtually all the remainder of her life in Italy, nor that she would become the reigning symbol of the Hollywood on the Tiber epoch.

War and Peace may only have represented profit for the Wayne-Fellows producing firm, but it happened to be an important break for Anita. The role of Princess Hélène was not large, but what was significant was that she had her first real occasion to appear in a truly prestigious cast: Audrey Hepburn, Henry Fonda, Mel Ferrer, Vittorio Gassman, working with a highly-respected director like King Vidor, in an epic based on one of the greatest works of literature ever written. She gave her role elegance, quality and depth. For the first time, she had an opportunity to demonstrate acting ability.

That same year her first marriage took place. She had met Anthony Steel, the London-born star, when she appeared opposite him in the English-made *Valerie*, a psychological Western directed by Gerd Oswald. This was one of Anita's "friendships" that Anita decided to turn into matrimony. Impetuously, she and Steel decided to get married in Florence.

Florence had rarely seen such excitement since the Medicis were holding court and Savanorola was being burnt to a crisp during the Renaissance. The wedding was arranged for the splendid medieval Palazzo Vecchio, now the Town Hall, in the magnificent Piazza Signoria. The ceremony took place in the historic Red and Gold Room, where Pope Leo XII once reigned, and the mayor of the ancient city, resplendent in his robes of office, performed the rites. Anita wore an exceptional gown for the occasion, one shoulder covered, the other bared.

The wedding proved to be a mere preview of Anita's clamorous effect on Italian journalists and photographers. Some two hundred panting, perspiring, persistent newsmen fought their way into the ceremonial chamber as thousands of Florentines milled in the courtyard of the Palazzo and in the Piazza Signoria.

After the nuptial vows were exchanged and the mayor had dutifully kissed Anita on both cheeks in devoted fatherly fashion, the beautiful wedded couple, with the aid of smiling, festive carabinieri, forced their way through cheering, applauding crowds. They mounted a flower-bedecked, horse-drawn carriage and started a triumphant drive through the narrow Florentine streets, flamboyantly imbibing champagne during their ride.

By nature, Italians love weddings, more so if they are not their own. They adore full-blown Viking blondes and any kind of spectacle, so the constantly augmented crowd of Florentines delightfully followed the honeymoon carriage and joined in the general merriment.

For a brief period following the raucous wedding, Anita and Tony returned to Los Angeles. Anita appeared to have settled for relatively uneventful domesticity. She enjoyed playing "house" for a husband. Her image was subdued. She was a married woman and a housewife above all, and would of course work when required. Still, she was Anita Ekberg, always looked at, sought after and much in demand for stories and photographs. Steel's star was waning in his native England and never really existed in Hollywood. He was less and less able to cope with his role as "Mr. Ekberg," seeking more and more solace in the bottle, sometimes also in violence.

"Tony was intelligent and charming," Anita said. "He drank five or six glasses of whiskey and became even more charming. But with the seventh, he became bad, ugly. He often struck me." Anita became genuinely frightened of him, and though she was not yet seeking an end to her marriage realized that distance between her and her husband was advisable.

When Anita was offered a now-forgotten Italian film entitled *The Sign of the Gladiator*, opposite French actor Georges Marchal, scheduled for Rome shooting in 1957, she jumped at the opportunity. Batjac certainly had no objection, since it meant some $75,000 to add to its bleak bank account. That all the picture was destined to do was glut the over-strained market for product exploiting the glories and gories of ancient Rome mattered not one bit to either Anita or Batjac. Anita's role of a highly-sexed Amazon princess clothed in a series of diaphanous, pastel-colored chiffon tunics called primarily for heavy-breathing close-ups with her French co-star.

Sans Steel, Anita arrived in Rome accompanied by Lisbeth Haggstrom, her longtime Swedish personal secretary. Ekberg was greeted by a battery of photographers, her producers, and since at the time she was a William Morris client, of course by Hank. Hank thought he was prepared for the jutty protruding from her front, but he was still startled. But what surprised him most was her soft voice, her femininity and facial attractiveness. Her eyes were magnificent, clear, deep pools of infinite blue, and her skin was pure porcelain. Hank glanced at her famous breasts. No question they were awesome, no wonder that they warranted the enormous publicity and were the primary attributes that gave her the opportunity for a career, he thought. But as startling and exciting as they certainly were, he asked himself were they more fortune or misfortune by overwhelming the singular loveliness of her face?

Hank escorted his two charges to the comfortable penthouse apartment the KLA office had found for them on Via Tagliamento, not far from KL's Corso Trieste headquarters. Fortunately, Anita and Liz were pleased with the choice. Things seemed to have begun on the right foot.

Hank then gave Anita the script, which she had not yet read, but that, unfortunately, he had. "Anita, there's no point in playing games. It's crap. Unadulterated. I'm sorry but that's the way it is."

"I know it," Anita replied with a sigh. "It always seems to be that way. But at least I'm out of that California hellhole."

"While you're doing it, we'll work on getting you better things. That is, if you want to stay."

"Yes please," Anita responded. "I do want to stay. Really I do. I loved Rome when I was here for *War and Peace*. I loved Italy from the first moment. You know the sensation you get sometimes, that a place is right for you. Yes, certainly I want to stay. Besides, what have I got to look forward to in Hollywood? Nobody cares about me there. Batjac just passes me from one lousy film to another, one part more ridiculous than the next. They couldn't care less and I don't think William Morris does either. They just go along with what Batjac tells them. I'd like a real chance someday. Please. Try to do something."

The phone rang one evening around nine o'clock at the Via Aicccio apartment. As soon as Hank said, "*Pronto, chi parla*?" he heard Anita's tearful voice in lament. "What kind of men are there in this town? Maybe it's true what I hear, that all Italian men are queer!"

Hank was flabbergasted by Anita's outburst. "What's the matter? What's happened?"

"Liz and I have been cooped up in this flat night after night ever since we arrived in Rome. I thought I was going to be so happy here, and do you know that not one male has called to invite us out to dinner or on the town or to anything! What's all this bull about Latin lovers? It's all a myth! I'm ready to climb the walls! You've got to do something!" There was a pause in the diatribe. "What about my partner Georges Marchal?" she finally asked, her voice muted.

"Well, what about him?" responded Hank.

"Is he that way? I mean, is he queer, too? He's never asked me out on a date and he's not married."

That's good sound illogic, thought Hank. It was his first awareness that Anita had her own method for classifying the male of the species, and it couldn't have been simpler. Class A included those who courted or paid homage to her. Those who didn't had no class. They were automatically judged as homosexual or, in some cases, deformed or impotent. In spite of the peculiar viewpoint revealed by her remarks, Hank understood her frustration. After all, she was the alluring Anita and it really didn't seem suitable that she should be allowed to vegetate in what was presumed to be a love-drenched Rome full of potent Italians who had trained for life to thrill the female.

More and more, Hank and Gene realized that the happenstance of their being two Americans based in Rome added heavily to their responsibilities as agents for the flock of personalities that, like birds fleeing the winter season, came to nest in the city. Agents anywhere have been forced to understand that most clients were incapable of separating business and personal needs, and thus subjected their representatives to a variety of roles that range from priest or psychiatrist to pimp. But KL's was a special case, a diverse situation.

The artists who came from abroad to become KL's charges were suddenly uprooted. Almost all of them were excruciatingly fragile or insecure, and they found themselves far from their familiar atmosphere, faced with a foreign language, confronted with a totally different method of work. Customs and lifestyles were not the same. Currency and rates of exchange confused them and fears of being cheated or being taken advantage of strengthened paranoic tendencies. Above all, there was the absence of an established social life, at least in the initial period. The dependence on K and L, therefore, was for them essential, and by circumstance inevitable. K and L also became a substitute for family, the living presence of roots, the familiar voice, the physiognomy of America, a home away from home. K and L never considered it their duty to assume the odious pimp role, but in Anita's case, Hank sensed that loneliness and isolation, and positive action was called for. He told Anita that he would see what he could do. As he hung up, his mind was immediately on Walter Chiari. All Hank had to do, of course, was find him, a maddening and time-consuming operation that sometimes took weeks.

Fortunately, it happened to be one of the rare nights that Walter was at home eating with Mamma and other family members. The moment that Hank mentioned Anita, Walter stopped stuffing pasta down his throat. As soon as Hank, with considerable circumlocution and embarrassment, began to explain the purpose of his call, Walter broke in.

"Hold it, Hank. Hold it," Chiari said. "You're telling me that this *favolosa* package of feminine pulchritude is desolating *tutta sola* in Roma. Am I right?"

"You're right," replied Hank, somewhat relieved, unprepared for the discourse that was to follow. Walter proceeded in his florid English, full of syllables, studded with adjectives, his vocabulary a salad with its special Chiari dressing: one-fourth dictionary-learned, one-fourth conversation-developed, one-fourth poetry-inspired, the rest instinctual histrionics.

"Italian males are a special breed of the human species, their primary attributes being noses, blood, daydreams and genitalia. Before I go on, let me note that the last four syllables of the fourth basic characteristic, i-ta-li-a, happen to be the name of their country. Hardly a mere coincidence, in my opinion.

"Their noses have become inflated through centuries of trying to absorb the aroma of the female. As they catch the scent, their blood heats to the point that they begin to beat their chests and scream Tarzan-like, as if possessed by primordial lust. Curtain drops. End of the show. If they really had the courage, they would immediately stop their grunts and groans, quickly stop fantasizing over oversized mamilla, forthwith cease to play with themselves in frustration, and, twelve deep, be at Anita's front door.

"But *carissimo mio*," Walter went on and on in his diss-ertation, "you have to understand that here we are confronting a special factor. This particular female is so formidable, so unapproachable, that most Italian men end up with an inferiority complex which compounds the inferiority complex they already have. They fear that they will not come up to Anita's regal expectations or are convinced she has so many admirers handsomer, sexier, richer than they are, there is no point even to try."

The Maestro of Grandiloquence continued. Hank never thought of interrupting. "All Italian men are in love with their mothers. They have never outgrown breastfeeding and they worship those marvelously comforting, so fulfilling milk stations protruding from the front of a woman. Breasts! Teats! Nipples! What images, what joys those words conjure up in the spirit, the memory and the dreams of the male. What, I ask you, is the fundamental symbol of Rome? Forget emperors, conquests and SPQR. What else but Romulus and Remus avidly sucking the teats of the She-Wolf who saved their lives? Mamma Roma! Mamma mia! Anita!

"Hank, my dear, dear friend, your problem is solved. Anita's problem is solved. I will assume full responsibility and discharge it so as to bring honor to all my Italian brethren. Just give me Anita's phone number and put your mind at rest. I promise you that Anita's wandering in the desert is over," concluded the Professor of Pyrotechnic English.

And Anita's desert-wandering *was* over. All kinds of oases began to spring up for her.

Innumerable photos of Anita's nocturnal escapades began highlighting covers of Italian magazines. She was in newsreels. She was discussed on television newscasts. Then a particular scandal occurred that became hot copy the world over, and was one of the events that inspired Fellini's *La Dolce Vita*.

On the night of November 7, 1958, young and wealthy Peter Howard, American playboy, dilettante actor and scion of the Vanderbilt family, decided to have a private party in honor of Contessa Olghina de Robilant. He chose an obscure restaurant-club called Rugantino, which was located in Rome's predominantly working-class neighborhood of Trastevere, situated across the Tiber and proud of a heritage that led its population to claim arrogantly that they were the first and true Romans. Howard's guests included such distinguished or notorious night owl personalities as painter and feminist Novella Parigini; noted woman-about-town Linda Christian; model-actress Elsa Martinelli; daughter of the infamous Benito, Annamaria Mussolini; her cousin, Raimonda Ciano; Principe Pier-Francesco Borghese, whose family rivaled the Massimos, Orsinis and Pignatellis in pretension of most ancient roots and bluer blood; and of course, Miss Anita Ekberg, who, by the way, was still Mrs. Anthony Steel. Naturally, the presumed "private" party was quickly ferreted out by several sensation-hungry photographers, who needed no briefing to know that with such a cast of characters, there would be some kind of a newsworthy show on display.

The party accelerated like a Ferrari in heat when a champagne-plied Anita, susceptible always to a syncopated beat, found herself alone on the dance floor, moving to the exciting samba rhythms of the Italian band. As she kicked off her shoes, her blonde mane flying and her *décolletage* heaving, she went into an "improvised dance that made 'Little Egypt' seem like a girl scout," to quote one of the press services reporting the festa. The fragile shoulder straps of her gown broke loose from their moorings. The alcoholized spectators were on their feet and on chairs, applauding and cheering. "Take it off, Anita," they shouted. "More! More! More! *Tutto!*" they excitedly egged her on. The photographers were in ecstasy as they shot every bounce, curve and shake of the way-gone Anita.

Anxious to cash in on the inevitable notoriety, Aïché Nana, a Lebanese bellydancer who happened to be present, decided to compete with Anita's uninhibited gyrations. Jumping onto the dance floor, Nana stripped right down to her excuse for a G-string and immediately indulged in a series of Arabian-Night bumps and grinds while writhing on the floor. The photographers went frantic, the place went wild, and Anita, never one to be upstaged by anybody's twitching belly button, went on doing her thing, but with a new spurt of exuberance. Suddenly there was panic. The police rushed in to put a stop to the "indecent spectacle" and participants were ordered to leave on their own volition or be transported by paddy wagon to jail.

The following morning, every wire service in Rome had a set of the Rugantino party stills, concentrating on the bounce of Anita and the bumps of Aïché. For days, every Italian newspaper was filled with stories on the scandalous event, unaware that it was simply doing research for the eventual Fellini film, as, of course, did Titus Petronius Arbiter nearly two thousand years before. He, virtually before anyone, foresaw the decline and destruction of the Roman Empire through the rising moral chaos. "Rome is a cesspool of vice and carnality, of sexual excesses and unbridled sensuality, of profligate amusements to which the leisure classes devote themselves, giving themselves over exclusively to the pursuit of pleasure in all its forms."

It was as if Titus Petronius and Federico Fellini were seated at a small corner table, unobtrusive and unseen, watching as yet another generation, in another era, proved that history was always repeating itself.

Providing readily salable and highly spiced copy, Anita's private life was constantly being chronicled. Such reporting could not fail to reach the attention of husband Tony, who returned to Rome to make an attempt at reconciliation. Unfortunately, Steel's drinking had become even more compulsive and was clearly ravaging his physique and once healthy attractiveness. Anita's undiminished vitality and increasing fame made the differences between them even more marked. He could not control his envy. He was eaten by jealousy and felt impotent in his effort to compete with Anita's innumerable admirers. He was unable to suppress his drunken violence, even in public. Photographers snapped pictures of Steel slapping Anita, which were widely circulated in the scandal sheets of the world. They also appeared on the sacred walls of Fellini's private office, which were covered with news stories, photos of incidents, pictures of actors and actresses, faces of people of the streets. The great director would share his life with this collage of humanity until, through a process of elimination, it included only those who were to remain integral to the film he was bearing in month-to-month pregnancy.

Anita's relationship with Steel at this ugly point in their marriage became a focal point of *La Dolce Vita*, with Lex Barker, the former Tarzan, impersonating the role of Anita's husband. Anita, though mortified by the public displays of drunkenness and violence of which Steel was guilty, still felt sorry for him, still cared for him. Even though his physical mistreatment of her continually distressed her, she could not bring herself to a definite decision to end the marriage. Tony, fortunately, had to leave for a film engagement, allowing Anita a chance to breathe a heaving sigh of relief.

Photographer Pierluigi Praturlon was a good friend of both Ekberg and Fellini. It was Pierluigi who unwittingly provided another event that contributed perhaps the most important element of *La Dolce Vita*. His enterprise simultaneously increased the probability that not Monroe, Taylor, Gardner, Bardot, Hayworth, Mansfield, Dors or other famed sex symbols of world cinema would be Federico's choice as symbol of his masterwork, but that it would be no other than… Ekberg.

Pierluigi had scheduled a photographic series of Anita against various Roman backgrounds. Even though it had already been immortalized for filmgoers around the world in *Three Coins in the Fountain*, the Fontana di Trevi was the one Pierluigi had in mind.

"It was four o'clock in the morning," he recalled to Gene, "but it was still hot and humid. Anita and I had danced for hours at Il Rancho Grande. She sat on the edge of the fountain, which was still brightly lit. As I was getting my equipment ready, she silently watched the gushing water, listening to its sound. She took off her shoes and stuck her feet into the water to cool them.

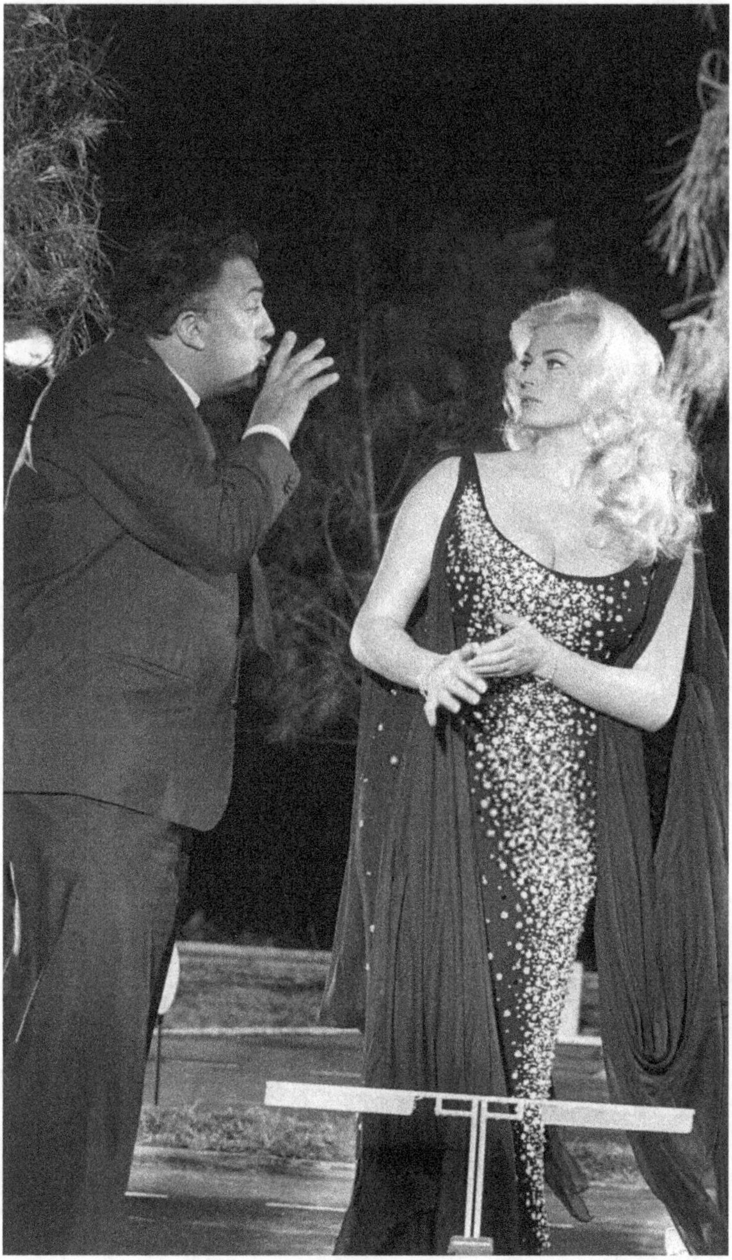

Federico Fellini and Anita Ekberg

The next thing I knew, she had lifted her dress and was wading in the fountain, totally oblivious to me and the only others in sight – two young *carabinieri*, who, open-mouthed, watched with incredulous eyes what they were sure was an apparition. I immediately started to click away with my Leica when I got such a funny feeling inside of me. I was a kid, taking part in a fantasy. Such wonderful joy surged through me as I watched Anita so childlike and natural in her spontaneity. Such moments don't happen very often in life.

"I happened to see Federico a few days later," continued Praturlon. "I started to tell him about Anita, that night, how I felt. He listened intently, asked questions. He asked to see the pictures and came over to my studio to look at them. He was absolutely ecstatic. What he saw, Federico told me, was the exact quality, the perfect essence, that he needed for *La Dolce Vita.*"

"It's Federico Fellini calling," Franca said to Hank on the Via Lisbona intercom. "Are you sure it's really Fellini?" a surprised Hank asked, since he and the director had never before had direct contact. "That's what he said," replied KLA's empress of the reception room. "Put him through," ordered Hank, wondering what the master of cinema wanted.

Hank decided to show off his now efficient Italian. "Signor Fellini, this is Hank Kaufman. I'm very pleased to hear from you."

"Do you prefer to speak English?" asked the director.

"*Come vuole Lei*," Hank continued in Italian.

"I think we speak in English. I have difficulty but I like to try. Tell me, Kaufman, it's true, yes, that you are the representative of Anita Ekberg?"

"Yes, it's true," replied Hank, his heart quickening.

"All right. I would like for you to come and see me, please. As soon as possible. Tomorrow? Three o'clock – is possible for you at my office? You know where is the Studio Safa Palatino, of course?"

"Of course. I'll be most happy to be there."

Three o'clock the following day. Hank was sitting in Fellini's Safa Palatino office raptly listening to and watching the director as he outlined the nature of his new film, from time to time glancing at the wall covered from ceiling to floor with photos and newspaper items, several of which were about Anita.

"The role is of a visiting Hollywood star, one of those... how you say – sex bombs. The pin-ups that the whole world knows and loves. You see them more and more on the Via Veneto. More and more they are part of the general Roman life and landscape. I do not want to show this star only like a pin-up, only an image to give a sexual thrill. I want to reveal to the public what is the inside of such a *creatura*, who she is, what she is hidden in her fantastic body. I want to... can you say 'open up the petals' of the flower?" Hank nodded his head, too fascinated to want to interrupt. "To open up the petals of the flower to show that her life, her personality, her *anima*, her thoughts and dreams are not the same, they are very different from the body exterior, the sexual image the spectator only sees. The spectator will have another pair of eyes to look inside of her, and with his two pairs of eyes, he will see a woman more glorious, more splendid, than before."

Hank was entranced, not only by what Fellini was describing but by the man himself. He seemed both gentle and strong. His voice was soft but it vibrated with currents and colors and enveloped the listener with visual images and poetic visions that he sensed came both from long thought and spontaneous invention of the moment. Hank saw the opportunity for Anita as God-given. Here was a rare opportunity for an actress virtually categorized as a commodity, artificially used in stereotyped roles, to be brought to life, fashioned by one of the great masters of world cinema. Fellini finished the discussion, more aptly described as a performance, by requesting that Hank arrange for him to meet with Anita as quickly as possible, with the hope of spending a great deal of time listening to and studying her.

Hank immediately arranged to go over and see Anita, who couldn't understand the urgency. Euphoric, still under Fellini's influence, it never entered Hank's mind that Anita wouldn't turn flip flops, somersaults and pirouettes in samba syncopation when she heard of Fellini's interest in her.

She was colossally unimpressed, as unaware of Fellini's reputation as she was of his existence. Wrapping herself up in the aura of grand Hollywood star in the grand Hollywood tradition, she left Hank wide-eyed, open-mouthed and incredulous.

"I won't meet him, not until I read a script. You know I don't talk to directors until I have read a script." Like *Sign of the Gladiator* which you rushed to Rome to do without having read a line of it, thought Hank as he listened to Anita's drivel. "What is he, another of those kind who just wants to make passes at me or ogle my body?" she asked haughtily. "You tell that Mr. Fellini that if he wants me, he's going to have to send me the script."

Hank started to explain to her who Fellini was. She wasn't listening. Hank tried to express to her Fellini's way of working. "He doesn't develop shooting scripts," Hank began. "He has a vision of what he expects to achieve. He knows both the horizons and the structure of his project. He sees his characters in action and situation, and has his story line at his command," Hank went on. "All of this goes into the overall design he has formulated in his brain and part of which he has put on paper. But the film itself, in the shooting, in its day-by-day development, becomes the creative act that gives his cerebral composition its flesh and blood, a collective process shared by Fellini, his cameraman, his writers, his technicians, his performers."

Anita was listening but not listening. Hank, so concentrated in his effort, was unconscious of Anita's lack of interest. "The image, the visual, the improvised, the unexpected, the spontaneous have to come out of the collaboration, not out of a script. This space for invention and inspiration is what permits Fellini's unique powers of oration to function and his genius to flower."

Hank thought that he had been nothing less than sensational in his description of Fellini and his method of work, and couldn't have been more pleased with his success in convincing Anita. He looked at her in self-satisfaction, waiting for her reply. It came and went. "I want to read a script," she repeated, Scandinavian, stubborn and Hollywood imperious. Hank was on the verge of explosion. He rose to go, deliberately avoiding the usual both-cheek kissing routine. As he was about to leave, he turned to look at her. "How can you be such an idiot?" he spat out, and slammed the door behind him.

Foul-tempered and embarrassed, he phoned Fellini the next day and was put through to him immediately. He asked the director whether he might come over to the Studio. "But did you speak to Anita?" Fellini inquired. "Yes," Hank replied, his heart sinking. "So what did she say?" pressed Fellini. "Please,

Federico, don't ask me anything now. Let me come and see you and I'll tell you," pleaded Hank. Miffed at all the mystery, Fellini nevertheless conceded.

Hank found himself once again in the Great Man's office with the floor-to-ceiling display on the wall and all those awards and trophies that honored his films *The White Sheik*, *I Vitelloni*, *La Strada*, *Nights of Cabiria* and others. Christ, Hank thought, how shall I do this? Our first direct contact with Fellini and I've got to report on Anita Ekberg's ridiculousness. I'm likely to get thrown out, and fast.

As Hank began to stammer his explanation, trying to be as protective of Anita as possible, he realized that Fellini wasn't in the least disturbed. Fellini, in fact, was vastly amused. He could have taken the boastful egomaniac route and dramatically pointed at all the awards and made a long address about all the great stars and actors in all categories who had written, phoned or told him that they would be thrilled to work for him script unseen and without salary, just for the magical experience of appearing in one of his pictures. On the contrary, he said: "If that's what the lady wants, that's what the lady will get." He called into the room Clemente Fracassi, his production chief. "Our little tramp Ekberg," he said affectionately, as if he were referring to a naughty daughter, "wants a script. Prepare it."

In a matter of days, Hank had in his hands the sequence of the film that recounted the Roman visit of the Hollywood movie star. Fellini of course drew heavily on actual personalities and events. The film star character that he wanted Anita to portray was a composite of many all too familiar to those close to the Roman film arena, in proportions of 75 percent Anita and 25 percent all-the-others. In outline, it seemed clichéd and virtually constituted invasion of privacy to the extent that it was based on so much of Anita's own personality and experiences.

When Anita read the material, she was outraged. She let all her fury spill out on both Fellini and Hank. "He's not serious, that genius of yours," she screamed at Hank. "He is making *fun* of me. He just wants to use me. He just wants to ridicule me and exploit me. The answer is no, no, NO! It's cheap. It's vulgar and if he tries to put this on the screen, I'll sue him, that's what I'll do. He even dares to call the character Anita!"

Hank sat quietly, listening to her diatribe. He decided on a different tactic. Let Anita shout, scream, stamp her feet and tear the script to bits and he wouldn't say a word or bat an eye. It was useless to repeat, once again, that the sequence had neither value nor meaning in itself, that she simply had to put herself into Fellini's hands and trust that he would create a marvelous character as part of an extraordinary film. The only way to overcome what seemed an insurmountable barrier was to get Anita and Federico together, and leave it up to the director's talent for spell-weaving.

"I'm going to tell Federico that you think the script is disgusting, that you think he's only trying to use you and that you're outraged. Since he's a real gentleman, he'll be very upset, and since he adores women, he'll be even more upset. He won't have any problem getting the biggest star in the business to play the part. He just happens to admire and want *you*. But I'll just have to tell him it's out. He'll have to take Marilyn Monroe or Ava Gardner." Anita was not looking at Hank but she certainly was listening. "Don't worry, honey, we'll find something else that you'll go for." Hank rose to leave, but took it slow.

There was quiet in the room. As Hank neared the door, after having done the brushing on Anita's two cheeks, he heard that child's voice, whispered and hoarse. "Wait a minute," she said.

"Anita, why don't you just meet the man, for Christ's sake?" Hank said, moving towards her and putting his arm on her shoulders.

"You called me an idiot the other day," she said, pouting.

"Well, darling, sometimes you are. You at least could have given some thought to my advice. I only ask you to do one thing. Meet Fellini. Let him talk to you and you do all the talking you want to him. How about it?"

After a moment, Anita nodded her head and whispered, "All right. If you think I should, I'll meet him."

And she did. And he was charmed and charming. And she was charmed and charming. A real affection grew between them. It was one of the few times that Anita didn't put a man on trial to ascertain his masculinity, impotency or homosexuality. The friendship was not confused with romance or affair. It was warm and free and the more she was exposed to Fellini, the more she grew to like, respect and trust him.

Federico agreed to change the name of the character to Sylvia instead of Anita. He agreed to other changes, but none of them really mattered, and in reading the sequence it was only slightly different and in any event had no real relevance until the magic of Fellini and of Peppino Rotunno and the other collaborators on *La Dolce Vita* began the actual creation through lights, camera and images.

KLA and Fracassi worked out the deal. The film was to be bankrolled by Angelo Rizzoli, the wealthiest picture financier and by far the most powerful publisher in Italy. He finally agreed to pay Batjac the highest weekly remuneration yet paid it for the loan-out of her services. Back to her Hollywood-star pretentiousness, Anita made demands on dressing room accommodation, exclusive services of a hairdresser and makeup artist, private car, and chauffeur, living expenses and other prerogatives. Fellini's strong conviction that Anita was the one to bring the character to vivid fruition made Fracassi and Rizzoli malleable, and the contract was finally agreed to by KLA and the production, and was ready for signature.

Anita, who, together with Batjac, had to sign the contract, refused. All her doubts were revived. Tony Steel had returned during that critical period, and whether he had any effect on provoking this new crisis was never ascertained. Anita was living in a certain amount of fear. She sought to avoid being alone with Tony, never knowing what she was going to face in abuse or violence. She returned to her apprehensions on her role and her sequence in the picture. Over and over again she kept repeating that she was being ridiculed, she was being used, she would be a laughing stock. Fracassi phoned Hank to ask for the signed contract. Fracassi got excuses. Fellini himself phoned. He also got excuses. Anita refused to answer Federico's calls. Hank pleaded with her. He brought Gene into the pleading act. They both appeared at her apartment. Tony was not there. She was near tears, in desperation, worry, confusion and fear. She began again on the reasons for her not doing the film. Gene lost his patience. He asked Hank to take the contract out of his briefcase, which Hank did.

"Are you going to sign this contract?" demanded Gene.

"I can't. I can't let them..."

"We've heard all that, Anita," Gene broke in, furious. "I'm going to tell you something right to your face and I don't give a damn whether you like it or don't. You haven't got a career anymore. There's only one way for you to go and that's down. You have absolutely nothing to lose by doing Fellini's picture and almost certainly a hell of a lot to gain." Gene turned to Hank. "Am I right or wrong, Hank?"

"You're right."

"So for the last time. Will you sign this contract?"

Anita looked at Gene, her eyes blazing in fury, but when she spoke her voice was low. "You can't talk to me like that."

"As long as we're responsible for you, I *can* talk to you like that, and I *am* talking to you like that. All right, Anita. You're going to do the picture. If you won't sign the contract, I, as your authorized agent, am going to on your behalf. It may not be legal, but I'll take that chance."

Then, taking out his pen, he signed "Anita Ekberg by Gene Lerner, Authorized Agent." Anita watched silently, stunned and angry. Gene handed Hank the contract, who quietly stuck it into his briefcase.

"We're going now, Anita," Gene said. "We'll give the contract to Fracassi and advise Batjac the deal is closed."

Hank was already on his feet. He kept staring at Anita, wanting to take her in his arms. She was clearly suffering, over Tony, over the uncertainties of her life, over Gene's brutally frank statements.

"Anita dear," Hank said softly. "I told you that you had to trust us. I know we're doing the right thing for you. You may not feel it now, but once you're involved with the picture, I'm convinced that you'll be glad. If you need anything, we'll be at home. Just give us a call."

Hank then went to Anita, hugged her, kissed her on both cheeks. She accepted his show of affection without looking at him. Gene knew it was best for him to make no such effort. He simply said, "Goodbye Anita," as he and Hank left.

Several days after Hank had delivered the contract and officially informed Batjac, Fellini invited Anita and Hank to lunch. Only at the last minute was Hank sure that Ekberg would join them. Her mood was radically different. She was smiling, gushing with conversation, extremely affectionate with Hank. The lunch was at L'Escargot on the Via Appia Antica, and the greeting between Anita and Fellini was of two loving friends who had not seen each other for decades.

Fellini was the first to recommend a regional specialty of the house, the ricotta and spinach malfatti. When the steaming dish was brought to the table, Anita, whose knowledge of Italian at

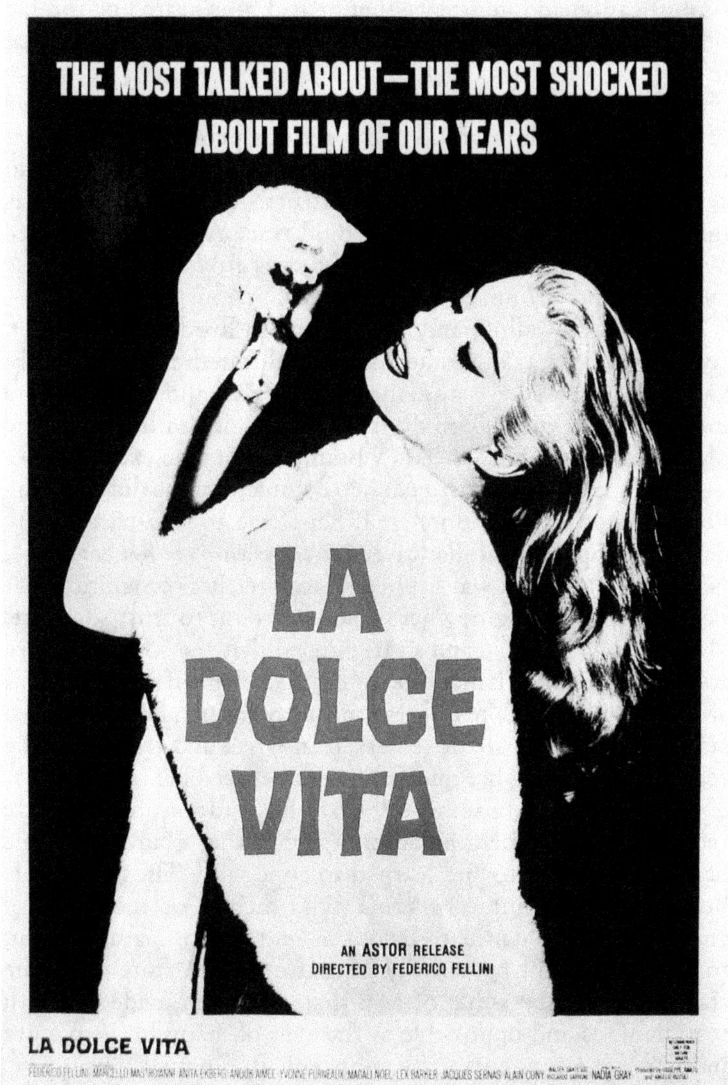

that time was rudimentary but colorful, pointed to the malfatti and let out a high-pitched shriek. "Look, they look like little dicks!" she exclaimed. Fellini burst out laughing, thoroughly amused. And as breakfast progressed, he became increasingly cheerful. He felt he had found in Anita the perfect fusion of sophistication and innocence that he had been searching for. He became more and more convinced that she would be sensational in his film.

The snobs were appalled at the idea that an innovative director like Fellini would show serious professional interest in an actress they considered to have very modest talent, an actress who had been entirely constructed by publicity. It was inconceivable to them that he would want Anita for *La Dolce Vita*, a film that, even before it began, was arousing such intense curiosity and promised to become one of his masterpieces – scandalous, revealing, and a milestone in his directing career. Even today, Anita's wonderfully uninhibited and stunningly varied performance astonishes the viewer and prompts the question: how did Fellini do it? What magic did he use? How did he manage to make her so vibrant, so spicy, so exciting?

Anita learned to trust Federico completely. She did anything he asked her to do, and more. It happened to be a particularly dark, unhappy time in her life. Her concern over her marriage, her worry over what was happening to Steel, her recognition that her career was going nowhere made her want to trust someone. She was so vulnerable and so frightened that she sought to have someone in whose hands she could place herself and who was able and willing to take full responsibility for her. Her emotional state required that she lose herself in work and transform the realities suffocating her into fantasies that freed her.

And Fellini understood that, he understood *her*. He recognized the Ekberg paradox, which earlier Hank and Gene had been exposed to and learned to cope with. The formidable body encased a simple *bambina*, who thrived on the ordinary and the basic. To dance, to be out in, and part of, nature, to eat, to make love, not necessarily in that order. In spite of all the star pretentiousness that often afflicted her and made her both so ridiculous and impossible in the eyes of many in the picture industry, she was curiously innocent, instinctual, impulsive, and so transparent in her efforts at guile that she seemed a child caught in the pantry trying to steal a piece of candy. She was not without feminine wiles, but if she really cared for a man, she was incapable of anything like female guile. Fellini referred to her as "a child of nature, a Flemish Renaissance woman in the wrong place and in the wrong century."

Anita was indefatigable, collaborative as she had never before been on a picture. The remarkable Fontana di Trevi night scenes, in which she frolics so blissfully with Marcello Mastroianni, were shot during several successive icily humid nights in a freezing February climate. The two stars were each furnished with hip-high rubber boots to wade through the penetratingly cold fountain waters over and over again for repeated takes. Anita found the boots inhibitive. After a few minutes, she yanked them off. "I have to feel free and I can't move with these heavy boots on," she told Fellini. One night she was talking to Hank about her childhood in Sweden with moving nostalgia. "I would throw myself into the freezing, ice-covered sea," she recalled. "I adored those first moments of being paralyzed by the cold and slowly, slowly getting used to it and no longer feeling it. Jesus, it was exhilarating."

After each frigid take, she and Mastroianni were quickly wrapped in blankets, whisked into their portable dressing rooms in the Piazza for resuscitation and preparation for the next shot. Anita was instantaneously stripped, dried, massaged and frictioned and her insides warmed by shots of cognac before she was whisked back once more into the bitter cold, ready once again to pretend that the dancing through the waters of Trevi was taking place on a steaming summer Roman night.

Mastroianni received similar treatment, but he preferred vodka, and if one minutely examines the close-ups of the scene, one will perceive glints in the eyes of the protagonists which were not provoked by acting bravura or directorial genius. "Marcello was terrified of all those dunkings," Anita said, "but Federico called me 'that incredible Viking' and couldn't understand how I was able to stand it. To me, it was great fun. And all of those people - thousands of them – staying up half the night, sometimes till dawn, to watch and cheer us on." It was something of a repeat of the night shooting of *The Naked Maja* and its scenes of folk-dancing with Ava Gardner as willing participant. Here again, filming became a thrilling stop for Rome-by-Night tourist buses.

The *Dolce Vita* excitement coincided with developments that profoundly altered both Anita's and Hank's and Gene's personal and professional lives. Anita finally received her divorce from Tony Steel. While retaining a certain friendship for him, she was relieved of what was a heavy burden and more than welcomed her release from a marriage that had seemed doomed from the start. And Anita was the cause for the definitive break between Kaufman-Lerner Associates and the William Morris Agency.

In 1960, William Morris had suggested a buyout of KLA, with Hank and Gene entering into personal employment agreements as vice presidents and continental managers of William Morris International. There were months of meetings between Hank and Gene on the one hand, the Lastfogel-Stoller-Lefkowitz-Stoller quartet on the other. In their numerous policy talks, Hank and Gene repeatedly stressed the crucial point that they were to maintain final responsibility for the careers of Italian artists who required particular handling for the development of their local and international potential, like Brazzi, as well as for the careers of foreign artists living and working mainly in Europe, like Anita.

WMA said they understood, and agreed. If the Agency didn't have such faith in KLA, why would he want to make Hank and Gene a part of the William Morris family, President Lastfogel asked?

Before coming to an absolute conclusion, Gene told Lastfogel that he preferred to return to Rome, where it had all begun, and there, in that effervescent and beautiful city that had brought Hank and him fortune, there, on the soil of Italy, together with Hank, make the decision of such import.

In a matter of days, the decision was made for then.

In the negative.

Phil Kellogg advised K and L that WMA client Robert Fellows, who now owned what was left of Ekberg's contract with Batjac, intended to lend Anita's services out for another of those banal, second-rate, wooden-role Hollywood pictures. Kellogg told Hank and Gene to inform Anita that she was required to report for the film.

Gene and Hank were enraged. There was no question that Fellows wanted Anita back in Hollywood to cash in on the fame she had achieved in Italy and Europe, and the William Morris office was certainly not standing in Fellows' way. To permit Anita to go back for such a film was, in Gene's and Hank's minds, an obnoxious contradiction to what seemed to be her new career potential and a serious setback to her rising earning power.

In Gene's and Hank's view, William Morris had breached a fundamental principle of the understanding reached for its buyout of KLA. They came to the conclusion that the plan could not function to their satisfaction or be of sufficient value to the many important and rising clients under their aegis.

And so, in March 1961, came the end of the nearly six-year WMA-KLA association. Before the dissolution, however, KLA was able to relieve Anita of her Fellows-Batjac contract, and, with its break with William Morris, could accept her as its exclusive, worldwide client. She could at last proceed with her career as member of the KLA family without further obligations either to Fellows, Batjac or William Morris.

KLA proceeded to form an association for the United States with the Ashley-Famous agency, now called International Creative Management, the most powerful talent agency in the world. Olga Horstig remained firm in her alliance with KLA. When, to their profound disappointment, Christopher Mann decided to continue his WMA association and thus work with the new Rome branch of William Morris, Hank and Gene made a partnership deal with the influential London-based Grade Organisation, headed by Leslie Grade and Robin Fox. The agreement left KLA totally independent, with Hank and Gene retaining majority control of their firm's stock. Part of the deal stipulated that either Hank or Gene would spend up to three years in London, working in overall liaison between KLA, Grade and Ashley-Famous. Always as partner in KLA, Gene accepted the task. From 1964 to 1967, he made his working and living headquarters in the British capital.

The spectacular success of *La Dolce Vita* was followed by another Fellini-Ekberg collaboration. He offered her the starring role in his segment of the three-part *Boccaccio '70*, produced by Carlo Ponti. Fellini cast Anita as a larger-than-life billboard pin-up, advertising milk. The billboard comes to life, allowing a gigantic Anita to dwarf the City of Rome with her pendulous presence. Her breasts filled to overflowing, spilling out over her skin-tight, astral-studded velvet gown, the lettered slogan "BEVETE PIU' LATTE" ("DRINK MORE MILK") appears beneath her outstretched figure and we hear a musical jingle repeating the words.

The Fellini-Ekberg combination succeeded once again. Federico seemed to be the only director who understood how to penetrate the Ekberg facade and how best to utilize and project both her symbolic appeal and external attributes. The two Fellini pictures gave Anita momentum for a revitalized international career through much of the 1960s. It embraced a number of films that neither broke box office records nor aroused critics to bravos over Anita's performances. They were, however, films of dignity, several of which recognized Anita as an actress, not merely a figure or figurehead.

Among them were *4 for Texas* for Robert Aldrich and Warner Bros., her re-entry to Hollywood at the highest salary of her career, all of it hers and all of it tax-free. She returned to Movieland U.S.A. as a triumphant international film queen, with $2,000 in weekly living expenses, three first-class round-trips to include herself, Liz Haggstrom and a companion who soon thereafter became husband number two, a limousine and chauffeur at 24-hour-a-day disposition, personal hair stylist and makeup artist of her choice, special costuming, and of course equal co-star billing with Frank Sinatra and Dean Martin.

There were also *Call Me Bwana*, made in London opposite Bob Hope; *The Alphabet Murders*, an Agatha Christie mystery, co-starring Margaret Rutherford and Tony Randall, also filmed in London, an M-G-M production for which Anita received a weekly salary nearly five times higher than what was paid for her appearance in *La Dolce Vita*; *Behind Closed Doors*, Dino Risi's Italian comedy; *Three Etc.'s and the Colonel*, an Italian farce co-starring Vittorio de Sica; a big-budget European co-production of *The Mongols*, co-starring Jack Palance; and *Woman Times Seven*, the Shirley MacLaine starrer directed by de Sica, in which Anita and a number of male stars like Rossano Brazzi, Peter Sellers and Vittorio Gassman made guest appearances. There were also well-paid television appearances, including commercials, in Italy, England, France, Germany and the United States. And always, everywhere was that unforgettable image of her in *La Dolce Vita*, the euphoric liberated Viking goddess rising from the waters of the Fontana di Trevi, as if to lead one and all to break the shackles of their everyday realities.

"What those 1960 years accomplished was to bring me more money than I had ever amassed in my life. I was rid of my Batjac contract so I could keep everything that I earned. I never before had any financial security. Up to then, it was always a struggle to make ends meet on the weekly salary I was getting from Batjac. It gave me such a wonderful feeling."

It was Hank and Gene who convinced Anita to invest some of her earnings in land and in a home, the first in her life that was all her own. She bought two extensive plots of beachfront acreage on a stretch of rugged sand dunes sixty miles south of Rome, and finished the construction of her villa by the end of 1963. It was just across the road from K and L's Casa Bianca in Sabaudia.

The Swedish-Malibu-style house that she built embodied her personal vision of the ideal home. The spacious expanse of the stone cantilevered structure overhanging the dunes consisted mainly of one gigantic room, which included a large salon area, library, dining space and open kitchen. Electronically operated sliding glass panels surrounded it, opening onto a magnificent long terrace overlooking the Tyrrhenian Sea, which lapped her property. Facing west, the total effect was, indeed, dramatic, particularly as dusk gathered and the glowing sun slowly fell into the Mediterranean blue. The only other rooms were a large master bedroom with a queen-sized bed, a dressing room and, of course, bathrooms. When visitors expressed surprise over the lack of guest rooms, Anita explained with candor, "I built this house to be alone with the man I choose to love and live with."

After the divorce from Steel, her liaisons continued to provide enough sensational copy to satisfy the demands of the locally based press and press services and to amuse an avid public. One which was handled with discretion, little known to the outside world, was her 1962 romance with Sean Connery, when she was shooting *The Alphabet Murders* in London. Anita fell in love and, according to her, was led by Connery to believe that they would be married. When the news broke that he had married Diane Cilento, with whom he had been having a serious romance, Anita was devastated. She phoned Gene to commiserate. "I can't believe it. It just can't be true. It can't be. He told me we would get married. I'm just not fortunate. I'm honest, and men take advantage. When it comes to real love, I'm always duped."

When Anita really loved, she loved with sincerity and profundity of heart, and made every effort to avoid indiscretion. For her, real love was a private matter. When Tyrone Power died in 1958, Anita was making *The Dam on the Yellow River*, her second Italian film after *Sign of the Gladiator.* Gene heard the news on his way to visiting her at Cinecittà. All he knew was that Anita and Power had worked together and that it was likely that they had an affair. Anita was sitting at her dressing table being made-up when he mentioned the news to her and was startled by her reaction. Her face turned white and her whole body began to tremble as she burst into agonizing sobs. She fell into Gene's arms, weeping desperately, gasping out words that she seemed to have hidden in the deepest recesses of her soul.

"I loved him. Oh, God, how I loved him. Do you know how good he was? So few men in this world are good. He wanted us to get married. We would have, but his wife wouldn't give him a divorce, even though their marriage was already on the rocks. The bitch saw photos of me in Ty's apartment. She tore them to shreds and threw the pieces into the street. In the end, we had to give up. Oh, Gene, you don't know, you don't know the terrible pain it caused me... We would have been so happy. So happy!"

None of Anita's relationships was treated with such tact and secrecy as the one with Gianni Agnelli, head of the far-flung Fiat industrial empire, and one of the outstanding business leaders of the world. Many of the press and most of the "in" set knew of it, but it was treated as sacrosanct. He was married to an extraordinary woman, whom no one wanted to distress. He had a statesman's prestige that not even opponents, rivals or enemies saw any point in besmirching. And he had personal qualities as a man that were praiseworthy.

Anita saw a true friend in Agnelli and her love for him was based on that recognition. She was ever anxious to protect his reputation. She fully understood what was at stake. She knew there was not the remotest possibility of marriage. They did not see one another frequently, though they were from time to time seen together on one of Agnelli's elaborate yachts. Their other meetings were carefully hidden but they were in constant telephonic contact. Anita's reference to Ty Power's goodness also applied to Agnelli. He further supplied Anita with the emotional substance of a father figure, a strikingly handsome, debonair and distinguished one at that. Theirs was not an affair as cynics would define it, nor a romance that scandalmongers could lasciviously gossip over. It was a rare rapport between a man and a woman based on reality and had its roots in essentials of love: respect, understanding, communication, tenderness and the absence of exploitation one of the other, and to this day, the rudiments of that rare rapport endured.

One day a radiant Anita showed Hank a pair of turquoise and gold earrings. "Gianni gave them to me," she said happily. "Aren't they exquisite?" She then became pensive. "I know that if I wanted to play it right, I could have been rich like Paulette Goddard or Zsa Zsa Gabor long ago. I could have had all the expensive jewels I wanted. And yachts, real estate. Stocks and bonds. All of those things. But I'm not able to play that game. I just don't know how. I suppose I'm stupid. Other women do it, but I just can't."

In 1963, Franco Silva, a handsome Italian hunk of an actor who had not yet, not ever would shake the world with his on-screen talent, had been discarded by Anita after a much-publicized entanglement. He didn't like it. He allegedly tried to blackmail her for $20,000 in return for keeping her Agnelli relationship secret. Furious, Anita hauled him into court. Of course, the press was overjoyed by the delectable party Anita provided them with and gave full play to the sensational event. However, Agnelli's name was not referred to in the proceedings or in the press, though innuendos that led to his person were frequent enough. Much to Anita's distress, Silva was eventually acquitted of attempted extortion and she was persuaded to drop the case.

Notoriety of a different nature took place in the Calabrian town of Castrovillari, where Anita was shooting *A Porte Chiuse*. She was accompanied to the location by her then escort, Marchese Antonio Gerini, one of the upper echelon in the playboy category. When the inhabitants of the province got wind of Anita's presence, they descended en masse to get a closer look as Anita, accompanied by the marquis, was driving through the town. The crowd blocked her silver-colored Ferrari. Some were shocked by her half-unbuttoned blouse that left much of her bosom revealed. There were shouts of "sinne."

Anita, in panic, tried to drive through the throng to escape. Stones began striking the car. Anita, half-hysterical, kept going forward and brushed against several persons among the hundreds who choked the piazza. She was later taken to court for damages, a case which was quietly settled. Several of her accusers said that they had actually tried to stone her because she was a "scarlet woman," "a whore." Later, in an article in the important Italian weekly *L'Europe*, she was accused of "systematically indulging in adultery." She sued the publication and the matter was settled by written retraction.

On April 9, 1963, Anita made the unfortunate decision of marrying a tall, blandly good-looking Roman hanger-on and would-be actor named Rik Van Nutter, who was totally American in spite of the European twist to his name. Their wedding was no exciting Florence carnival with horse-drawn carriage and champagne-quaffing as thousands cheered. It was an imitation of the Mel Ferrer-Audrey Hepburn nuptials. Without benefit of press or photographers, Anita became Mrs. Van Nutter in a secret ceremony at Lugano, Switzerland.

It was not too many years later that Anita commented, "I'm just not fortunate in love. The men who really made me happy were the men I didn't marry." And once she unexpectedly turned to Gene after a moment of silence to say: "Would you be surprised if I told you that the greatest love of my life was an Italian?"

Anita gave herself completely to Rik. She persuaded K and L to take him on as a client, which they did only to please her. He was dubbed Mister Toothbrush, because of his amazing white teeth and his appearance in a toothbrush commercial. KLA did succeed in providing him with a few job opportunities. The only role pompous Rik really played was that of husband, and in that role he wildly over-acted. He knew more about films, scripts and careers than anybody. By 1967, he had alienated Anita from Hank, Gene and other friends, and professional advisers like attorney Vittorio Ripa di Meana and publicist Giorgio Conti, who had also been extremely close to her.

Anita loved to cook for her Rik and for herself. She spent hours in the huge, open kitchen of the seaside villa, making all sorts of delicacies: wonderfully-spiced sausages, marvelous Swedish liver pates, exquisite sauces for pastas of various types. Rik kept not only that flashing glitter of teeth but also his slender figure. On the other hand, Anita's figure began to expand and expand and expand to accommodate all of her appetizing concoctions and the vodkas she found so refreshing. In the latter 1960s, her body widened more and more towards travesty. She became more and more wary of her former friends, the press, and Rik was definitely not opposed to keeping her isolated from other influences. Fearing ridicule, she went to great lengths to protect her privacy, a privacy she had so frequently scorned in the past.

She and Rik waged open warfare against the members of the fourth estate. When they discovered reporters or *paparazzi* lurking around the villa or hiding in the surrounding dunes, she and Rik attacked them with BB shots from a rifle or arrows from bows. They planted a high-powered telescope on the terrace to spy on intruders in the area. For Rik, all this was something of a mad Lewis Carroll game, but for Anita, it was a perilous move towards total paranoia.

The press of course was not without its own weapons or resources. It sought revenge. When Anita dared to descend to her private beach for a swim in the sea on a scalding summer day, she defensively covered herself with a loose-fitting man's shirt to hide the growing bulges in her body. Photographers from hidden perches used their telescopic lenses to catch her in the most unflattering poses possible. Once in the water, she immediately fell on her haunches, hoping to conceal her fatness. The photographers simply waited to catch her every time she rose. She had already lost the battle to preserve the figure that had drawn so many thousands of pilgrims to the shrine of the Fontana di Trevi and that had been a universal symbol of the Rome envisioned by Fellini.

In Rik's rash efforts to insert himself in running Anita's career, controlling her finances and dominating her personal life, he brought ruin to the much-enamored Anita. By 1970, she was jobless. When her beloved villa was impounded by the Italian Internal Revenue for her failure to pay tax on her earnings, she found herself homeless, and soon thereafter, she was also husbandless. Newspapers carried the following Reuters dispatch dated March 2, 1971:

> Anita Ekberg, recently divorced from Rik Van Nutter, whom she married in 1963, is seeking a court injunction to stop Van Nutter from removing and selling property which she claims is hers. The property, consisting of furniture, home furnishings and personal items, was stored in a warehouse in the South of France after she and Van Nutter had separated.

What the newspapers did not say was that all of Anita's belongings had been removed from the villa in the darkness of night to avoid attachment by the tax authorities and that Rik had removed whatever monies still remained in their joint account.

"Rik was gentle," Anita later said. "But he did nothing, except to live on my earnings. He had more clothes than I did and far more time to enjoy himself. But he was gentle! When after seven years I decided I'd had enough of him, he left, taking with him our bed, the sheets, covers, and most of my other things, including the pots in which I had planted herbs and even rolls of toilet paper. Rik was gentle, but above all, he was certainly a farsighted type."

Disenchanted, humiliated, Anita found herself homeless and penniless. Notwithstanding the catastrophe she had made out of her life, she was still able to state that "Rome is the only place where I really feel some semblance of home. I realize that my vogue and cult are finished. So why can't they leave me alone now? Why am I still a target for them?" The reference was to the press. Cruelly and crudely, it sought to inflate the parody that Anita had at last become. She turned into a recluse in the modest house in Mentana, her constant companions only her Great Dane dogs, busying herself with occasional gardening. "See my hands, how horrible they are? That's from cultivating roses and working the earth," she told an interviewer in May 1972. "I've broken all my nails, but *pazienza*. There are so many plants that need taking care of. They're easily worth a few torn nails."

Her figure had grown to monstrous proportions. She defensively referred to the rolls of flesh as "not fatness, but development. Anyway, who ever said that bones were beautiful," she asked? She often alluded to making a comeback, but it was only daydreaming and empty talk. For years, she continued to live in sloth and solitude, with an occasional lover sharing her bed.

Finally, in 1978, aged 47, she somehow found the determination. She spent two months in a Swiss clinic, going through the ordeal of losing fifty pounds, and later was to lose another fifteen. She first tried a nightclub engagement, as "symbol of the sexy female of the Sixties." Her five-night engagement ended after three. The German press was devastating. It criticized everything. Her repertoire of old songs. Her limited dancing. Her body covered from top to bottom in chiffon, when the public came to see some *décolletage* and some legs. "Nothing was shown, certainly nothing of glamor, sensuality or talent."

Anita then appeared on Italian television. She came across with considerable charm, sense of humor and dignity in the telecasts, and as a result, received a good deal of favorable publicity. It was then that Angelo Frontoni persuaded Anita to do a series of nudes for Italian *Playboy*. Many of his photos, some of them showing every aspect of her body in tasteful diaphaneity, were superlative. It was almost as if Anita had re-entered that astonishing body of a score of years before and had somehow rekindled the translucent sweetness of a face not yet splattered by the mud of life. *Playboy* paid the highest price in its history for the Frontoni series, and it provoked a flurry of interest in Anita among film producers.

Anita was signed for an Italian film entitled *The Murdering Nun* that was shot in Central Africa. The picture opened in Italy in the winter of 1979. The critics wrote excretions of disgust over its offensive story and insipid vulgarity. They destroyed the film. They destroyed Anita.

There was no such thing as comeback from comeback.

In 1980, Anita turned 50. She might have insisted that it was only her 45th or 48th... whatever. Still envisioning herself a star, she found her way to celebrate in spite of her profound emotional wounds and choking solitude. "Fellini ruined me," she had said. Nevertheless, she lifted her glass of vodka to commemorate the Rome and the Anita he had created, both of which were dead, or which had never actually lived.

Fellini gave Ekberg a certain immortality. He transfigured her into an exaltation of sensuality. He presented her as the female sexual ideal of an epoch. She was for him, for millions, the Deity of Desire. A symbol, an ideal, even a goddess may perish, but the woman must live. Fellini's most recent fantasy-epic had its world premiere in Rome in 1980, twenty years after that momentous first showing of *La Dolce Vita*. He gave his new film the title of *City of Women*. He found no role, no place in that new city, for the woman named Anita Ekberg.

Gone was the midnight frolicking in the Fontana di Trevi and the uninhibited dancing and drinking until dawn, gone the admiring crowds that followed the star wherever she went, chanting "Anitona" or singing "Bevete piu latte!" Gone the impetuous girl-woman, who reveled in snow and sun, field and sea, riding, boating, swimming, running until she had no breath, a joyfully abandoned daughter of nature. And gone was the woman named Anita Ekberg, to live among her thorns and plants in Genzano, the town outside of Rome to which she recently moved.

As Fellini's *La Dolce Vita* myth crumbled and his Viking goddess toppled from her throne, the 1960s slithered into the 1970s. The motion picture camera twisted its lenses into stilettos to murder make-believe, adopting its role of documenter of events, mercilessly sharpening its focus to reveal that the positive print in the projector of time and history had become hopelessly snarled. The silver screen of Hollywood on the Tiber no longer had its tarnish, and its sheen was turning to mold. Cinecittà, the palantine of Hollywood on the Tiber's dominion, stood decaying in silence, an empty, ghostlike obituary to the epoch, awaiting its fate as sycophant to television, massive housing project or mausoleum.

The ultimate rise of the Roman Empire through camera and celluloid had taken its inevitable fall.

"Today, the customers of our newsstand are people you would never recognize," said ageing Raffaella Gigli, proprietor of the Via Veneto kiosk on the corner of Via Ludovisi, shaking her head sadly. "From those worldly, sophisticated people of those days, we only get occasional crumbs. The carefree, devil-may-care personalities of that period are all in flight, wanderers in their darkness. The famous now live only in their memories, having hidden themselves away in their shuttered homes.

"Nightlife, if you want to call it that, now consists of rowdy bunches of soccer fans, chanting, waving their pennants and piercing your ears with their horn-blasting until the early hours. Since the time of the *dolce vita*, I haven't seen faces you would find in every newspaper and every magazine. Of the old-timers, only Fellini still comes by," Signora Gigli concluded, her face consumed by memory.

The Via Veneto, the Via Imperiale of Hollywood on the Tiber, had become its Sunset Boulevard.

But the faces of many more mere participants of Hollywood on the Tiber become luminous when the epoch is mentioned today. Even though the babble of voices that a world would recognize with palpitating heart has disappeared in haunting echo, eyes of the partakers of the era glow in tearful nostalgia.

They spend endless hours in recall of wondrous happenings and titillating events that emblazoned Rome's ultimate renaissance. Moist tongues caress the magic names of the deities and idols who were there. Story after story, reminiscence after reminiscence, revelation after revelation, cascade from intoxicated lips.

They see Rome once again in all her Glory, delighted by the play of klieg lights that blotted out centuries of wrinkles and millennia of darkness and disinterest. Once again, Narcissus, adoring his reflection in the massive artificial lake constructed by Metro-Goldwyn-Mayer at Cinecittà. Once again Courtesan, abandoning herself to the marvelous sensation of make-believe through the sorcerous ministrations of makeup artists, hairstylists and costumiers.

As they look back into the past, as they are clutched by their recollections of Hollywood on the Tiber, they seem to be seeing neither history nor fact, but a spectacular epic with a cast to outrank any ever assembled in the annals of show business, and through the mists of nostalgia, they are unable to see that the title of the sensational, unrivaled colossus is...

THE END.

Epilogue

KAUFMAN-LERNER ASSOCIATES
Via Lisbona 12
Rome, Italy

February 5, 1970

Mr. Hank Kaufman
Whitehall Hotel
85-97 New South Head Road
Rushcutters Bay
Sydney, Australia

Dear Hank,

Your cable arrived yesterday. I'm glad you arrived without mishap after the hysterical departure. Wasn't it great that the new Jumbo 747 happened to be on exhibition at Fiumicino when you left? After you took off, I managed to sneak aboard for an inspection. Unbelievable. More unbelievable than realizing it's supposed to fly! I'm dying to get on one as fast as I can.

Sydney, Melbourne, Djakarta, Denpasar, Bali, Manila, Tokyo, Hong Kong, Bangkok, San Francisco, Los Angeles, Boston, Miami, New York, London, Paris, then back again to Rome. With your trip-around-the-world, you satisfy another of your dreams. You have always had them, always will have them. So many of them have been and will be fulfilled.

So, five days ago, January 31, 1970, almost eighteen years after we first put up the brass plaque on the outer gate of Via Aiaccio 12-bis, we are no longer talent agents. I say "Thank God," because Kaufman-Lerner Associates as an entity for the future still exists and Via Lisbona 12 as headquarters for things to come remains.

Though I could not bring myself to talk about it, I realize what a dreadful day that Friday was for you. And for Barbato, who was trying so hard to hide his sadness. And Marion, our employees, many of our clients and even some of the industry. It was also, in certain ways, a dreadful day for me. Watching our three suites of offices and nineteen rooms diminished to a single five-room studio-garçonnière suffocated me. Every time a photo came down from the walls, intense memory overwhelmed me. Each time the movers took a filing cabinet full of correspondence and documents to truck to Sabavuia for storage, an important event was replayed.

And yet, from time to time, I felt surges of happiness. As the offices became emptied of our history, they seemed to become packed with more and more of the personalities we cared so much about, the producers with whom we fought the hardest, directors, writers and others we worked with. And they were all so entertaining and charming and affectionate. We seemed to be whirling in a huge fiesta. We were the hosts of a grand party, a very special, very joyful, Cocktailus Romanus. The biggest and most successful of them all.

I wanted to come over to you to say, dear Hank, that the years have passed incredibly, and they were incredible years. We have had such a fabulous life experience. We have come such a long way. We have been part of, and partners in, a remarkable flash of history. And with the curtain now down, we can in humility and in pride take our bows with grace, dignity and gratitude.

We started here in '53 with absolutely nothing and we ended with a very great deal. We could have continued indefinitely, but we came to Rome to build, not just to survive. The day had come to take yesterday gently into our arms and carry it as gently into tomorrow.

It's too early to make a scientific analysis of the period we have lived through, but someday it will be done. So much didn't work. Why? So much went wrong. Why? So much waste, graft, corruption, exploitation. We know why. So much sacrifice of serious, principled, talented artists. Unforgiveable. Still, with so much hope, enthusiasm and effort, why were there so few positive results to be recorded in the history of world cinema? With perhaps nearly one billion dollars available, with such overwhelming richness in artistic resources, why proportionally did so little of quality, importance and permanence emerge? It seems that the aberrant, speculative phenomenon that began around 1950 never had a structure and only a rare few saw the need for one. It was a Humpty Dumpty who had never been put together even before its fall.

We strenuously tried to merge the mentalities and sensibilities of Americans and Italians (and other Europeans) towards the achievement of a common goal in our 18-year experience. To be Americans by birth, education and culture and to have lived so long among and almost as Europeans is a hell of a wonderful combination. I am convinced that our future should be based on this fusion to which we were exposed and which, through our work, through our being what we are, we actively developed. We must go ahead with your idea to do a New York show on Kurt Weill, whose life and art so marvelously intermingled Europe and America. "The mythical city, the city of nets, the city of pleasure, where the only sins are to be unhappy or poor." Those Weill-Brecht words from their Mahagonny might well have applied to the Rome of our epoch, non sei d'accordo? Yes, we've got to try to do that Kurt Weill show.

And we must stop talking and start doing something about another of those remarkable "fused personalities." We have talked about Josephine Baker for so many years and we're going to have to find a way to get her to agree to our doing a film or Broadway musical on her amazing life adventure. All the way from the poverty and anonymity of St. Louis, Missouri to the Empress of Paris, a spectacular troubadour of song and dance known all over the world and an undisputed war heroine for the Allied cause against Hitler. It's a tremendous story and we're going to be the ones to do it!

Tomorrow I'm off to Sabaudia. Marion is already there putting Casa Bianca into gleaming order. There's a family named Hobart who now own the Ekberg villa. I'm told that Peter Hobart is a young industrialist from Ohio and that his wife Anna is Italian and has serious interest in sociology, psychology and psychiatry, and that they're both delightful "merged personalities." They have two children. I shall call on them.

The weather is continuing to be glorious for this time of year. I will take a walk down the beach to Mount Circe and have a long, long talk with Ulysses' spellbinding goddess. And I shall watch the sun slide behind the Tyrrhenian Sea and wait for the red, orange, yellow, purple afterglow against the Western sky. And I might even try a poem or two after so many years.

I definitely am going over to San Felice to see Magnani. I feel an impelling desire to embrace and be embraced by that unbelievable, stupendous, crazy Romana and to thank her, not only for what she herself is and symbolizes, but for what she brought to our lives. Anna and Open City. There never would have been a KLA and Rome if it hadn't been for her, and for it.

Write as often and as much as you wish. And enjoy yourself, carefree and adolescent. The dreams you still want to fulfill will be waiting for you when you return.

Un abbraccio forte, forte, come sempre,

Gene

Acknowledgements

We wish to express our deep regrets for not having had the opportunity to mention in the book, for example, the following: all our associates, such as Michele Pietravalle, Ferdinando Ghia, Valentina Sturla, David Lewis, Nino Castellet, William Packer, and Claudio Giglioli, as well as all our assistants and employees like Annie Kisray, Malini Kenny, and Jan Lawler. All our clients worldwide, particularly those from Italian cinema, such as Rik Battaglia, Franco Brusati, Maria Grazia Buccella, Danilo Donati, Cesare Danova, Pietro Germi, Terence Hill, Sylva Koscina, Tomas Milian, Anna Moffo, Milly Monti, Luciana Paluzzi, Gabor Pogany, Teddy Reno, Luisa Rivelli, Carlo Rustichelli, Jacqueline Sassard, Delia Scala, Catherine Spaak, Agnes Spaak, Ornella Vanoni. All the Italian producers with whom we have had, sooner or later, valued relationships, such as Peppino Amato, Alfredo Bini, Mario Cecchi-Gori, Vittorio Cecchi-Gori, Tonino Cervi, Nino Crisman, Marcello Danon, Pier Giuseppe Gurgo-Salice, Maurizio Lodi-Fé, Fulvio Luchisano, Maleno Malenotti, Antonio Musu, Luciano Perugia, Luigi Rovere, Nello Santi, Rudy Solmson, Nicolo Theodoli, Giorgio Venturini, Italo Zingarelli. And all the prestigious Italian artists, directors, screenwriters, operators, set designers, costume designers, and musicians, skilled and great, esteemed and admired, whom we unfortunately did not have the pleasure of listing as clients of Kaufman-Lerner Associates.

Index